THE IMPACT OF HUMAN R
ON ARMED FORC

This book considers those aspects of human rights law which may become relevant to the activities of armed forces whether they remain in barracks, undertake training or are deployed in military operations within their own State or outside it. The unique nature of military service and of military courts gives rise to human rights issues in respect both of civilians and soldiers, whether volunteers or conscripts, who find themselves before these courts. Rowe examines these issues as well as the application of international humanitarian law alongside the human rights obligations of the State when forces are training for and involved in armed conflict; where armed forces are deployed in situations of civil disorder; and where States contribute armed forces to multinational forces.

This is a timely study in light of the allegations of ill-treatment by soldiers of civilians following the war in Iraq and the detention of 'unlawful combatants' in Guantanamo Bay. It will have broad appeal, for scholars in human rights, international law and military studies, and anyone concerned with policy relevant to the armed forces.

PETER ROWE is Professor of Law at the University of Lancaster. He has been Chairman of the United Kingdom Group of the International Society for Military Law and the Law of War, and has published widely in these areas.

THE IMPACT OF HUMAN RIGHTS LAW ON ARMED FORCES

PETER ROWE
University of Lancaster

CAMBRIDGE
UNIVERSITY PRESS

CAMBRIDGE UNIVERSITY PRESS

Cambridge, New York, Melbourne, Madrid, Cape Town, Singapore, São Paulo

Cambridge University Press
The Edinburgh Building, Cambridge CB2 2RU, UK

Published in the United States of America by Cambridge University Press, New York

www.cambridge.org
Information on this title: www.cambridge.org/9780521617321

First published 2006

Printed in the United Kingdom at the University Press, Cambridge

A catalogue record for this book is available from the British Library

ISBN-13   978-0-521-85170-1 hardback
ISBN-10   0-521-85170-X hardback

ISBN-13   978-0-521-61732-1 paperback
ISBN-10   0-521-61732-4 paperback

This book is dedicated to Anne, Tim and Katherine.

CONTENTS

PREFACE

This book attempts to consider those aspects of human rights law which may become relevant to the activities of armed forces whether they remain in barracks, undertake training or are deployed in military operations within their own State or outside it. In particular, it considers, from a human rights perspective, the position of members of those armed forces and those with whom they will come into contact during some form of military operation.

The unique nature of military service and of military courts gives rise to human rights issues in respect of those who serve in armed forces, whether as volunteers or as conscripts, and of civilians who find themselves placed before military courts. Chapters 1 to 4 explore the application of human rights standards in this military context.

It is often, however, part of the function of armed forces to take part in armed conflict, or at least to train for such a possibility. In this case international humanitarian law will also apply alongside the human rights obligations of the State in certain circumstances. Since the former body of law draws a distinction between international and non-international armed conflicts, whilst the latter does not, I have considered it appropriate to make such a distinction in order to consider the different nature of, and issues involved in, such conflict from both a human rights and an international humanitarian law standpoint. Chapters 5 and 6 respectively tackle these different types of armed conflict but the latter chapter deals also with issues involved in civil disorder which does not reach the threshold of an armed conflict.

The practice of States in deploying contingents of their armed forces to multinational forces has become a common feature of modern international relations. By its very nature armed forces will be acting outside their own territory and they may be involved in the arrest and detention of civilians. Particular issues of the application of human rights and, possibly, international humanitarian law will arise in addition to the law of sending and receiving States, matters which are explored in chapter 7.

This book does not set out to compare different military legal systems throughout the world. To attempt to do so would not only have involved some form of selection and but it would also have run the risk of inaccuracies since the military legal systems are usually embedded within the national law of the State concerned and an understanding of that law would have been required. Nor does it attempt to describe all modern non-international armed conflicts. Instead, issues have been explored which, it is hoped, will find resonance in the armed forces of most States.

This concentration on issues has enabled consideration to be given to the various human rights instruments without an over-concentration on any one of them. There are, of course, many differences among them, both in procedural and in substantive terms. For these reasons a decision of one human rights body could be followed by another but it may not be. Moreover, the context in which they operate will also have some bearing on their significance to the role of armed forces. Professor Harris summed up the position when he concluded (in D. Harris 'Regional Protection of Human Rights: The Inter-American Achievement'; in D. Harris and S. Livingstone (eds.), *The Inter-American System of Human Rights* (Oxford: Clarendon, 1998), p. 2) that 'human rights issues in the Americas have often concerned gross, as opposed to ordinary, violations of human rights. They have much more to do with the forced disappearance, killing, torture and arbitrary detention of political opponents and terrorists than with particular issues concerning, for example, the right to a fair trial or freedom of expression that are the stock in trade of the European . . . Court.' It is not, therefore, surprising to see decisions of the Inter-American system taking a prominent role in chapter 6 while those of the European Court appear more relevant to chapters 1 to 3.

Senior members of armed forces may take the view that the whole idea of human rights is a dangerous one if it gets a hold on those responsible for discipline and for ensuring those armed forces are able to discharge their duties. I hope that this work will dispel such an idea and show that, in a military context, the relevant norms of human rights law can lead, like those of international humanitarian law, to a control on the actions of soldiers and a resulting enhancement of military discipline.

This book will, it is hoped, prove of interest to those who direct the policy of the armed forces within individual States, to those who apply it and to scholars who seek an understanding of how armed forces may be subject to control by international (and national) legal norms.

I should like to acknowledge my gratitude to a number of people who have widened my horizons and who have helped me to formulate my views. Discussions over many years with military lawyers have, I hope, led me to take a realistic view of the issues faced by law in the context of armed forces. Professor Timothy McCormack invited me to become the inaugural Sir Ninian Stevens Visiting Scholar to the Asia-Pacific Centre for Military Law at the Faculty of Law, University of Melbourne for part of the 2002–3 academic year. While there I benefited greatly from discussions with him and with his colleagues, Bruce Oswald, CSC, and John Tobin. John also read and commented on a draft of chapter 6. Errors remaining are my responsibility.

I am grateful also to Lorna Pimperton of the University of Lancaster Law Library who assisted me to place the text in the form required by my publishers, to my colleagues in the Law School who have helped me in many ways and to Finola O'Sullivan of Cambridge University Press who helped me to transform an idea for a book into this final form.

I have attempted to state the law as at 1 January 2005, although where possible some later cases have been added since that date.

Human rights within the context of members of armed forces

One might be forgiven for thinking that the very nature of human rights is not a primary consideration for the armed forces of a State which has established them for at least one purpose, to fight a war on its behalf. The fighting of war necessarily involves loss of life, injury to individuals and the destruction of property. There is, it might be argued, little room to consider the human rights of those within the armed forces or those who come into contact with them during a war, whether of an international or of a non-international kind. To provide some amelioration of the condition of the victims of the war, to control the methods of war and to limit its consequences, particularly as they affect civilians or civilian objects, States have, over a period of time, agreed by treaty to a wide body of international humanitarian law.

International humanitarian law has been defined as

> 'international rules, established by treaties or custom, which are specifically intended to solve humanitarian problems directly arising from international or non-international armed conflicts and which, for humanitarian reasons, limit the right of Parties to a conflict to use the methods and means of warfare of their choice or protect persons and property that are, or may be, affected by conflict.'[1]

This international humanitarian law has been drawn up for application in time of war (or armed conflict as it is usually called in modern times).[2] It is not entirely clear whether international humanitarian law gives the soldier

---

[1] Y. Sandoz, C. Swinarski and B. Zimmerman, *Commentary on the Additional Protocols of 8 June 1977 to the Geneva Conventions of 12 August 1949* (Geneva: International Committee of the Red Cross, 1987), p. xxvii. This link with an armed conflict is not, however, required in respect of genocide or crimes against humanity. See the Rome Statute 1998 of the International Criminal Court, Arts. 6 and 7 respectively.

[2] International humanitarian law comes into effect when the conditions of common Arts. 2 and 3 to the Geneva Conventions 1949 apply. These require an international or a non-international armed conflict to be in existence or a declaration of war (if the armed conflict is of an international character). See also Additional Protocol I 1977 (international armed

any 'rights' under it.[3] The general structure of this body of law is to impose obligations upon States, although individuals may take their benefit (such as by being treated as a prisoner of war) and those who infringe them may be personally liable. An important provision in the Geneva Conventions 1949, however, is that a [soldier] 'may in no circumstances renounce in part or in entirety the *rights* secured to [him] by the present Convention'.[4] These 'rights' within the Geneva Conventions 1949 (Geneva Convention for the amelioration of the condition of the wounded and sick in armed forces in the field, Geneva, 12 August 1949, in force 21 October 1950, 75 *United Nations Treaty Series* (UNTS) 31 ('First Geneva Convention 1949'); Geneva Convention for the amelioration of the condition of wounded, sick and shipwrecked members of armed forces at sea, Geneva, 12 August 1949, in force 21 October 1950, 75 UNTS 85 ('Second Geneva Convention 1949'); Geneva Convention relative to the treatment of prisoners of war, Geneva, 12 August 1949, in force 21 October 1950, 75 UNTS 135 ('Third Geneva Convention 1949'); Geneva Convention relative to the protection of civilian persons in time of war, Geneva, 12 August 1949, in force 21 October 1950, 75 UNTS 287 ('Fourth Geneva Convention 1949') are not of the same nature as those within human rights treaties. A soldier cannot enforce them directly through legal avenues as might be possible through human rights treaties.[5] While he is, for example, a prisoner of war he has the '*right* to make known to the military authorities in whose power [he] is [his] requests regarding the conditions of captivity'.[6] There is no corresponding 'right' to humane treatment although the detaining State

---

conflicts) and Additional Protocol II 1977 (non-international armed conflicts). Both these Protocols widen the applicability of international humanitarian law. See Art. 1(4) of the First Protocol.

[3] For a discussion of the meaning of 'rights' see J. Raz, 'Legal Rights' (1984) 4 *Oxford Journal of Legal Studies* 1 (who refers to the extensive literature on this topic); R. Higgins, *Problems and Process, International Law and How we Use it* (Oxford: Oxford University Press, 1994), pp. 96–110.

[4] The four Geneva Conventions 1949, Arts. 7, 7, 7 and 8 respectively. See also Arts. 6, 6, 6, 7 respectively ('rights which it confers on them') and the third and fourth Conventions, Art. 78 for further examples of where the term 'right' or 'rights' is used. Compare the fourth Geneva Convention, Art. 47: 'shall not be deprived . . . of the benefits of the present Convention'.

[5] Depending upon the national law of a particular State he may, also, bring an action in the courts alleging a breach of international humanitarian law towards himself. See, for example, *Kadic* v. *Karadzic* (1995) 34 International Legal Materials (ILM) 1592. Compare the attempts by British former prisoners of war to bring an action in the courts of Japan seeking compensation for their treatment in Japanese prisoner of war camps during World War II (see chapter 5 below).

[6] The third Geneva Convention 1949, Art. 78.

is under an obligation to ensure this.[7] Too much can be made of the use or the non-use in the Geneva Conventions 1949 of the term 'right' as indicating a right given to an individual compared with an obligation imposed upon the State concerned.[8] The practical reality of the situation is that there are very limited means provided by these Conventions to a protected person to enforce the treatment of him which these Conventions require of the detaining State.[9]

In cases where an armed conflict is taking place international humanitarian law may, however, be relevant and enable an individual indirectly to enforce 'rights' given by this body of law under a relevant human rights treaty.[10] Human rights law has been developed largely for application in time of peace, although it was envisaged that it would also have some relevance during wartime.[11] In time of war (or, more accurately, in time of an international armed conflict) international humanitarian law has been declared to be, in certain instances, the *lex specialis* giving meaning to terms such as 'arbitrary', the right to life and the treatment of detainees in human rights treaties.[12] In turn, international human rights law has

---

[7] The third Geneva Convention 1949, Art. 13.

[8] The same is true of the use of the term 'is entitled to'; see, for example, the third Geneva Convention 1949, Art. 14(1). Compare Y. Dinstein, 'Human Rights in Armed Conflict' in T. Meron (ed.), *Human Rights in International Law* (2 vols., Oxford: Clarendon Press, 1984), vol. II, p. 347, who takes the view that 'many provisions in the four Geneva Conventions clearly create rights of states'. Dinstein is referring here to the rights of the State of which the victim is a national. The possessor of this 'right' will, unlike the victim of a breach of international humanitarian law, have a greater opportunity to enforce it (through diplomatic means).

[9] See R. Provost, *International Human Rights and Humanitarian Law* (Cambridge: Cambridge University Press, 2001), p. 28. This work provides an excellent account of the relationship between human rights and international humanitarian law.

[10] There is a considerable overlap of protection of individuals given by human rights treaties and to protected persons (or civilians) within international humanitarian law. For a rejection of the view by Columbia that the Inter-American Commission on Human Rights did 'not have competence, in the processing of individual petitions, to apply international humanitarian law', see Report No. 26/97, Case 11.142 (Columbia) at paras. 198–9. Compare *Coard* v. *United States of America* Report No. 109/99, Case 10.951, 29 September 1999; *Bankovic* v. *Belgium et al.* Application No. 52207/99, Admissibility, 12 December 2001, (2002) 41 ILM 517.

[11] The issue of whether human rights are founded upon the individual treaties or pre-existed them is well discussed by M. Craven, 'Legal Differentiation and the Concept of the Human Rights Treaty in International Law', (2000) 11 *European Journal of International Law* 489 at 493.

[12] *Legality of the Threat or Use of Nuclear Weapons*, Advisory Opinion (1996) International Court of Justice. Reports of Judgments, Advisory Opinions and Orders, vol. I, 226 at para. 25. See also the 1950 Convention, Art. 15 in the case of a derogation from Art. 2 of the Convention; *Coard* v. *United States* (n. 10 above). This is discussed in more detail in chapter 5.

played a significant part in the development of international humanitarian law.[13]

In an application made by an individual to a human rights body reliance upon international humanitarian law may also be seen where the armed conflict was of a non-international nature. The Inter-American Commission on Human Rights has taken the view (in 1998) that

> 'it is primarily in situations of internal armed conflict that human rights and humanitarian law converge most precisely and reinforce one another . . . both common Article 3 of the Geneva Conventions [1949] and the American Convention on Human Rights [1969] guarantee these rights [the right to life and physical integrity] and prohibit extra-judicial executions, and the Commission should apply both bodies of law'.[14]

A breach of international humanitarian law is designed to lead to the trial and punishment of an individual perpetrator while a breach of a human rights treaty is intended to lead to the State being liable either to pay compensation to the victim[15] (along with the prosecution of an individual) or being called upon to change its practices.[16]

International humanitarian law and human rights possess sufficient differences to lead to the conclusion that they do not represent the same forms of legal protection to individuals while deriving from separate sources. Provost summed up the position well when he commented that

---

[13] See, for example, *Prosecutor* v. *Tadic* IT-94-1-AR 72, 2 October 1995, para. 97 (1996) 35 ILM 35; United Kingdom Ministry of Defence, *The Manual of the Law of Armed Conflict* (Oxford: Oxford University Press 2004), para. 1.8 and for an excellent discussion of this issue, T. Meron, 'The Humanization of Humanitarian Law' (2000) 94 *American Journal of International Law* 239.

[14] Report No. 26/97, Case 11.142 (Columbia) 13 April 1998, para. 147. The Commission found there to be an 'internal armed conflict' [*sic*] to be in existence and therefore common Art. 3 to the Geneva Conventions 1949 applied, at para. 202. See also *Abella* v. *Argentina*, Report No. 55/97, Case 11.137, 18 November 1997.

[15] This is the remedy available to the European Court of Human Rights established by the European Convention on Human Rights and Fundamental Freedoms 1950 (hereafter, the 1950 Convention). See also the practice of the Inter-American Commission on Human Rights, established by the American Convention on Human Rights 1969 set out in Report No. 26/97, Case 11.142 (Columbia) at para. 189. In para. 193 the Commission concludes that 'monetary compensation is not generally sufficient in a case which would have required a criminal investigation and the sanction of those responsible'.

[16] A further difference lies in the fact that (generally) international humanitarian law has been designed to protect the nationals of a State different from that of the State taking action. See the definition of 'protected person' in the Geneva Conventions 1949. This view has, however, been challenged by the Appeals Chamber of the International Criminal Tribunal for the former Yugoslavia (ICTY). See, in particular, *Prosecutor* v. *Tadic*, Appeals Chamber Judgment IT-94-1-A, 15 July 1999, para. 166, (1999) 38 ILM 1518; *Prosecutor* v. *Delalic et al. (Celebici Case)* Appeals Chamber, 20 February 2002, para. 58.

there were 'significant differences between human rights and humanitarian law . . . each displays a peculiar richness and resilience likely to be
weakened, if anything, by over simplistic or over enthusiastic attempts to
recast one in terms of the other'.[17]

Some have thought this risk to be so serious that it might lead to a
merger between the two systems 'to such an extent that it would become
unpractical [sic] to apply them'.[18] This must surely be to overstate the case
if the warning given by Provost is heeded and individual human rights
treaties are considered in detail. To do so is to implant the concept of
'human rights' within its legal base. The International Court of Justice
(ICJ) has stated that 'law exists, it is said to serve a social need; but precisely
for that reason it can do so only through and within the limits of its own
discipline. Otherwise, it is not a legal service that would be rendered.
Humanitarian considerations may constitute the inspirational basis for
rules of law ... Such considerations do not, however, in themselves amount
to rules of law.'[19]

It should not be thought that the mere enactment into law (whether
in an international or national form) of a 'human right' is sufficient, by
itself, to guarantee the enjoyment of that right. Even if it is clear that the
armed forces have denied an individual his or her rights there may, in
some contexts, be many procedural or other impediments lying in the
way of a remedy against the State involved. It may be that effort should be
directed towards training members of armed forces to comply with the
human rights obligations of their State.

Human rights in the armed forces

The detailed treatment of human rights is, generally, a post-World War
II development. Although the term was little used in the context of the
armed forces before then the soldier[20] was not wholly at the mercy of his
military superiors acting to enforce military discipline. He would, most

---

[17] Provost, *International Human Rights*, p. 349.
[18] 'Application of International Humanitarian Law and International Human Rights Law to
UN-Mandated Forces: Report of the Expert Meeting on Multinational Peace Operations'
(2004) 86 *International Review of the Red Cross* 207, 211.
[19] *The South West Africa Cases* [1966] ICJ 1, paras. 49, 50.
[20] This term is used throughout as a convenient way of referring to a member of the armed
forces. It does not draw any distinctions between different roles played by soldiers, i.e.
those who are trained to come into contact with the enemy and those who provide support
functions, or military police. It could cover, for instance, border guards and troops of a
ministry of internal affairs. For convenience, references to the masculine gender include
the feminine except where the context provides otherwise.

probably, have had certain rights to make complaint about his treatment.[21] This right to make a complaint was, however, unlikely to have been an effective means of challenging what we would now think of as a breach of his human rights.[22] There was no objective standard of treatment, which a human rights treaty could provide, to which a soldier (in particular) was entitled. Although all armies would have operated under a system of military discipline different armies treated their soldiers differently. Military punishments varied and often reflected and exceeded the degree of severity of criminal sanctions available in the civilian courts. The infliction of the death penalty or of corporal punishment was not uncommon.[23]

Although the term 'human rights' of the soldier was not spoken of the armed forces would normally wish to treat its soldiers 'fairly' or with 'common humanity' if only to ensure recruitment of a sufficient number of soldiers or to retain those whom it had trained. Whilst these considerations might have been less pressing where the State conscripted those who would form its junior ranks, a certain degree of fair treatment of soldiers by those in authority over them was essential to ensure that the army acted with some measure of efficiency.

It is, perhaps, not too great an exaggeration to conclude that as the fundamental purpose of an army is to fight during an armed conflict an individual's needs are treated as subservient to this purpose. Where he is a volunteer he could be expected to have joined the armed forces with the knowledge that his interests would have to be subsumed to the greater interests of those armed forces. The armed forces possess another characteristic different in degree from all other forms of employment. This is its hierarchical structure based on rank and the obligation to obey

---

[21] For an example, see the Army Act 1881 (United Kingdom), s. 43. A number of other States followed the British example in their own military law. Within this family of military law there are few 'rights' as such given to soldiers, although there are many 'duties' placed on them. The 'rights' of soldiers should not be confused with 'privileges' given to certain groups of soldiers, usually dependent on rank. These 'privileges' can be withdrawn at any time. The pattern in the twenty-first-century German army has been to give soldiers a greater number of specific 'rights': see G. Nolte and H. Krieger, 'Comparison of European Military Law Systems' in G. Nolte (ed.), *European Military Law Systems* (Berlin: de Gruyter Recht, 2003), pp. 74–6.

[22] For the practical difficulties of low-ranking sailors making complaints of bullying in the Royal Navy in the 1920s see L. Gardiner, *The Royal Oak Courts Martial* (London, William Blackwood, 1965), p. 98 where such individuals were 'branded as sea-lawyers for laying complaints'.

[23] Tying a soldier to a gun carriage for long periods was practised during World War I. By 1881 in the British army punishments could not be of 'a nature to cause injury to life or limb', the Army Act 1881, s. 44 (apart from the death penalty).

orders given by a person more senior in rank or seniority to the recipient of the order. This requirement to obey orders has been described as 'the essence of efficiency in a military unit'[24] and it cannot be ignored when the acts of an individual soldier are being considered.

The armed forces of many States operate within this type of hierarchical structure with a broad distinction between commissioned officers, non-commissioned officers (NCOs) and the lowest ranking soldier. Although both categories of officers are required to show qualities of leadership commissioned officers will, generally, have received a longer period of education and will be expected to lead a greater number of men than NCOs. It is common for these officers to be recruited directly into the armed forces without progressing from the ranks of NCOs. In those States relying upon some form of conscription it is normally the case that commissioned officers will be volunteers, whilst the NCOs may be comprised of some conscript soldiers.[25] Within the broad category of commissioned officers and NCOs there will be a range of ranks, dependent upon seniority and aptitude.

Within a military structure this difference in rank brings with it different roles and responsibilities.[26] The requirement to obey orders without discussion, in an appropriate case, is considered vital to most (if not all) military systems.[27] A failure to obey an order from a soldier higher in rank will usually amount to a serious military offence. The need to endow the

[24] *R. v. Her Majesty's Attorney General for New Zealand* (Judicial Committee of the Privy Council, London, 17 March 2003) *per* Lord Scott at para. 41, who concluded that this relationship between superior and subordinate created a 'presumption of undue influence' in relation to a contract of confidentiality put to a soldier by his superior officer to sign. On this point Lord Scott dissented from the majority of the Board, who took the view that there 'was no order in the sense of a command which created an obligation to obey under military law', (Lord Hoffman at para. 20). See, generally, N. Keijzer, *Military Obedience* (Alphen aan den Rijn: Sijthoff & Noordhoff, 1978); M. Osiel, *Obeying Orders* (New Brunswick: Transaction Publishers, 1999).

[25] For an account of the Soviet armed forces in 1988, see C. Donnelly, *Red Banner: the Soviet Military System in Peace and War* (Coulsdon: Jane's Information Group Ltd, 1988) who shows that the 'great majority of junior NCOs in the Soviet Armed Forces' were conscripts.

[26] See, generally, N. Dixon, *On the Psychology of Military Incompetence* (London: Futura Publications, 1979). Dixon notes that 'since men are not by nature all that well equipped for aggression on a grand scale, they have to develop a complex of rules, conventions and ways of thinking which, in the course of time, ossify into outmoded tradition, curious ritual, inappropriate dogma and that bane of some military organizations, irrelevant "bullshit"' (p. 169).

[27] To understand the reality of military life in an all-volunteer army it is necessary to consider the 'power' of ordinary soldiers as a group who 'negotiate' their working relationships with superiors 'in which a relaxed interpretation of military law is traded-off for effective role performance': J. Hockey, *Squaddies: Portrait of a Subculture* (Exeter: University of Exeter

giver of the orders with some degree of status within the organisation has led to different forms of punishment where that individual (compared with a person of the lowest ranks) has been in breach of the military code of discipline. Thus, commissioned officers will, commonly, be treated differently from the lowest ranking soldiers. They will also have responsibilities not to abuse their status to influence, for example, the religious thinking of subordinates.[28] Military organisations will, usually, consider it inappropriate to treat all ranks equally in relation to certain aspects of military life.

The treatment of individuals on a basis of equality is, however, a fundamental principle of most, if not all legal systems. It certainly is in international law. International humanitarian law requires protected persons under the Geneva Conventions of 1949 to be treated without, for example, 'any adverse distinction based, in particular, on race, religion or political opinion'.[29] It is not surprising to see human rights treaties containing a similar message,[30] although such rights to equal treatment may not amount to a free-standing right. The right to equal treatment may also be given in other international instruments, an example being under the law of the European Union.[31] In addition, national laws may impose obligations of equal treatment in different ways.[32]

Differences in rank or seniority in the armed forces may lead to different treatment by military superiors of soldiers. This is usually more marked in armed forces than in comparable civilian occupations. Whilst it might

---

Press, 1986), p. 159. Where they feel they are being ordered to undertake unnecessary or petty duties they can be unco-operative without disobeying orders, see *ibid.*, p. 74 under the sub-heading 'Privates' Power and the NFI'. On active duty where their lives are being threatened the formality of the hierarchical structure is likely to be relaxed, *ibid.*, p. 101. See also chapter 5.

[28] See *Larissis* v. *Greece* (1999) 27 EHRR 329, para. 51.

[29] The fourth Geneva Convention 1949, Art. 27. See also the third Convention, Art. 16; second Convention, Art. 12; first Convention Art. 12; Additional Protocol I 1977, Art. 75(1); Additional Protocol II 1977, Art. 4.

[30] The International Covenant on Civil and Political Rights 1966 (hereafter '1966 Covenant'), Art. 3; the 1950 Convention, Art. 14 (and Protocol 12); American Convention on Human Rights 1969, Art. 1; African Charter on Human and Peoples' Rights, 1981, Arts. 2 and 3.

[31] See Council Directive 76/207/EEC of 9 February 1976 on the implementation of the principle of equal treatment for men and women as regards access to employment, vocational training and promotion, and working conditions, OJ 1976 No. L39 p. 40, 14 February 1976. See also the Convention on the Elimination of Racial Discrimination, 1966; Convention on the Elimination of All Forms of Discrimination against Women, 1979.

[32] See, for example, the Canadian Charter of Rights and Freedoms, 1982, s. 15; Constitution of the Republic of South Africa 1996, Chapter 2, s. 9.

be expected that soldiers of the same rank should be treated equally the need to enforce a hierarchical system within a military discipline structure normally ensures that senior non-commissioned or commissioned officers have certain 'privileges' denied to those inferior in rank. Volunteer soldiers may be treated differently from conscript soldiers, both within the same armed forces and as between different armed forces. The reason for this lies in the different nature of each type of military service.

The volunteer soldier

The conversion of armies from a conscript to a volunteer soldier base is becoming more common.[33] Where this is the case the terms of service must be sufficiently attractive to enable recruitment to take place of a sufficient number of individuals with the ability to train in the skills required. In addition, the conditions of military life must be such that trained individuals are encouraged to remain in the armed forces for a period acceptable to both the soldier and to his employers.

By enlisting in the armed forces the adult volunteer soldier must be taken to have consented to certain aspects of military life. It is not difficult to conclude that he has accepted that the military discipline system will apply to him, that he will have to follow orders, wear a uniform, attend parades and be called upon to take part in armed conflict should this occur during his military service. It is unlikely, however, that he will be given, prior to his recruitment, a list of activities that he will be required to perform as a soldier or the conditions under which he will live.[34] He will, for instance, not be required formally to agree, as part of his enlistment process, those activities in which he will take part and those in which he will not.[35] His knowledge of what military life is like will, most probably, be drawn from recruitment films, brochures or other publicity and from

[33] In Europe, Belgium, France, the Netherlands and Spain have ended conscription, respectively in 1992, 2001, 1996, 2001. It is expected that Portugal, Italy, the Czech Republic and Russia will act similarly in, respectively, 2003, 2006, 2006 and 2010: 'Human Rights and the Armed Forces' Seminar Information and Discussion Paper (Council of Europe, 5 December 2002), p. 3.

[34] The Optional Protocol on the Rights of the Child 2000, Art. 3(3)(c) requires that children under eighteen who volunteer for the armed forces must be 'fully informed of the duties involved in such military service'. *Quaere* whether this can be otherwise than in fairly general terms.

[35] It is possible that in some armed forces he will be recruited only for particular tasks or for service in particular locations. Thus, an army doctor may be recruited only to perform medical services and a chaplain or other religious adviser to perform religious activities for those professing his particular religious faith.

recruitment personnel. He may have heard of the nature of military life from serving or former soldiers. He is unlikely to be in the same position as a person who wishes to know the terms of a particular civilian employment before he commits himself to it. In an application for civilian employment he may be provided with a draft contract and a detailed job description along with the nature of any training to which he must submit himself.

It is difficult to conclude that, by the mere fact of joining the armed forces voluntarily, a person has consented to all the treatment to which he is subjected in the armed forces, or that he has waived those of his human rights available to him as a civilian. He will not have waived any specific human rights available to him by enlisting although those rights must be considered in a military context. No human rights instrument provides directly for this. The 'particular characteristics of military life' may, however, be taken into account and treatment which would amount to a breach of the human rights of a civilian may not draw the same conclusion if the individual is a soldier.[36] An example of this is the acceptance, certainly by the European Court of Human Rights, of military courts to try soldiers and, in appropriate cases, to deprive them of their liberty. It is difficult to imagine the Court accepting 'courts' established by civilian employers having the same consequences.

A particular aspect of this issue is the treatment of soldiers who admit to being homosexual or who are found to be such. A soldier in many States has, like a civilian, a right to a private life. This would encompass his sexual activities providing they were engaged in during off-duty hours and in private. Where it is well known that the armed forces of a particular State do not permit homosexuals to serve the question arises as to whether, by enlisting, a soldier has agreed that he may be dismissed should his homosexuality become known. Has he, in other words, consented to waive his right to a private life by joining the armed forces with knowledge of this attitude towards homosexuals? Should the answer be in the affirmative the mere fact of voluntary enlistment into the armed forces would carry great significance in the human rights obligations owed by the State to its soldiers, even if the attitude of the armed forces to homosexuals had been specifically brought to the attention of all recruits. In this case it might be expected that the State would be required to spell out clearly that by joining the armed forces the soldier's human right to a private life in so far as he admits to being a homosexual has been waived. The difficulty

---

[36] This is the case under the 1950 Convention. See *Engel et al.* v. *The Netherlands* (1976) 1 EHRR 647, para. 54.

with this approach is that the State is unlikely to be willing to 'bargain' with the potential recruit, who is left with the alternative of not joining the armed forces or joining on the terms that he gives up his right to a private life for the whole period of his military service, which could be a whole working lifetime. It is not surprising, therefore, to see the European Court of Human Rights in 1999 concluding that the mere fact of joining the armed forces with knowledge about its attitudes to homosexuality did not lead to a waiver of the right to a private life.[37]

It is suggested that the principle adopted by the Court in these cases, namely, that a soldier does not waive his rights given by a human rights instrument, merely by voluntarily joining the armed forces with knowledge of this attitude, is correct. The alternative is to assert that the act of voluntary enlistment has a profound effect on those rights. To adopt this approach would lead to the need for further inquiry, such as whether the soldier knew he was waiving a particular human right and whether he knew the extent and the consequences of such a waiver. Even if these conditions were satisfied a State could, in effect, deny a soldier his human rights given by an appropriate human rights instrument by claiming that he had, upon enlistment, waived those rights which the armed forces consider are incompatible with military service. Were this to be the case the State would find itself in a position similar to that which would apply if it had entered a reservation to the human rights treaty to the effect that it did not apply, or applied only to a limited extent, to its soldiers.[38] To rely upon a waiver of rights by a volunteer soldier would, however, mean that a restriction of the soldier's human rights would not apply to conscript soldiers who can hardly be said to have voluntarily consented to any waiver of their rights. In armed forces which rely on conscription there will exist a combination of conscript and volunteer soldiers. Any reliance upon the alleged waiver of rights by a volunteer soldier would therefore be unsatisfying if the armed forces wished the position of volunteers and conscripts to be the same on this point.

States party to human rights instruments other than the European Convention on Human Rights 1950 may find that their decision-making bodies would form a similar view to the Court not only in respect of homosexuals within the armed forces but also on the general point of the

---

[37] See *Smith and Grady* v. *United Kingdom* (2000) 29 EHRR 493; *Lustig-Prean and Beckett* v. *United Kingdom* (27 September 1999); *Perkins* v. *United Kingdom* (22 October 2002); *Brown* v. *United Kingdom* (8 July 2003) and, for more detailed treatment, chapter 2.

[38] Compare the position of derogation notice, which can only be issued where there is a war or other public emergency.

lack of significance, in terms of human rights obligations, of the enlistment process.

It is, of course, possible that a soldier may waive on specific occasions certain rights available to him during the course of his military service. He may, for instance, waive his right to be tried by an independent and impartial tribunal by agreeing, instead, to be dealt with by his commanding or other senior officer by way of a summary procedure.[39] It may be necessary to inquire, however, whether his consent has been freely given to waive a right given to him by a human rights treaty. A relevant consideration would be whether he has received any independent advice as to the advantages and disadvantages in waiving a right given to him by a human rights treaty. Given the nature of the military discipline system and the hierarchical structure of military life a soldier of low rank may find it difficult freely to waive his rights without such advice.[40]

The conscript soldier

The fact that many armed forces in Europe, at least, were comprised of conscripts led the framers of the European Convention in Human Rights 1950 and of the 1966 Covenant to recognise the realities of the structure of those armed forces. The prohibition of slavery and forced labour was drawn in such a way as to exclude 'any service of a military character or, in case of conscientious objectors in countries where they are recognised, service exacted instead of compulsory military service'.[41] Compulsory military service is not, therefore, by its very nature an infringement of the human rights of those subject to it. There are a number of reasons why States in the modern world may wish to retain some form of conscription, although there is currently a strong tendency to abolish it.[42] They may

---

[39] Military discipline is discussed in chapter 3. It is clear that any waiver must be established in 'an unequivocal manner', see *Ocalan* v. *Turkey* (2003) 37 EHRR 10 at para. 116.

[40] The unequal nature of the relationship may also explain why prisoners of war are not permitted to renounce any of the 'rights secured to them' by the third Geneva Convention 1949, see Art. 7; the fourth Convention, Art. 8.

[41] The same wording is to be found in the 1966 Covenant, Art. 8(3)(ii) and in the American Convention on Human Rights 1969, Art. 6(3)(b).

[42] Particularly in Europe. For the implications of abolishing conscript service see K. Coffey, *Strategic Implications of the All-Volunteer Force* (Chapel Hill: University of North Carolina Press, 1979). In the United Kingdom conscription (or national service) was ended in 1960. See, generally, Defence: Outline of Future Policy, Cmnd 124 (1957), para. 41. There has often been opposition to conscription within States: see M. Useem, *Conscription, Protest and Social Conflict* (New York: John Wiley, 1973), chapter 1.

see it as an education process for their young people[43] or as an obligation of all citizens, *qua* citizens, whatever their background or educational achievements.[44] More mundane reasons might underlie the whole basis of conscription. These could include the costs of maintaining a standing army. It has been the practice of States to pay conscripts a small wage. The costs of an all-volunteer army of the same size would be very much more expensive.[45] They could also include the fact that the State may have taken the view that conscripts can be required to undertake tasks which volunteers would not be willing to do.[46]

The nature of conscription is often referred to as 'the citizen in uniform'.[47] This implies that the civilian retains many of his rights when he is conscripted into military service. If the volunteer soldier is also a 'citizen in uniform' there can be no difference between the two classes of soldier in this regard.[48] If the phrase means that the soldier's human rights are the

---

[43] See G. Nolte and H. Krieger in Nolte, *European Military Law* (n. 21 above), pp. 85–6. Other ways of expressing the same idea, such as conscription would 'do the average young man a lot of good', can be seen in J. Western and P. Wilson in R. Forward and B. Reece (eds.), *Conscription in Australia* (St. Lucia: University of Queensland Press, 1968), p. 227. This study also shows that only a minority of those affected by conscription in Australia (at the time) opposed it, *ibid.* at p. 231. Since military training (whether as a volunteer or as a conscript) affects, generally, adolescents it has been suggested that it marks a transition from 'being a boy to being a man': Hockey, *Squaddies* (n. 27 above), p. 34. Such broad generalisations have been challenged by B. Johnson (ed.), *All Bull: the National Servicemen* (London: Quartet Books, 1973), pp. 13–14. In modern conditions they fail to take into account the presence and influence of women in the armed forces: R. Howes and M. Stevenson (eds.), *Women and the Use of Military Force* (Boulder: Lynne Rienner Publishers, 1993), p. 209.

[44] This obligation may take other forms, such as the imposition of a legal duty to vote in elections, to serve on a jury or even to assist the police if called upon to do so.

[45] In order to end conscription in the United States the 'basic pay for recruits would have to be increased by 75 per cent': Coffey, *Strategic Implications*, p. 39; Forward and Reece, *Conscription in Australia*, p. 137. For the economic consequences of conscription against paying sufficiently high salaries to attract the number of volunteer soldiers required see Forward and Reece, *Conscription in Australia*, p. 83.

[46] Dmitri Mitrofinov, a Duma Deputy, is reported as saying: 'if there is another Chernobyl and we have to send in the army, you think contract soldiers will agree to this?' *The Times*, 25 April 2003. They may, however, do so if higher wages are paid to them and greater precautions are taken to protect them from the risks involved.

[47] Compare G. Nolte and H. Krieger in Nolte, *European Military Law* (n. 21 above), p. 370 where the 'post-war military policy [in Germany is] characterised by the concept of the soldier as a "staatsbürger in Uniform"'.

[48] Compare L. Besselink in Nolte, *European Military Law* (n. 21 above), p. 580 who argues that in the Netherlands volunteers have 'in a certain sense given up being a citizen – while conscripts have been involuntarily drafted – they have in a sense remained citizens'. *Quaere* the limits within a democracy of the imposition of compulsory military service on a minority (those within the relevant age range) by the majority.

same as a civilian it is clearly inaccurate. Indeed, one of the purposes of initial military training is to achieve what Hockey has called 'civilian role dispossession'.[49] If the phrase means that the soldier's human rights are the same as the citizen except where restrictions on those rights are clearly justifiable it merely means that the category of soldier is not the same as civilian. Both are 'citizens'. The phrase is likely to conjure up a political philosophy rather than a legal classification. It will involve concepts such as the sharing of a political philosophy between the armed forces and its civilian society and the positive notion that all citizens should serve in the armed forces but in a practical world only those able and capable can actually do so.[50]

The formulation in the human rights treaties refers to service of a 'military character'. Does this mean service which can be shown objectively to have a military purpose or does it mean that any service of whatever nature performed whilst a person is a member of the armed forces is excluded from the definition of slavery or forced labour? Since the presence of this exclusion from slavery or forced labour appears in a human rights treaty it is likely that it would be construed strictly by any adjudicatory body. The nature of conscript armies is usually that they are larger in terms of the number of the lowest ranking soldiers compared with more senior ranks than all-volunteer armies. To some extent this is understandable since their size will depend upon demographic considerations and, in particular, the numbers of young people of military age.

Conscript soldiers can, in practical terms, provide a ready form of labour available to the State to use for any purpose it directs assuming that these orders emanate through the military chain of command. Through this means a State might order soldiers to build roads, harvest crops,[51] act as servants to officers for their private parties, wash officers' cars or take their dogs for a walk. Whether any of this work can be said to be of a 'military character' is doubtful. This term is linked to the nature of lawful military orders. An order, for instance, by an officer to a low-ranking soldier to wash the officer's car would normally be considered to be an unlawful order since there is no military purpose to be served by its

---

[49] Hockey, *Squaddies* (n. 27 above), p. 23.

[50] For a view of how an 'army can qualify for the description "citizen"' see J. Haswell, *Citizen Armies* (London: Peter Davies Ltd, 1973), p. 13.

[51] See *Black Book on Rights of Conscripts in Central and Eastern Europe* (Stockholm: European Council of Conscripts Organisations, 1996), para. 1.2.

implementation. It cannot be said to be work of a 'military character' and the mere fact that the person giving the order and the soldier to whom it is given are in a military relationship does not make it so. The same can be said of the order to build roads or to assist with the harvest.[52]

It is not uncommon in some States for the armed forces to be deployed during times of national emergency ranging from civil disorder, which the civilian police are unable to control, to the use of the armed forces in time of floods or other national emergency and to their use to replace striking workers. In these cases it might be argued that there is a proper role for the armed forces in the protection of the lives of citizens where no other body is able to perform such service.[53] A specific legal instrument might be necessary to deem the work to be of a military character so as to ensure that orders given to soldiers are lawful military orders, of which a failure to obey would amount to a military offence.

It seems relatively easy to take the position that work required of conscript soldiers which has no military purpose would not appear to be work of a 'military character', despite the fact that the work is done by soldiers on the orders of military superiors. The reason that this statement is expressed in this way is due to the nature of military activities. The proper role of the armed forces within a State will vary depending upon the specific constitutional arrangements in existence. In some States it may be legitimate to use the armed forces for a certain purpose but be constitutionally improper in another State. Use of the armed forces, for instance, to harvest crops may be constitutionally permissible in one State and unconstitutional in another. It is difficult to conclude that work by members of the armed forces of a type permitted within the constitution of the State concerned would not be work of a military character.[54] Again,

---

[52] See the case referred to by L. Besselink in Nolte, *European Military Law* (n. 21 above), p. 606, of a soldier who was ordered to take part in a private production of a film which, it was alleged, would have 'a positive effect on the image of the armed forces'. It was held that the order to do so was not a lawful order.

[53] See *ibid.* where the argument is expressed as 'contributing to the protection and safety of society'.

[54] Although compare the Parliamentary Assembly of the Council of Europe Resolution 1166 (1998) which stressed that 'conscripts are not deployed for tasks not compatible with the fact that they have been drafted for national defence service': Council of Europe Parliamentary Assembly Recommendation 1380 (1998). This leaves open the question of the limits of 'national defence'. For a wide view see the statement of the Indian armed forces at www.mod.nic.in/aforces/welcome.html. The role of the East Timor army includes 'support [to] the government during national disasters and other emergencies', see

the armed forces can, for instance, argue that work which does not appear to be of a military nature needs to be completed since it might be of some value to them in the future. The building of roads may be seen as possessing a military advantage since it will enable military vehicles (as well as other vehicles) to use them.[55] In all these cases the work is done within a military context where the soldiers will be subject to their own system of military discipline. This context must be considered because there are relatively few instances of 'work' of the armed forces which are purely of a military character. Thus, the firing of a tank's guns or the launch of munitions from an aircraft or a submarine would be but many other activities carried out by the armed forces have civilian counterparts. To drive a military truck is not dissimilar from driving such a vehicle for a civilian employer, to build barracks is similar to civil construction and to engage in physical fitness exercises may be little different from comparable civilian activities. What distinguishes these types of work as possessing a 'military character' is that they can be seen to possess some military purpose (even if this term is construed widely) carried out within the structure of military discipline. The conclusion must be drawn that work involving washing an officer's car or taking his dog for a walk would be difficult to justify as having any military purpose. Other work carried out by soldiers in which there might be a national interest in its completion might be considered as work of a military character when its full context is considered.

States may choose the form of conscription. They may decide to enlist males only or both sexes, only those between certain ages, or they may draw the names of conscripts from a random group such as those born on particular dates.[56] They may offer wide or narrow exemptions or deferments of military service[57] and they may provide various alternatives to military service by way of conscientious objection or substitute military service. States may also limit conscript soldiers to homeland service and

---

J. McClelland, 'Starting from Scratch: the Military Discipline System of the East Timor Defence Force' (2002) 7 *Journal of Conflict and Security Law* 252, 256. An 'emergency' may be that which the government styles as an 'emergency'. See, generally, G. Nolte and H. Krieger in Nolte, *European Military Law* (n. 21 above), pp. 34–51. The changing nature of 'military work' is discussed in C. Moskos, J. Williams and D. Segal (eds.), *The Postmodern Military* (Oxford: Oxford University Press, 2000).

[55] There are certain similarities here with the determination of whether, for instance, a road can be a 'military objective', see Additional Protocol I 1977, Art. 52(2).

[56] For an example, see the practice in Australia in 1964, Forward and Reece, *Conscription in Australia* (n. 43 above), p. 106, of placing marbles with dates on them in a lottery barrel.

[57] For examples see *ibid.*, at pp. 109, 116–17.

not require them to serve in an armed conflict abroad in which the State is involved.[58]

A State will, however, be expected to act fairly in selecting those for conscript service where full participation of the whole age group is not required. Should only those from a particular ethnic, or of a poor, background be required to perform military service or a disproportionate number of such individuals be refused exemptions or deferments from military service an issue of the infringement of their 'human right' to be treated equally with other comparable members of the population may arise.[59]

It is difficult to say that an individual has a human right to be treated equally with others in the matter of whether he is required to perform military service. Within the 1950 Convention, Article 14 which prohibits discrimination is not a free-standing provision and can only be invoked in relation to a Convention right or freedom. There is none applicable upon which Article 14 could be based since Article 4 (dealing with service of a military character) does not give any right or freedom to an individual. The same structure can be found in the other relevant treaties.

It is, perhaps, not surprising to find that an individual who claims that he was unfairly selected for military service will find it difficult to argue that his State has infringed his human rights in this regard. It has been common in some States to require only men to serve. This would have been the position at the time of the drafting of the various human rights treaties. States would hardly wish to find themselves being challenged on the ground that men had been discriminated against compared with

---

[58] This issue can have a high political profile. Examples would include the sending of conscripts of a number of nations to fight during the Korean war and United States and Australian conscripts to fight during the Vietnam war.

[59] See I. Kiss, 'Rights of Conscripts in Peacetime: Obstacles to and Opportunities for Providing Judicial and Non-Judicial Solutions in East European and Central Asian Countries' in B. Vankovska (ed.), *Legal Framing of the Democratic Control of Armed Forces and the Security Sector: Norms and Reality/ies* (Belgrade: Geneva Centre for the Democratic Control of Armed Forces and Centre for Civil-Military Relations, 2001), pp. 45, 49. Kiss comments on the admission into the army of those who are medically unfit for military service. See also *Compulsory Military Service in Central and Eastern Europe, a General Survey* (Utrecht: European Council of Conscripts Organisations, 1996) which comments that 'selection centres are allegedly catching anybody they can who is not smart and/or rich enough to obtain an exemption, and the military are happy when the quantitative requirements are met, without bothering about the quality of the draftees' (p. 9). The Monitoring Committee of the Parliamentary Assembly of the Council of Europe was informed that 'in 2001 only 12 per cent of those eligible [in the Russian Federation] for the army or navy are likely to be conscripted', Doc. 9396, 26 March 2002, para. 73.

women of the same age group since only the former were required to undertake military service. It is more likely that any challenge on this basis would be based upon national law (such as a Constitution) or an international instrument to which the State is a party requiring equal treatment between men and women.[60]

Many (but not all) States provide some means by which those who have a conscientious objection to military service can comply with conscription without actually being enlisted in the armed forces. These systems are designed to ensure that the freedom of conscience of potential recruits is respected.[61] They also provide a means whereby those who will not submit themselves to military service after being compelled by the State to do so do not gain an advantage over those who do submit themselves.[62] Some States will require the individual to prove that he has a conscientious objection, which could be on the grounds of religious,

[60] For an example see EU Directive 76/207/EEC and discussion below. G. Nolte and H. Krieger in Nolte, *European Military Law* (n. 21 above), p. 87 conclude that 'military service is not an obligation for women in any of the countries under review'.

[61] See the 1966 Covenant, Art. 18 (and General Comment No. 22, para. 11); the 1950 Convention, Art. 9; the American Convention on Human Rights 1969, Art. 12; the African Charter on Human and Peoples' Rights 1981, Art. 8. This right must be read, however, in the light of the relevant provision relating to compulsory military service which, in itself, does not give a right to be a conscientious objector. The Committee on Legal Affairs and Human Rights of the Council of Europe, 'Exercise of the Right of Conscientious Objection to Military Service in Council of Europe Member States', Doc. 8809, 13 July 2000, recommends the incorporation of the right of conscientious objection to military service into the 1950 Convention 'by means of a protocol amending Arts. 4.3(b) and 9', para. 6. For a general summary of conscientious objection under human rights instruments see E/CN. 4/2002/WP.2 (14 March 2002); H. Gilbert, 'The Slow Development of the Right to Conscientious Objection to Military Service under the European Convention on Human Rights [2001] EHRLR 554. See also Keijzer, *Military Obedience* (n. 24 above), chapter 5 (which also deals with conscience issues of serving soldiers); C. Evans, *Freedom of Religion under the European Convention on Human Rights* (Oxford: Oxford University Press, 2001), pp. 170–9.

[62] In theory this may be true. In practice, however, the number of those who avoid any form of military or civilian service (where it is available) is large. In 'several Eastern European countries . . . conscripts frequently avoid doing military service. In these countries between 10% and 20% of conscripts are actually enlisted for military service. Since all defaulters cannot be prosecuted, some states make an example of only a few by bringing them to court or declare amnesties': Committee on Legal Affairs and Human Rights of the Council of Europe (see n. 61) at para. 18. For an account of attempts by the Russian authorities to arrest those avoiding military service see *The Times*, 21 November 2002; 'Conscription Through Detention in Russia's Armed Forces' (2002) 14 Human Rights Watch, no. 8 (D) November. The need to avoid what may be seen as an unfair advantage may also explain the reluctance by the appropriate medical authorities to declare that a person is medically unfit for service.

ethical, moral, humanitarian or philosophical beliefs, to serving in the armed forces and if he cannot do so he will be required to serve.[63] Some States may recognise the only ground for conscientious objection to be one based upon a religious conviction. Even then they may draw distinctions between different religions, permitting one form of religious belief but rejecting others.[64] They may also accept a conscientious objection to service in the armed forces but not to service only in a particular theatre of operations.[65]

The national law of a State may permit those who are recognised to be conscientious objectors to perform some form of non-combatant military service or a civilian alternative service, even at the election of the individual.[66] The State will normally provide that the terms of this alternative service are to be no more favourable than those pertaining to military service. This is difficult to achieve since the discipline imposed in substitute service will normally be less onerous than in military service unless the period of alternative service is made longer than military service.[67] It may also need to be longer to equate with any form of reserve liability of

[63] See the Council of Europe Resolution 337 (1967) para. 1. The issue of conscientious objection to a particular military action by a volunteer soldier is discussed in chapter 2; it is also recognised by the Committee on Legal Affairs and Human Rights of the Parliamentary Assembly of the Council of Europe (see n. 59) at para. 5.

[64] For an account of the differences in this regard between the Amish and the Seventh Day Adventists in the United States, see *The Times*, 3 April 2003 and between Roman Catholics and Jehovah's Witnesses (or 'followers of other faiths') *Bustos* v. *Bolivia*, Report No. 52/04, Petition 14/04 (admissibility), 13 October 2004, para. 32.

[65] See the *Zonstien et al.* v. *Judge-Advocate General* (the Israeli Supreme Court sitting as the High Court of Justice) HC 7622/02, 23 October 2002 (reservists' refusal to serve in the occupied territories). The Court concluded that selective conscientious objection would have the result that 'the army of the nation may turn into an army of different groups comprised of various units. To each of which it would be conscientiously acceptable to act in certain areas, whereas it would be conscientiously unacceptable to act in others' (para. 16). It also drew a distinction between a political objection to service in a particular area and a conscientious objection to carry out political decisions: *ibid*. See also *Gillette US*, 401 US 437 (1971) and 'Vietnam and Conscription' in Useem, *Conscription, Protest* (n. 42 above), chapter 3.

[66] The advantage to the individual of the latter alternative is that he will not have to prove a conscientious objection. A State may provide various forms of civilian service. For an analysis of the practice in the member States of the Council of Europe see the Committee of Legal Affairs and Human Rights of the Parliamentary Assembly, n. 61 at paras. 18–45.

[67] The Council of Europe Resolution 337 (1967) stipulates that 'the period to be served in alternative work shall be at least as long as the period of normal military service', para. C.1, and in the Document of the Copenhagen Meeting of the Conference on the Human Dimension of the CSCE (1990) it is stated at para. 18.4 that it should be of 'a non-punitive nature'.

the conscript who performs military service. This lengthened period has been found by the European Court of Human Rights to be acceptable as being within the margin of appreciation of States providing it does not have a punitive character.[68] Some States have not provided any form of alternative to military service through an alleged fear that the conditions of service would be seen to be incomparably better than in the armed forces.[69]

An individual subject to conscription will normally be subject to criminal prosecution if he fails to report for military service. Should he be convicted a period of imprisonment can be expected.[70] The State may designate the offence as a civilian one or the military offence of desertion. The opportunity to prove he is a conscientious objector and that (where it is available) he should serve his time in an alternative organisation will therefore be of crucial importance. The provision of an adjudication body (and any appeal body) which is independent of, and impartial from, the executive will be as important on this issue as it is if a soldier is faced with a criminal trial for refusing military service.[71]

Whether a soldier has consented to certain treatment or has waived his rights by voluntarily joining the armed forces has been discussed above. None of these issues will apply to a conscript soldier through the mere fact of becoming a soldier. The fact that he has not chosen to become a conscientious objector or has not chosen an alternative military service cannot be taken as suggesting that he has 'volunteered' for military service.[72] He can, like his volunteer counterpart, waive certain rights which he might

---

[68] Kiss in Vankovska, *Legal Framing* comments that 'in Georgia conscript military service is one year and six months, while the term stipulated for the alternative service equals three years, i.e. almost [*sic*] twice as long' (p. 49). See also CCPR/CO/POL/Rev. 1, 5 November 2004, para. 15.

[69] See Kiss in Vankovska, *Legal Framing* at p. 49. The States to which she refers are Armenia, Uzbekistan, Azerbaijan, Kazakhstan, Georgia, Ukraine, Russia and Latvia. For pressure to do so see the Council of Europe Resolution 337 (1967); the Final Act of the 1990 Copenhagen Conference of the CSCE, para. 18.4; the UN Commission on Human Rights (Doc. E/CN. 4/1993/L.107) of 8 March 1993, para. 3. In relation to Cyprus see CCPR/C/79 Add.88, 17 and for the view of the Human Rights Commission in relation to Turkmenistan see E/CN.4/RES/2003/11, para. (d).

[70] For examples under the 1950 Convention see *Tsirlis, Kouloumpas and Georgiadis* v. *Greece* (29 May 1997) and *Stefanov* v. *Bulgaria* (3 May 2001); *Thlimmenos* v. *Greece* (6 April 2000).

[71] See the Council of Europe Resolution 337 (1967) para. 3; the Committee on Legal Affairs and Human Rights of the Parliamentary Assembly of the Council of Europe (n. 61) paras. 24, 26; 'Issue of the Administration of Justice Through Military Tribunals', E/CN.4/Sub.2/2003/4, 27 June 2003, paras. 38–9.

[72] See the Report of the European Committee of Social Rights to the Committee of Ministers on 21 April 2001 at para. 22.

otherwise have during the course of his military service subject to adequate safeguards to ensure that any waiver is free and informed. There is no reason to suggest that his ability to waive rights is any different from the volunteer during his military service.[73]

The volunteer soldier must be taken to have recognised the fact that he may be called to take part in an armed conflict and this is a risk foreseen by him. Indeed, he may hope that he will be called upon to do so in order to put all his training into practice and to be able to advance more rapidly in his military career. No such weighing of risks and advantages will normally apply to the conscript soldier. He will not be taking part in an armed conflict through any choice of his but because his national law has compelled him to do so.[74]

International humanitarian law draws no distinction between volunteer and conscript soldiers. This is not surprising since the Geneva Conventions of 1949 were drawn up at a time when most of the major military powers had in place some form of conscripted military service and the two World Wars had been fought by large numbers of conscript soldiers.

It may be argued that a State which relies upon conscript soldiers during an armed conflict (whether international or non-international) might be tempted to take less care over their lives since the very system of conscription ensures that there will be a ready stream of replacements for soldiers killed or wounded. A comparison might be drawn between, on the one hand, conscript infantry soldiers and highly trained fast jet pilots on the other. The latter group will have taken a considerable time to train and will have cost the State a great deal of money to do so. They will be much more limited in number. Once they are killed, wounded or captured the State may have no effective air power at its disposal. Commanders planning a military operation involving such individuals will have to weigh up carefully the risks of losing aircrew and aircraft very carefully. The same considerations need not apply to conscript soldiers. This is not to

---

[73] This conclusion might, however, be subject to qualification if a system of institutional bullying or ill-treatment of conscript soldiers is in place where the soldier is serving. For further discussion see chapter 3.

[74] Compare the powerful arguments presented by E. Pargeter in her novel, *The Soldier at the Door* (London: Headline Book Publishing, 1955) through the voice of a mother whose son had been killed in battle: 'He didn't want to be put in a spot where he might have to kill somebody else or be killed himself. He never did anything to ask for that, nor did he deserve it. He only went [to fight in the Korean war] because he had to, because they're all taken by law, whether they like it or not. He never had any choice in the matter. And he's dead . . . is that murder? . . . and over and above that, there's the making them kill other people' (p. 47).

suggest that States relying on some form of conscription will act in this way, although some might.[75]

A State engaged in an international armed conflict against one which relies upon conscript soldiers may find that these soldiers easier to kill in large numbers than volunteer soldiers. Conscript soldiers may have received little effective training compared with volunteers. They may have been concentrated in large numbers at a particular defensive position and threatened with severe penalties for themselves or their families if they do not do their utmost to defend a particular military position. A feature of such treatment in recent armed conflicts is for soldiers to surrender in very large numbers[76] and for large numbers of conscript soldiers to be killed.[77]

It might be argued that a State should take note of the fact that a large number of enemy soldiers are conscripts who have been compelled to join the armed forces and may have been threatened with severe military punishments for 'failing to comply with their duty'. Were the State to take such notice, in an appropriate case, it might be expected to adapt its methods and means of combat to protect the lives of these conscripts wherever it can, consistent with its overall objective of achieving success in battle and protecting its own armed forces. Aerial bombing of their positions is likely to cause a considerable number of casualties especially if this is carried out by high-flying bomber aircraft using non-guided weaponry.[78] To attack such forces on the ground through the use of infantry and armoured vehicles as an alternative would cause additional casualties on the side of

---

[75] See, for example, a report that Iraqi officers who had surrendered to coalition forces in 2003 and had left their conscript soldiers 'hungry, poorly armed and almost destitute for weeks, judging by the state we saw them in': *The Times*, 22 March 2003. For discussion of a soldier's right to life and the obligations of his own State see chapter 3.

[76] This was a feature of the Falklands/Malvinas war in 1982 and the Gulf war 1991. Surrender was deemed a feasible option only because the soldiers concerned believed they would be treated within the terms of the third Geneva Convention 1949 when they came into the hands of the enemy. This can be compared with the position of United States conscript soldiers during the Vietnam war where they had no such belief.

[77] For a discussion of the relatively high ratio of conscripts to volunteer Australian soldiers killed in South Vietnam in 1966–7 see R. Forward in Forward and Reece, *Conscription in Australia* at pp. 126–7 and of United States conscripts killed in the Korean war; Useem, *Conscription, Protest* (n. 42 above), pp. 82, 107. This latter study also links the draft, education and family income levels to casualty rates.

[78] The bombing of Iraqi positions by high-flying aircraft was a feature of the Gulf war in 1991, see F. Hampson, 'Means and Methods of Warfare in the Conflict in the Gulf' in P. Rowe (ed.), *The Gulf War 1990–91 in International and English Law* (London: Routledge and Sweet & Maxwell, 1993), p. 103.

the attackers. The only alternative might be a pro-active drive to enable the conscripts to surrender.

Non-nationals as members of the armed forces

There is no restriction in international law on a State recruiting non-nationals into its armed forces if those individuals are fully incorporated into the armed forces.[79] France recruits foreign nationals into its Foreign Legion and Gurkhas, who are nationals of Nepal, are recruited into the British Army.[80] The Russian army is reportedly seeking to recruit as volunteers nationals of States formerly part of the USSR.[81] All the soldiers concerned will, clearly, be volunteers and, as members of the armed forces of the receiving State, will be owed the same human rights obligations as nationals. Whether they are treated equally with other members of the armed forces who are nationals of the State will depend on the national law concerned.[82]

Ethnic minorities as members of the armed forces

It will often be a political goal to ensure that the armed forces are comprised of a representative mix of all ethnic groups comprising the State. This may be seen as an equality issue but it may also be seen as necessary for 'political and economic reconstruction and future conflict prevention [to ensure] proper integration of minorities in society, including the military sector'.[83]

Women members of the armed forces

The incidence of women serving in the armed forces of States varies considerably. In Europe the effect of Directives from the European Union concerned with equal treatment of men and women has resulted in States having to assess whether there are good reasons for preventing

---

[79] Should they be a member of the armed forces of a party to an international armed conflict they will not be mercenaries, see Additional Protocol I 1977, Art. 47(e).

[80] See *R. (Purja and others)* v. *Ministry of Defence* [2004] 1 WLR 289, CA.

[81] *The Times*, 25 April 2003.

[82] See *R (Gurung et al)* v. *Ministry of Defence* 2002 WL 31784511.

[83] 'Human Rights and the Armed Forces' (Office of the Commissioner for Human Rights, the Council of Europe) paper prepared for a seminar in Moscow, 5–6 December 2002.

women from volunteering for service in the armed forces or for service in particular units. The acceptance of women into the armed forces is seen as an equal treatment rather than a human rights issue.[84] Some States prevent them from volunteering to be infantry soldiers[85] whilst other States impose no such restrictions.[86] A further beneficial consequence of the wider participation of women in the armed forces of a number of States has been to reduce the need to reach military force level targets through some form of conscription. It is recognised that women members of the armed forces may be captured during an international armed conflict and taken prisoner of war. The third Geneva Convention 1949 directs States to take particular measures where women combatants become prisoners of war.[87]

Once the State has accepted that women may become soldiers it will owe then, as a group, obligations different from men soldiers. Experience has shown that in an armed forces environment women members are at some risk from sexual predations of men soldiers. This may take the form of sexual harassment, sexual assault or rape.[88] The armed forces will need to put in place procedures to protect women soldiers from this type of activity. It will not be sufficient for them to assert that they have prohibited sexual harassment or rape and that harsh penalties can be imposed under military law. The State will be liable for the activities of other soldiers if those in command where the victim is located did not do 'all that could reasonably be expected of them to avoid a real and immediate risk [of

---

[84] See, however, the African Charter on Human and Peoples' Rights 1981, Art. 18(3).

[85] The United Kingdom is an example. See *Sirdar* v. *Army Board* [2000] IRLR 47. Germany permitted women to serve only in the 'medical and military music services' until the decision of the European Court of Justice in *Tanja Kreil* v. *Federal Republic of Germany* [2002] 1 CMLR 1047. See also the Committee of Women in the NATO Forces (NATO website). See, generally, M. Segal in R. Howes and M. Stevenson, *Women and the Use of Military Force* (Boulder: Lynne Rienner Publishers, 1993) pp. 86, 91; G. Nolte and H. Krieger in Nolte, *European Military Law*, p. 86.

[86] Israel is an example. See CCPR/C/ISR/2001/2, 4 December 2001, paras. 34, 35. They may not, however, be represented in the senior leadership of the armed forces, see A/52/38/ Rev. 1, Part II, 12 August 1997: Concluding Observations of the Committee on the Elimination of Discrimination Against Women: Israel, para. 158.

[87] See Arts. 25, 130. See also the first and second Geneva Conventions 1949, Art. 12; Additional Protocol I 1977, Art. 76; the Rome Statute of the International Criminal Court 1998, Art. 8(2)(b)(xxii). M. Segal in Howes and Stevenson, *Women and the Use of Military Force*, p. 90 shows that two women of the United States armed forces were taken prisoner of war in the Gulf war 1990–1. One was taken prisoner in the Iraq war in 2003.

[88] Consensual sexual activity between soldiers is discussed in chapter 3.

INDIVIDUALS WITH DISABILITIES

degrading or humiliating treatment] of which they have or ought to have knowledge'.[89]

In practical terms it will not be easy to show such knowledge on the part of the State (acting through its armed forces). Individual women may be reluctant to make a formal complaint if they fear that their military careers might be jeopardised by doing so.[90] The facts would need to suggest also that there was 'a real and immediate risk' of degrading or humiliating treatment. This would be difficult to establish in most cases.

Individuals with disabilities

On occasions, individuals with some form of disability have sought to join the armed forces. At first sight it might appear that, the ultimate purpose of the armed forces being to engage in combat, there would be no scope for those with disabilities to serve in them. This is, however, too sweeping a conclusion since the nature of an individual's disability will be relevant, there may be anti-discrimination legislation within the State and there are a number of roles within the armed forces where participation in combat is not, in practice, expected.[91] The role of the armed forces will differ among States and it will, generally, be for them to determine the standards of health and fitness for potential recruits. They will be expected to determine whether the role, for example, of a military musician is one primarily as a musician or as a soldier. Different physical abilities may be needed for each role.[92] It seems clear, at least under the 1950 Convention,

---

[89] *Osman* v. *United Kingdom* (2000) 29 EHRR 245, at para. 116, a decision of the European Court of Human Rights, the principles of which may be adopted by other human rights bodies.

[90] See *Gagnon* v. *Canadian Human Rights Commission and the Canadian Armed Forces* (Canadian Human Rights Tribunal) 14 February 2002, which involved 'unacceptable discriminatory behaviour' by commissioned officers following a complaint of sexual harassment by the complainant's wife, also a serving soldier. See also *Levac and the Canadian Human Rights Commission* v. *Canadian Armed Forces* (Human Rights Tribunal) 2 February 1995, http://www.chrt-tcdp.gc.ca/decisions/docs/levac2-e.htm (dismissal due to heart problem); J. Chema, 'Arresting "Tailhook". The Prosecution of Sexual Harassment in the Military' (1993) 140 *Military Law Review* 1.

[91] See *Canada (Human Rights Commission)* v. *Canada (Armed Forces)* [1994] 2 FC 188, Robertson JA (dissenting).

[92] For an example, see *Canada (Human Rights Commission)* v. *Canada (Armed Forces) and Husband* [1994] 2 FC 188 (dealing with alleged discrimination against an applicant, whose eyesight did not reach the minimum standards for military service, for a career as a musician in the Canadian Armed Forces).

that that Convention 'does not guarantee the right to serve in the armed forces or to be recruited in public service employment.'[93]

Child soldiers

There has been a campaign for some time to persuade States not to recruit child soldiers into their armed forces.[94] One of the difficult issues has been the age at which a person is considered to be a 'child' soldier. In Additional Protocol I 1977, to the Geneva Conventions 1949 the minimum age for recruitment was set at fifteen[95] and in the Optional Protocol to the Convention on the Rights of the Child on the Involvement of Children in Armed Conflict 2000 (Optional Protocol 2000), parties have agreed not to permit children under the age of eighteen to take a direct part in hostilities.[96] This Protocol also permits, with certain safeguards, States to recruit individuals younger than eighteen into their armed forces but specifically directs that no compulsory recruitment should take place under this age.[97] A further difficulty has been the recruitment of child soldiers to serve in armed groups. The Optional Protocol purports to prohibit armed groups from recruiting individuals under the age of eighteen years.[98] The culmination of this development has been the inclusion in the Rome Statute 1998 of the International Criminal Court of the war crime of 'conscripting

---

[93] See *Marangos* v. *Cyprus*, Application No. 31106/96, 20 May 1997, admissibility, para. 2; *Leander* v. *Sweden*, 26 March 1987, paras. 59, 71.

[94] There have been various calls on States to deal with this issue. See, for example, 'Report to the Secretary-General on Children and Armed Conflict' (United Nations Security Council (UNSC), S/2002/1299, 26 November 2002) paras. 27–68; A/58/546-S/2003/1053, 10 November 2003, para. 45; the Amman Declaration on the Use of Children as Soldiers, 10 April 2001, which refers to previous declarations from regional conferences. The United Nations Secretary-General has directed that all members of national contingents on peace support operations be at least twenty-one years of age. See, generally, G. Machel, *The Impact of Armed Conflict on Children*, UN Doc. A/51/306, 26 August 1996, para. 62; B. Thompson, 'Africa's Charter on Children's Rights: A Normative Break with Cultural Traditionalism' (1992) 41 *International and Comparative Law Quarterly* 432; G. Goodwin-Gill and I. Cohen, *Child Soldiers* (Oxford: Oxford University Press, 1994).

[95] Article 77(2). See also the United Nations Convention on the Rights of the Child 1989, Art. 38.

[96] Article 1.   [97] Articles 3 and 2, respectively.

[98] Article 4. The State itself is required to 'take all feasible measures to prevent such recruitment' (Art. 4(2)). On ratification of the Protocol Mexico declared, in CCPR/C/LKA/2002/4, 18 October 2002, para. 461 that the responsibility 'for non-governmental armed groups for the recruitment of children under 18 years or their use in hostilities lies solely with such groups and shall not be applicable to the Mexican State as such'. For the difficulties of applying the provisions of a treaty to an armed group see chapter 6.

or enlisting children under the age of fifteen years into the national armed forces (or into armed forces or groups)'.[99]

Although these principles are not stated directly in a human rights instrument they have been considered to reflect such a basis. It appears that the 'United States in particular took the view that [the insertion of the war crime of enlisting children under the age of fifteen] did not reflect customary international law and was more a human rights provision than a criminal law provision'.[100] It is significant that (at least) some States perceive this restriction on recruiting or enlisting children as being primarily for their protection rather than, in the case of an armed conflict, the victims of their actions.[101] The war crime set out in the Rome Statute 1998 applies only where the State is engaged in an armed conflict and it will not therefore prohibit recruitment of soldiers under the age of fifteen during peacetime.[102] In this case the State will only be under an obligation to prevent this if it is a party to the Optional Protocol 2000 and it fails to take 'all feasible measures to ensure that members of its armed forces who have not attained the age of 18 years do not take *a direct part in hostilities*'.[103]

---

[99] Article 8(2)(b)(xxvi) and Art. 8(2)(e)(vii).

[100] R. Lee, *The International Criminal Court, The Making of the Rome Statute, Issues, Negotiations, Results* (The Hague: Kluwer International, 1999), p. 117. See also Human Rights Committee General Comment No. 17, para. 3. Compare the (majority) view of the Appeals Chamber of the Special Court for Sierra Leone, *Prosecutor* v. *Norman*, Case No. SCSL-2004-14-AR72(E), 31 May 2004, paras. 33, 51, which held that the appellant could be tried for the offence of 'conscripting or enlisting children under the age of fifteen years into armed forces or groups or using them to participate directly in hostilities' since, by 1996, this offence had become part of customary international law.

[101] See, for example, the dissenting opinion of Justice Robertson in *Prosecutor* v. *Norman*, Case No. SCSL-2004-14-AR72(E), 31 May 2004, who commented that the conscripting or enlistment of children under the age of fifteen was to put 'at risk the lives of those who have scarcely begun to lead them' (para. 45). At para. 38 he described this prohibition 'against child recruitment . . . as a human rights principle'. The prohibition on recruitment or enlistment of children under eighteen years is contained in the Optional Protocol to the Convention on the Rights of the Child on the Involvement of Children in Armed Conflict 2000. Compare the prohibition in Additional Protocol I 1977, Art. 77, of the use of mercenaries.

[102] This is the effect of Art. 8(2)(b) even though sub-para. (xxvi) refers to conscription or enlistment of children under the age of fifteen 'into the national armed forces or using them to participate directly in hostilities'. The same principle applies in non-international armed conflicts: see Art. 8(2)(c) and sub-para. (vii). Compare circumstances where the recruitment into national armed forces or into armed groups occurred prior to the onset of an armed conflict.

[103] Emphasis supplied. For the understanding of the United States of this term see its declaration upon ratification of the Protocol. By January 2005 there were ninety-one States

A State party to all the relevant treaties[104] which did not foresee itself being involved in an armed conflict would not be constrained by international law from recruiting fourteen-year-olds into its armed forces, even although there may be sound practical reasons for recruiting soldiers only from those aged eighteen or above. It might have in mind that soldiers under fifteen could be employed, for example, in a military cookhouse and, were an armed conflict (whether international or non-international) to arise, such child soldiers would be discharged, be placed in the reserves or be confined to non-combat-type duties until they reached the age of eighteen.[105]

It is also difficult to argue that the human rights of the fourteen-year-old soldiers have been affected adversely merely by the fact that they had been recruited by the State into its armed forces, especially where they and their parents had agreed to the recruitment. This view is based upon the assumption that the consent of the child and his parents is voluntary. It would remain so despite the motive for all to agree is one of poverty.[106] In a State not party to the Optional Protocol 2000, where the child is conscripted into the armed forces during time of peace, it will be difficult to conclude that the human rights of the child have been adversely affected given the acceptance of service of a military character as a general exemption from the prohibition on forced or compulsory labour.[107] In order, however, to give some practical edge to the attempt

party to this Protocol. A new international coalition was formed in 1998 which commented that 'the latest research on child soldiers estimated that more than 300,000 children under 18 years old are fighting in armed conflicts around the World': see http://web.amnesty.org/802568F7005C4.

[104] The Geneva Conventions 1949, their Additional Protocols 1977, the UN Convention on the Rights of the Child 1989 and its Optional Protocol 2000; the African Charter on the Rights and Welfare of the Child 1990, OAU Doc. CAB/LEG/24.9/49 (1990).

[105] See the view of Justice Robertson in his dissenting opinion in *Prosecutor v. Norman*, Case No. SCSL-2004-14-AR72(E), 31 May 2004 at para. 9. Some States party to the Optional Protocol have made declarations to the effect that, although they may recruit soldiers under the age of eighteen, they are either involved in compulsory training until that age or their law specifically prohibits persons under eighteen being involved in armed conflict.

[106] See also the view of Justice Robertson, *ibid.*, at para. 8, although he was discussing the nature of 'voluntary enlistment' in a non-international armed conflict. Article 3 permits voluntary recruitment providing it is 'genuinely voluntary', Optional Protocol 2000, Art. 2. All States party to the Optional Protocol require the consent of the parents of a child recruited under the age of eighteen: see declarations and reservations to the Protocol.

[107] See, for example, the 1966 Covenant, Art. 8; the 1950 Convention, Art. 4(3)(b); the American Convention on Human Rights 1969, Art. 6(3)(b). *Quaere* where the conscription involves, say, ten-year-old children in which their education continues whether two provisions of the 1950 Convention, namely Arts. 4(3)(b) and 8(1), would be in conflict with each other. This would depend upon the (perhaps) unlikely possibility that the State could show that the conscription was necessary on grounds of 'national security'.

to ban the recruitment or enlistment of children under eighteen years into armed forces the Optional Protocol requires that States ratifying the Protocol indicate the minimum age of voluntary recruitment.[108]

Since, unlike States, rebels do not possess standing armies they are unlikely to 'recruit' children under fifteen in the absence of an armed conflict. In the event of a non-international armed conflict experience has shown that their recruitment is not uncommon. This is discussed further in chapter 6.

---

[108] Article 3. A number of States party to the Optional Protocol permit recruitment into the armed forces at the age of sixteen. See the declarations and reservations of Bangladesh, Canada, Chile, El Salvador, United Kingdom. Conscription of children under eighteen is prohibited: Art. 2.

2

The human rights of members of the armed forces

Human rights issues relating to particular groups of individuals who wish to join, or who form part of, the armed forces have been discussed in chapter 1. This chapter will consider the human rights obligations of a State towards its soldiers otherwise than through the disciplinary process, which is discussed in chapter 3. The human rights of soldiers during armed conflict and in multinational forces will be discussed in chapters 5, 6 and 7. The current chapter will therefore concentrate on the human rights of soldiers during peacetime service.

The right to life

It appears trite to say that, if necessary, a soldier is expected to 'sacrifice' his life in the service of his country.[1] Whilst it is accepted by soldiers that they will have to risk their lives in time of armed conflict and they may well be killed or wounded this is not so readily accepted in times of peace. In practice, however, a soldier is more likely to be killed[2] during peacetime than during an armed conflict. This is due to a number of factors, such as the statistical unlikelihood of a particular soldier being involved in an armed conflict, the experience of modern international armed conflict where casualties on the part of soldiers are low and the fact that military service can be inherently dangerous. In attempts to imbue training with the realism of an armed conflict soldiers are expected to carry out physical activities bearing little direct comparison with civilian life. Apart from

[1] *Quaere* whether a soldier ever 'sacrifices' his life, in the sense of voluntarily giving up his life for 'the sake of something else more important or worthy' (Oxford English Dictionary).

[2] Since it is difficult to map a particular human right obligation on a State to prevent a soldier being injured, concentration is given to the loss of life of soldiers. The State may provide compensation schemes for soldiers injured during peacetime activities. For an example see the Crown Proceedings (Armed Forces) Act 1987 (United Kingdom) but not during wartime: see *Mulcahy v. Ministry of Defence* [1996] 2 All ER 758 where a soldier was injured in battle conditions during the Gulf war 1991; *R. v. Ministry of Defence, ex parte Walker* [2000] 2 All ER 917, injury by warring factions in Bosnia.

strenuous exercise these activities may involve climbing cliff faces at night, training in the jungle or low flying in mountainous terrain. In addition, initial recruit training is often made deliberately rigorous to inculcate what are seen as the basic skills of military life and to determine (where recruitment is voluntary) whether particular individuals are unsuitable for further service.

It is unlikely that a State will deliberately deprive a soldier of his life during peacetime unless it has retained the death penalty for particular military offences.[3] A soldier is much more likely to be killed through recklessness or negligence on the part of his military superiors or colleagues or through the deliberate actions of his fellow soldiers. Although an unintentional killing of a person during an official form of military training may involve the application of a human rights provision designed to protect life, it is unlikely to do so unless the risk of death was very likely to occur and could, with reasonable action, have been prevented.[4] The European Court of Human Rights has confirmed that it is not necessary to show that the failure to prevent the killing amounted to 'gross negligence or wilful disregard of the duty to protect life'.[5] In these circumstances the killing might also be said to be 'arbitrary'.[6] The death of a soldier resulting from such conduct would be likely also to attract the attention of those responsible for enforcing the criminal law. An investigation into the death might establish the commission of a criminal offence rather than the breach of a human rights obligation owed by the State to that particular soldier.

The killing of one soldier by another as a result of acts which in themselves breach the military discipline code is a much more likely occurrence. This can take the form of bullying, initiation ceremonies or other unlawful activities. The fact that it occurs at all is perhaps not surprising. Young

---

[3] For discussion see chapters 3 and 5. *Quaere* whether a breach of the fair trial provisions of a human rights instrument would lead to a breach of the right to life if the death penalty is imposed.

[4] See, for example, *Stewart* v. *United Kingdom* (1984) 39 DR 162, para. 15, a decision of the European Commission on Human Rights. It concluded that 'the concept that "everyone's right to life shall be protected by law" enjoins the State not only to refrain from taking life "intentionally" but, further, to take appropriate steps to safeguard life': *ibid.* at para. 14. This case was concerned with the application of Art. 2(2) of the 1950 Convention.

[5] *Osman* v. *United Kingdom* (2000) 29 EHRR 245, para. 116; *Z* v. *United Kingdom*, Applic. No. 29392/95, para. 73.

[6] This is the test for a deprivation of the right to life under the 1966 Covenant. To bring Art. 4 of this Covenant into line with Art. 2 of the 1950 Convention it would be necessary to construe 'arbitrary' as meaning the 'authorities did not do all that could be reasonably expected of them to avoid a real and immediate risk to life of which they have or ought to have knowledge': *Osman* v. *United Kingdom* (2000) 29 EHRR 245.

men are often accommodated in a limited space, loyalty to a particular regiment or unit is actively encouraged, access is often available to lethal weapons and military training is expected to develop aggressive tendencies in soldiers. In addition, the commanding officer of the military unit, upon whom rests the obligation to maintain discipline, will need to delegate to subordinates the maintenance of that discipline throughout the whole unit. The commissioned officers are likely to delegate to a non-commissioned officer (for example, a sergeant) or even to more senior recruits the 'duty' to ensure that order and military discipline occurs amongst the soldiers for whom they are responsible. The risk to an individual soldier of being killed by another soldier in these circumstances is greater where his status in the military hierarchy is the lowest. A recruit is much more likely to suffer in this way than an established soldier.

For the State to be responsible for a breach of its obligation to respect the life of the soldier it will need to be shown that the armed forces acted in breach of the soldier's right to life. The commanding officer of the unit concerned could, of course, argue that neither he nor any of his commissioned officers sanctioned the unlawful acts on the part of subordinates and that the killing of the soldier could not, therefore, be laid at the door of the armed forces. The killing, it might be argued is no different from one committed by one soldier against another off the barracks for an entirely private purpose.

These arguments will often not reflect the realities of military life. Where the soldiers are conscripts the risk of an unlawful killing of a soldier may be higher than in armed forces reliant upon volunteers. Since by the very nature of conscription most individuals will not wish to be soldiers the military regime may be made deliberately harsh in order to maintain control of individuals.[7] Since this form of control will be labour intensive the actual implementation of such a policy depends upon the delegation of tasks to a relatively low level in the military hierarchy. The practice of this may involve commissioned officers turning a blind eye

---

[7] See, generally, D. Brown, '*Dedovshchina:* Caste Tyranny in the Soviet Armed Forces' (1992) 5 *Journal of Soviet Military Studies* 53; I. Kiss, 'Rights of Conscripts in Peacetime: Obstacles to and Opportunities for Providing Judicial and Non-Judicial Solutions in East European and Central Asian Countries' in B. Vankovska (ed.), *Legal Framing of the Democratic Control of Armed Forces and the Security Sector: Norms and Reality/ies* (Belgrade: Geneva Centre for the Democratic Control of Armed Forces and Centre for Civil-Military Relations, 2001), p. 45. Kiss comments that 'Dedovshina [sic] has become an almost integral part of the armed forces, and presently is widespread in the post-Soviet armies, especially the Russian army . . . it has become an officers' tool for controlling recruits' (p. 45). Further discussion of the military discipline system in relation to conscript soldiers can be found in chapter 3.

to the way in which senior recruits or non-commissioned officers treat conscript soldiers. If questioned about the activities actually taking place the former are likely to say that they do not condone bullying or physical violence against recruits and, indeed, that they have expressly forbidden it to occur. They may also take the view, in the alternative, that in their armed forces new conscript recruits have traditionally been treated in this way with the result that the armed forces as a whole have benefited since all senior recruits will have passed a tough challenge.

There is not only the risk that conscript recruits will be killed by other soldiers but also the risk that a combination of bullying and poor living conditions will lead soldiers to commit suicide. A pattern of suicides would suggest to senior officers that military discipline, in the form of protecting soldiers from other soldiers, has broken down and that action needs to be taken by them to restore discipline.

The European Court on Human Rights has faced a number of situations where the acts of individuals not acting as the agents of the State have nevertheless led to the responsibility of the State for a deprivation of the right to life of an individual. In none of these cases has the actor, who actually caused the death, been acting purportedly on behalf of a State organ. In one case he was a prisoner,[8] in another, an unidentified group[9] and in another a soldier of the same rank as the deceased who was acting for his own private purposes.[10] The Court has stressed that the State may be responsible for a breach of human rights to a person within its jurisdiction where the 'authorities knew or ought to have known at the time of the existence of a real and immediate risk to the life of an identified individual or individuals from the criminal acts of a third party and that they failed to take measures within the scope of their powers which, judged reasonably, might have been expected to avoid that risk.'[11] In *Yavus* v. *Turkey* a soldier was shot and killed by an army firearm in his barracks by another soldier who had been convicted of wilful homicide prior to being conscripted into the army. The killer was not permitted to have a firearm with him while in the part of the barracks concerned and he had obtained the ammunition for it improperly. The Court held that Turkey was not in breach of its obligations to the deceased since the

---

[8] *Osman* v. *United Kingdom* (2000) 29 EHRR 245. For the acts of other private individuals see *Cyprus* v. *Turkey* (2002) 35 EHRR 30, para. 81.

[9] *Kaya* v. *Turkey* (28 March 2000).

[10] *Yavus* v. *Turkey*, 25 May 2000 CD353. The killing was the 'result of a private vendetta over the supply of drugs' (at p. CD359).

[11] *Osman* v. *United Kingdom* (2002) 35 EHRR 19, para. 116.

applicants had 'failed to show that the authorities knew or could be taken to have known that there was a real and immediate risk to the life of [the deceased soldier]'.[12] The result might have been different if the military authorities had known that the killer was suffering from a mental disorder which might have induced him to kill a colleague.

These cases illustrate how difficult it would be to hold the State liable for a breach of the right to life owed to soldiers. Despite the killer in *Yavus* having a conviction for wilful murder (for which he had served eight years in prison) and having access to lethal weapons, the military authorities could not reasonably have foreseen the real and immediate risk to the deceased. Nor was it sufficient in *Osman* where the killer was known to the police as someone who might have been harassing the victim.

The key element is the real and immediate risk to an individual of which they have or ought to have knowledge. This may occur if senior officers become aware of a pattern of conduct on the part of their subordinates which has resulted in the death of one or more soldiers. In this case they might reasonably be expected to do something to prevent 'a real and immediate risk to life of which they have knowledge'. It will, however, be difficult to show an 'immediate' risk unless the officers have knowledge of a specific activity which is likely to cause a real risk to the life of a particular recruit or a group of recruits.[13]

The incidence of deaths amongst recruits in some States is reported to be high. It has been suggested, for instance, that the number of recruits who died as a result of 'harassment between conscripts [between 1985 and 1991] is 15,000'.[14] This would appear to be an unsubstantiated number. The Monitoring Committee of the Parliamentary Assembly of the Council of Europe was informed that in '2000, 68 persons were acknowledged to have died as a result of violence in the [Russian] army'.[15]

Deaths and the suicides of soldiers will, most often, occur within the military barracks. It will therefore often fall to the military authorities to conduct (at least preliminary) investigations into the death of an individual soldier. In some cases the death may appear to have been caused

---

[12] At p. CD359.

[13] An example might be where senior officers know that a particular recruit is to be forced to take part in 'Russian roulette' with live ammunition in a firearm.

[14] *Black Book on Rights of Conscripts in Central and Eastern Europe* (European Council of Conscript Organisations, 1996) at http://www.xs4all.nl/-ecco/cee-blackbook.html, p. 22. The comment made by Kiss in Vankovska, *Legal Framing* at p. 45 that 'according to a recent assessment of the Russian army, one or two cases of conscript murder invariably occur each day' is difficult to accept.

[15] Doc. 9396, 26 March 2002, para. 67.

through a tragic accident with firearms or other military equipment or through what appears to be a suicide quite unrelated to the activities of any other soldiers.[16] In other cases evidence may point to the involvement of other individuals in the death. Where this occurs the risk that any military police investigation may be perceived to be unwilling to uncover the whole circumstances of the death through fear of causing some form of blame to fall on senior officers may be considerable. It is, in reality, unlikely that there will be sufficient evidence to justify serious charges under the criminal law or the military discipline code against these senior officers since their involvement will be of the nature of an omission rather than of an actual act which has contributed to the death. In the armed forces of some States a board of inquiry (or something similar) will be charged with the task of investigating a particular incident, whether the cause of an air accident, the loss of equipment or it may be convened to investigate the circumstances surrounding the death of a member of the armed forces while in military barracks.[17] The importance of an independent investigation into the death of an individual has been stressed, particularly by the European Court of Human Rights, as a corollary of the right to life within the 1950 Convention.[18] This is unlikely to be satisfied by a military board of inquiry drawn from the same unit as the deceased since it lacks the necessary ingredient of independence from those it is purporting to investigate.[19]

[16] With the strict military discipline applied in many (if not most) States in recruit training and the fact that this will be an experience quite different from that which a recruit has experienced prior to his military service the possibility of suicide cannot be discounted. Experience, however, has shown that a deliberate killing can be made to look as if the death was caused by suicide; see the *Black Book* (n. 14) at p. 22. Careful investigation becomes essential where the facts suggest that a soldier has killed himself.

[17] This may be more likely where the death occurs abroad. Where it takes place in the territory of the State concerned a relationship with the civil authorities will normally be set out in the national law.

[18] See, for example, *McKerr* v. *United Kingdom* (2002) 34 EHRR 20, para. 112 and earlier cases cited there. See also the Convention against Torture 1984, Art. 12; Human Rights Committee General Comment No. 6, para. 4.

[19] In Report No. 74/2001, Case 11.662 (Columbia) the Commission has referred on several occasions to the unsuitability of military courts as a forum for examining alleged violations of human rights committed by members of the armed forces or National Police': para. 24 In Report No. 26/97, Case 11.142 (Columbia) the Inter-American Commission on Human Rights concluded (in 1998) that 'because of its structure, the military investigation [of alleged extra-judicial investigations] was neither independent nor impartial. The proceedings also clearly denied the petitioners their fundamental right to an effective judicial remedy, as they were not permitted to be a party to the case. Another serious defect in the military proceedings was the exclusion of available evidence from eye witnesses'

Where the inquiry is conducted by the civilian authorities this requirement of independence is likely to be met. It may take the form of an
inquest into the death of the soldier. A difficulty to be faced is that the
military authorities are likely to have been on the scene first and they
may have carried out their initial investigations. A poorly led inquiry
may cause relevant evidence (such as clothing or paperwork) to be
destroyed or to go missing.[20] There may also be an inadequate autopsy
of the body or a refusal to permit an independent forensic pathologist to
examine it.[21]

Torture, degrading or inhumane treatment

Chapter 3 will consider this issue where punishments have been imposed
informally by a non-commissioned officer as part of a purported exercise
of disciplinary powers. There may, in practice, be little difference between
the role played by of these non-commissioned officers and other senior
recruits but this chapter will consider specifically the actions of the latter.

One example might be taken to illustrate the issue. This is of a soldier
required by more senior soldiers to masturbate in front of all his colleagues.[22] It does not take a great leap of imagination to conclude that
this would 'grossly humiliate' the victim and thus amount to degrading
treatment.[23]

The arguments discussed above relating to whether senior officers of
the armed forces may cause the State to be liable for a breach of the
human rights of recruits (in particular) apply also to allegations that
individual soldiers have been subjected to torture, degrading or inhuman
treatment by their soldier colleagues. The treatment of recruits has been
reported as including hitting soldiers with a 'belt with iron pieces on it'[24]
and 'position Alpha' where the victim is required to 'bend forward and

---

(at para. 139). Caution should be exercised in concluding that all military investigations
of military conduct are incompatible with human rights standards. The structure of the
investigation will be crucial.

[20] An allegation made in *The Times*, 2 October 2002, concerning the deaths of more than
one recruit at Deepcut military base in the United Kingdom.

[21] See *Manual for the Effective Prevention and Investigation of Extra-Legal Arbitrary and
Summary Execution* (UN Doc. E/ST/CSDHA/.12, 1991) and cited in *Salman v. Turkey*
(ECtHR) 27 June 2000, para. 73.

[22] See the *Black Book* (n. 14) p. 21.

[23] See *Smith and Grady v. United Kingdom* (2000) 29 EHRR 493 and chapter 3 where the
nature of degrading punishments is further discussed.

[24] *Black Book* (n. 14) p. 21.

receive a forceful kick with the point of the boot in the tailbone'.[25] The threat of such treatment could amount to torture if it is carried out with the 'consent or acquiescence of a public official or person acting in an official capacity'.[26] Since it is unlikely that senior officers will have 'consented' to the acts alleged to amount to torture the issue will revolve, in practice, around whether they have 'acquiesced'[27] in them. An initial assessment would require a senior officer to know that the acts were actually taking place. Should this be so he has the power to prevent such acts through the military discipline system to a much greater extent than would a civilian employer.[28] By deliberately failing to do so it could be reasonably inferred that he has acquiesced in them. Both he and the person carrying out the torture would commit a criminal offence if the State to which they belong is a party to the Convention Against Torture and other Cruel, Inhuman or Degrading Punishment 1984 and has implemented its obligation to ensure that torture is an offence under its national law. Whether the State itself is in breach of its obligations to the soldier concerned not to engage in torture (certainly under the 1950 Convention) will depend on whether the inactivity of the senior officer can be imputed to the State. It would appear that a much greater degree of knowledge is required of that officer. He must know that there is a real and immediate risk to a particular individual or group of individuals.[29] This will be much more difficult to establish than his acquiescence in torture being committed by a recruit upon another recruit.

---

[25] D. Brown, '*Dedovshchina*: Caste Tyranny in the Soviet Armed Forces' (1992) 5 *Journal of Soviet Military Studies* 53, 63. Compare 'Prevention of Torture in the Armed Forces of the Slovak Republic' in CCPR/C/SVK/2003/2, 6 August 2002, paras. 51–4.

[26] The Convention Against Torture and Other Cruel, Inhuman or Degrading Treatment or Punishment (1984), Art. 1(1). The Committee Against Torture concluded that the 'systematic mistreatment and beating of recruits in the armed forces [in the Ukraine] constitutes a flagrant violation of the Convention [Against Torture]': UN Doc. A/52/44. 1 May 1997, para. 136.

[27] The Oxford English Dictionary defines this as 'agree, especially, tacitly, raise no objection'. For an obligation upon armed forces commanders to prevent 'bullying' see CCPR/C/CZE/2000/1, 4 May 2000, para. 135.

[28] The acts concerned would not amount to the infliction of a 'lawful sanction' even though they might be carried out in some general way so as to promote that which military law seeks itself to promote, namely military discipline. No justification for torture is permissible: see the 1984 Convention, Art. 2(2).

[29] For the obligation of the State to conduct an investigation see Art. 12. For the principles of liability under the 1950 Convention see *Osman* v. *United Kingdom* (2000) 29 EHRR 245, para. 116. For an application of this principle to a killing of one conscript soldier by another see *Yavuz* v. *Turkey* (n. 10 above).

It should not be thought that the problems alluded to above apply only in armed forces which rely upon conscription for their recruitment. Some forms of degrading or inhuman treatment can be found, especially in initial recruit training establishments, but they are more likely to be carried out by non-commissioned officers than by other recruits.[30] This is due, to some extent, to the fact that recruits of different seniorities are unlikely to share the same accommodation or to train together.[31] This is, from a practical view, significant since most acts of degrading or inhuman treatment are likely to occur at night or before soldiers report for duty. It is also due to the fact that most volunteers will wish to get through their military training successfully in order to pursue their chosen careers in the armed forces and will not wish to jeopardise this goal through being disciplined for a 'bullying' incident.

A situation similar in all-volunteer armed forces to conscription occurs where soldiers are recruited on a voluntary basis but, as part of their terms of service, are not permitted to leave for a fixed period. This may be as a result of their age on recruitment or a recognition that as military training is required to be tough it is in the interests both of the recruit and of the armed forces that they should remain long enough for a proper assessment to be made by both sides as to whether the recruit is suitable for military service. Where the recruit is unwilling to remain in military service he may find himself the subject of degrading treatment both by his colleagues (who consider that he is letting down their platoon during recruit training) or by non-commissioned officers. A major difference, however, between a volunteer recruit in these circumstances and a conscript recruit is that the former is more likely to be able to go absent without leave, since leaving the barracks will normally not be as easy to achieve for the latter. Whilst the volunteer may be able to avoid degrading treatment by going absent without leave he may be subject to a loss of liberty when he returns, since he will have committed a military offence. The conscript will find that he cannot so easily escape from such treatment if it is a feature of recruit training in his own armed forces.

A further difference between all-volunteer armed forces and a conscript force is that commanders in the former type generally have more incentive to ensure that bullying of recruits does not occur since they are dependent upon the conditions of military service being sufficiently attractive to

---

[30] For discussion of whether acts which might be degrading to a civilian employee would be so regarded in military service see chapter 3.

[31] Compare the system of dedovshchina which is dependent on the fact that two cohorts of conscripts are recruited annually, see Brown, '*Dedovshchina*', 57.

young people, who might have a choice of different occupations to enter, to encourage them to join and to remain in the armed forces. Any allegation made of bullying in the armed forces is likely to attract widespread media attention, certainly in some States, with a foreseeable drop in the number or quality of volunteers for service. In conscript armed forces, on the other hand, the continual flow of recruits can lead to less concern over the treatment of individuals within military service. This is not to say that it always does but the attitude of commanders to recruitment can be quite different in each type of armed forces. More so is this the case in conscript armed forces where the number of men recruited each year is determined less by the actual needs of the armed forces than by the numbers of young men in the population at that time.[32]

It is, perhaps, too easy to blame the ill-treatment of recruits upon poor leadership exhibited by senior officers. Whilst this may be the case in some instances,[33] experiences of well-disciplined armed forces show that the practice is difficult to eliminate completely unless this particular aspect of the culture of the armed forces is changed.

Deprivation of liberty

In the absence of any disciplinary proceedings soldiers may argue that in the course of their military service they have been deprived of their liberty. To test the limits of this term two examples will be taken. It is not uncommon, particularly in conscript armies during recruit training, that soldiers are not permitted to leave the barracks.[34] They may have been sent 'to serve as far away from home as possible [and the conscript] may get no leave at all throughout his term of service'.[35] Again, in the naval services of States sailors may be at sea for long periods of time with no, or very limited, opportunities for shore leave. Although the term 'deprivation of liberty'

---

[32] There are, of course, variations in the practice of States as to the basis on which compulsory military service is imposed. Some may permit wide latitude for exemptions either to military service or to alternative military service (or both); others might permit long periods of deferral for education purposes. See, generally, chapter 1.

[33] This is argued to be the case in the *Black Book* (n. 14).

[34] See I. Kiss in Vankovska, *Legal Framing*, who comments 'it became clear from interviews with conscripts that they are given leave once in a two–three month period and sometimes even less frequently, instead of having a free day once a week' (p. 50); *Compulsory Military Service in Central and Eastern Europe, a General Survey* (Utrecht: European Council of Conscripts Organisations, 1996), p. 7.

[35] C. Donnelly, *Red Banner: the Soviet Military System in Peace and War* (Coulsdon: Jane's Information Group, 1988), pp. 175, 178. This must be taken to reflect the position as at 1988.

must be considered in its military context,[36] different considerations apply in each of these examples. It has been stated that if a soldier is free to carry on his normal military duties and is, for instance, not locked in a room he will not be deprived of his liberty even though he is not permitted to leave the barracks.[37]

The confinement of soldiers (usually conscripts) to their barracks for long periods of time, perhaps punctuated by short periods of leave, for no military purpose other than as a means of control over them is difficult to see otherwise than as a deprivation of their liberty. It can be no answer to argue that soldiers can move about in a relatively large area. If this were to be the case it would be necessary to lay down limits as to what the minimum area for this free movement should be and to exclude any areas out of bounds to them.

It is necessary not only to consider the area in the barracks to which soldiers have access but also the length of time for which this confinement to barracks is to last. The shorter the period of time the greater the possibility that the State could argue that such confinement bears a military purpose. It might be argued, for instance, that a very short period of confinement to barracks is necessary at the start of recruit training to ensure that the recruits are able to give their undivided attention to their military duties in order to instil in them the necessary qualities of the ethos of military service, which will apply in war as well as in peacetime. There must, however, be a limit to this period, recognisable in all armed forces. The longer this period of confinement the easier it would be to conclude that the soldiers have, effectively, been deprived of their liberty, especially if no recreational facilities are provided in the barracks and no military duties are required of them during a significant period of that time.

The formulation of this principle is not without its difficulties. A State could argue that it, in relation to its conscript soldiers, it must be the judge as to what military duties are required of them and the time over which they may be imposed, even though to civilians the tasks the soldiers are required to perform appear to have no purpose. Should the matter come up for judicial determination it will be for a court or other adjudicatory body to assess all the facts in order to determine whether, in reality, the confinement to barracks amounts to a deprivation of the soldiers' liberty.

A sailor whose ship (or submarine) is required to remain at sea for long periods of time without calling in at any port can hardly claim to be deprived of his liberty while on board that ship or boat merely because he

---

[36] *Engel* v. *Netherlands* (1976) 1 EHRR 647, para. 54.   [37] *Ibid.* at para. 61.

cannot leave his place of 'employment'. Where he is a volunteer he must be taken to have consented to his confinement. Where he is a conscript this element of consent will be missing but it can be more easily argued by the State concerned that its defence interests require the ship (or boat) to be at sea for this length of time. There is, in consequence, an objective justification for the fact that the sailor is unable to leave the vessel for the period of time that it is at sea and there is not, therefore, any deprivation of his liberty.[38]

Right to privacy

It is often difficult to think of a soldier possessing a private life while he is on military premises.[39] He may be accommodated in dormitory barracks (or on board ship or boat) with the minimum of personal space.[40] If he is a conscript soldier he may spend only very short periods of time off the barracks, if he is given leave. His military duties may last for most of the time in which he is not permitted to be in bed. This is not to suggest that this reflects the conditions of all members of the armed forces in all States, although it does apply in some States at some (or all) of the time of military service.[41]

It can be seen from this that the recognition of the private life of a conscript soldier is often quite different from that of the volunteer. The issue of the retention of the volunteer in military service will often prove as important as his initial recruitment and the conditions of his service must be conducive to this. No such considerations apply to the conscript soldier. Any discussion of the right to privacy of soldiers is therefore much more likely to be relevant where that soldier is a conscript rather than a volunteer.

---

[38] Other facts may be important, such as whether a conscript sailor is denied leave while the vessel is at a foreign port when volunteer sailors are allowed such leave. A justification for the difference in treatment as between these two groups might be required should the matter come before a human rights body since it may be argued that, by this fact, the State has deprived the conscript sailor (although not the volunteer) of his liberty.

[39] Despite the fact that in the British Army the lowest rank is known as a 'private soldier'.

[40] The limits of the personal space of a soldier within barracks may be relevant in terms of a power to search this space without judicial authorisation. For an example see the Armed Forces Act 2001 (United Kingdom), s. 15.

[41] The armed forces of most States will restrict the private life of a soldier during initial military training more than when the soldier is fully trained. See J. Hockey, *Squaddies: Portrait of a Subculture* (Exeter: University of Exeter Press, 1986), p. 24 for an account of what the author describes as 'an end to privacy'.

A clear separation between the private life of a soldier and his military life is difficult to draw. A civilian will normally have defined hours of work or a contractual minimum and maximum number of hours' work with clear holiday entitlements. It will, in other words, be relatively easy to determine which part of a day he is employed and which part is his private time. Soldiers, whether conscripts or volunteers, may be required to be on duty for long periods of the day or be subject to such call at any time of the day or night. They may also be required to spend large amounts of time separated from their families at various times during military service. It is difficult to find a civilian occupation that would impose such restraints on the private life of an employee. Even if it did, the civilian employee would normally be entitled under his contract to give a short period of notice to terminate his contract. If he were to be absent from his employer's business without leave he would not, unlike the soldier, commit a serious offence.

Whilst the various human rights treaties require a State to respect a person's family and private life[42] the characteristics of military life must be considered. Certain acts by military superiors may be considered not to be a breach of a human rights instrument although they could be described as degrading treatment if carried out in a civilian context. The human rights instruments permit interference with the right to a private life in defined circumstances if such interference is necessary in a 'democratic society in the interests of national security'[43] or such as is not 'arbitrary or unlawful'.[44] An order to a soldier to travel with his unit to a military base abroad in order to prepare for an armed conflict could clearly be justified and therefore a non-interference with his private life, although he will be separated from his family.[45] Similar orders, which lead to a separation of a soldier from his family, will fall into this category if such a separation is necessary for training purposes. It has become common in Europe, with the independence of a number of States from the former USSR, for the armed forces of one State to train for weeks or months in the territory

---

[42] The 1966 Covenant, Art. 17; the 1950 Convention, Art. 8; the American Convention on Human Rights 1969, Art. 11.

[43] The 1950 Convention, Art. 8(2).

[44] The 1966 Covenant, Art. 17; The American Convention on Human Rights 1969, Art. 11(2).

[45] Compare the position, however, if the soldier is a single parent and the effect of the order to travel from the family home is to deny the child access to his or her sole parent. This may be a real practical problem where the soldier concerned is a reservist and is called up for service.

of another State.[46] This will invariably lead to a separation between the soldier and his family.

Any justification of an interference with the private life of a soldier based on his agreement to it is unsatisfactory when the nature of conscript service is considered. A volunteer will, no doubt, appreciate that military service may entail periods of separation from his family. Should this occur on a scale greater than he had anticipated he will have the option, normally, of giving notice to terminate his service. The law of his State will determine the 'right' he has to terminate his military service. The conscript, on the other hand, has no right to terminate his military service prematurely. He has not consented to any separation from his family for long or short periods, even if he accepts that he must perform his conscripted military service. Should this non-interference with a soldier's private life through separation from his family be based upon agreement or consent this cannot be its basis for the conscript. The justification for this separation must therefore be based upon whether it can be shown by the State to be necessary in the interests of national security or upon the separation not being arbitrary or disproportionate.

A purported justification that conscript soldiers must be based far away from their homes or must live within the barracks is unlikely to stand up to scrutiny unless there is a national security interest involved or the decision to do so can be shown not to be arbitrary.[47] The term 'national security' must have a meaning different from 'whatever the defence ministry decides', even though, of course, the actions of that ministry will affect national security. A further issue arises, namely, the willingness of a judicial body to probe into the actual needs of an alleged claim of national security made by the government. On the one hand it may be argued that only the government knows what national security demands. It has access to intelligence information which the courts may be reluctant to press the government to disclose. On the other hand to argue along these lines is to make the term 'national security' a non-justiciable one, a result hardly envisaged by the drafters of a human rights instrument, such as the 1950

---

[46] The arrangements are made on the basis of the Participating for Peace programme of NATO: see the Agreement Among the States Parties to the North Atlantic Treaty and Other States Participating in the Partnership for Peace Regarding the Status of their Forces (19 June 1995).

[47] Restrictions on the opportunity to live in married soldiers' quarters might infringe the right to a private life: *R. (on the application of Purja et al.)* v. *Ministry of Defence* [2004] 1 WLR 289, CA.

Convention.[48] Indeed, the European Court of Human Rights concluded that the claims of the United Kingdom on the grounds of national security to discharge homosexual members of the armed forces should not be upheld.[49] The significance of this conclusion should not be underestimated. It shows that this Court will weigh seriously the claims of a State to be acting in its national security interests against the aims of the 1950 Convention, and, if necessary, come to a different conclusion.[50]

Issues of national security may also be raised by a State where it seeks to intercept and to read the correspondence of soldiers. There may be grounds for doing this where the soldiers concerned are located within a combat zone or in an area from which they may launch, or defend, an attack and there is a risk that this correspondence will be intercepted by the enemy State. Were this to happen the enemy might learn military security information to the detriment of the State of the correspondents, either directly or indirectly (when it comes to the knowledge of the intended recipient). With the modern systems of communications consisting of mobile telephones and email in addition to the older form of soldiers' letters the means of communicating information has expanded greatly. A State which foresees the risks of sensitive information coming into the hands of an enemy is faced with a number of choices to restrict it. It could prohibit soldiers possessing mobile phones and permit correspondence by email or by letter if it is able to make secure these methods of communication.

A military commander who argued that he did not want his soldiers in barracks to communicate with their families by any means would find it difficult to justify this action in terms of 'national security'. The most likely situation envisaged here is where conscript soldiers wish to let their families know the conditions in which they are required to perform their military service. They might want to let others know of the poor food, living conditions, the treatment they are receiving from other conscripts or the nature of their daily life. The only plausible ground upon which a commander could argue for such a position is that if this information became widespread the ability of the State to secure the presence of individuals for conscripted military service would be compromised, through an increase in those failing to attend for their military service.

---

[48] Article 8(2). Although the term is not mentioned specifically in this context in other human rights instruments it is likely to be a factor in determining whether an interference with privacy is 'arbitrary'.
[49] See *Smith and Grady v. United Kingdom* (2002) 29 EHRR 493, para. 89.
[50] See the powerful dissent of Judge Loucaides in *Smith and Grady v. United Kingdom, ibid.*

A restriction on the correspondence from conscripts would be likely to add very little to this perceived risk, however, since they could communicate this information while on leave. To accept the commander's view would, in effect, be to increase the chances of a denial of the soldier's rights under a relevant human rights instrument, especially if the interference with his correspondence is coupled with an expanded view of what amounts to 'official secrets'. In many States the disclosure of official (or military) 'secrets' is considered to be a serious offence, even though the motive for doing so is not financial gain but to draw to the public's attention matters which the person disclosing believes to be in the public interest.[51]

States may take different views as to whether the sexual activities of a soldier come within his private life or whether their effects have some significance in the military context. This is not a topic of relevance only to members of the armed forces. A civilian who performs acts of a sexual nature in his place of work is likely to be disciplined if they affect the working environment. If the acts are consensual they may, depending on their nature, affect the ability of the employer to conduct his business. If they are not consensual the perpetrator may be disciplined for conduct ranging from harassment to sexual assault.

In the armed forces additional factors come into play. The private time of a soldier may be less clear in the military context and the importance of maintaining military discipline is likely to be stronger than the maintenance of discipline in civilian employment. A sexual relationship between, for instance, a commander and a low-ranking soldier might be considered by senior military officers to be unacceptable, even if it is carried on solely off the barracks and during the off-duty time of both concerned. A variation on this relationship might be one between a soldier and the commander's husband or wife, where no evidence of it is exhibited in the military working environment.

Any attempts to prohibit these relationships would appear to give rise to a claim that the soldier's right to privacy has been denied. In the absence of any effect on the military working environment (which will be the case if the relationship is kept secret by the parties concerned) any argument for making such activities a disciplinary offence must be based upon the need to ensure the maintenance of military discipline or the highest standards of professional personal conduct, in particular, the avoidance of an abuse of authority. Where this relationship is unknown in the military unit concerned there is little risk of a detrimental effect on discipline.

---

[51] See *Hadjianastassiou* v. *Greece* (1993) 16 EHRR 219, para. 46.

There is, however, the risk that it will become known. Even if it is known that a commander is having a sexual relationship with a low-ranking soldier it is likely to have an effect on discipline if the latter is perceived to be treated differently by that commander, or by his (or her) subordinates, from other soldiers. It might also be argued to limit the effectiveness of the commander if he (or she) might be tempted to make decisions which would favour the low-ranking soldier in a war situation and, in consequence, place other soldiers' lives at risk. The latter argument appears to be hypothetical unless the evidence shows that, in the circumstances, it is a real possibility.

Where the relationship is between a commander's husband or wife and a soldier subordinate to that particular commander different considerations come into play. The only possible effects on military discipline could come from the commander's subordinates knowing of this fact and, as a consequence, failing to follow his (or her) orders or from the commander treating the soldier concerned differently from other comparable soldiers. In this connection there may be an unwitting element of gender imbalance between a commander who is a female and one who is a male. Where the commander is a female and her husband is conducting a sexual relationship with a low-ranking soldier the effect of that fact on the willingness of the other soldiers to follow the commander's orders may be non-existent. Where the gender roles are reversed the effect on a largely male soldier corps may be perceived differently. In some societies this fact may compromise the role of the commander but in others it is unlikely to do so. A commander who treated the lower-ranking soldier in a discriminatory way as a result solely of his participation in the relationship would be likely himself to undermine his ability to maintain military discipline.

A State which prohibited these sexual relationships solely on the purported ground of maintaining military discipline might find itself with a difficult argument to make should the issue come before a human rights body.[52] Were it to prohibit them on the ground that it wished to set

---

[52] A comparable situation can be seen in the attempt to prohibit homosexuals from joining or remaining in the armed forces of the United Kingdom. See *Smith and Grady* v. *United Kingdom* (2000) 29 EHRR 493. See also G. Rubin, 'Section 146 of the Criminal Justice and Public Order Act 1994 and the "Decriminalisation" of Homosexual Acts in the Armed Forces' [1996] *Criminal Law Review* 393 (who sets out statistical information at pp. 395–6). In the United States armed forces application of the policy of 'don't ask, don't tell' towards homosexuality is illustrated by *Turner* v. *Department of Navy et al.* (United States Court of Appeals, 15 April 2003) which makes no reference to the 1966 Covenant on Civil and Political Rights.

a standard of acceptable and unacceptable conduct on the part of the members of its armed forces the result might be quite different. This will, however, depend upon whether those members are volunteers and therefore have the ability to consent to being judged by this professional standard or whether they are conscripts with no choice at all on this issue.[53]

The arguments in relation to different rank sexual relationships do not apply where the individuals are of the same rank and they conduct their relationship off the barracks and in off-duty times. Any attempt to prohibit this conduct in these circumstances would be extremely difficult to justify before a human rights body. That is not to say that an attempt might not be made on the ground that soldiers might be distracted from their military duties through concern over their sexual partner serving in the same unit as themselves during wartime. Similar arguments were made about homosexual relations but these were rejected by the European Court of Human Rights in 1999.[54]

Should the armed forces be deployed to a State some distance from the home State of the soldier he may be required to submit to inocula-tions or injections to protect him from particular diseases while serving there. Many (if not most) will have no objections to this requirement and will submit themselves for such medically-administered treatment. Others may refuse. Where there is concern that the enemy will use chem-ical or biological weapons the State may require all its soldiers in the zone of possible military action to take medically prescribed tablets or inoculations to protect them against the consequences of the use of such weapons. Whether a soldier has a 'right' to refuse such medically admin-istered treatment depends upon the extent of his right to privacy as set out in his military law.

It might be argued that, in the exercise of his right to privacy, the soldier has the right to decide what substance is administered into his body. Any forced submission would amount to a criminal offence in the national

---

[53] For an example see *R* v. *Army Board of the Defence Council ex parte D.B.* 2000 WL 1212969 where a British Army officer was invited to resign on the grounds that his behaviour fell below the standards expected of such officers, and for a description of the 'Tailhook affair' in 1991 see R. Howes and M. Stevenson, *Women and the Use of Military Force* (Boulder: Lynne Rienner, 1993), p. 211; J. Chema, 'Arresting "Tailhook": The Prosecution of Sexual Harassment in the Military' (1993) 140 *Military Law Review* 1; D. Jones, 'Fraternization: Time for a Rational Departure of Defence Standard' (1992) 135 *Military Law Review* 37.

[54] See the argument advanced by the United Kingdom to justify its ban on the recruitment or retention of homosexual members in its armed forces, *Smith and Grady* v. *United Kingdom* (2000) 29 EHRR 493, para. 77.

law of many States. If this is the case the soldier cannot be ordered by a military superior to submit himself for such medical treatment although the order may be given through what is perceived to be the best interests of the soldier. Such an order would be illegal since it will involve the commission of a criminal offence.

A soldier who fails to submit himself to such medical treatment is a potential risk to military efficiency should chemical or biological weapons be used since he will tie down other armed forces personnel in caring for him. In consequence he is likely to be sent back to his home State as being unfit for service in that particular region.[55] He may also be charged with a military offence.[56] It is, however, difficult to accept that a soldier has a right to a private life which can be understood as being sufficiently wide to cover a decision not to permit medically-administered substances being put inside his body and then accept that he may be punished for exercising this 'right'.

Experience from the Gulf war 1990–1 has shown that a number of soldiers have attributed their medically prescribed injections and pills designed to combat the effects of the potential use of chemical or biological weapons to their subsequent illnesses. The effects of such treatment have become known as 'Gulf war syndrome' and litigation has begun in some States by former soldiers seeking compensation.[57] The knowledge that soldiers have drawn such conclusions from their medically administered

---

[55] It is reported that 'Australian sailors on their way to the Middle East were ordered home after refusing anthrax [inoculations]': *The Times*, 13 February 2003. See the Australian Military Regulations, Statutory Rules 1927 No. 149, as amended, regulation 435.

[56] *R v. Sergeant (Retired) Michael Kipling* (2002) CMAC 1 (Canada). The primary issue in this case was whether the National Defence Act, RS 1985, c. N-5, s. 126, which imposes an obligation on a soldier to comply with the order to submit to a vaccination unless he has a reasonable excuse, was applicable. A new trial was directed on the facts of the case. The soldier's argument in terms of his human rights was based upon the Canadian Charter of Rights and Freedoms 1982, ss. 7, 12, and 15. In the Charter there is no specific right to private life. In relation to anthrax vaccinations the United States District Court for the District of Columbia issued a preliminary injunction on 22 December 2003 stating that the 'defendants were enjoined from inoculating service members without their consent', *John Doe et al. v. Donald H. Rumsfeld*. The unusual nature of injunctive relief against the military is explored in the opinion of Sullivan, District Judge. Summary judgment was given for the plaintiffs on 27 October 2004. It is likely that this decision would have been otherwise had disciplinary proceedings been brought against service members for refusing to obey a military order to be inoculated.

[57] See *Secretary of State for Defence v. Rusling, President of the Pensions Appeal Tribunal (England and Wales)* 2003 WL 21236566, Newman, J. who expressed the view that his decision was 'not a decision which determines the existence or non-existence of Gulf War syndrome as a "single disease entity"' (para. 81).

treatment in 1990–1 may lead a (small) number to resist such treatment should the situation be repeated.[58]

It is a traditional requirement of the profession of arms that soldiers wear uniform and do so with great attention to detail in terms of what is considered by particular armed forces unit to be acceptable. In some units this can reach fastidious proportions. Some will prescribe hair length, whether beards are acceptable and the extent to which the wearing of personal jewellery is permitted. In addition, physical and cultural differences between men and women might suggest a gender-based approach. Whilst women will not grow beards they may wish to have their hair longer and wear a greater range of personal jewellery than men.[59] It might be thought that the volunteer has agreed to any restrictions on his or her personal liberty but no such agreement will arise merely from the nature of conscript service. The volunteer who, for instance, wishes to grow a beard which his particular armed forces forbid could argue that he has not waived his right to a private life merely by joining the armed forces.[60] It is unlikely that he will have had drawn specifically to his attention on joining that he will not be permitted to grow a beard. The State may take the view that any restriction on growing a beard or long hair or the wearing of jewellery is not 'arbitrary'[61] or is in the interests of 'national security' in a 'democratic society'[62] in that the personal smartness (as defined by the State concerned) of soldiers is an important indicator of military efficiency and discipline in a body where tradition bears a strong influence. It may also seek to argue that where its soldiers are stationed abroad they must display a sartorial and a personal appearance similar to

---

[58] Specific problems in relation to deployment to the Gulf region in 2003 have been the fear of soldiers that a certain number of days should elapse between inoculations and of informed consent by soldiers, *The Times*, 13 February 2003.

[59] The equal treatment of men and women in the law of States may cause some rethinking of issues such as the length of hair and the wearing of personal jewellery. See *Sirdar* v. *Army Board and Secretary of State for Defence* [1999] All ER (EC) 928 and *Raderman* v. *Kaine*, 411 F 2d 1102 (1969).

[60] A waiver of rights must be shown to be 'unequivocal', *Pfeifer and Plankl* v. *Austria* (25 January 1992) para. 37 (with which few human rights bodies would disagree). The European Court of Human Rights has held that the mere joining of armed forces voluntarily knowing that they have a policy of dismissing homosexuals did not result in soldiers having waived their right of a private life: *Smith and Grady* v. *United Kingdom* (2000) 29 EHHR 493. *Raderman* v. *Kaine* concerned a reservist who 'made the choice some time ago to join a reserve unit. Concomitant with this decision was the knowledge that he would be subject to any rules and regulations concerning his appearance for six years' (411 F 2d 1102 (1969) at 1106).

[61] See the 1966 Covenant, Art. 17; the American Convention on Human Rights 1969.

[62] The 1950 Convention, Art. 8.

the soldiers of other States with whom they come into contact.[63] Neither of these grounds is convincing since, at least in the case of the European Convention on Human Rights 1950, it can hardly be said that such restrictions evince a 'pressing social need'[64] or that they are in the interests of national security. Nor is it sufficient to argue that the soldier's hair will not be cut or jewellery removed against his wishes but that he will suffer some other detriment by refusing to co-operate with his military superiors in this regard. Such a detriment could involve administrative dismissal from the armed forces, military punishments or a career disadvantage. Should one or more of these detriments occur to a volunteer soldier purely as a result of one of the issues discussed above it is difficult to accept that this would not involve a breach of his right to a private life. A stronger ground for a State to use is that the growing of a beard or long hair or the wearing of jewellery make it difficult to wear protective equipment (such as nuclear, biological and chemical headgear) and that the wearing of jewellery may cause a risk to the health or safety of the soldier when taking part in military activities. This ground would not cover a general prohibition applicable to all soldiers at all times.

There can be no argument that a conscript has agreed to such restrictions. The fact that soldiers do not generally complain of such issues is, of course, not conclusive evidence that such interference by the military authorities could not amount to infringement of the private life of the soldier.

Freedom of thought, conscience and religion

This right is referred to in various human rights instruments.[65] Historically, it was common in most States for the armed forces to call upon their own deity to guide their arm in battle. It was more common for the army to be composed of soldiers all of the same faith. In more modern times this

---

[63] See H. Besselink in G. Nolte (ed.), *European Military Law Systems* (Berlin: de Gruyter Recht, 2003), p. 597 who refers to a Dutch case where a soldier refused to have his hair cut when required to serve abroad. The court held that there had been no 'infringement of his right to privacy . . . because he had not been forced to cut his hair' although he was required to remain in Holland.

[64] The benchmark of proportionality against which the interests of a democratic society are measured, see *Voigt* v. *Germany*, 26/9/1995; ref: 17851/91, para. 53.

[65] The 1966 Covenant, Art. 18; the 1950 Convention, Art. 9; the American Convention on Human Rights 1969, Art. 12; the African Charter on Human and Peoples' Rights 1981, Art. 8.

link has, in some cases, been less clear with a number of soldiers having different religious beliefs from the majority of their soldier colleagues or having no religious belief at all. The obligation to treat all soldiers in the matter of their religious beliefs equally brings with it an obligation to provide facilities by which these different religions may be practised. Prayer rooms may need to be provided and priests to be appointed, especially where the soldier is unable to cater for his religious needs in off-duty times.[66] There may also be a need to provide facilities for the soldier to receive food consistent with his particular religious practices.[67]

The link between the armed forces and a deity is particularly strong during wartime where loss of life among soldiers is expected to occur. The right of the State to impose limitations on a soldier's manifestation of his religion is curtailed by human rights treaties.[68] None of these limitations refers to national security as a ground for restricting the manifestation of religious beliefs. The point can therefore be made with some certainty that a soldier has the right to manifest his religious beliefs providing they do not cause a breakdown of 'order' within the military environment.[69] This may be unlikely to occur unless an armed conflict is predominantly seen by (at least) some soldiers as a religious one.

During peacetime a unit of the armed forces may be required to be part of a civic ceremony during which there is a religious element. A soldier with no religious beliefs at all or one who professes allegiance to a different religion may object to taking part in the religious aspect of the ceremony. Whilst it seems clear that an order from a military superior to a soldier to change his religion would infringe his rights in this regard an order to enter, with his military unit, a building belonging to a different religion in which all that is required of the soldier is his presence would not necessarily do so, although it may be considered to be insensitive.[70]

---

[66] For the permission given by a Royal Naval commander to a member of his crew to practice Satanism on board ship see *The Times*, 25 October 2004.

[67] For an example see H. Besselink in Nolte, *European Military Law*, p. 595 where the author cites a case involving a 'Jewish navy corporal who for religious reasons wished to eat and drink kosher food only, which was not served'. He was awarded compensation for the cost of preparing his meals on the basis of equality with other soldiers.

[68] See note 65 and, respectively, Art. 18(3); Art. 9(2); Art. 12(3); Art. 8.

[69] The need to preserve 'order' is a ground for the State to limit this right. In this context 'order' must encompass military discipline. For examples, see *Kalac* v. *Turkey* (1997) 27 EHRR 552; *Sen* v. *Turkey*, Application No. 45824/99.

[70] See, generally, G. Nolte and H. Krieger, 'European Military Law: General Comparative Report' in Nolte, *European Military Law*, pp. 88–9. A soldier may object to being ordered to enter a building of the same religion as himself but of a different sect of that religion.

It is very common in States which adopt some form of compulsory military service to provide for an alternative to military service for those who have objections on grounds of conscience to serving in a military armed force. The practice of States will vary as to the nature of this service and how the individual is required to show that he has a conscientious objection to military service. These issues are discussed in chapter 1. What is less common is for States to provide a means by which soldiers who have volunteered for service in the armed forces are permitted to leave if, on grounds of conscience, they feel unable to take part in a particular military operation.

It must be assumed that an order to take part in such a military operation is not an order to take part in an activity made illegal either by the national law of the State or by international law.[71] Should the alternative to the exercise of his conscience be to absent himself without leave or desert from his armed forces he will commit a serious disciplinary offence. This may, in effect, prevent him from exercising his right of conscience since the penalties involved will match the seriousness of the offence in military terms.

The application of the freedom of conscience may operate differently upon the conscript from the volunteer to the armed forces. The latter may be expected to take into account that he will be required, from time to time, to take part in activities that, although not unlawful, might be considered to be contrary to his conscience. He can take this into account in his decision whether to join the armed forces. The conscript soldier has no choice unless he is able to opt for some form of substitute military service or he can show that he is actually a conscientious objector to military service and is able to avoid it. In all-volunteer armed forces the issue may be resolved by invoking military considerations and providing some form of tribunal to assess such cases. The military considerations may revolve around the need to allow a soldier to leave the armed forces if he is, in effect, unable to perform properly his military duties. In a conscript army there is the additional factor that a soldier who is permitted to exercise his freedom of conscience may attain an advantage over those who make no such claim. The former will be able then to achieve what most will seek, namely, dismissal from the armed forces or removal from unpleasant

---

[71] See, for example, the order to shoot and kill those attempting to escape from the German Democratic Republic prior to unification with the Federal Republic of Germany in *K-H.K.* v. *Germany* (22 March 2001), para. 75.

duties. For this reason the opportunity to take such a course may be more limited than in all-volunteer armed forces.[72]

Freedom of assembly and association

This right is recognised in various human rights treaties.[73] There is specific reference to the armed forces only in the 1950 Convention which stipulates that the relevant Article (11) 'shall not prevent the imposition of lawful restrictions on the exercise of these rights by members of the armed forces . . .' In all treaties the right may be restricted in the interests of 'national security or public safety, for the prevention of disorder or crime'.[74]

The numbers of those subject to military discipline will be much greater than those responsible for upholding it. As a result the armed forces have always feared the risk that soldiers (or sailors) will act together in defiance of the orders of a superior in the military chain of command. The weight of numbers could, in most cases, lead to senior officers losing control of an army unit or, in the case of the navy, a ship. It is not surprising, therefore to see in the military law of most States a restriction on the assembly of members of the armed forces where at least one of the aims is to defy the authority of officers charged with the responsibility of maintaining military discipline and carrying out the functions entrusted to that military unit.[75] It is known (at least in Anglophone States) as mutiny and is considered to be a serious military offence.

Its potential as a means of preventing any action (or inaction) being taken by those who meet together is considerable given that, should it be proved, the soldiers concerned will face severe penalties. In addition,

---

[72] A soldier who deserts (in this case from the Russian Federation army) his armed forces 'should not be denied refugee status if return to his home country would give him no choice other than to participate in the commission . . . on a sufficiently widespread basis . . . of act(s) in breach of the basic rules of human conduct generally recognised by the international community': *Krotov* v. *Secretary of State for the Home Department* [2004] EWCA Civ 69, *per* Potter LJ at paras. 39, 51; *Sepet and Bula* v. *Secretary of State for the Home Department* [2003] 1 WLR 856. For issues of a belief by British soldiers in the illegality of the war in Iraq see *The Times*, 30 May 2003.

[73] The 1966 Covenant, Art. 21; the 1950 Convention, Art. 11, the American Convention on Human Rights 1969, Arts. 15 and 16; the African Charter on Human and Peoples' Rights 1981, Arts. 10 and 11.

[74] In all, except the African Charter on Human and Peoples' Rights 1981, the restrictions must be set against the interests of a democratic society.

[75] Individual States will formulate this restriction in different ways.

the very nature of the requirement[76] to obey (lawful) orders of a military superior makes compromise or negotiation difficult, if not impossible, where the military superior indicates that there is no room for discussion of his orders.

This restriction on the right of assembly can be used to conceal poor physical treatment of soldiers, particularly, conscripts, unpopular activities required of soldiers, poor leadership displaying, for instance, discriminatory treatment of certain soldiers or the giving of irrational orders and poor management of the armed forces by the government of the State (such as a failure to pay the soldiers on time or at all). Whilst soldiers may be permitted by the military law of their State to make an *individual* complaint about their treatment in the hands of superior officers it may not permit collective complaints.[77] If the soldiers cannot raise their concerns as a group others may have to do it for them. In some States with conscript armed forces mothers of soldiers have taken on this role and, on occasion, they have attracted considerable publicity both within and outside the State.

In some other States unions of soldiers are permitted. Indeed, there may be separate unions for different groupings of soldiers, for example, officers and conscripts.[78] This is quite a different situation than a State permitting members of its armed forces to join a civilian union. In those States permitting military-specific unions there will invariably be lawful restrictions on a union calling out its members on strike. There may also be restrictions on political activity taking place on the military base, soldiers taking part in demonstrations off the base while in military uniform and on 'industrial action' taking place while on duty.

Other States will take the view that, as a general principle, unions of soldiers should not be permitted. This view will generally be based on the fact that their soldiers normally have a right to complain to their commander if they have a grievance and to superior commanders if the grievance is against the soldier's commanding officer. This, they will argue, should be sufficient to deal with grievances, along with the responsibility placed on more junior officers to ensure the welfare of their men. Another

---

[76] Backed up by a military offence of refusing to obey a lawful order.

[77] For an example of the treatment of what was perceived as a group complaint see L. Gardiner, *The Royal Oak Courts Martial* (London: William Blackwood, 1965), p. 212.

[78] For a survey of the position in NATO States in 1986 conducted by the United Kingdom Government for a report to Parliament, see *Special Report from the Select Committee on the Armed Forces Bill 1985–86*, HC 170 (London: HMSO, 1986) p. 162; *Rekvenyi v. Hungary* (2000) 30 EHRR 519.

reason for prohibiting military unions, although often concealed, is the perceived fear of commanders that to do so would lead to a collective challenge to their orders and, in consequence, to the maintenance of military discipline and the efficiency of the armed forces being impaired.[79]

It has been shown above that the various human rights instruments permit some interference with the right of assembly. A common ground upon which restrictions may be imposed is that of 'national security'. If these human rights instruments are to have any real effect it will be necessary to require the State concerned, in the event of a complaint, to show objectively why the interests of national security require a particular restriction on this right. It has been argued above that the term, 'national security' must mean more than 'the view of the defence ministry' and a human rights court or body may take a view different from that of the State.[80] It is possible that, for instance, the European Court of Human Rights could decide, should a suitable case[81] be brought before it, that a State had not made out sufficient grounds to show that its national security interests required the total prohibition of unions amongst its soldiers if there is a demand by those soldiers for such an opportunity. The practice of a number of other States shows that military unions are permitted but are subject to greater restrictions on their activities than would be their civilian counterparts.[82] The Court might find comfort in this position.

Freedom of expression

In relation to this right (or freedom of speech) there are no specific references to the armed forces in the various human rights instruments,[83]

---

[79] See Parliamentary Assembly of the Council of Europe Recommendation 1572 (2002) calling for a right of association of members of the armed forces.

[80] See *Smith and Grady* v. *United Kingdom* (2000) 29 EHRR 493, para. 99.

[81] This may be more likely to involve conscript soldiers, who cannot be said to have consented to the restrictions on assembly. It is unlikely that the Court would take the same view in time of war.

[82] *Quaere* whether the 'imposition of lawful restrictions on the exercise of these rights by members of the armed forces' (Art. 11(2) of the 1950 Convention) would permit a restriction which is judged by the Court to interfere with the rights concerned although the national law provides for restrictions. See, generally, G. Nolte and H. Krieger in Nolte, *European Military Law Systems*, pp. 83–5; N. Jayawickrame, *The Judicial Application of Human Rights Law* (Cambridge: Cambridge University Press, 2002), p. 759; *Rekvenyi* v. *Hungary* (2000) 30 EHRR 519.

[83] See the 1966 Covenant, Art. 19; the 1950 Convention, Art. 10; the American Convention on Human Rights 1969, Art. 13; the African Charter on Human and Peoples' Rights 1981, Art. 9.

although this freedom may be restricted in the interests of national security.[84] In the military context the exercise of this right may be seen in the form of a letter addressed to a soldier's superior officer or to a person outside the armed forces, or a leaflet or newspaper distributed to other soldiers on a regular or on an irregular basis. It may also involve a soldier expressing his opinion about his treatment or the conditions of military life to his superiors or to his soldier colleagues.[85] It may involve a soldier criticising publicly the direction of the armed forces or the Head of State or being disrespectful to a more senior soldier.[86]

The nature of 'national security' has been discussed above. It seems clear that military discipline *could* be undermined by the exercise of this freedom of expression in the form of a document of some sort.[87] A document which, for instance, advised its readers not to obey the orders of a particular commander would have this consequence, whereas one that merely described life in the armed forces might not. A document which commented that the commander's spouse was having a sexual relationship with a low-ranking soldier might have a greater tendency to undermine the authority of the commander if that commander is a male than if a female.[88] Rather like restrictions on the freedom of assembly, restrictions on the freedom of expression may be used by a higher military authority to conceal matters of concern to soldiers as a particular group. Military punishments are likely, for example, to be imposed for individual acts involved in disclosing military 'secrets' or for challenging the orders of a superior officer or even for 'undermining the morale' of the armed forces. In a memorable phrase the European Court of Human Rights has commented that the freedom of expression 'does not stop at the gates of army barracks'[89] and it has shown itself particularly adept at drawing the line between an acceptable and an unacceptable interference with the freedom of expression. In coming to a view different from the State it has been able to show that it will only be satisfied that the interests of national security

---

[84] This limitation does not occur in the African Charter on Human and Peoples' Rights 1981.

[85] Since this section deals with the freedom of expression in a military context it is not concerned with those limitations on the freedom which would apply to civilians also.

[86] See, for example, M. Davidson, 'Contemptuous Speech Against the President' (1999) *The Army Lawyer* 1, which discusses the First Amendment (freedom of speech) to the United States Constitution and its applicability to members of the United States armed forces. For an offence of using 'insubordinate language' to a superior officer see the Army Act 1955 (United Kingdom), s. 33(1)(b).

[87] See *Engel* v. *Netherlands* (1976) 1 EHRR 647, para. 100.

[88] This 'unequal treatment of men and women' is discussed above.

[89] *Grigoriades* v. *Greece* (1997) 27 EHRR 464, para. 45.

necessary in a democratic society require a limitation on this right if this is proved objectively to be so.[90] It may be satisfied that a restriction is necessary where the manifestation of the freedom resulted in the disclosure of what objectively could be considered to be military secrets or a description of how particular military duties are performed.[91] It would, of course, be relatively easy for the armed forces to conclude that anything which takes place while a soldier is on duty or on a military base is an 'official secret' the disclosure of which could be lawfully prohibited. Taken literally this would, for example, prevent a conscript soldier disclosing to his mother that he is beaten regularly by more senior conscript soldiers or that he does not get enough food or he received very little medical attention for an injury to him which occurred while he was on duty. A State which adopted such an approach to official secrets would be likely to cause a human rights body to weigh the claimed official secret and set it against the permitted limitation of the 'national security' interests of the State.

It is not sufficient in a military case to concentrate on the right of the soldier making the disclosure. The person or organisation to whom the disclosure has been made may also be significant. There is, for instance, a considerable difference between disclosing how the armed forces treat their soldiers to a member of parliament and to an official of a foreign State. There is also a difference between the disclosure of treatment in one part of the army to other soldiers of a different unit and the same disclosure to the national press.

Following a particular military operation a former (or even a serving) soldier may wish to publish a book for sale to the general public concerning that operation and much of its detail. Should the government concerned take the view that its publication would be undesirable, a contest between the freedom of expression of the soldier and the security interests of the State will have to be resolved. In most cases the writer of the book will have left the armed forces and any requirement of confidentiality will apply, therefore, to an individual who is no longer subject to military law. Whether the State can interfere directly by preventing publication or indirectly by requiring the author to hand over all profits obtained from the sale of the book will depend, first, upon the nature of any limitations imposed by the national law on the particular publication (in the form of

---

[90] Compare *Vereinigung Demokratischer Soldaten Österreichs and Gubi* v. *Austria* (12 December 1994), para. 38.
[91] See, for example, *Hadjianastassiou* v. *Greece* (1993) 16 EHRR 219.

contractual arrangements, or otherwise).[92] It will also be necessary to test the national law conclusion against any human rights instrument to which the State is a party. The key issue will be whether such a restriction on the freedom of expression is in the interests of national security. Should the reason for a State to act in this way be a fear of compromising the activities of special forces in any future military operation[93] the longer the period between the activities the book describes and its publication the less likely that a State would be able to prove any real risk to national security so as to justify a restriction on the freedom of expression. It seems clear that a human rights body would be likely to investigate the particular circumstances of any purported restriction on the freedom of expression rather than relying merely on a confidentiality clause which a soldier had been required to sign as a condition of his remaining in the particular special forces unit.[94]

In some States there exists an armed forces ombudsman to whom soldiers may be able to make a complaint of their treatment in the armed forces without first having to raise the complaint with military authorities.[95] In practical terms this may prove to be an effective means by soldiers of enforcing their human rights, although a particular application to the ombudsman may be couched in other language.

Propaganda for war is specifically prohibited in the 1966 Covenant.[96] Whilst this will be an activity normally carried out (if at all) by the government of the State soldiers may be used for such purposes in the national media. A soldier ordered to make propaganda statements would need to show that that order was an unlawful one if he is not to be charged with a military offence by his refusal.[97]

---

[92] For an example see *R. v. Her Majesty's Attorney General for New Zealand* (Judicial Committee of the Privy Council, London, 17 March 2003), which concerned a book about the activities of the United Kingdom special forces in the Gulf war 1990–1.

[93] As it was in *R. v. Her Majesty's Attorney General for New Zealand* case (*ibid.* at para. 17).

[94] In *R. v. Her Majesty's Attorney General for New Zealand* (*ibid.*) the appellant was required to sign the confidentiality clause binding himself for the rest of his life, with return to his unit (and thus a transfer from his special forces unit) as the consequence of not signing. The effect of such an order was discussed in chapter 1.

[95] See, for example, Ireland (see the Ombudsman (Defence Forces) Bill 2002 and debate in the Dail Eireann, 11 December 2003, which Bill excludes the ombudsman considering an action which 'affects national security or a military operation': s. 5(1)(c)). The position in other States in Europe is commented on by G. Nolte and H. Krieger in Nolte, *European Military Law* (n. 63 above), p. 111. An ombudsman for the Canadian forces was established in 1998 and in Australia by an amendment to the Ombudsman Act 1976, s. 19B.

[96] Article 20(1). See also the American Convention on Human Rights 1969, Art. 13(5).

[97] In some States it will be difficult to show that such an order is illegal if implementation of the obligation has not been incorporated into national law. Moreover, the line between

The soldier's human rights during wartime

In a number of the human rights instruments the State may derogate from certain rights in time of war[98] or other public emergency threatening the life of the nation. Some of the occasions on which a derogation might be made are discussed in chapter 5. It may also do so in respect of the right to privacy, to freedom of conscience and religion, to freedom of association and assembly and to the right of expression. It may, however, only do so to 'the extent strictly required by the exigencies of the situation'.[99] It will not be difficult for a State to come to the conclusion that it needs to restrict these rights of non-nationals, such as prisoners of war or protected civilians[100] but it may not wish to do so in respect of is own soldiers.

In the absence of any such derogation a State's national security interests will differ as between peace and war. It may be that it would prefer, as a matter of policy, to rely upon its national security interests to impose any restrictions on these rights rather than to issue a derogation notice.

It is much more likely that a human rights body would decide a particular case in a way which did not conflict with the claimed exigencies of the situation or the national security interests of the State if that State was involved in war. A State has, therefore, a considerable degree of latitude to restrict the human rights it owes its soldiers during war or other public emergency threatening the life of the nation should it so wish.[101]

---

propaganda and other information can be a difficult one to draw since the former, in modern times, is normally used in a pejorative sense. Military forces may, for instance, engage in psychological operations prior to or during a time of armed conflict in which they broadcast messages on a wavelength accessible to the local population. They are likely to argue that this is not propaganda.

[98] This term is taken to refer to an international armed conflict, see chapters 5 and 6 for further discussion.

[99] The 1966 Covenant, Art. 4(1); The 1950 Convention, Art. 15(1); the American Convention on Human Rights 1969, Art. 27(1) which includes 'for the period of time'.

[100] For further discussion see chapter 5.

[101] The State may also restrict the jurisdiction of an armed forces ombudsman 'if an order [to a soldier] is issued in the course of a military operation', see Ombudsman (Defence Forces) Bill 2002, cl. 4(2)(c).

3

Human rights and the disciplinary process

It is axiomatic that the armed forces of a State must be a disciplined body. They possess weapons, equipment and training normally unequalled by any other organ of the State. Without some form of effective control over their activities the armed forces could achieve anything within their physical power and skills. They could, in other words, take over and replace the government of a State from elected politicians but they could not replace those who, for instance, carry out medical services for the whole population, unless all, or a substantial number of, medical personnel were conscripted into the armed forces.

Whilst there may be a number of factors contributing to the fact that, generally, the armed forces of a State do not do what they could actually do, i.e. take over the government of the State[1] this chapter will concentrate on the disciplinary process within the armed forces as a means of controlling their activities.

It is difficult to imagine any group or any body that would benefit if the armed forces disintegrated into an undisciplined body. In the absence of those who would use parts of the armed forces for their own political purposes the State, the civilian population, members of the armed forces themselves and the wider international community have an interest in ensuring that the armed forces of any particular State are a disciplined body.

In a democracy it is well understood that the government must exercise control of the armed forces. Individual States will do this in different ways. In many, if not most, the constitutional arrangements will require it. Treaties to which the State is a party may set out circumstances when the State has agreed to contribute the use of its armed forces abroad.[2] The

---

[1] See, generally, S. E. Finer, *The Man on Horseback* (Baltimore, Harmondsworth: Penguin, 1976).

[2] See, for instance, the Agreement Between the Parties to the North Atlantic Treaty Regarding the Status of Forces, 19 June 1951, 199 UNTS 67, or various other status of forces agreements. See, generally, D. Fleck (ed.), *The Handbook of the Law of Visiting Forces* (Oxford: Oxford University Press, 2001).

government of the State will, therefore, ultimately be responsible not only for the actions of its armed forces abroad but also to ensure that they are in a condition to achieve the tasks set for them by that government. It will, for instance, have to ensure that: members of the armed forces receive their pay on time; recruitment and retention of personnel is adequate for the tasks required of them; and that their equipment is of a standard appropriate for the roles expected of them. Each of these factors illustrates the fact that the discipline of the armed forces of a State is not the sole responsibility of the armed forces themselves; the actions of the State may be crucial in achieving a disciplined body.

If we pursue these factors a little further we can see that if the State is unable to pay the members of its armed forces their salaries on time it will take a considerably high level of discipline to ensure that they continue to perform the tasks expected of them. In peacetime members of the armed forces may be willing reluctantly to accept this if they perceive that the State itself is in a difficult position and is genuinely unable to do so. They may, in practice, be able to make up the shortfall (if there is merely delay in paying their salaries) by taking civilian jobs in their free time. Not all members will be able to do this and it is likely that the ability to do so will, generally, follow rank seniority lines. A colonel, for instance, might be able to make up the shortfall in his salary by obtaining civilian employment, but a conscript soldier might not. It is, perhaps, also necessary to consider the status within the State of the officer corps. Where this is high, officers may be willing to accommodate a government unable to pay them on time if they can foresee that this is a temporary difficulty.[3] Where, on the other hand, the status of the officer corps is low, or has been perceived to have been lowered by changes in the political system of the State, they may be less willing to accommodate the government. In these circumstances their attitude will be transmitted directly or indirectly to their subordinates with a consequent effect on discipline.

The State will determine the structure of the armed forces. Where the armed forces are composed of conscripts they will usually be quite different in nature from a disciplined body comprised entirely of volunteers. A particular State may have relatively little concern over the terms and conditions of service of conscripts, over retention rates or the perceived harshness of the military discipline system. In a system providing an endless supply of soldiers little thought needs to be given to making the job an attractive one or, indeed, what the conscripts are required to

---

[3] In this connection high social status is equated with high morale.

do. Since the recruits are not volunteers it has traditionally been the case that the only way to keep them in order is through a harsh disciplinary system.

Where recruitment to the armed forces is purely on a voluntary basis the government will need to pay attention to the terms and conditions of service in the armed forces, including the harshness or otherwise of the military disciplinary system, if it is to maintain recruitment at the level it requires. The problem is, however, not as simple as this. Within the armed forces of any State there will be tasks much sought after and others which are less popular. In many States the opportunity to be trained as a military pilot is much sought after and standards to be achieved by recruits for pilot training are often very high. The skills acquired can relatively easily be transferred to the civilian sector at some later stage. The role of an infantry-man is often not seen as so attractive with demand for it being often lower and the standards of educational achievement and ability being less than for the military pilot. Both the infantryman and the military pilot will, however, be subject to the same (or similar) disciplinary system. Whilst differences in rank in an all-volunteer force may justify some differences in the actual application of the disciplinary system they cannot justify, for instance, harsh discipline for non-commissioned officers and a weak disciplinary system for commissioned officers. In addition, retention of trained personnel (not least because of the costs of training) becomes a major issue for the government. A perception that the disciplinary system is fair to all servicemen and women is essential if recruitment and retention of all types and skills is to be maintained.

Poor morale in the armed forces may well lead to a breakdown, to some extent, of discipline, caused by a number of factors, including the unwillingness of the government to provide the necessary standard of equipment for the armed forces to carry out the functions allocated by that government to them. This may range from unsafe equipment, to lack of training time on, for instance, flying tasks because of lack of sufficient fuel, to inadequate military equipment or accommodation and rations of soldiers.

Where a State wishes to change recruitment of the members of its armed forces from a conscript to a voluntary basis, a goal being pursued by many States in Europe and elsewhere,[4] many changes in the structure of the armed forces will be required. One of these will be the nature of the disciplinary system.

[4] See chapter 1.

What is military discipline?

Within a State military discipline is likely to be perceived as the most stringent form of professional discipline. Other professional bodies, employers or voluntary organisations will also possess a form of discipline. These may range from religious orders, employers, schools, to the police, the fire services and other quasi-military organisations, such as coast guards. For a serious breach of discipline a member of one of these organisations may lose his ability to work in that profession again, his actual employment, his chances of promotion or he or she may be fined.

Military discipline shares with its various forms of civilian counterpart any one of these consequences in a particular case. How, then, can it be argued that military discipline, as a disciplinary system, is *sui generis*? One answer is that it has traditionally been this way, certainly from the nineteenth century onwards. In some States soldiers were largely recruited from individuals who had, in reality, very little choice between joining the army or starving to death. In practical terms they were a form of quasi-conscript. In other States a form of conscription had actually been introduced.[5] In both cases those who actually had a choice would have swelled the ranks in a desire for adventure, some form of booty or to travel beyond their immediate environs. The officer corps, certainly in Europe, was derived from individuals belonging to a higher social class than the 'common' soldier and expected to treat its social inferiors in ways which would be considered unacceptable today.[6] In structure there was little significant difference between the army and the navy of a State, if the latter existed.

It is too easy to conclude that military discipline in the nineteenth and twentieth centuries uniquely exhibited harsh penalties for relatively non-serious offences. So did the civilian society in many States. In England, for instance, the death penalty or transportation to a colony was available to the courts for what would now be considered to be relatively minor criminal offences. Military discipline held on to harsh penalties much longer than did the civilian courts and the armed forces imposed these penalties on their own members within the confines of military barracks. In States having a form of conscription dismissal from the armed forces for a serious breach of its disciplinary code was not a practical solution.

---

[5] This may have varied from the twentieth-century form of conscription which applied to the whole of the State. It could, for instance, have involved 'press-ganging' individuals in the locality of a port for naval service.

[6] See J. Haswell, *Citizen Armies* (London: Peter Davies Ltd, 1973), chapter 2.

This would be the position also if the offence was committed during wartime. Penalties had therefore to be developed to match the seriousness of the offence. The move to all-volunteer armed forces in the latter half of the twentieth and the early twenty-first centuries led to changes to the disciplinary system but the principle that the armed forces retained control over their disciplinary systems prevailed, as did the acceptance that some acts would have to be prohibited which were not punishable in one form or another in a civilian profession.

Not only were some acts prohibited by the armed forces' disciplinary system which were not prohibited in the civilian sphere but a wider range of punishments was developed. These could include those recognisable by civilian professions such as dismissal, a fine or a reprimand affecting chances of promotion or reduction in rank (or grade) but there were others, such as the death penalty for certain military offences, corporal punishment, detention (not to be confused with imprisonment), the imposition of menial tasks[7] and restrictions in movement, given that the soldier was considered to be employed twenty-four hours a day. In some States the armed forces are permitted to try criminal offences committed within a military context by their own courts. The nature of the supervisory powers possessed by the civilian courts over their military counterparts will also vary.

In addition to these differences, military discipline has to be conducted, on occasion, in times of war or 'warlike'[8] activities. Whilst it may be debated whether the military discipline system is created essentially for war or warlike conditions or whether it is created for peacetime service the essential fact is that it has to operate more frequently in the latter than in the former circumstances. Indeed, most armies in the world do not experience war or warlike conditions. Those which do, do so relatively rarely. For most members of the armed forces at any one time there is little risk that they may actually have to engage in military operations against an enemy. The risk of a soldier losing his life in battle may, in many States, be considerably less than the risk to a police officer of being killed in the course of his or her duty. The difference between the police disciplinary system and that of the armed forces is that the

---

[7] An example which appears in more than one military system is the order to clean a floor (or toilets) with a toothbrush.

[8] See *R. v. Brocklebank* (1996) 134 DLR (4th) 377, Decary J, para. 29. Lawyers would prefer to speak of armed conflicts (of an international or a non-international character) or of military activities similar to an armed conflict.

latter (it would probably be generally recognised) is designed for war or warlike activities, although it is recognised that it must operate in peacetime also.

It might be argued, however, that since war or warlike activities are, in reality, a rare occurrence for most armed forces a peacetime disciplinary system might be adopted and should war or warlike operations be required some legislative machinery might be employed to convert a peacetime disciplinary system onto a war footing. This would enable, it may be argued, the disciplinary system to match better the actual conditions of service in the armed forces. It would assist with recruiting and retention in all-volunteer armed forces since military service could be made similar to some form of civilian employment. The nearest comparator in civilian employment might be the police force, whose members are, themselves, subject to a disciplinary code.

Some States have argued that this two-tier disciplinary system is highly undesirable.[9] First, it may be difficult to distinguish 'peace from war'. The certainty offered in distinguishing between the two when States were in the practice of declaring war has largely disappeared. It is more common to expropriate the word 'war' to refer to action against a noun[10] in addition to military action against a defined State. States may become involved in a non-international armed conflict or even in assisting the police force to quell civil disorder within the bounds of its territory. The armed forces may form a part of a United Nations or other multinational force. To those caught up in these activities on the part of the armed forces it may look very similar to a war. Secondly, since most members of the armed forces at any one time will carry out their military service in peacetime conditions they will also train in these conditions. If the mission of their armed forces[11] is primarily to oppose those who threaten the State or its interests it is argued that they should train for these conditions and be subject to a disciplinary system that will actually apply in wartime. The breakdown of military discipline in wartime may be disastrous not only for the State concerned but also for innocent civilians. The former may face national defeat and the latter the risk of death, injury or damage

---

[9] See, for example, 'Military Justice in the Australian Defence Force' (Joint Standing Committee on Foreign Affairs, Defence and Trade) presented to both Houses of the Australian Parliament on 21 June 1999, para. 4.32; Special Report from the Select Committee on the Armed Forces Bill, Session 2000–2001, vol. II, HC 154-II (2001) p. 146 (United Kingdom).

[10] Such as the 'war against terrorism' or even the 'war against drugs'.

[11] It should not be thought that the mission of the armed forces of every State is identical.

to their property from the rapacious acts of an undisciplined armed force.

The reality of the situation for most States is neither black nor white; there will be changes in the disciplinary system if the State moves from peace to war (however defined). These changes may be structural, such as the imposition of different military courts to operate in war conditions,[12] or practical, such as the closer control over the movements of military personnel during wartime.[13] It is likely, however, that most States will wish to keep their military disciplinary system broadly similar for these two contrasting conditions.

Finally, the attitude of members of the armed forces is worth considering. Where the armed forces consist of volunteers only it is reasonable to infer that the disciplinary system is acceptable to them, otherwise they would not have joined. They may be presumed to have agreed, by joining, to subject themselves to a disciplinary system more stringent than any other operating within the civilian sphere. It must be assumed that each individual has thought it necessary to become subjected to such a code, if only for his or her own safety given that military activities can often prove to be dangerous. To argue that by accepting this type of employment members of the armed forces have also accepted the risks of being treated unfairly under it, or that they can be dealt with in any way that their superior officers consider appropriate, is to misunderstand the nature of their voluntary acceptance of military service. The operation of the armed forces, particularly in the way it treats those subject to its disciplinary code, will be controlled to a greater or lesser extent by that code or by national law generally.[14] The advantages of a disciplinary code to an individual following any particular occupation or even leisure activity in

---

[12] Or whether one soldier can sue another for negligence committed in the course of his duty.

[13] The requirement to serve twenty-four hours a day (subject to sleep and meal times) may need to be implemented. When members of the armed forces are off duty in peacetime there may be minimal control by superior officers as to how much alcohol is consumed by them. In war or warlike conditions all alcohol may be prohibited or closely monitored.

[14] In practice, however, private soldiers may have more 'unofficial power' and may operate 'a negotiated order . . . in which a relaxed interpretation of military law is traded-off for effective role performance', J. Hockey, *Squaddies: Portrait of a Subculture* (Exeter: University of Exeter Press, 1986), p. 159. For suggestions as to an appropriate code of ethics for soldiers see M. Friedland, *Controlling Misconduct in the Military* (Study Prepared for the Commission of Inquiry into the Deployment of Canadian Forces to Somalia) (Ottawa: Minister of Public Works and Government Services, 1997), pp. 20–2.

civilian life are as applicable to members of the armed forces as they are to civilians.[15]

In armed forces comprised of conscripts the position appears to contrast with that for volunteers. The conscripts have not voluntarily joined the armed forces but in many States they are permitted to make a choice between military service and a civilian substitute or alternative service. If they decide to accept the obligation to serve in the armed forces, rather than in the substitute service, they have exercised some choice. The freedom to choose is not, of course, of the same nature as that of the volunteer and it may be no real choice at all if the conscript has no conscientious objection to military service but merely would not have chosen this type of employment at all.

Armed forces subject to a disciplinary system under international law

It may be thought that international law would have no interest in disciplinary systems within the armed forces of States in much the same way as it has no interest in the disciplinary systems of State police forces. From the early part of the twentieth century, however, treaties have required the armed forces of States to possess a disciplinary code if that State wishes the members of its armed forces to be treated as prisoners of war if they are captured. There is therefore a *quid pro quo* for prisoner of war status, that individuals can be punished under their own disciplinary system for breaches of international humanitarian law (or the laws of war) and that a superior officer is responsible for those under his command.[16] Those outside the disciplinary code of any armed forces, such as the mercenary or the civilian who takes an active part in hostilities, will not be entitled to prisoner of war status if captured. Neither will they be considered to be lawful combatants.

Although international law may consider it important that a member of the armed forces be subject to military discipline, it may also be concerned to impose limits on that jurisdiction. Noting a tendency in some States

---

[15] An example might be the interest which all employees have in ensuring that those who shirk their work and thereby place it on others should be disciplined. See J. Hockey, *Squaddies*, who argues that (at least in the British army) the working relations among private soldiers are based upon 'reciprocity'.

[16] See the Regulations Annexed to the Hague Convention (IV) 1907, Art. 1; the third Geneva Convention 1949, Art. 4(2); Additional Protocol I 1907, Art. 43.

for military courts to exonerate military personnel for breaches of the human rights of civilians, calls may be made to restrict such jurisdiction in circumstances where civilian courts are considered to be the appropriate forum.[17]

The influence of human rights on the disciplinary systems of the armed forces

From a superficial level the point might be made that the human rights of soldiers is an oxymoron. The reality of military life is that a soldier's life must be tough if he is to become a 'tough soldier' ready to join battle and defeat enemy soldiers. Sacrifices of various kinds are expected from him and this type of regime has worked in the past (at least for some States) in bringing victory in war. Human rights in the workplace may be fine for civilians but military life is, and should be, quite different. A 'civilianisation' of the military, it might be argued, will only lead to defeat in war.

A moment's thought will show that such an attitude is untenable in the twenty-first century, providing the nature of these human rights is considered within a military context.[18] An army which declared that it would ignore the human rights of its soldiers during its disciplinary procedures may find it difficult to recruit and retain them where it depends upon voluntary enlistment. Where the army is comprised of conscript soldiers the State might be expected to guard them against infringements of their human rights through the military disciplinary process since it has compelled them to join the armed forces.

It is, however, surprising that it should take so long for the applicability of human rights principles to be recognised in military disciplinary procedures.[19] This is particularly so in western Europe where for most

---

[17] For a summary of relevant international instruments (particularly in respect of disappearances) see 'Issue of the Administration of Justice Through Military Courts' E/CN.4/Sub.2/2003/4, 27 June 2003, paras. 40–4. See, however, the Rome Statute of the International Criminal Court, 1998, Art. 17(2) where an armed conflict has taken place.

[18] The military context will include, where appropriate, peacetime and war or warlike conditions.

[19] The creation of a new army is likely to bring human rights to the fore. See J. McClelland, 'Starting from Scratch: The Military Discipline System of the East Timor Defence Force' (2002) 7 *Journal of Conflict and Security Law* 253, 258. This might be compared with existing armed forces which become the armed forces of a new State, such as the Ukraine and Moldova. See, generally, E. Fidell, 'A Worldwide Perspective on Change in Military Justice' in E. Fidell and D. Sullivan (eds.), *Evolving Military Justice* (Annapolis: Naval Institute Press, 2002), p. 209.

States the European Convention on Human Rights has been in force from the early 1950s and most have relied upon conscription for at least some of the period since then. There are a number of reasons why this should be so. In some States the military disciplinary procedures deal only with relatively minor military offences; any allegation of a serious nature against a soldier will be dealt with by the civilian courts.[20] In other States, where the military disciplinary procedures can result in serious penalties, the drive to make the disciplinary procedures compliant with the human rights standards of the 1950 Convention has been carried out largely by soldiers themselves. Typically, they have been disciplined and have then brought an application to the Commission (when it was in existence) or to the Court of Human Rights alleging a breach of their human rights. When the Court has decided the case the relevant States have then altered their procedures to try to ensure compliance with the Convention. The fact that soldiers themselves have taken the initiative shows how the development of human rights principles to the military disciplinary procedures has been slow. A volunteer soldier who wishes to remain in the army is likely to want to take his punishment and get on with his military career. A soldier who wishes to leave the army or who has been dismissed from it is more likely to consider bringing an application under the Convention to challenge the procedures involved in his case.

A conscript might be expected to make a challenge more readily given his involuntary submission to military discipline procedures. The experience under the 1950 Convention, however, suggests otherwise. Conscript soldiers appear to have accepted that they may be punished within the military structure. It may be that, in some States, they do not have access to independently-minded lawyers who can advise them as to their 'rights' nor to conscript organisations which can take up a case on their behalf.[21] Conscript soldiers appear to have been more concerned with another issue, namely, their wish to publish within the barracks, or more generally

---

[20] See, generally, G. Nolte and H. Krieger, 'Comparison of Military Law Systems' in G. Nolte (ed.), *European Military Law Systems* (Berlin: De Gruyter Recht, 2003), pp. 160–70.

[21] See I. Kiss, 'Rights of Conscripts in Peacetime: Obstacles to and Opportunities for Providing Judicial and Non-Judicial Solutions in Eastern European and Central Asian Countries' in B. Vankovska (ed.), *Legal Framing of the Democratic Control of Armed Forces and the Security Sector: Norms and Reality/ies* (Belgrade: Geneva Centre for the Democratic Control of Armed Forces and Centre for Civil-Military Relations, 2001), p. 55. Kiss concludes that 'there is a general need for training special attorneys in the protection of conscript rights'.

in the armed forces, their views about military service or particular aspects of it (including the way they are treated).[22]

In many armies soldiers are disciplined by a mix of informal and formal procedures. The former usually consist of soldiers superior in rank to the soldier being disciplined imposing some form of treatment on him which is permitted by the most senior ranks in the army. The formal procedures will typically involve a hearing by a military court (or court-martial) or a semi-formal hearing by the soldier's commanding (or other senior) officer. There may or may not be a system of appeals for the soldier to use.

Informal disciplinary systems

In terms of its frequency a soldier is likely to be subjected to many more informal disciplinary procedures than occasions when he is to be dealt with formally. The use of the term 'informal disciplinary procedures' is intended to exclude acts by soldiers superior in rank to the individual soldier subjected to them which are illegal, such as any use of violence in the form of bullying, initiation ceremonies or otherwise. It is intended to refer to orders by a non-commissioned officer to a soldier for whom he has responsibility to perform acts ostensibly as a punishment for failing to perform his duties as a soldier to an acceptable standard. At one level this may appear to be a form of 'extra training', at another, punishment. It is not, of course, uncommon in many professions for a person under training to be required to perform a particular duty again or to be sent for further training to achieve an acceptable standard. The difference in the armed forces is that this punishment may take the form of what would be considered in civilian life to be demeaning or even life-threatening in some circumstances.

Examples of this type of punishment would include a soldier, whose responsibilities do not normally include cleaning the toilets, being required to do so with a toothbrush[23] or cutting the grass with nail scissors. It would also include him being required to repeat a demanding physical activity with the risk of exhaustion being foreseeable. The person giving the order may well have done so with the intention of making the individual a better soldier or one who will obey military orders without

---

[22] See chapter 2 for further discussion.

[23] This form of 'punishment' appears from the literature to be (or to have been) common in the former Soviet Union and in the United Kingdom. See respectively, D. Brown, 'Dedovshchina: Caste Tyranny in the Soviet Armed Forces' (1992) 5 Journal of Soviet Military Studies 53, 61; The Times, 11 February 2003. It also appears in a cartoon within a report written by the Parliamentary Commissioner for the Armed Forces in Germany.

questioning them. He may characterise this punishment as having both deterrent and rehabilitative aspects.

The human rights issue that might arise in these circumstances is whether these forms of punishment could amount to torture, degrading or inhuman treatment. Cleaning the toilets and cutting the grass with a toothbrush and nail scissors respectively might be argued to be degrading treatment.

Degrading treatment must be such as to 'arouse in its victims feelings of fear, anguish and inferiority capable of humiliating and debasing them . . . it is sufficient if the victim is humiliated in his or her own eyes'.[24] Could it be said that to be ordered to clean the toilets with a toothbrush is degrading treatment of the soldier? Were he to be ordered to do this same function with appropriate equipment the answer would clearly be in the negative if soldiers were expected to clean the toilets themselves. It is not difficult to imagine a situation where even this could be degrading to an individual. Suppose a general ordered the commanding officer (a lieutenant colonel or equivalent) of a unit to clean the toilets of the most junior soldiers of that unit. It is difficult to escape from the conclusion that, even with all the necessary equipment to do so, this would be humiliating to him, especially if this was required to be performed in the sight of junior soldiers. It might appear also to be humiliating to the soldier ordered to do this for disciplinary reasons if he is provided with a toothbrush to accomplish it and at least some of his colleagues see him having to accomplish the task. The argument against this position is to accept that the human rights of soldiers must be considered within a military context. If in military life (in the particular unit concerned) it is normal for soldiers to be ordered to do this and many, if not most, recruits have been ordered at one time or another to do so the degree of humiliation may be reduced. Soldiers may actually see it as unpleasant but not humiliating.

Soldiers ordered to repeat or to carry out a strenuous physical exercise for the purpose of ensuring that they can do so, or do so properly, may have their lives put at risk if they are physically incapable of doing so safely. Through exhaustion or otherwise they may die while performing such activities. This would amount to a deprivation of the soldier's right to life if the non-commissioned officer who ordered it ought to have known of a real and immediate risk to the life of the soldier.[25]

---

[24] *Smith and Grady* v. *United Kingdom* (2000) 29 EHRR 493 at para. 120.
[25] *Osman* v. *United Kingdom* (2000) 29 EHRR 245, para. 116 and see chapter 2. The circumstances of military training would also have to be taken into account. Where the suffering of the soldier was intentional it might amount to torture. In this case the issue would turn on whether the order could be described as a lawful sanction.

To both the soldier and the superior indulging in this type of activity there are, paradoxically, advantages. The soldier avoids any entry in his records of a disciplinary offence[26] and the superior avoids the bureaucracy involved in bringing formal disciplinary proceedings. There is obviously a risk in these circumstances that these advantages could lead, for example, to beatings behind the barrack block when formal disciplinary proceedings should have been initiated. This risk might materialise if the culture of a particular unit encourages it or where the State has imposed what are perceived by the armed forces to be difficult bureaucratic procedures in the course of taking formal disciplinary proceedings against soldiers.[27]

Formal disciplinary procedures

These procedures will normally be set out in legislation or in some other official publication and can, in consequence, be subjected to scrutiny by parliament or some other body. This publication will usually include the offences which may be committed, the procedure to be followed and the individual, court or tribunal to deal with charges laid against a soldier and the punishments available. The respective limits of the jurisdiction of military processes and concurrent jurisdiction of the civilian police and courts will need to be established formally since most soldiers will spend most of their military service within the territorial limits of their own State.[28]

Disciplinary punishments imposed by senior officers

In the armies of most States a soldier may be dealt with by his commanding (or other senior) officer for breaches of discipline.[29] There will be some

---

[26] See Hockey, *Squaddies* (n. 14 above), p. 20 (which refers to the British army where volunteer soldiers will often wish to keep their discipline records clear for promotion purposes). Where the soldier is a conscript this type of behaviour is unlikely to be accepted freely.

[27] In an attempt to give formal 'rights' to a soldier, for example, to obtain legal advice the commander may perceive this as a challenge to his authority to maintain discipline in his unit and thus seek to avoid formal procedures.

[28] For an example see the functions of the East Timor Defence Force in McClelland, 'Starting from Scratch' (n. 19 above), p. 257.

[29] In India this is styled a 'summary court-martial': the Army Act 1950 (India) s. 116. In the United States it is termed 'Article 15 [of the Uniform Code of Military Justice] non-judicial punishment'. It was established by the United States Congress 'as a device for protecting the service member from the stigma of a court-martial, with consequent likely loss of later civilian job opportunities, and also protecting the military from the effect of a court-martial on the member's efficiency and morale': *Turner* v. *Department of Navy et al.*, United States Court of Appeals, 15 April 2003, p. 6. For the position in Europe see

formality to this process, including the framing of a charge of committing a specific military offence. Senior officers will generally see this process as having many advantages. These summary proceedings can be held quickly and will avoid the formality of military court proceedings. Since commanding (or other senior) officers will be responsible for discipline in their units the process provides a means whereby they can enforce directly this discipline on their subordinates. Commanders will, almost certainly, hold a strong conviction that in matters of military discipline (relevant for war and peacetime service) soldiers must be shown firm but fair treatment, with little room for what might be considered as court-room argument. The summary hearing will normally therefore often exclude lawyers on either side. The soldier may or may not be permitted to be accompanied by a 'friend' but essentially the proceedings involve his commanding officer on one side and him on the other. A good commanding officer may take the view that to be fair to a (perhaps inexperienced) soldier in these circumstances he will need to make sure that the latter understands fully the nature of the charge, that any areas of disputed facts are dealt with thoroughly and that he advises him of any further action he may take, if he is not satisfied with his treatment.[30]

Some may argue that this procedure differs little from that before a senior manager in civilian employment for a particular breach of discipline. In these circumstances discussion of the human rights of the employee being disciplined would be unlikely to figure prominently although some form of observance of the rules of 'natural justice' might. Are the disciplinary processes sufficiently different in the armed forces so as to make the issue of human rights of the soldier appearing before his commanding officer different not only in degree but also in quality from a disciplinary process in civilian employment? The answer will be in the affirmative if the offence or punishment available to the senior officer is such as to amount to a criminal charge or a deprivation of the soldier's liberty, neither of which will apply in the case of a civilian employer.

G. Nolte and H. Krieger 'Comparison of European Military Law Systems' in Nolte, *European Military Law*, chapter 2. It is assumed the soldier is given a hearing. Compare the position in Georgia, CPT/Inf (2002) 14, 25 July 2002, para. 179.

[30] For an account of the procedure in the newly established East Timor Defence Force, see McClelland, 'Starting from Scratch' (n. 28) p. 265 and for the new Iraqi army see 'Creation of a Code of Military Discipline for the New Iraqi Army' CPA/ORD/7 August 2003/23, s. 11. Where the summary offence could be considered to be of a criminal, rather than of a disciplinary, nature a failure to permit legal representation may be a breach of the 1950 Convention, Art. 6(2)(c): *Ezeh and Connors* v. *United Kingdom*, Application Nos. 39665/98; 40086/98, Grand Chamber, 9 October 2003.

In civilian employment it is generally easy to draw a distinction between a criminal offence and a breach of a disciplinary code, although there might be some overlap. The punishments available to a criminal court will be more severe than those available to a civilian employer. In the military context, however, a wider range and severity of punishments is available to the senior officer. It may therefore be more difficult to draw a clear line between those punishments which might be considered to be criminal and those which, although described as disciplinary, are in reality little different from criminal punishments.[31]

An example might suffice to illustrate the point. A soldier is found guilty by his commanding officer of being absent without leave (a purely military offence) and he is ordered to be detained in a locked room in the barracks for ten days. Although the offence charged is not a criminal one the punishment imposed, detention in a locked room, looks very like the type of punishment that might have been imposed by a criminal court for a breach of the criminal law. There can be little doubt that in a State complying with its human rights obligations under a relevant human rights instrument the defendant in a criminal court would be entitled to be treated in accordance with those human rights.

Whilst a 'criminal charge' will be considered in the light of the nature of the charge and the severity of the punishment imposed on the soldier and not merely on the label that States accord to a particular offence, as military or criminal, some distinctions between the two can be easily made.[32] Thus a deprivation of liberty for a period other than a very short one would indicate that the offence charged is in reality a criminal one but the imposition of a fine or a reduction in rank is not quite so easy to determine. A fine of a month's pay might be fairly substantial in the armed forces of some States and a decision to reduce a person in rank is also likely to have severe financial consequences depending by how many ranks the soldier is reduced. It is likely that severe financial penalties such as these would also cause the charge to be considered in reality as a criminal one.[33]

---

[31] In the Royal Navy a commanding officer had the power to impose a period of imprisonment (in a civilian prison) on a sailor but this was removed in the Armed Forces Act 1996. The conditions of detention may involve degrading or inhuman treatment, see, for an example, CPT/Inf (2004) 25 (Armenia) 28 July 2004, para. 198.

[32] See *Engel et al.* v. *Netherlands* (1976) 1 EHRR 647 at para. 59. Compare *Lauko* v. *Slovakia* (2001) 33 EHRR 40 at para. 58, which refers to the legal rule being directed towards all citizens and not towards a given group possessing a special status; *Kadubec* v. *Slovakia* (2001) 33 EHRR 41 at para. 52.

[33] Compare the view of the Abadee Report, *A Study into the Judicial System under the Defence Forces Discipline Act [Australia]1997*, p. 46 which concluded that the 1966 Covenant, Art. 14 applied only to criminal charges and not to disciplinary offences.

A deprivation of liberty in civilian life is relatively easy to determine. It is unlikely that a civilian employer could lawfully deprive an employee of his liberty.[34] In the armed forces, on the other hand, a soldier's movements may be restricted quite lawfully under his system of military discipline. He may be ordered not to go to a particular place, to remain in barracks overnight or for longer periods. He may be ordered to remain in a particular place, such as a trench, for a number of days. Alternatively, he may be locked in the guard-room or in another place of detention. While in detention his pay may or may not be stopped. A simple distinction between a deprivation of liberty and a mere restriction of movement is whether the soldier is locked in a room so that he cannot physically escape.[35] In all the other cases given above the soldier could regain his liberty although he would be likely to be have committed the military offence of failing to obey orders if he did leave the place in which he is ordered to stay.

In the armed forces of a number of States the power of a senior officer to order the detention of a soldier has been retained. Detention might not be seen by the commander primarily as a punishment but as a means of ensuring the greater military effectiveness of the soldier by requiring him to undergo further military training whilst he is in detention. For this purpose to be achieved, ironically, the period of detention must be of sufficient length to enable further training to take place. Whatever the intentions of his commanding officer the soldier is likely to perceive it as a punishment even though he may later recognise, paradoxically, that the additional training he acquired while in detention might have improved his chances of promotion. He will see it as punishment simply because any further training will be unlike any other military training undertaken since, as the soldier is in detention, he will not be at liberty to go where he pleases in his off-duty time. In addition, if his pay is stopped whilst in detention it will be difficult to convince the soldier that this is necessary to train him.

It is, of course, possible for a military legal system to provide for additional training to be imposed by a senior officer in consequence of a breach of military discipline, in much the same way that a civilian employer might require an employee to undergo additional training if he is found to have

---

[34] Compare, however, the decision to keep a miner in his underground place of employment until the end of his hours of work despite his demand to be brought to the surface immediately.

[35] See *Engel et al.* v. *Netherlands* (1976) 1 EHRR 647 at para. 59; *Voulanne* v. *Finland* 265/87, ICCPR A/44/40, 7 April 1989 at para. 9.5. A further factor would be whether the punishment 'clearly deviat[ed]' from the normal conditions of life within the armed forces of the Contracting States': *Engel et al.* v. *Netherlands* (1976) 1 EHRR 647 at para. 59.

been in breach of his disciplinary code. A commander is likely to be able to order this additional training without invoking the summary disciplinary procedures. Where these are applied it is because the soldier has committed a disciplinary offence and his treatment is intended to reflect the perceived necessity to uphold military discipline, which implies at least an element of punishment.

The difficulty posed here is that if the detention amounts to a deprivation of liberty imposed upon a soldier by his senior officer this will interfere with the soldier's rights, under various human rights instruments, either on the ground that such a punishment can only be imposed by a court[36] or that the soldier must be able to challenge the lawfulness of his detention before a court.[37] Despite the relative formality of proceedings before a senior officer they cannot be classified as a 'court' or he be termed a 'judicial officer' since the commanding officer is responsible for discipline in his unit and is therefore acting in an executive rather than in a judicial manner when he enforces military discipline.[38] A State which wishes to retain the power of a senior officer to impose a punishment of a deprivation of liberty on a soldier can continue to do so providing it gives the latter certain procedural choices. First, it may offer him the right to trial by military court instead of being dealt with by his senior officer. This opportunity to elect trial by military court is preferably given as soon as the soldier is brought before the senior officer and not merely at the moment the punishment is to be announced.[39] By deciding not to elect trial before a military court the soldier will, in effect, be

[36] Article 5(1)(a). Compare the 1966 Covenant and the American Convention on Human Rights 1969, Arts. 9 and 7 respectively which suggest that if the deprivation of liberty follows from an application of the national law concerned it will not breach these Articles.

[37] The 1966 Covenant, Art. 9(3); the 1950 Convention, Art. 5(3); the American Convention on Human Rights 1969, Art. 7(5).

[38] See, generally, *Hood* v. *United Kingdom* (2000) 29 EHRR 365 at para. 58; *Jordan* v. *United Kingdom* (2001) 31 EHRR 6; *Duinhoff and Duijf* v. *The Netherlands* (1984) 13 EHRR 478; *Pauwels* v. *Belgium* (1988) 11 EHRR 238; *de Jong, Baljet and Van Den Brink* v. *The Netherlands* (1984) 8 EHRR 20. In *Turner* v. *Department of Navy et al.*, United States Court of Appeals, 15 April 2003 the commanding officer was described as serving 'simultaneously as prosecutor, judge and jury', p. 2. In CAT/C/44/Add.6, 12 February 1999, Finland confirmed that it had altered the law to permit confinement of a soldier only through the order of a court, para. 26.

[39] In the United Kingdom the Armed Forces Discipline Act 2000 imposed a requirement that the opportunity to elect trial by court-martial should be given as soon as the soldier appears before his commanding officer and not later in the proceedings. In *Turner* v. *Department of Navy et al.*, United States Court of Appeals, 15 April 2003 the serviceman concerned did not have a right to elect trial by court-martial.

waiving his right to be tried by a court.[40] It will be necessary to show that this waiver of rights has been given freely by the soldier with a full understanding of the effects of his choice.[41] This may be more difficult to establish where, as is common, the soldier does not have access to a lawyer in respect of a charge brought initially before his commanding officer.

Secondly, whether he is given a right to elect trial by military court or not he may be given the right to appeal from the decision of his commanding officer to a military court or some other court. Where the decision to deprive a soldier of his liberty is confirmed by that court the soldier will therefore have no grounds of complaint that his right to liberty has been improperly denied to him. It might be expected that in the armed forces of some States a right given to a soldier to appeal from the decision of his commanding officer to a court would be seen as a means of reducing the ability of the latter to enforce discipline within his unit and thus the effectiveness of the system of military discipline as a whole. In addition, it is likely that any appeal from the commanding officer will only be made where the punishment is considered severe, such as a relatively lengthy period of detention, a large fine or a reduction in rank having a serious financial impact on the soldier. These cases reflect the most severe breaches of discipline that a commanding officer can deal with and any 'interference' by a court will only be seen to weaken the authority of the latter to deal with serious breaches of discipline. A system of appeal might also be seen as introducing a bureaucratic process in a system designed for speed of discipline and punishment.

The United Kingdom is one State which wished to retain the power of a commanding officer to impose a period of detention (amounting to a deprivation of liberty) on a soldier. It has squared this with its obligations under the 1950 Convention by providing both an opportunity on the part of the soldier to elect court-martial instead of being dealt with by his commanding officer and an appeal to a new court, the Summary Appeal Court, which was established in 2000.[42]

---

[40] *Pfeifer and Plankl* v. *Austria*, Judgment, 25 January 1992 at para. 37.
[41] See M. Friedland, 'Military Justice and the Somalia Affair' (1998) *Criminal Law Quarterly* 360, 393–5.
[42] For an empirical study of the operation of this court see P. Rowe, 'A New Court to Protect Human Rights in the Armed Forces of the UK: the Summary Appeal Court' (2003) 8 *Journal of Conflict and Security Law* 201. The Abadee Report (n. 33 above) in Australia did not recommend an appeal, considering that 'the advantages . . . [were] outweighed by the disadvantages', recommendation 30.

Although there were arguments presented in Parliament against the establishment of such a court[43] the experience of its working shows that the court is likely to have a beneficial influence on the summary process itself by laying down principles with which commanding officers would be unlikely to disagree. These include emphasis that where two soldiers are charged together who differ in rank (and therefore in pay) any financial penalty should reflect this difference, that the financial consequences of a reduction in rank should be considered and that a deprivation of liberty might not be appropriate for 'minor' breaches of discipline.

It is common in the armed forces for soldiers of different ranks to be dealt with differently by their commanding officer. There may be a disciplinary process applicable to commissioned officers only and a different one for soldiers and non-commissioned officers. Can a member of one of these groups argue that the procedure by which his alleged breach of discipline has been dealt with discriminates against him on the ground of his rank, that it does not deal with all members of the armed forces equally? To take one example, a soldier may be sentenced to detention (involving a deprivation of his liberty) but a commissioned officer cannot receive such a punishment in the military law of a number of States. The European Court of Human Rights has accepted that in military discipline systems a State can draw distinctions between those of different rank on the ground that different responsibilities are imposed on different ranks.[44]

A number of States, party to the European Convention on Human Rights 1950, have entered a reservation to the effect that the provisions of Articles 5 (deprivation of liberty) and 6 (fair trial) do not apply to the enforcement of military discipline. Where this is the case the States concerned have made a judgment that the wider need to enforce the military discipline system prevails over these particular human rights of those serving in the armed forces. The consequences of such a reservation are discussed below.[45]

The role of the commanding officer is essential, in some States, in setting in motion the disciplinary process against a particular soldier. His pivotal

---

[43] See for example, *Hansard*, HL, vol. 607, col. 684, 29 November 1999, Lord Inge (a former Chief of the Defence Staff).

[44] See *Engel v. Netherlands* (1976) 1 EHRR 647 at para. 72. Under the 1950 Convention there is no express principle stated that everyone is 'equal' as compared with the prohibition on 'discrimination' in the form of 'other status' (Art. 15). Compare the African Charter on Human and Peoples' Rights 1981, Art. 3: 'every individual shall be equal before the law'.

[45] Ten States have made some form of reservation in this connection. They are the Czech Republic, France, Lithuania, Moldova, Portugal, Russia, Slovakia, Spain, Turkey, Ukraine. France, Ireland and the United Kingdom have individually made some form of reservation to the 1966 Covenant relating to discipline in their armed forces.

role may, however, also have the effect that he can prevent a prosecution from commencing or even condone what might be considered to be a serious charge.

Military courts

Military courts take various forms in different States. It is perhaps surprising that the armed forces should be permitted to exercise military discipline through the medium of a 'court'.[46] In the army of the United Kingdom this process developed in early modern times, largely because the army was employed abroad and not within the State, and it has been exported to a number of other States. It might, however, be argued that use of the noun, 'court' (even as a prefix to 'martial') is not significant and that others such as 'tribunal' or 'disciplinary hearing' would imply equal status. Whilst other terms may be used the concept of a court or tribunal implies some form of legislative establishment of the body. In this it can be contrasted with the disciplinary hearing established by an employer. It also implies that the military court is of a judicial or a quasi-judicial nature. The term 'military court' will be used in this chapter to refer to any form of body established by a constitution or by legislation to determine a charge against a soldier under the military law of his State.

There are a number of features of military courts which are different from civilian courts. It is common for military officers to comprise the whole or part of the court. There are good reasons for this. The court will have been established to enforce military discipline in one form or another and who, it may be argued, other than military officers, would be qualified to make decisions on military discipline? Many of these military offences will have no civilian counterpart and, as it has been shown above, the forms of punishment available to a military court will differ considerably from those available to a civilian court. It has to be said also that the status of military officers both within the wider society of a number of States and compared with members of the armed forces who are not commissioned officers has been such as to prove acceptable for even junior officers to sit on military courts.[47]

---

[46] Such a power may, in some States, be restricted to wartime, see CCPR/CO/81/BEL, 12 October 2004, para. 10.

[47] A distinction may be drawn between eligibility to sit on a military court of a junior officer (say, two years' commissioned service) and of the same power possessed by middle-ranking or senior officers only. Justification for this wider eligibility is frequently based upon the fact that training to be member of a court-martial is given in initial officer-training programmes.

This composition of a military court will also apply where the court can deal with what is formally a criminal offence and where it can impose punishment which in reality is more akin to a penalty imposed by a court hearing a criminal case.[48] A criminal offence committed by a soldier within a military context is no less a breach of discipline than a purely military offence and so it is not surprising to see the court being comprised of military officers.[49]

In the light of the above it might be thought that there is no role for non-commissioned officers on the panel of a military court. It is difficult to accept that a military court can ever be comprised of the 'peers' of an accused soldier since in the military system differences in rank can be of much greater significance than differences in grade within civilian employment. There is a good reason why this should be so. In the armed forces the concept of superior orders is well-grounded. Those superior in rank give orders to those inferior in rank; the differences between the giver and the receiver of the order might be only one rank. In some cases there might be no difference but the giver is of greater seniority in that rank than the receiver of the order. Even if a commissioned officer of middle rank is an accused in a military court it is difficult to say that the military officers comprising the court are his peers if they are superior in rank to him. The alternative is to say that a peer for a commissioned officer is any other commissioned officer of whatever rank.

It is not unknown in some armies for non-commissioned officers to serve on military courts.[50] They may automatically be listed to appear in a particular court session or become a member only at the request of an accused soldier. In both cases it is likely that they will form the minority of members of the court. It is difficult to explain why this should be so unless

---

[48] Examples of States where a military court can deal with an offence against the criminal law include Australia, Canada, the United Kingdom and the United States. For the position in Europe see Nolte, *European Military Law*, chapter 2. For an overview of military jurisdiction in relation to members of armed forces see 'Issue of the Administration of Justice Through Military Tribunals' E/CN.4/Sub.2/2003/4, 27 June 2003, paras. 20–70.

[49] The punishment imposed by a military court might be more severe than for a comparable offence tried by civilian courts if it is *perceived* by the former that the offence is more serious if committed in a military context. Examples might be the theft of personal property from a fellow soldier and the possession of controlled drugs by an aircraft mechanic. *Quaere* whether in a comparable situation a civilian court might not take the same view as to the seriousness of the offence.

[50] This is possible, for example, in the United States and the United Kingdom military justice systems. It has been rejected in Australia although recommended by Brigadier, Hon A. R Abadee, 'A Study into Judicial System under the Defence Force Discipline Act', August 1997, paras. 25, 26.

the view is accepted that the major responsibility for the enforcement of military discipline belongs to commissioned officers.

It might be thought that civilians would have no part to play as members of a military court. Unlike military officers they have no direct responsibility to enforce military discipline. If they are present there must, therefore, be another reason for this. It can only be to provide the contribution of a legally-qualified individual, who may or may not have experience in the ordinary criminal courts. The advantage to be gained from the presence of a lawyer is to ensure, as far as possible, that the soldier receives a fair trial. The presence of a civilian lawyer might also contribute to the acceptability within the State of soldiers being tried by military courts. This individual may take the role of legal adviser to the court[51] without being a member of it or the role of the presiding judge, who as a member of the court, will have a vote on the decisions of the court.[52] Alternatively, there may be a mix of civilian judges and military officers, or a military judge[53] sitting with other military officers.

For those looking at military courts from the standpoint of the human right to a fair trial the issue revolves around whether such courts have the necessary qualities of independence and impartiality (both actual and perceived). These two essential ingredients of a fair trial are requirements not only of human rights instruments but also under international humanitarian law where a protected person may be placed on trial.[54]

It might be thought that a military court could not satisfy these requirements since the whole, or the majority, of the court is comprised of military officers, who remain part of the general military hierarchy, obliged to follow the orders of their military superiors. They are, in turn, dependent upon their superiors for promotion. In many States these military court members will be sitting in court on one day and will return to their normal military duties the next. This mixing of court duties with normal

[51] Another variable feature is a power to decide issues such as the admissibility of evidence or to rule on points of law which the other members of the court must accept, or merely to advise the court on these issues with the decisions being theirs.

[52] In some States the legal adviser may have a vote only on sentence and not on guilt or innocence. An example is in the United Kingdom, introduced by the Armed Forces Act 1996.

[53] This is the practice in Canada and in the United States military courts. It was also the practice in Royal Naval courts-martial (United Kingdom); see *Grieves* v. *United Kingdom* (Grand Chamber, 16 December 2003).

[54] For human rights instruments see the 1966 Covenant, Art. 14; the 1950 Convention, Art. 6(1); American Convention on Human Rights 1969, Art. 8(1). The African Charter on Human and Peoples' Rights 1981, Art. 7(1)(d) refers only to an 'impartial' court or tribunals. For international humanitarian law see chapter 5.

military activities can lead to an allegation of 'command influence' where court members decide a particular case on the basis of some express or implied view of the case taken by a superior officer who is not a member of the court.[55]

Even without considering command influence as such it is the practice in some States for the decision of a military court to be 'subject to confirmation'. This means that the senior officer who convened the court (but who was not a member of it) is required to approve the decision or alter it[56] prior to its promulgation. It is also possible for this senior officer to refuse to confirm the finding with the result that the soldier may have to be tried again. In States where this practice, which is of a long-standing nature,[57] continues it is difficult to see that the military court is independent of the chain of command (represented by the confirming officer). Although, if any changes are to be made to the decision of the military court, these will work in the accused soldier's favour, the fact is that an executive officer (the confirming officer) has interfered with the decision of a judicial or quasi-judicial body.[58] The term 'judicial' or 'quasi-judicial' body has been used to reflect that a military court dealing with an offence against the criminal law of the State or one which has seriously detrimental consequences to an accused[59] is expected to possess these twin requirements of independence and impartiality. If they do the process can be described as 'judicial' or at least 'quasi-judicial' and thus clearly distinct from decisions made by the executive, or in this context, the chain of command.

---

[55] In *Morris* v. *United Kingdom* (2002) 34 EHRR 52, the European Court of Human Rights drew attention to 'the risk of outside pressure being brought to bear on the two relatively junior serving officers who sat on the Applicant's court-martial' (para. 72). Compare the view, expressed by the Grand Chamber, in *Cooper* v. *United Kingdom*, Application No. 48843/99 (3 December 2003), para. 124. By Art. 37(a) of the Uniform Code of Military Justice (United States) it is a military offence to attempt to influence the decision of a court-martial. The fact that intelligent and usually well-educated military officers might be influenced in performing their duty in a military court suggests that it is the military system itself which might create the need for protection rather than the weaknesses of individual court members.

[56] There will normally be a requirement that any alteration must be no more severe in finding or sentence than the original decision of the military court.

[57] In the United Kingdom it was such but was abolished by the Armed Forces Act 1996 following the decision of the European Commission of Human Rights in *Findlay* v. *United Kingdom*, Application No. 22107/93 (which decision was approved by the Court of Human Rights in (1997) 24 EHRR 221).

[58] See *Morris* v. *United Kingdom* (2002) 34 EHRR 52 at para. 73. Compare the view of the Grand Chamber in *Cooper* v. *United Kingdom* (n. 55 above) at para. 133.

[59] See *Engel* v. *The Netherlands* (1976) 1 EHRR 647 at para. 59.

In considering whether military courts possess these twin requirements of independence from the executive (or, indeed, anyone else) and impartiality it is necessary to look at the issue from the point of view of a reasonable person acquainted with all the relevant facts. If there is to such an individual the *appearance* of a lack of independence or impartiality this will be sufficient to show that the court lacks independence or impartiality or both.[60] Whilst it will be relatively rare for a member of a military court to display lack of impartiality towards an accused soldier the appearance of such may be sufficient to show that the latter may not receive a fair trial.

There are a number of ways to show actual and perceived independence and impartiality of the members of a military court who are also serving members of the armed forces. They should not, for instance, be drawn from the same chain of command of the accused or mingle socially during their call up for military court service with such members.[61] They should not be assessed by their military superiors in respect of their performance as a member of a military court or receive any performance-related pay which is derived in whole or in part from court duties.[62] They should receive instruction as to their duties and the importance of the separate function they are required to perform whilst a member of a military court.[63]

One additional means of showing that the members of a military court are impartial is to make call up for such service dependent on a random process. This could be achieved through a number of means. If a random procedure is adopted it would be a complete answer to a query whether a particular member of the court has been selected on the basis that he has a reputation as being 'hard on discipline' or hard against particular types of military offence.[64]

One other particular danger to be foreseen by the trial of individuals by military courts is that of the trial being held behind closed doors. Military courts are more prone to this danger than their civilian counterparts

---

[60] *Findlay* v. *United Kingdom* (1997) 24 EHRR 221 at para. 76; *R.* v. *Genereaux* (1992) 1 SCR 259.

[61] This can be a real risk since a military court is likely to be held in the military base to which the accused soldier is attached. It would be natural for the visiting military officer who is to sit on the military court to socialise with fellow officers at that base.

[62] See *R.* v. *Genereaux* (1992) 1 SCR 259.

[63] *Morris* v. *United Kingdom* (2002) 34 EHRR 52 at para. 72. Compare *Cooper* v. *United Kingdom* (Grand Chamber, 16 December 2003), para. 122.

[64] The fact that the members of the court-martial were appointed on an *ad hoc* basis was not decisive in *Morris* v. *United Kingdom*, para. 70.

since in the former it is possible that all participants in the military court process are not only members of the armed forces but also of that part of the armed forces to which the accused belongs. As a matter of practicality the holding of secret courts would not be difficult. All human rights instruments require that trials be held in public. Unlike a civilian court a poll of civilians unconnected with the proceedings attending a military court in any part of the world is likely to show very small numbers (if any in most military trials). This is often due to the fact that these trials will generally be held on military premises to which the public usually do not have access, or easy access. States can avoid criticism on this account if they publicise the timing and location of a military court, inviting the public to attend if they wish.

Unlike in proceedings before a senior officer, or indeed, any other commissioned officer who deals with disciplinary matters, prosecuting and defending lawyers are common in the military courts of some States. It might be wondered why they should be present at all. If the military court has jurisdiction to deal with military and not criminal offences a competent military officer, who is not a lawyer, might be thought to be able to provide all the assistance an accused soldier might need. He could speak to the court on behalf of the accused and put forward any grounds for mitigation. Moreover, should there be a legally-qualified judge (whether military or civil) that individual could be considered to be responsible for ensuring the accused soldier receives a fair trial.[65]

The fact that lawyers are permitted in military courts of some States (for both prosecution and defence) suggests that their presence is necessary to offer some further form of protection to the accused soldier in a military court trial where the nature of the offence is likely to be more serious than the breaches of discipline dealt with by senior officers. The lawyer for the prosecution performs this function by supporting only a case against the soldier which can be justified, on a legal basis, in accordance with the military disciplinary code. The lawyer for the defence is present to ensure that the prosecution is challenged to prove its case and to put the best defence available to the court.

There are, of course, many variations on this practice. Where the military court possesses jurisdiction to deal with criminal offences the need for lawyers as advocates is much clearer. Even more so is this the case where the nature of the criminal offence is serious. Where lawyer advocates are

---

[65] It is not uncommon in some States for a judicial officer to bear the responsibility in non-criminal cases of ensuring the proceedings are conducted fairly, in the absence of legal representation on both sides.

present the prosecution is likely to be brought by a military lawyer. The defence, or the accused soldier, may be permitted (or even financially assisted) to employ a civilian lawyer. The employment of the latter may, or may not, be impracticable where the military court is held outside the territory of its own State. Where lawyers are permitted to appear in military courts it is possible that all the personnel of the military court, the court itself, prosecution and defence lawyers, all witnesses, any experts and the accused soldier, are all members of the same organisation. There will be differences in rank among these members, with the significance that this possesses in the military context and most (if not all) participants will be required to take up their normal military duties after the military trial has been concluded.[66]

In the light of this there is a risk that an accused soldier will not *appear* to receive a fair trial. He will usually be the most junior in rank of all the participants and is prey to the risk that the members of the court will consider primarily the needs of the armed forces. The presence, therefore, of independently-minded and impartial lawyers as actors in the process is an important ingredient to a fair trial. One way by which the prosecuting lawyer can be separated from the court itself is to take the unit comprising of military lawyer prosecutors outside the military chain of command so that decisions to prosecute are made independently by these lawyers.[67] Should defence lawyers be civilians further independence from the chain of command is established.

Although some human rights instruments[68] require an accused to have a defence lawyer in certain circumstances the provision of lawyers and any further protection of the accused, such as the establishment of an independent military prosecutor, are also the result of a desire to ensure that military trials are perceived by all concerned and the wider society as being fair.

Where the offence charged is a purely disciplinary one these proceedings differ markedly from those which would be held for a comparable breach of discipline by a civilian employer.[69] Apart from the differences

---

[66] This was the case in *Grieves* v. *United Kingdom* (2004) 39 EHRR 2, para. 12.

[67] This is the practice in the United Kingdom, established by the Armed Forces Act 1996, in Australia and in Canada.

[68] See the 1966 Covenant, Art. 14(3)(d); the American Convention on Human Rights 1969, Art. 8(2)(d). Compare *Amnesty International et al.* v. *Sudan* (African Commission on Human and Peoples' Rights) Communication No. 48/90, para. 66.

[69] An example would be a soldier who is charged with a disciplinary offence by failing to keep proper accounts of a social facility available to soldiers and his civilian counterpart facing disciplinary proceedings for a similar matter.

alluded to above there is the range of penalties available to a military court. These will include, as discussed above, some which are similar to those available to an employer's disciplinary hearing but others which are quite distinct and are of a more severe nature.

A further failing to which military courts may succumb is delay. It is a common requirement in human rights instruments that a trial should be within a reasonable time or be held without undue delay. There may be various reasons for delay within a military context. The military police may have no right to charge a soldier[70] and other processes, such as the convening of a military court, may not move quickly.[71]

The idea that a soldier found to have infringed his military discipline code by a military court should have a right of appeal may strike some in the armed forces as being unnecessary. The argument might run along the following lines. The soldier has been given a fair hearing; the charges preferred by a military prosecutor (assume this prosecutor to be independent of the chain of command) have been proved beyond reasonable doubt. The soldier has been defended by a lawyer (assume this to be a civilian lawyer) and he has been convicted. An appeal would only undermine the military court in its interpretation of the military discipline system. The members of the military court are more closely involved with the actual enforcement of discipline than are any members of an appeal court. They have a much better idea of the punishment to impose than do those more isolated from discipline on a day-to-day basis.

Should this argument be accepted there could never be an appeal, certainly where the offence is of a purely military nature, from the decision of a senior officer or a military court. An appeal from a military court is a fairly recent phenomenon in some States, the reasons for denying it being one or more of those set out above.[72] It should not be thought that the issue is a simple one of whether there is an appeal or not. There can

---

[70] See, for example and comment, *R. v. Greig*, 17 October 2000 (United Kingdom), at http://web.onetel.com/-aspals/cases.htm

[71] In some States the role of judicial officers, independent of the military chain of command, will be important in ensuring that a person charged is brought as quickly as possible before a military court.

[72] F. Wiener, *Civilians under Military Justice, the British Practice since 1689 Especially in North America* (Chicago: University of Chicago Press, 1967) at p. 232 summed up the position as follows: 'with surprising unanimity, the common law world concluded virtually at the same moment in time [early 1950s] that, just as war is too important to be left to the generals, so military justice is too vital to be entrusted only to judge advocates'. Compare *Constitutional Rights Project and Civil Liberties Organisation v. Nigeria*, Communication No.148/96, 15 November 1999, paras. 9–10.

be variations on any right of appeal. It could, for instance, be limited to appeals against conviction of certain offences only, or against the finding of guilt only and not against the punishment imposed, or a right for both the prosecution and the accused to appeal or for the accused only.

When it is borne in mind that the right to a fair trial existing in human rights instruments applies only where the offence charged is a criminal one[73] or where it is in reality of a criminal nature[74] any right to an appeal must relate to the same type of offence.[75] Apart from this limitation on appeals from military courts there are no further restrictions, such as an appeal against the finding of guilt only. Whilst the human rights treaties give the convicted person the right to appeal,[76] there is no restriction in these instruments in giving the right to a prosecutor to appeal against a finding of not guilty or against the leniency of the sentence imposed by the military court.

The pattern of appeal against the decision of a military court is likely to vary from one State to another. In some the appeal court may be comprised solely of civilian judges, in others, a mix of civilian and military judges or military judges alone. Where civilian judges participate in appeals from military courts the reason for involving them may lie in the fact that the State accepts that some civilian scrutiny of military trials is desirable. Its desirability may be seen in ensuring that a soldier has received a fair trial in the military court or to provide some re-assurance to society generally that the system of military courts is (ultimately) under civilian control in the same way as the armed forces themselves are under civilian control.

---

[73] The 1966 Covenant, Art. 14(1) and the 1950 Convention, Art. 6(1) refer to a criminal charge. The American Convention on Human Rights 1969, Art. 8(1) refers to an 'accusation of a criminal nature' and the African Charter on Human and Peoples' Rights 1981 to 'legally punishable offence', Art. 7(2).

[74] See *Engel* v. *Netherlands* (1976) 1 EHRR 647 at para. 59. In this case the nature of military punishments becomes significant.

[75] See the 1966 Covenant, Art. 14(5); the Seventh Protocol (1984), Art. 2, to the 1950 Convention; the American Convention on Human Rights 1969, Art. 8(2)(h); the African Charter on Human and Peoples' Rights 1981, Art. 7(1)(a).

[76] An issue that might arise here is whether the 'right to appeal' means that a convicted person has the right for his case to be heard by the appeal court or tribunal itself or whether it is sufficient that one judge of that court determines whether to grant leave to appeal or even that the whole court decides not to grant leave, in which case the appeal itself is not heard. Compare the language of the 1966 Covenant, Art. 14(5) with the Seventh Protocol, Art. 2 to the 1950 Convention, the latter of which provides that 'the exercise of this right, including the grounds on which it may be exercised, shall be governed by law'. The American Convention on Human Rights 1969 and the African Charter on Human and Peoples' Rights 1981 use terminology similar to that of the 1966 Covenant.

Where the appeal court is comprised solely of military judges the position is not quite so clear. That court, itself, must be able to show the same degree of independence and impartiality required of the trial court. Should there be a further right of appeal to a court in which civilian judges are in the majority the presence of military judges alone in the lower of these two appeal courts is not as significant as it would be if there were to be no further right of appeal. In the absence of a further appeal the soldier will have been dealt with solely by military officers, albeit as the court itself, prosecutor, possibly defence adviser and the appeal court. Although it might be argued that a military legal system which comprises civilian lawyers or judges is preferable to one that does not there is, by the mere fact that there is no civilian involvement in a military trial, a breach of the human rights of the soldier.

The position of a protected person tried by a military court of a State occupying territory has been discussed above. Whilst the State may be able to provide a military court to try him the provision of an appeal court within occupied territory may be more difficult.[77] Since the right of appeal is, in these circumstances, a provision contained in a human rights instrument it is possible for the occupying State to issue an appropriate derogation notice in respect of the particular rights from which it wishes to derogate. International humanitarian law does not require a protected person to have a right of appeal from a military court but he should, nevertheless, be permitted to petition the competent authority of the occupying State.[78] If a derogation notice is issued the effect will be, therefore, that the protected person will have no right of appeal from the decision of a military court.

The death penalty

The imposition of the death penalty may be a punishment available to a military court. Although there have been attempts to abolish this particular penalty for all offences,[79] States have been given the option to restore

---

[77] Courts must be held in the territory occupied but appeal courts should 'preferably' be held there, see the fourth Geneva Convention 1949, Art. 66.

[78] *Ibid.*, Art. 73. Additional Protocol I 1977, Art. 75 is silent on the issue of an appeal.

[79] See the Second Optional Protocol (1990) to the 1966 Covenant; the Sixth Protocol (1983) and Protocol 13 (2002) to the 1950 Convention; the Protocol to the American Convention on Human Rights to Abolish the Death Penalty (1990). See, generally, W. Schabas, *The Abolition of the Death Penalty in International Law* (3rd edn, Cambridge: Cambridge University Press, 2002).

it[80] in 'time of war . . . for a most serious crime of a military nature committed during wartime'.[81] Many States are not party to these additional
protocols and they can, like those which have restored the penalty, provide
for the death penalty in their national law as a punishment which may be
imposed by any court, including a military court.

Where the death penalty is available to the military courts of a State
there are no specific human rights treaty obligations with which to comply before those courts impose it. Indeed, the pattern of the human rights
instruments is to make no distinctions among the various penalties available to any form of court. There are, for instance, no obligations to ensure
that if this penalty is to be imposed by a military court the accused soldier has had the benefit of legal representation, at least one member of
the military court is a civilian lawyer or the appeal court is comprised
of a majority of civilian judges. It is therefore possible for a State party
to a major human rights instrument to provide in its national law for a
military court (assuming it is objectively perceived to be independent and
impartial) to impose the death penalty on a soldier who has received no
legal representation, providing that this penalty is confirmed by an appeal
court (however comprised).[82]

It may seem paradoxical that the human rights instruments provide
very little in the way of limitations on the use of the death penalty where a
State seeks to apply it during 'wartime' whilst international humanitarian
law imposes stringent requirements if the person convicted by a military
court is a protected person. The fourth Geneva Convention 1949 stipulates
the type of offence for which the death penalty might be imposed and the
modalities involved.[83] The effect of these two contrasting positions is that
a State may lawfully[84] impose the death penalty on one of its own soldiers
for any military offence whereas the range of offences for which it may

---

[80] Either unconditionally or conditional upon a suitable reservation. Compare, respectively,
the Second Additional Protocol to the 1966 Covenant and the Sixth Protocol to the 1950
Convention. In all cases the death penalty, if restored, must be included in the national
law of the State concerned. By Protocol 13 (2003) to the 1950 Convention participating
States have agreed to abolish the death penalty in all circumstances. No derogations or
reservations are permitted by this Protocol.

[81] Second Additional Protocol to the 1966 Covenant. The Protocol to the American Convention of 1969 is similar.

[82] Assuming an appeal in made. This appeal court must also exhibit the features of independence and impartiality required of the trial court.

[83] See Art. 68. Additional Protocol I 1977, Art. 75 is silent on the issue.

[84] This assumes that its national law permits this penalty. For guidance on safeguards in
respect of the imposition of the death penalty see Human Rights Commission Resolution
2003/67. The issue is also discussed in chapter 5.

impose this penalty on a protected person is much more limited and, in addition, certain procedures have to be followed.

Reservations to human rights treaties

It has been indicated above that a State might take the view on accession to a human rights instrument that it does not want its military discipline systems to come within the regime of that instrument. Ten States have entered appropriate reservations to the 1950 Convention on ratification of it.[85] The majority have not done so. The effect of entering such a reservation is that it would appear to leave the whole system of military justice outside the 1950 Convention. This is more wide-ranging than a derogation notice since this notice may be issued only in very limited circumstances under those human rights treaties which permit it.

Should an application be brought to a human rights body by a soldier from a State which has made such a reservation it is likely that that body would interpret the reservation strictly against that State. It might, for instance, come to the conclusion that a State which purported to exclude its enforcement of military justice procedures from the light of the relevant human rights treaty had, in fact and law, done so only in respect of military[86] and not criminal offences. It might also take the view that a particular military punishment involves inhuman or degrading treatment and this had not been included within the reservation.[87] Moreover, it is always possible for another State to object to the reservation on the ground that it runs counter to the object and purpose of the human rights instrument concerned, which has been designed to protect those who may suffer at the hands of the State. Following up this theme, it may draw a distinction between conscript and volunteer soldiers and uphold the validity of the reservation only to the latter, since the former have no choice whether to accept military employment under such conditions.

Visiting forces

It is common for one State to station its soldiers on the territory of another State, with its consent. The States concerned normally enter into a status of forces agreement whereby the receiving State will grant the right of the

---

[85] See note 45 above. The view has been expressed in the United Kingdom Parliament in 2002 that the United Kingdom might withdraw from the 1950 Convention, enter a reservation in respect of its armed forces and rejoin the Convention immediately afterwards. France, Ireland and the United Kingdom have made some form of reservation to military discipline in the 1966 Covenant.

[86] Assuming that the penalty involved for such an offence was akin to that imposed as a criminal penalty, see *Engel* v. *Netherlands* (1976) 1 EHRR 647 at para. 59.

[87] From which there can be no derogation.

sending State to hold its military courts in the territory of the former.[88] Both States may, or may not, be parties to the same human rights instruments. Some status of forces agreements might make reference to human rights but this is likely only where the soldiers of the sending State are to be tried in the courts of the receiving State for an offence against the law of that State.[89]

The receiving State may take the view that once it has granted permission for the sending State to hold its military discipline procedures on its territory it has no further concern with those procedures. In particular, it may argue that it is for the sending State alone to satisfy itself that it has complied with its human rights obligation to its own soldiers. This may not, however, be the legal position. First, consider where both the receiving and sending States are parties to the same human rights instrument. The receiving State will owe an obligation under the relevant human rights treaty to secure to those within its (territory) and jurisdiction the rights granted by the treaty. The soldiers of the sending State are within the territory of the receiving State; whether they are within its jurisdiction is less clear. In one sense they are. If a soldier of the visiting force is arrested outside his military base by a police officer of the receiving State and is subjected to degrading or inhuman treatment in the police station that soldier must be held to be within the jurisdiction of the receiving State, so that this State will be responsible under the human rights treaty for his treatment. If, on the other hand, the soldier is subjected to a military punishment which amounts to degrading or inhuman treatment following conviction by a military court of his own State the question of whether that soldier is within the jurisdiction of the receiving State is less clear. He is clearly within the jurisdiction of his own State but can he be within the jurisdiction of another (the receiving State) simultaneously? The answer would seem to be in the affirmative where the receiving State has not granted exclusive jurisdiction to the sending State for any crimes committed by members of those visiting forces. In this situation the receiving State can place soldiers of the visiting force on trial for alleged breaches of the criminal law of that State. It may have agreed merely to a convenient arrangement for prioritising claims to prosecute between itself and the sending State's military authorities.

---

[88] They will also come to an agreement about any conflicts of jurisdiction. See, generally, Fleck, *The Handbook of the Law of Visiting Forces* (see n. 2 above).

[89] An excellent example of such an agreement is the Status of Forces Agreement between the United State and South Korea, 9 July 1966. See also the Agreement Between the Parties to the North Atlantic Treaty Regarding the Status of Forces, 19 June 1951, 199 UNTS 67, Art. VII (9).

Should the sending and receiving States be party to the same human rights instrument the issue revolves around whether the receiving State will also be responsible for the breach of human rights committed by the military authorities of the visiting force while on the territory of the receiving State. At first sight it would appear not to be responsible. The breach of the soldier's human right not to be subjected to degrading or inhuman treatment has been committed by the armed forces of another State. The receiving State authorities might, however, have become aware that a particular military punishment was employed by the visiting force authorities and that this punishment had the prohibited effect. Is the receiving State to stand idly by while a breach of human rights is committed on its territory and within its jurisdiction? Since it is the territorial State it could insist on an alteration to the status of forces agreement by a memorandum of understanding or otherwise to ensure that this particular practice does not occur on its territory. One example of a punishment which a military court of the visiting force might impose in this connection is the death penalty on one of its soldiers.[90] If the procedures involved, such as a relatively long period of uncertainty as to whether the punishment would be carried out, amounted to torture, degrading or inhuman treatment the receiving State might be expected to make representations about this to the sending State authorities. As long as the treatment on the territory of the State had the effect outlined it would be irrelevant that the death penalty was actually carried out in the soldier's home State and not on the territory of the receiving State.

A more common situation is where the receiving State, party to a human rights treaty, is aware that the military courts of the visiting force do not give the appearance of independence and impartiality when dealing with criminal offences or military offences having similar attributes. It may be politically difficult[91] for the receiving State to require the visiting force to change its military court structure as a condition precedent to entering into a status of forces agreement. Should the argument referred to above

---

[90] It is not uncommon for a status of forces agreement to stipulate that the military authorities are not permitted to execute a death sentence imposed by a military court on the territory of the receiving State. For an example see Agreement Among the States Party to the North Atlantic Treaty and other States Participating in the Partnership for Peace Regarding the Status of their Forces, Brussels, 19 June 1995; Additional Protocol, Art. 1.

[91] It should not, however, be assumed that the political circumstances surrounding a status of forces agreement are uniform across a variety of States. If the receiving State is in a strong political position compared with the sending State it may be able to insist on terms that it would be unable to do if the relative strengths of the parties were reversed.

be accepted, namely, that the members of the visiting force remain within the jurisdiction of the receiving State in addition to the jurisdiction of their own State, the receiving State would bear some responsibility for the breach of the human right to a fair trial of a soldier of the visiting force. This is not to suggest that the visiting force, which may not be a party to the human rights instruments in question, somehow becomes a party to it in these circumstances. The effect of continuing to hold its military courts in the territory of the receiving State is to place the latter State in breach of its obligations to the visiting force soldier simply because he is within the jurisdiction also of that State.

It has been assumed above that the sending State continues to owe the human rights obligations it has accepted by treaty to its own soldiers when they are stationed abroad. It would be surprising if it were otherwise. Where these obligations attach to individuals within the 'jurisdiction' of a State there can be little question that this is so. Any requirement that the individuals must also be within the 'territory'[92] of the State concerned might suggest that when soldiers are stationed abroad the human rights obligations of their own State to them no longer apply. A State not wishing to come to this conclusion could argue either that 'territory' in this connection includes its military bases abroad or that, despite the wording of the 1966 Covenant, it will accord all its human rights obligations to its soldiers abroad.[93]

The second of these alternatives might prove to be more attractive to the State concerned since the first will lead to further legal complications. The notion that the territory of the State automatically extends to its warships abroad and, by implication, to its military bases abroad, has been rejected by at least one judicial decision of persuasive force.[94] It is unrealistic to accept that a State agreeing to the presence of a visiting force has ceded part of its territory to that State for the duration of the agreement. A State which enters into a treaty by which it grants exclusive rights to a part of its territory to another State for a long period of time is unlikely to have accepted that that land is, for the duration of the treaty, the territory of the other State.[95]

---

[92] See the 1966 Covenant, Art. 2. Compare the 1950 Convention, Art. 1; the American Convention on Human Rights 1969, Art. 1.

[93] See Human Rights Committee General Comment No. 31, which must be taken to refer also to the armed forces of the sending State.

[94] *Chung Chi Cheung* v. *R.* [1939] AC 160.

[95] See, for example, the Treaty of Establishment 1960 in respect of the United Kingdom. Sovereign Base areas in Cyprus and the Cyprus Act 1960, s. 2(1).

4

Civilians before military courts

Within a State the activities of civilians may impinge upon the armed forces in various ways. This chapter will consider how, if at all, civilians may come within military jurisdiction and the effects of having done so. Chapters 5, 6 and 7 will deal, *inter alia*, with the way in which international and national law requires civilians, having no connection with the armed forces, to be treated by soldiers during an armed conflict or civil disturbance within a State and when taking part in multinational forces.

Although civilians might perform some functions previously carried out by members of the armed forces[1] or they might accompany them within their own State or abroad they will not necessarily be members of those armed forces. The very notion of subjecting civilians to military jurisdiction, otherwise than during armed conflict, appears to be illogical.[2] They are not being trained for war for which adherence to a military discipline system is considered to be a necessary prerequisite and the justification for its application. Within the territory of their own State civilians can be placed on trial for any alleged breaches of the criminal law committed by them and be tried by the ordinary civilian courts. Even where there is an armed conflict taking place (whether of an international or of a non-international kind) and the civilian courts are continuing to operate it is difficult to find a convincing reason why they should, instead, come under military jurisdiction. Practice among States is not, however, always based upon such logical arguments.

---

[1] It is likely, certainly in Europe, with a move from conscription to all-volunteer armed forces that some tasks previously performed by military personnel will be carried out by civilians. In Iraq in 2004 there were examples of civilian contractors carrying out functions previously thought to be purely military, such as 'defusing bombs ... and providing security for convoys' (*The Times*, 2 April 2004), under the headline, 'Pentagon's civil soldiers'.

[2] There is, however, a long history of British practice of such jurisdiction. See F. Wiener, *Civilians under Military Justice, the British Practice since 1689 Especially in North America* (Chicago: University of Chicago Press, 1967). The practice of other States is discussed at p. 233.

What is a 'military court'?

There will be general agreement that a court comprised entirely of military personnel,[3] established by the national law of the State concerned as a court,[4] with jurisdiction over other military personnel for breach of the military code of discipline would amount to a military court. This would remain the position if a civilian judge was appointed to advise the court and even to take part in its findings and its sentencing. It may remain a military court even if the majority of its members are civilians providing the national law so designates it and the person appearing before the court is a member of the armed forces. It is likely to be described as a civilian court even if the defendant is a member of the armed forces but where the membership of the court is entirely civilian.[5] In a number of States this will occur at the level of an appeal from a military court.

The military members of a court may be officers or, more rarely, non-commissioned officers. The significance of this fact resides not only in the rank involved but in the level of education received by each category. It is trite to argue that officers alone have a responsibility for discipline which justifies their presence in military courts. Non-commissioned officers also bear responsibility for discipline within their command.[6] The fact that more senior personnel also bear responsibility does not detract from responsibility at lower levels (whether as junior officers or as non-commissioned officers) of the rank structure. Officers, however, will have, generally, spent a longer period in education than non-commissioned officers. As a group they may be better educated than a cross-section of civilians (such as might form a jury in a State adopting such a method of trial). In some States the military officers serving on military courts may themselves be trained as judges; in other States they may be military officers without any such experience. Again, in some States all defendants, who are members of the armed forces, appearing before military courts

---

[3] The term 'military personnel' is used here to reflect the fact that although membership of military courts is often the exclusive preserve of officers in some States, non-commissioned officers may also be members (see below). The term 'officer' will be taken to refer to a commissioned officer in the armed forces.

[4] That law is likely to provide that a senior officer may exercise some form of summary jurisdiction over minor breaches of the relevant military law without his actions being described as a 'court'. See, generally, chapter 3.

[5] Compare the 'Creation of a Code of Military Discipline for the New Iraqi Army', CPA/ORD/7 August 2003/23, s. 5(4) and (5) where 'military judges will be selected from sitting civil judges'.

[6] They may also be criminally liable for the acts of those under their effective command and control, see the Rome Statute 1998, Art. 28.

may be entitled to legal or other representation, often not available without payment by the defendant before a civilian court. The value of this representation may, however, be queried if it is provided exclusively by military lawyers who are not permitted by their military hierarchy to be sufficiently independent of their chain of command.

The national law of a State may provide that, in certain circumstances, a civilian may be tried by a military court. That court may be comprised totally of military personnel or by a combination of military and civilian members. It may be convened with a civilian judge or president of the court or with a military officer as chairman of the court.

Where a purported 'military court' is not established by the law of the State concerned it is difficult to accept that it is a 'court' (or tribunal) at all. An *ad hoc* group of military personnel who purport to try a captured fighter or a fellow prisoner of war for alleged breaches of military law while in a prisoner of war camp could not amount to a court or tribunal. The fact that the decision of a military court may be altered by a senior member of the armed forces or by a government official may suggest that it lacks even the essential characteristics of a court or tribunal.[7] A practical problem may arise for the armed forces of some States where international law requires a State to determine an issue judicially but the national law of that State has not implemented such a right into its national law or created any procedures for such a judicial process.[8]

The term 'military court' will be used in this chapter to refer to a court, established by the national law of a State, whose membership includes one or more military members, convened to try a civilian.[9]

---

[7] See *Morris* v. *United Kingdom* (2002) 34 EHRR 52 at para. 73 but compare *Cooper* v. *United Kingdom* (2004) 39 EHRR 8 at para. 133. The latter decision shows that the alteration by a non-judicial official of a purported judicial decision may be acceptable if the final decision rests with an independent and impartial court. See also discussion of Military Order No. 1 (United States) below.

[8] Examples would include Geneva Convention III 1949, Art. 5 (and Additional Protocol I 1977, Art. 45); Geneva Convention IV 1949, Arts. 66, 71; Regulations Annexed to Hague Convention IV 1907, Art. 30. The issue is likely to arise most starkly where the armed forces are operating outside the jurisdiction of their own State.

[9] There will inevitably be borderline cases, such as *Constitutional Rights Project* v. *Nigeria* (African Commission on Human and Peoples' Rights) Communication No. 60/91 where a civilian was tried by a court comprising a judge, an officer of the armed forces and a police officer for an offence under the Robbery and Firearms (Special Provisions) Act 1984.

The theoretical basis for the trial of civilians by military courts within their own State

The practice of States[10] shows that the trial of civilians by military courts may arise, for example, where a person, drafted for military service, claims to be a conscientious objector, where a civilian commits an offence jointly with a member of the armed forces,[11] where he injures or kills a soldier,[12] commits what is deemed to be an offence against the armed forces itself,[13] when he is accused of treason or breach of national security[14] or even where an offence is considered serious.[15] In addition, a civilian may be the dependant of a soldier or be a civilian contractor employed by the armed forces and, for this reason alone, be subject to the jurisdiction of a military court.[16]

It might also be argued that in some States it is necessary to try civilians by military courts if the offence charged is considered to be a 'terrorist' one. At one end of the spectrum the armed forces may be granted exclusive jurisdiction over the campaign against terrorism within the State. In this model the fight against 'terrorists' is carried out by the armed forces rather than by a civilian police force. Thus, suspected terrorists will be fought (in a way similar to that which may occur during a non-international armed conflict), caught and detained by soldiers rather than by police officers.[17] It would appear, so it may be argued, reasonable to permit the armed forces to follow through this process and to try such individuals. It is not difficult

---

[10] See, generally, *Military Jurisdiction and International Law, Military Courts and Gross Human Rights Violations*, Vol. 1 (International Commission of Jurists), 24 February 2004.

[11] See, for example, CCPR/CO/71/UZB/Add.1, 17 October 2002, which deals with Uzbekistan.

[12] See the attempts by Chile to reduce the jurisdiction of military courts for such offences, CCPR/C/SR.1733, 3 March 2000, paras. 34–6.

[13] Commission on Human Rights E/CN.4/Sub.2/2003/4, 27 June 2003, para. 14.

[14] A civilian charged with treason could be tried by a military court in Peru, *Castillo Petruzzi et al. Case* (Inter-American Court of Human Rights) (1999) Ser. C, No. 52, para. 127. For an example, in relation to Israel, see CCPR/C/SR.1676, 28 September 1998, para. 53.

[15] See *Constitutional Rights Project* v. *Nigeria* (n. 9 above). In *Loayza Tamayo* (Inter-American Court of Human Rights) (1997) Ser. C, No. 33 a civilian was tried first by a military court and then by a civilian court for different, but similar, offences.

[16] These individuals are often described, particularly in the earlier literature, as 'camp followers'. In modern times, however, many States will permit military jurisdiction over such individuals only where the breach of military law is committed abroad (see below).

[17] See *Civil Liberties Organisation* v. *Nigeria*, Communication No. 151/96, African Commission on Human Rights, 15 November 1999, para. 26: 'While being held in a military detention camp is not necessarily inhuman, there is the obvious danger that normal safeguards on the treatment of prisoners will be lacking.'

to find what some may consider plausible reasons for trial by military court. Members of the ordinary criminal courts might be threatened by members of a 'terrorist' organisation if a guilty verdict is returned against one of their number. This risk will be greater where these court members are jurors and are not professional judges (although this distinction may, in the circumstances, be purely theoretical). It might also be suggested that the only 'safe' forum to give evidence of a national security nature is before a military court where, for instance, the authorities are unwilling to produce the evidence in a form normally accepted in a civilian court. There may be other practical reasons such as the relative anonymity of military compared with civilian courts, their potential speed of operation, the fact that a military court may be permitted to sit in any location and at what would be considered by a civilian court, unusual times, along with the possible lack of access by an accused to civilian defence lawyers. These arguments might be taken further to permit the armed forces to imprison persons without any form of trial or only those whom their courts have convicted.[18]

Retreating from this position a State may provide for the armed forces and the civil police and judicial system to operate co-operatively. Its national law may require suspected terrorists to be handed over by the armed forces to the civilian police for trial by a civilian court. It may also provide that the civilian court will be comprised of one or more military judges.

A State willing to do so should be able to find alternatives to military jurisdiction through changes to the civilian judicial system, if necessary. There is no overwhelming reason why conscientious objectors, or those who commit offences jointly with soldiers or against them need to be tried by a military as compared with a civilian court. In relation to terrorist offences a criminal court could be comprised of one or more professional judges instead of relying upon lay persons to decide the issue of guilt or innocence.[19] It is usually easier for the State to protect the security of judges than it would be to protect a juror. There is the additional safeguard to an accused in the requirement of the judge or judges to give reasons for a finding of guilt, which a jury is not normally required to do. Consistent with the human rights obligation of the State to ensure an accused receives

---

[18] For discussion of the rights of detainees held by armed forces during an international armed conflict see chapter 5 and for a non-international armed conflict, chapter 6.

[19] This may not be possible in some States owing to a constitutional obligation of the State to offer trial by jury to an accused unless he is serving in the armed forces, see *McElroy* v. *Guagliardo*, 361 US 281 (1960), Justice Clark at p. 284.

a fair trial an ordinary criminal court can hear evidence *in camera* where it is of a national security nature and where it perceives a risk to that security if a member of the public heard this evidence. It is normally possible for a State to pass quickly emergency legislation altering the admissibility, or other rules,[20] of evidence or the range of offences before civilian courts for certain types of offence where this is considered to be essential.

The trial of a civilian by a military court lends itself to the perception that the court is not independent of the executive arm of government. An intelligent reasonable person with knowledge of all the facts might conclude that the government had chosen a military court to try civilians simply because it did not trust the civilian judiciary or because it wished to control the way in which the evidence was given. The State may argue that it is unable to protect the judiciary, witnesses or police officers from terrorist violence but the burden must be upon it to show why it has chosen this method of trial when the alternative, trial by a civilian court, is still available.

A civilian placed on trial before a military court comprised of military officers only could argue that his right to an independent and impartial tribunal has been denied to him; 'that the armed forces have the dual function of combating insurgent groups with military force, and of judging and imposing sentence upon members of such groups'.[21] This would also be the case where a minority of the judges were civilians themselves. Where the civilian judges form the majority of the court a reasonable man might question why civilian judges do not form the sole membership of the court if they are as independent of the government as they would be if the court did not have a military judge.[22] This argument here is

---

[20] Such as hiding, by the use of screens and pseudonyms, the identity of witnesses from the accused. Compare the hiding of the identity of the judges (so-called 'faceless' judges) see E/CN.4/2004/60, 13 December 2003, para. 59; *Loayza Tamayo* (Inter-American Court of Human Rights) (1997) Ser. C, No. 33, para. 46(h) (Peru); *Cantoral Benavides Case* (2000) Ser. C, No. 69, para. 108 (Peru); *Castillo Petruzzi et al. Case* (1999) Ser. C. No. 52, para. 133.

[21] *Cantoral Benavides Case* (Inter-American Court of Human Rights) (2000) Ser. C. No. 69, para. 114; *Castillo Petruzzi et al. Case* (1999) Ser. C. No. 52, para. 130. There is much support for this proposition in statements made by human rights bodies. See, for example, Human Rights Committee General Comment No. 13, para. 4; Concluding Observations of the Human Rights Committee: Lebanon, CCPR/C/Add.78, 1 April 1997, para. 14; *Report on Terrorism and Human Rights*, Inter-American Commission on Human Rights, OEA/Ser. L/V/II.116 Doc. 5 rev. 1 corr., 22 October 2002, para. 256; E/CN.4/2004/60, para. 60.

[22] This was the case in *Incal* v. *Turkey* (2000) 29 EHRR 449; *Zana* v. *Turkey, Application No. 29851/96*, 6 March 2001, para. 23. See also *Ocalan* v. *Turkey* (2003) 37 EHRR 10, para. 120 and for discussion as to whether the applicant had waived his right to an

based on the assumption that the presence of the military judge amongst a majority of civilian judges in, for instance, the National Security Court of Turkey infects the whole court and not merely that particular judge.[23] This is a strange conclusion to reach, particularly in view of the fact that the president of that court (from which a large number of applications have been brought to the European Court of Human Rights) must be one of the civilian judges. It suggests that the risk of the president and the other civilian judge being 'influenced' by the military judge or being unable to put out of their minds those 'considerations which ha[ve] nothing to do with the case' is so great that the composition of the court will lead objectively to 'a legitimate fear'[24] that the court lacks independence and impartiality. This argument has not been accepted where a civilian judge acts in the same way as a president of a court giving directions on points of law but is outnumbered by military judges in a military court.[25]

If it is assumed that a particular military court has acquired a sufficient degree of independence and impartiality to be consistent with human rights instruments[26] and it is an 'integral part of the general judicial system'[27] why should that independence and impartiality alter depending upon whether the accused is a soldier or a civilian? It might be argued that the volunteer soldier has consented to a military trial should he transgress

---

independent and impartial tribunal, para. 116. See also *Constitutional Rights Project* v. *Nigeria* (African Commission on Human and Peoples' Rights) Communication No. 60/91, para. 14 (the court comprised a civilian judge, a military officer and a police officer).

[23] In *Incal* v. *Turkey* (2000) 29 EHRR 449 the Court took the view that the presence (alongside two civilian judges) of a military judge in the National Security Court might allow *the court* (and not merely the military judge) 'to be unduly influenced by considerations which had nothing to do with the nature of the case' (para. 72.) Compare the dissenting view (of eight judges). In *Ocalan* v. *Turkey* the Court seemed to base the problem on the mere fact of the presence of the military judge confirmed by the Grand Chamber, 12 May 2005 at para. 118. Turkey has decided to abolish the State Security Court, see Parliamentary Assembly, Council of Europe, Resolution 1380 (2004), para. 9.

[24] *Incal* v. *Turkey* (2000) 29 EHRR 449, para. 72. A similar argument has been accepted by the Court of Appeal in England, see *Lodwick* v. *London Borough of Southwark* [2004] ILR 884, 9 EWCA Civ 306 but on the ground that the claim of bias was made against the legally-qualified chairman of a tribunal.

[25] Quite the opposite: 'The lack of a civilian in the pivotal role of Judge Advocate [a civilian judicial officer presiding over Army and RAF courts-martial in the United Kingdom but not in Royal Naval courts-martial] deprives a naval court-martial of one of the most significant guarantees of independence enjoyed by the other services' courts-martial' *Grieves* v. *United Kingdom* (2004) 39 EHRR 2, para. 89.

[26] For an example see *Cooper* v. *United Kingdom* (2004) 39 EHRR 8.

[27] See Commission on Human Rights, E/CN.4/Sub.2/2003/4, 27 June 2003, para. 7.

his military law[28] but a conscript soldier has not given any such consent. Nor has the child dependant of a soldier serving abroad who may be tried by a military court for crimes committed in the area where his father is serving.[29] If, on the other hand, military courts are unable to provide a fair trial even to soldiers, the effects of trying civilians in this forum should be no greater nor lesser a breach of that individual's human rights. There is, perhaps, a greater *perception* of the lack of independence and impartiality of a military court when it is trying a civilian. Such a perception calls for 'sufficient safeguards' to be taken to show that, objectively, the members of the court are independent and impartial of the executive, in much the same way as for the trial of a soldier by a military court.[30]

There is no reason in principle why, if such safeguards are taken where a military court, established by the national law of the State, tries a civilian that court cannot be an independent and impartial tribunal. It is too easy to conclude that a civilian can never receive a fair trial by an independent and impartial court if he is tried by a military court.[31] This would be a surprising conclusion given that the Geneva Conventions 1949 themselves permit the trial of civilians by a military court.[32] The key issue is not the status of the court as a military one or the role of the military officers[33] but

---

[28] See *Kalac* v. *Turkey* (1999) 27 EHRR 552: 'in choosing a military career Mr Kalac was accepting of his own accord a system of military discipline that by its very nature implied the possibility of placing on him certain of the rights and freedoms of members of the armed forces limitations incapable of being imposed on civilians', para. 28; *Engel et al.* v. *Netherlands* (1976) 1 EHRR 647 at para. 57.

[29] See R v. *Martin* [1998] 2 WLR 1, discussed below under the heading Trial of civilians who are nationals by a military court abroad.

[30] For a full discussion of these procedural steps see *Cooper* v. *United Kingdom* (n. 9) at paras. 106–26. See, generally, CCPR/C/26D/147/1983 (Uruguay), 1 November 1985; CCPR/C/79/Add.78 (Lebanon), 1 April 1997, para. 14; CCPR/CO/70/ PER, 15 (Peru) November 2000; CCPR/C/SR/1734 (Chile), 17 February 2000, paras. 14, 16; CCPR/CO/71/UZB Add.1 (Uzbekistan), 17 October 2002.

[31] See *Genie Lacayo Case* (Inter-American Court of Human Rights) (1997) Ser. C. No. 30, para. 84: 'the fact that it [trial of a civilian] involves a military court does not *per se* signify that the human rights guaranteed the accusing party by the Convention are being violated'.

[32] See, for example, Geneva Convention IV, Art. 66 and below. The use in that Article of the term 'non-political military courts' must be taken to mean military courts which are able to offer the accused an independent and impartial tribunal. Compare Geneva Convention III, Art. 84, which refers to an independent and impartial 'military court' trying a prisoner of war.

[33] Practice among States varies. Thus, in some, the majority of the Court is comprised of military officers who hold no judicial appointment, apart from their *ad hoc* appointment to a particular military court. In others, the membership may be comprised of military judicial officers.

whether there are, objectively perceived, sufficient safeguards to guarantee independence from the executive and the impartiality of the court.[34] In practice this may be difficult, although not impossible, to show. The lack of these sufficient safeguards is the real reason why military courts may fail to provide the necessary independence and impartiality of tribunals required by all human rights instruments. It is, however, clear that if such courts do not form part of the judicial system of the State concerned but are set up, or their jurisdiction is extended, by the armed forces themselves they will not have been established by law and could not therefore provide the right to a fair trial.[35] In these circumstances (and as discussed above) they may not be perceived as courts or tribunals at all, even although they purport to be so.[36]

It may seem ironic that a State faced with terrorist activity (however this is described) will be subjected to criticism for establishing military courts to try this type of defendant, even if these courts are able to function as independent and impartial tribunals, whereas that same State may not face the same criticism if it denies suspected terrorists any form of trial and imposes detention at the behest of an arm of the Executive.[37]

---

[34] The criticism of the trial made by Kafka was not based upon the status of the court but on the lack of any guarantees of fair trial, see F. Kafka, *The Trial* (London: Penguin Books, 1960), p. 117.

[35] The law of some States may permit a general officer commanding a region to establish military courts to try civilians where a proclamation of martial law has been made, in the absence of any statutory enactment, even if the civil courts are still sitting in the martial law area. This theoretical possibility may occur by the law of the United Kingdom. See *Marais* v. *General Officer Commanding the Lines of Communication and A.-G. of the Colony, ex Parte Marais* [1902] AC 109 (on appeal from the Supreme Court of Good Hope); *R.* v. *Allen* [1921] 2 IR 241. In practical terms it is likely that primary or secondary 'emergency legislation' will be enacted to deal with situations described as 'actual war' (*Marais*) and 'armed insurrection' (*Allen*). In this case, at least under the law of the United Kingdom, the statutory provision replaces any use of martial law under a military proclamation, *Egan* v. *Macready* (1921) 1 IR 265, which distinguished *Marais* (since the Restoration of Order in Ireland Act 1920 could not apply in the Cape of Good Hope) and it refused to follow *Allen*. O'Connor MR at p. 275 took the view that 'the claim of the military authorities to override legislation, specially made for a state of war, would seem to be a call for a new Bill of Rights'. A similar view was taken in the United States. See *Ex parte Milligan* 71 US 281 (1886), 285, Justice Davis.

[36] This was a view taken by Molony CJ in *R.* v. *Allen* [1921] 2 IR 241 at p. 270. So-called 'peoples' courts' may fall within the same category.

[37] To achieve this the State will need to issue an appropriate derogation notice (where this is permitted) from the trial provisions of the human rights treaties to which it is a party. See, however, *A and others* v. *Secretary of State for the Home Department* [2005] 2 AC 68.

There may, of course, be other breaches of the human rights of civilians committed by military courts, as with any civilian court.[38] One particular issue which might arise is the establishment by the national law of a State of military courts to try civilians who, when they committed the acts alleged to be criminal, would have been subject to the jurisdiction of a civilian but not a military court. This retrospective assumption of jurisdiction is unlikely, by itself, to amount to a breach of the human rights of those who appear before a military court providing that that court is able to provide a fair trial and the penalty imposed by that court is not a heavier one than that which was available to a civilian court at the time the offence was committed.[39] The availability to a military court of the death penalty for an offence which could not have attracted this penalty before a civilian court would clearly fall foul of this obligation. It is much more difficult to argue[40] that a sentence of imprisonment imposed by a military court, within the maximum term permitted to the civilian court when the offence was committed, would give rise to any such claim.[41]

In the event of a 'public emergency' within a State it is has been relatively common practice for the State to issue a derogation notice from relevant Articles of the 1966 Covenant. It is noticeable, however, that very few have done so in respect of Article 14, relating to the provision of an independent and impartial tribunal.[42] This may be because States do not consider that a military court per se would infringe Article 14 for soldiers or civilians or that they do not intend to subject civilians to military courts.

A trial by a military court may, however, lead to the opportunity to appeal to a civilian court. It had been shown in chapter 3 that in some

---

[38] Examples could be: inadequate time for a defence lawyer to prepare the case; failure to permit the defence lawyer to confer with his client in private; the speed by which procedural provisions are required to be submitted; failure to allow the defence to read the case against the accused; failure to permit cross-examination of soldiers; failure to provide a right of appeal and trial by 'faceless' judges and prosecutors: see *Castillo Petruzzi et al. Case* (Inter-American Court of Human Rights) (1999) Ser. C. No. 52, paras. 141, 161, 172.

[39] See the 1966 Covenant, Art. 15(1); the 1950 Convention, Art. 7(1); American Convention on Human Rights 1969, Art. 9. See also Additional Protocol I 1977, Art. 75(4)(c).

[40] Compare, however, if the detention or imprisonment is at a military prison where the conditions are much more harsh than in a civil prison.

[41] A further difficulty might arise where a civilian is tried by a military court and, for the same offence, a civilian court. The principle of *ne bis in idem* would be contravened.

[42] As at January 2005, twenty-two States had issued, at some stage, a derogation notice in respect of a public emergency (however described) within the State. Only a very few, including Nicaragua, Trinidad and Tobago and the United Kingdom (in relation to Northern Ireland) had derogated from Art. 14 to some extent. Turkey and the United Kingdom have made such a derogation from the comparable Art. 6 of the 1950 Convention.

States an appeal from a military court by a soldier is taken to a fully-civilian court. A State which provided for such an appeal could argue that any errors in the military court would be corrected on appeal and that this appeal court was an independent and impartial tribunal. This would, however, only be the case where an individual civilian's appeal related to a disciplinary matter and did not amount to a criminal charge.[43] Where the charge is of a criminal nature an accused 'is entitled to a first-instance tribunal which fully me[ets] the requirements of Article 6 para. 1'.[44] An appeal, on the other hand, to another military court clearly could not correct the breach of the right to a fair trial committed at the original military court level even if the appeal court itself satisfied all human rights fair trial requirements.

There is also a theoretical link between the trial of civilians by military courts and an investigation by the armed forces into the death, or other alleged breach of the human rights, of a civilian in the hands of the armed forces. There is no *a priori* reason why, as with the military courts, such an investigation cannot be an independent and effective one. Practice may, however, fall short of this theoretical position especially if the investigators are not able to show that they are independent from those whom they are investigating.[45]

Trial of civilians who are nationals by a military court abroad

In peacetime it is common in some States for the family and dependants of a soldier to accompany him to where he is to be stationed for any length of time abroad. The sending State may also employ its own nationals as civilian contractors, whose function is, for example, to service military equipment belonging to the sending State. The arrangements between the sending and the receiving State will normally be found in a status of forces agreement.[46] This agreement may provide for the sending State to

---

[43] In relation to the 1950 Convention see *De Cubber* v. *Belgium* (1984) 7 EHRR 236, at para. 32; *Zana* v. *Turkey*, Application No. *29851/96*, Judgment, 6 March 2001, para. 23.

[44] *Findlay* v. *United Kingdom* (1997) 24 EHRR 221 at para. 79.

[45] It is common practice for military police (or similar bodies) to investigate alleged offences committed by individual members of the armed forces. It has not been suggested that such investigations lack the necessary degree of independence merely because the investigators and those who are being investigated belong to the same organisation. For further discussion see chapter 2, n. 20.

[46] See, generally, D. Fleck (ed.), *The Handbook of the Law of Visiting Forces* (Oxford: Oxford University Press, 2001); S. Lazareff, *Status of Military Forces under Current International Law* (Leyden: Sijthoff, 1971); J. Woodliffe, *The Peacetime Use of Foreign Military Installations under Modern International Law* (Dordrecht: Nijhoff, 1992).

try civilian dependants or employees for certain crimes before a military or other court established by that State and operating on the territory of the receiving State.[47] The criminal offences with which these courts may deal are likely to be the same as those tried by a criminal court in the territory of the sending State itself.

The reasons for trying civilians who are nationals of the sending State before a military court of that State in the territory of the receiving State are often quite different from those applying to the trial of a civilian by a military court in his own State. When the armed forces are stationed abroad there is the perceived convenience of trying a civilian dependant of a soldier or employee before a court of his own State. He is spared the strangeness of a foreign court, which may be quite different from a court of his home State, in terms of procedure, the punishments available to it and the language in which proceedings are conducted. The justification for trying the civilian dependant before a military court (of his own State) therefore revolves around convenience to him, convenience to the armed forces, the fact that the crime is alleged to have taken place within the environs of the military base and the perceived morale-boosting value to soldiers that should their dependants be charged with a criminal offence it will be by a court of their own State.

It should not be thought that the arguments all point in the same direction. One consequence of accepting military jurisdiction over civilians who commit crimes within a military community abroad is that the alleged offender is denied the normal form of trial in his home State. Thus, in *R* v. *Martin* (1997)[48] a nineteen-year-old son of a soldier serving in

---

[47] The national law of the sending State may, however, prohibit its civilian dependants and workers being tried by a military court. This is the position in respect of the civilian dependants and workers of United States forces stationed abroad, see *Kinsella* v. *Singleton*, 361 US 234 (1960); *Grisham* v. *Hagan*, 361 US 278 (1960); *McElroy* v. *Guagliardo*, 361 US 28 (1960). Compare the Military Extraterritorial Jurisdiction Act 2000 (US). The national law of the United Kingdom permits such jurisdiction: see P. Rowe, 'The Trial of Civilians under Military Law: An Empirical Study' (1995) 46 *Northern Ireland Legal Quarterly* 405. It also has established a civilian court abroad, the Standing Civilian Court, Armed Forces Act 1976.

[48] [1998] 2 WLR 1. The jurisdiction of the British military authorities was based on the status of forces agreements, Agreement (with appendix) between the Parties to the North Atlantic Treaty regarding the status of their forces (London, 19 June 1951), 199 UNTS 67 and Agreement (with Protocol of Signature) to Supplement the Agreement between the Parties to the North Atlantic Treaty regarding the Status of their Forces with respect to Foreign Forces Stationed in the Federal Republic of Germany. (Bonn, 3 August 1959) 481 UNTS 262.

Germany was convicted by a British court-martial sitting in Germany on a charge of murdering a civilian in Germany. The effect of this assumption of jurisdiction by the military authorities was that he was 'deprived of the right, or at least the opportunity, of trial by jury [in England]'.[49]

In some status of forces agreements the receiving State will cede jurisdiction over civilian employees and dependants of soldiers stationed on its territory to the courts of the sending State for crimes that are service-connected. Crimes committed outside the normal environs of the military base will commonly come within the jurisdiction of the receiving State. In so far as a civilian employee or dependant is alleged to have committed such an offence he will be subject to the ordinary criminal courts of that State.[50]

The wife of a soldier who, for example, caused grievous bodily harm to her soldier husband in their house on the military barracks abroad may come within the jurisdiction of a military court of her own State (the sending State) if both the law of her home State and the relevant status of forces agreement permitted it. She may also come within the jurisdiction of the civilian courts of her home State if the national law of that State is wide enough to cover certain crimes committed extra-territorially.[51] The most serious offences may overlap in jurisdiction with the civilian court in the home State but the less serious ones may not.

The wife in the example above would have no choice whether to be tried by a military court or by the civilian courts of the receiving State. She would be tried by a court comprised of military officers, who, depending on the national law of the State concerned, might include one, or certainly

---

[49] [1998] 2 WLR 1 (HL), per Lord Slynn at p. 3. The accused was in England at the time of commencement of proceedings and he was returned to Germany to stand trial before a British court-martial. The House of Lords rejected a defence submission that the form of trial adopted in this case was an abuse of process (since the courts in England would also have jurisdiction to try him for the alleged offence committed in Germany). A powerful argument for the trial to take place in Germany was that the witnesses were located there and could not be subpoened to attend a trial in England. An alternative approach would have been for the German prosecutor to have commenced proceedings in the German courts.

[50] For an example, see the NATO Status of Forces Agreement 1951, Art. VII.3 and the Agreement Among the States Party to the North Atlantic Treaty and other States Participating in the Partnership for Peace Regarding the Status of their Forces 1995. Compare the Model Status of Forces Agreement for Peacekeeping Operations, UN Doc. A/45/594 (9 October 1990), Art. 47 which draws a distinction between military and civilian personnel, with exclusive jurisdiction being given to the sending State only in respect of the former.

[51] As it was in R. v. Martin [1998] 2 WLR 1 (murder committed by a British citizen outside the United Kingdom).

a minority of other civilians as members of the court. Although she may be represented by a civilian lawyer and a civilian judge might advise the court she will have her guilt or innocence determined by a body quite distinct from a normal civilian court in her home State or even in the receiving State. In States, for instance, which rely on jury trial this will have been replaced by a court of military officers (and possibly a civilian member).

It is likely, however, that this court will satisfy the requirements of an independent and impartial tribunal if it does so in its trial of soldiers. It might be argued that the wife of the soldier has consented to some extent to this procedure since she can be expected to know of it before any crime has been alleged against her. This leads to the theoretical conclusion that if she had not been prepared to be tried before a military court she would have had the option of not joining her husband abroad. Such an argument places the wife in a very difficult position, either to join her husband abroad and run the risk of being tried by a military court or living apart from him for the period of his service abroad. This could extend to a period of two or more years. By being forced to choose the latter course the State may be argued to be in breach of the right owed separately to the soldier and his wife to respect for his or her family life.[52] Where that dependant is the child of the soldier he or she is unlikely to have given any implied consent to be tried by a military court. A civilian worker, who is a national of the sending State and who is employed by the military authorities of that State, might be argued to be in the same position as the soldier in respect of his implied consent to be tried by a military court if he commits a crime within its jurisdiction while abroad.

An appeal from a military court sitting abroad is likely to be heard in the home State. Where this is a civilian court it will be able to provide a mechanism for a decision to be made by civilian judges in relation to the guilt or innocence of the dependant or civilian worker. It is, however, unlikely to be a retrial and the findings of the military court will be difficult to disturb in the absence of an error of law made by that court.

Should a State take the view that a military court is undesirable as a forum for trying a civilian under any circumstances it will need to provide

---

[52] This is, however, unlikely to succeed since a spouse must be taken to have consented, on marrying a soldier, to the possibility of temporary separation required for military operational reasons. In addition, the State has not 'deported' the soldier nor has it prevented the spouse from travelling to the receiving State. Compare *Winata* v. *Australia*, CCPR/C/72/D/930/2000 (2001).

some practical alternative. It could provide a civilian court[53] sitting abroad to hear all these criminal cases or it could stipulate in the status of forces agreement that as a sending State it wishes only to hold military courts on the territory of the receiving State in respect of those who are members of its armed forces. In this event dependants and any employed civilians will have to be tried by the courts of the receiving State or be sent to the sending State for trial there before the ordinary criminal courts of that State.

None of these options may be easy for a sending State. The acceptance of the need to provide a civilian court to operate on the territory of a receiving State will lead to a number of practical problems. It is unlikely that this court will have a sufficient caseload to justify its permanent presence in any particular location abroad unless the civilian judge is able to be employed on other judicial functions. A further difficulty is whether this court should be comprised of the same type of members as it would in the courts of the sending State. In particular, the issue would revolve around whether jurors could be listed to serve if that is the form of trial in the courts of the sending State and, if so, whether these jurors would travel from the sending State itself or whether they would be recruited from civilians of the same nationality living in the territory of the receiving State. The sending State may take the view that it is too disruptive of family life (and of military efficiency) to require a dependant to travel back to the sending State for trial before the courts of that State, even where those courts possess extra-territorial jurisdiction.

The option of accepting that a dependant or civilian component of the military force should be tried by the ordinary criminal courts of the receiving State for all alleged crimes committed on that territory may appear to be the easiest option. In reality, however, it treats the soldier and his wife, both of whom are nationals of the sending State, quite differently for a breach of the criminal law of the sending State and the receiving State. The soldier would be tried by a military court and his wife by a civilian court of the receiving State. Little difficulty with this would occur if it is accepted that the quality of justice in the military courts of the sending State and the civilian courts of the receiving State is equal. States in this position may not be prepared to accept that it is.[54]

---

[53] The United Kingdom has provided for a Standing Civilian Court (civilian judge sitting alone) to deal with relatively minor cases: Armed Forces Act 1976.

[54] It is not uncommon for each State to assert that its form of justice is 'the best in the world'.

The trial of civilians by military court in time of an international armed conflict

In times of international armed conflict a State may provide for the trial of its own citizens by military court or a court with at least some military involvement in it. This is unlikely to occur, however, unless a real risk of invasion and occupation is foreseen when the ordinary civilian courts may not be able to operate in an area over which actual fighting is taking place.[55] A further instance might be following the aftermath of a nuclear war where civilian society has been so disrupted as to make the re-existing law and criminal procedures inadequate to cope with the conditions then existing.[56]

Where the armed forces of one State occupy another State the occupier may have to establish 'non-political courts'[57] in order to enforce the law it has promulgated within the occupied territory.[58] In the absence of a suitable derogation notice during a period of an armed conflict a military court convened to try a civilian protected person would be required to display the same characteristics of independence and impartiality.[59] The major difference between such a court and the military courts convened to try its own soldiers is that the accused will not be a member of the armed forces of the State holding the military court nor a national of that State. In these circumstances the court must be reminded that the accused owes

---

[55] For an example, see the Emergency Powers (Defence) (No. 2) Act 1940 providing for 'war zone courts' should the United Kingdom be invaded by Nazi Germany. The proposed courts were military courts in the understanding of that phrase used in this chapter. See G. Rubin, 'If Hitler's Invasion Had Begun: British Plans for War Zone Courts 1940–1945' in K. O'Donovan and G. Rubin, *Human Rights and Legal History: Essays in Honour of Brian Simpson* (Oxford: Oxford University Press, 2000), chapter 4.

[56] See D. Bonner, *Emergency Powers in Peacetime* (London: Sweet & Maxwell, 1985), p. 10. This situation may be compared with the detonation of a 'dirty bomb' by international terrorists where the effects are likely to be much more limited.

[57] These may, of course, be military courts. It is argued above that the term, 'non-political' could be understood as meaning courts able to offer an accused an independent and impartial tribunal. See the fourth Geneva Convention 1949, Arts. 64, 65, 66; Additional Protocol I 1977, Art. 75. See also the trial of Eckehardt Weil by a British military court held in Berlin in 1971: A. Rogers, 'The Use of Military Courts to Try Suspects' (2000) 51 *International and Comparative Legal Quarterly* 967, 971.

[58] See also the Hague Regulations Annexed to Hague Convention IV 1907, Art. 43. The occupying State may, however, rely upon the courts of the occupied State to enforce its own penal provisions providing that these penal provisions do not 'constitute a threat to its security or an obstacle to the application of the [fourth Geneva] Convention': Art. 64 of that Convention.

[59] Additional Protocol I 1977, Art. 75(4). For the applicability of human rights treaties outside the territory of the State party to them see chapter 5.

no allegiance to the State by which is being tried.[60] The trial of a civilian protected person will almost certainly only occur in occupied territory.

It will also be necessary to provide that the trial is held in public.[61] This may be more difficult for the occupying force to accept since they may fear demonstrations by the local population or disruption of the trial. They may be able to show that the exclusion of the public is necessary in the interests of national security or public order.[62] There are further dissimilarities with the trial of a soldier before a military court of his own armed forces. The occupying State may assert that it cannot produce its own witnesses (almost always members of its armed forces) and the court should accept a transcript of their evidence on the grounds that to produce these soldiers in open court would compromise its security arrangements. The accused may also find difficulty in calling witnesses, especially if they are members of an organised resistance movement who, naturally, will be unwilling to appear as witnesses in the military courts of the occupying State.[63] The provision of lawyers, both for the prosecution and the defence,[64] will be as important as it is for the trial of a soldier by his own armed forces as a means of ensuring that the protected person receives a fair trial. In this matter international humanitarian law is, in theory, of more value to the protected person that any human rights provision since no derogation from the former is permitted.[65]

It will be shown in chapter 5 that protected persons tried by a State party to the 1950 Convention may come within the jurisdiction of that State if it is occupying the territory of another State.[66] It can reasonably be expected that a protected person tried by a military court will seek to challenge the compatibility of the court processes with the relevant provisions of human

---

[60] See the fourth Geneva Convention 1949, Art. 67.

[61] Although this is not specifically required by the Geneva Conventions 1949, nor by their Additional Protocols of 1977 (although see Art. 75(4) 'generally recognised principles of judicial procedure'), it is by various human rights instruments. See the 1966 Covenant, Art. 14; the 1950 Convention, Art. 6(1).

[62] Article 14(1) of the 1966 Covenant; Art. 6(1) of the 1950 Convention; Art. 8(5) of the American Convention on Human Rights 1969.

[63] On these issues human rights provisions are similar to those of international humanitarian law, see Additional Protocol I 1977, Art. 75(4)(g).

[64] The fourth Geneva Convention 1949, Art. 72.

[65] Y. Sandoz, C. Swinarski, B. Zimmerman (eds.), *Commentary on the Additional Protocols of 8 June 1977 to the Geneva Conventions of 12 August 1949* (Geneva: International Committee of the Red Cross, 1987), para. 3006.

[66] This will depend upon the subsequent interpretations of *Bankovic* v. *Belgium et al.* (2002) 41 *International Legal Materials* 517 in particular whether the principles within that case are limited to the 'legal space (*espace juridique*) of the Contracting States', para. 80.

rights instruments. In modern times it is common for non-governmental organisations specialising in human rights or for lawyers to take cases on behalf of individuals (whether nationals or not of the respondent State) to the European Court of Human Rights (where applicable) and to other human rights bodies where there is an individual right of petition. The rights given to civilians may thus be capable of enforcement despite the fact that the applicant is not of the same nationality as the occupying State and is located outside the territorial boundaries of that State.

Foreign civilians brought onto a military base

The detention of civilians captured outside the territory of the detaining State and transferred to a military base is uncommon. Following the military action undertaken by the United States armed forces in Afghanistan in 2001 a number of individuals, of varying nationalities, were captured by those forces. The overwhelming majority of these detainees were non-United States citizens and were transferred to Guantanamo Bay, a United States military base in Cuba.[67] They have been described by spokesmen of the United States government as 'unlawful combatants'.[68] On the assumption that they are not entitled to prisoner of war status they must be considered to be civilians. Should any of them be placed on trial the trial will be by a Military Commission established by the United States in 2001 to try non-citizens for 'violations of the laws of war and other offences triable by military commission'.[69]

It is for the Secretary of Defense to appoint the appointing authority who, in turn, appoints the members of the military commission[70]

---

[67] See the discussion of the relationship between Cuba and the United States over Guantanamo Bay in *Gherebi* v. *Bush and Rumsfeld*, United States Court of Appeals for the Ninth Circuit, 18 December 2003. See, generally, D. Rose, *Guantanamo: America's War on Human Rights* (London: Faber and Faber, 2004).

[68] Other terms used have been 'enemy combatants' and 'unprivileged belligerents'. For the treatment of those accorded the status of prisoners of war see chapter 5.

[69] Department of Defense Military Commission Order No. 1 (21 March 2002). The trial of non-United States nationals by Military Commission pre-dates the 2001 President's Military Order. For an example see *Ex Parte Quirin* 317 US 3 (1942). This trial and all subsequent proceedings took place within the territory of the United States. Many military commissions were conducted by that State (and a number of other States) of non-nationals in territory in Germany occupied by them following World War II.

[70] Department of Defense Military Commission Instruction No. 5 (15 March 2004) and Instruction No. 8 (30 April 2004) para. 3. Instruction No. 6 (30 April 2004) does, however, provide that 'the consideration or evaluation of the performance of duty as a member of a

and for him or the President to receive the record of the hearing and to make a 'final decision'.[71] It is difficult to argue that this form of trial would be able to convey the perception of an independent and impartial tribunal as required by all human rights treaties[72] and, through a more opaque phrase in the Geneva Conventions 1949, a 'fair and regular trial'.[73] Moreover, communications between defence counsel and the accused may be 'subject to monitoring or review by government officials using any available means, for security and intelligence purposes'.[74] The Council of Europe has also drawn attention to the fact that those tried by military commission will receive 'a different standard of justice than United States nationals, which amounts to . . . an act of discrimination contrary to the [1966 Covenant]'.[75]

A further legal difficulty in this situation is that the United States is not a party to the first Optional Protocol (1966) to the International Covenant on Civil and Political Rights 1966 by which those claiming to be victims of a breach of the Covenant may make an independent communication to the Human Rights Committee. Nor does it accept that the 1966 Covenant applies to the activities of its armed forces at Guantanamo Bay since this is not located 'within its territory and subject to its jurisdiction'.[76]

---

military commission is prohibited in preparing effectiveness, fitness, or evaluation reports of a commission member'. For a similar requirement see *Cooper* v. *United Kingdom* (2004) 39 EHRR 8, para. 125; *R.* v. *Genereux* (1992) 88 DLR (4th) 110.

[71] Military Order No. 1, para. 6(6).

[72] See, for example, discussion of the requirements of independence and impartiality at a court-martial in *Cooper* v. *United Kingdom* (2004) 39 EHRR 8, para. 104. The Court went on to conclude that 'such tribunals would only be tolerated as long as sufficient safeguards were in place to guarantee their independence and impartiality': para. 106.

[73] See the fourth Convention, Art. 147. Although the United States is not a party to Additional Protocol I 1977 it is commonly understood that Art. 75 reflects customary international law in its requirement of an 'impartial and regularly constituted court': C. Greenwood, 'International law and the war against terrorism' (2002) 78 *International Affairs* 301, 316. There is no separate requirement of 'independence' although 'fair . . . trial' is hardly possible without independence of the court from the executive.

[74] Department of Defense Military Commission Instruction No. 5, Annex B, para. I (30 April 2004).

[75] Parliamentary Assembly Resolution 1340 (2003) para. 8. This is to overstate the case. The status of an individual (whether a national or a non-national) may result in different jurisdictional bases of trial depending on this status. Thus, in some States a soldier may be tried by a military court and a foreign national civilian by a civilian court for the same act.

[76] See also the decision of the American Commission on Human Rights on a request for preliminary measures relating to detainees at Guantanamo Bay, 12 March 2002 and T. Meron, 'Extraterritoriality of Human Rights Treaties' (1995) 89 *American Journal of International Law* 78, 79.

That it denies the detainees concerned to be prisoners of war or civilian protected persons is sufficient (in the view of the United States) to exclude the application of the Geneva Conventions 1949.[77] The fact that they are non-United States nationals has led to a denial that they are entitled to the protection of the United States Constitution and federal law.[78] The detainees have therefore been described as being in a 'legal black hole',[79] denied even the standards of fair trial offered to United States armed forces by their Uniform Code of Military Justice.[80]

---

[77] See, however, the view of the European Council's Commission for Democracy Through Law (Venice Commission) CDL-AD (2003), 17 December 2003, para. 85.

[78] Following a number of test cases the United States Supreme Court has granted certiorari to bring before it the issue of whether a civilian can be tried by military commission in Guantanamo Bay, see *Hamdan* v. *Rumsfeld*, 22 November 2004. British citizens detained in Guantanamo Bay are unable to invoke the jurisdiction of the British courts: see *R. (Abbasi)* v. *Secretary for Foreign and Commonwealth Affairs and Secretary of State for the Home Department* [2002] EWCA Civ 1598.

[79] Lord Steyn, 'Guantanamo Bay: the Legal Black Hole' (2004) 53 *International and Comparative Legal Quarterly* 1.

[80] 10 USCA, para. 836; *Hamdan* v. *Rumsfeld* at para. D.

5

Human rights and international armed conflict

It may seem strange to think of the armed forces of a State having to consider the human rights both of enemy nationals and of its members during an international armed conflict in which they are involved. It will be well understood that for the duration of an international armed conflict international humanitarian law, which has been designed specifically to deal with just such a situation, will impose some legal limitations on the physical power of the armed forces. Members of the armed forces in most States will have been trained, to some extent, to abide by this body of law. They will know, for instance, that it is forbidden to kill unarmed civilians, to take part in any attack on them, to attack vehicles or buildings displaying the protective emblem, and to kill prisoners of war. Those higher up the chain of command will bear an additional responsibility to ensure compliance with this extensive body of law and may have lawyers to advise them.[1] In some States military exercises may well have had built into them: 'law of war scenarios' to test the ability of the armed forces to apply this law. Considerable effort is made by the International Committee of the Red Cross to advise States on their obligations under the Geneva Conventions 1949 (along with their Additional Protocols of 1977).[2]

What, however, of human rights? It is unlikely that comparable effort has been spent on the training of members of armed forces to respect the human rights of enemy nationals with whom they come into contact during an international armed conflict. It might be thought that this is

[1] Note, in particular, Arts. 57 (precautions in attack), 86, 87 (command responsibility) and 82 (legal advisers) all of Protocol Additional to the Geneva Conventions of 12 August 1949, and relating to the protection of victims of international armed conflicts (Protocol I) Geneva, 8 June 1977, in force 7 December 1978: (1977) 16 International Legal Materials (ILM) 1391, ('Additional Protocol I 1977').

[2] In particular, the Advisory Service on International Humanitarian Law (a unit within the Legal Division of the International Committee of the Red Cross). See, generally, P. Berman, 'The ICRC's Advisory Service on International Humanitarian Law: the Challenges of National Implementation' (1996) 312 International Review of the Red Cross 338.

not a real issue since international humanitarian law has been designed, as one of its purposes, to protect the 'victims of armed conflict' and there are many provisions within this body of law which might otherwise be styled as human rights.[3] It will be shown that this is too simplistic a view since the human rights treaties, to which States have become parties, will continue to apply to some extent during an international armed conflict.

As a matter of practice, soldiers will generally be more interested in international humanitarian law than in human rights for a number of reasons. International humanitarian law in one form or another has been part of the context of military life during international armed conflict from at least the beginning of the twentieth century.[4] In such conflicts soldiers have become increasingly well used to its basic principles throughout that century. This is particularly the case where the legal classification of the conflict is clearly an international one. In this situation it is not uncommon for opposing soldiers to respect each other and to apply, with little hesitation, these basic rules. More so is this the case if the armed conflict is of short duration. The human rights of foreign nationals with whom the soldier comes into contact have not been so well bedded into the military ethos of armed forces. The soldier may find it quite unrealistic to accept that he must respect the right to life of an enemy combatant.[5] In the armies of most States a breach of some (or all) of the rules of international

---

[3] For the relationship between human rights and international humanitarian law see Additional Protocol I 1977, Arts. 72, 75; D. Schindler, 'Human Rights and Humanitarian Law' (1981–2) 31 *American University Law Review* 935; L. Doswald-Beck and S. Vite, 'International Humanitarian Law and Human Rights Law' (1993) 293 *International Review of the Red Cross* 94; F. Hampson, 'Using International Human Rights Machinery to Enforce the International Law of Armed Conflicts' (1992) 31 *Revue de Droit Militaire et de Droit de la Guerre* 119; R. Provost, *International Human Rights and Humanitarian Law* (Cambridge: Cambridge University Press, 2002).

[4] See, for example, the various Hague Conventions 1907. See, generally, T. McCormack, 'From Sun Tzu to the Sixth Committee: the Evolution of an International Criminal Regime' in T. McCormack and G. Simpson (eds.), *The Law of War Crimes, National and International Approaches* (The Hague: Kluwer Law International, 1997), p. 31.

[5] There are, of course, limitations to this, which are discussed below. Apart from the issue of the jurisdiction of the human rights treaty concerned the fact that this right to life may be subject to an express derogation (under the European Convention for the Protection of Human Rights and Fundamental Freedoms, Rome, 4 November 1950, in force 3 September 1953, 213 *United Nations Treaty Series* (UNTS) 222 ('1950 Convention')) or is subject to the *lex specialis* of international humanitarian law (International Covenant on Civil and Political Rights, 16 December 1966, in force 23 March 1976, 999 (UNTS) 171 ('1966 Covenant')) makes it much less clear to the soldier than the relatively simple rule in international law that all combatants may be attacked.

humanitarian law will involve the personal responsibility of the soldier for his actions. He may be subjected to the disciplinary system of his own armed forces, the criminal law and legal system of his own State or that of another State or of an international tribunal. In a well-disciplined army the soldier may fear for his life, his liberty, his promotion prospects or his pocket and thus comply with the basic rules of international human-itarian law. Human rights law will often not be embedded within the disciplinary or criminal structures of the armed forces in the same way as with international humanitarian law. At least one of the reasons for this is that the structure of international humanitarian law lends itself to the prohibition of certain forms of conduct and thus the creation of criminal or disciplinary offences. This process has been greatly assisted by the Rome Statute of the International Criminal Court 1998.[6] The law of human rights, on the other hand, stresses the rights of individuals. Although there may be a corresponding duty on individuals to respect these rights, the criminal law or the disciplinary systems operating within the armed forces have been much slower in transforming these duties into offences for which individual soldiers may be charged.[7] Unlike interna-tional humanitarian law it is the State alone,[8] which will be responsible for breaches of human rights under the relevant treaty, even if its armed

---

[6] See Arts. 6, 7 and 8.

[7] Under English law see the Criminal Justice Act 1988, s. 134, relating to torture.

[8] See *Abella* v. *Argentina*, Report No. 55/97, Case 11.137, 18 November 1997 at para. 174, although individuals may be punished under their national law. The theoretical basis of the obligations under human rights and international humanitarian law is, however, the same. In international humanitarian law the State will also be responsible (which can include the payment of compensation) for the acts of its armed forces on the basis of a claim by another State only, Hague Convention IV 1907, Art. 3; Additional Protocol I 1977, Art. 91. See, generally, F. Kalshoven, 'State Responsibility for Warlike Acts of the Armed Forces' (1991) 40 *International and Comparative Law Quarterly* 827; L. Zegweld, 'Reme-dies for Victims of Violations of International Humanitarian Law' (2003) 85 *International Review of the Red Cross* 497, 507; 'German Federal Supreme Court: The *Distimo Mas-sacre Case* (*Greek Citizens* v. *Federal Republic of Germany*) (2003) 42 ILM 1030; Eritrea-Ethiopian Claims Commission, Partial Award on Prisoners of War (Ethiopia's Claim 4) (2003) ILM 1056; H. Kasutani in 'Correspondents' Reports' [Japan](1999) 2 *Yearbook of International Humanitarian Law* 388–90 (relating to compensation for 'comfort women' and allied prisoners of war under Japanese control in World War II). For the general responsibility of a State for its armed forces see the International Law Commission's Draft Articles on Responsibility of the State for Intentionally Wrongful Acts, 2001, as to which see J. Crawford, *The International Law Commission's Articles on State Responsibility* (Cambridge; Cambridge University Press, 2002), p. 96 for discussion of the acts of 'superior and subordinate officials'.

forces have acted 'outside the sphere of their authority or [where they] violate internal law'.[9]

The picture may well be quite different seen from the perspective of the victim of a breach of human rights during an international armed conflict. Where such a person has a right of individual petition to a human rights body[10] a claim for compensation may be brought by him against the State whose armed forces acted in a way to deny him (allegedly) a particular right given by the Convention. This may be seen, in some cases, to be a more important remedy for the victim than the knowledge that the soldier has been disciplined or prosecuted or that the State has been found to have been in breach of its obligations under the International Covenant on Civil and Political Rights 1966 (unless compensation is also available).[11]

The work of the media, particularly television, has had a profound effect on the conduct of international armed conflicts. When the actions of soldiers can be seen simultaneously, or shortly afterwards, on television it frequently follows that the propriety of their actions will also be discussed. The location of witnesses may then often be traced giving human rights organisations the opportunity to compile reports on particular incidents for widespread dissemination. These organisations are likely, due to the nature of their work, to concentrate on human rights violations in addition to breaches of international humanitarian law. The reports of the most respected of these organisations can have considerable influence within a State or world-wide and the armed forces of a State

---

[9] *Velasquez Rodriguez Case* (Inter-American Court of Human Rights), Judgment, 29 July 1988, para. 170. Thus, the State may be liable where its military courts fail properly to investigate, Report No. 40/03, Case 10.301, Inter-American Commission on Human Rights, 8 October 2003, para. 4.

[10] 'Human rights law . . . assumes that the individual has legally enforceable rights that he is able to assert': D. Schindler, 'Human Rights and Humanitarian Law' (1981–2) 31 *American University Law Review* 935, 941.

[11] Differences between the way in which the facts are established may be an important factor from the victim's point of view. A State may, at its discretion, pay compensation to the victim of the acts of its armed forces whether or not a breach of international humanitarian law or of human rights is admitted. For an example see D. Murphy, 'Contemporary Practice of the United States Relating to International Law' (2000) 94 *American Journal of International Law* 127; *The Times*, 8 January 2004 (in relation to the United Kingdom in Iraq; *Guardian*, 26 November 2003 (compensation paid by the United States for 'wrongful death claims' in Iraq). The national law of a State may permit a victim of a human rights or of an international humanitarian law breach to sue the perpetrator in its courts. For an example see *Kadic* v. *Karadzic* (1995) 34 ILM 1592; *Xuncax* v. *Gramajo* (1995) 886 F Supp 162; *Alvarez-Machain* v. *USA* (2003) 331 F 3d 604 and note the dissent of O'Scannlain, circuit judge at pp. 645–6 and, generally, C. Scott (ed.), *Torture as Tort: Comparative Perspectives on the Development of Transnational Human Rights Litigation* (Oxford: Hart, 2001).

would be wise to consider that the publication of such reports is a foreseeable consequence of their actions on the battlefield.[12]

Are human rights treaties applicable during an international armed conflict?

One view held by some States has been that international humanitarian law and not the human rights treaties govern international armed conflict.[13] To some extent this view has proved of some comfort to States. It has enabled them readily to become parties to human rights treaties, which may be a prerequisite to joining an international organisation or to recognition, with little concern about the effect of having done so should the State become involved in an international armed conflict. It has also enabled them to enter reservations to the Geneva Conventions 1949 and to Additional Protocol I 1977, which clearly apply during an international armed conflict. The pattern of reservations applicable to an international armed conflict is much greater in the latter family of treaties than in the former.[14] In practice, therefore, States have seen that they can accommodate their own national interests during an international armed conflict in these international humanitarian law treaties in which there are few[15] restrictions on the right of reservation.[16] Unlike these treaties, however, the human rights treaties do give an additional right to derogate from some rights and to issue a derogation notice in respect of 'war or other

---

[12] A good example of the use of an autopsy report obtained by Amnesty International can be seen in *Abella* v. *Argentina* Report No. 55/97, Case 11.137, 18 November 1997 at para. 406. The ICRC, however, makes confidential reports to States.

[13] In *Bankovic* v. *Belgium et al.* Application No. 52207/99, Admissibility Decision of 12 December 2001 (2002) 41 ILM 517, the respondent States argued that 'international humanitarian law . . . and, most recently, the International Criminal Court . . . exist to regulate such State conduct' [international armed conflict] (para. 43); *Legality of the Threat or Use of Nuclear Weapons*, Advisory Opinion (1996) ICJ Reports 226 at para. 24. The human rights treaties are silent as to the methods and means of warfare, *Abella* v. *Argentina*, Report No. 55/97, Case 11.137, 18 November 1997 at para. 161.

[14] No reservations could be traced by the author relating to conduct of an international armed conflict to the 1950 Convention or to the 1966 Covenant, nor where there any relevant derogation notices.

[15] See the Vienna Convention on the Law of Treaties, Vienna, 23 May 1969, in force 27 January 1980 (1969) 8 ILM 679, Art. 19.

[16] More recent treaties have not permitted reservations: see Ottawa Convention on the Prohibition of the Use, Stockpiling, Production and Transfer of Anti-Personnel Mines and on their Destruction 1997, Art. 19; the Rome Statute of the International Criminal Court 1998, Rome, 17 July 1998, 37 ILM 999, Art. 120. In the latter treaty a number of States have, however, made declarations and understandings.

public emergency threatening the life of the nation'.[17] Such a derogation must actually be made; it cannot be implied merely from the fact that the State is engaged in an international armed conflict.[18] It may, however, be queried whether a derogation notice issued in such circumstances would be considered effective, merely through the act of issuing it. A derogation notice affecting a State's own territory may be contrasted with one affecting the territory of another State which it occupies. In the latter case it is difficult to accept that the occupation of the territory will show a suitable emergency in the territory of the occupying State.[19] A derogation notice under a human rights instrument can only be seen as an example of acceptance of the principle that the ends justify the means. Since it must not be inconsistent with a State's other obligations under international law the protection of the human rights of an individual, where such a notice has been issued, is stronger when an international armed conflict is in existence than where it is not. This is because the State cannot derogate from its obligations under international humanitarian law.[20]

[17] The terminology varies in the individual human rights instruments, as do the rights from which there can be no derogation. See, generally, R. Higgins, 'Derogations under the Human Rights Treaties (1976–77) 48 *British Yearbook of International Law* 281; J. Hartman, 'Derogation from Human Rights Treaties in Public Emergencies' (1981) 22 *Harvard International Law Journal* 1; R. Macdonald, 'Derogations under Article 15 of the European Convention on Human Rights' (1997) 36 *Columbian Journal of Transnational Law* 225, who comments: 'the emergencies contemplated by the drafters are not necessarily those that confront the member states of Europe today' (p. 233). See also the Siracusa Principles (dealing with the 1966 Covenant) (1985) 7 *Human Rights Quarterly* 3; the Paris Minimum Standards of Human Rights Norms in a State of Emergency (dealing with the 1966 Covenant and the 1950 Convention) (1985) 79 *American Journal of International Law* 1072. See, however, T. Meron, *Human Rights Law-Making in the United Nations: a Critique of Instruments and Process* (Oxford: Clarendon Press, 1986), p. 86.

[18] *Cyprus* v. *Turkey* (1976) 4 EHRR 482 at para. 527. Under the 1966 Covenant, Art. 4 the public emergency must be 'officially proclaimed' thus deterring 'attempts to justify repressive action by a retroactive claim of derogation': Hartman, 'Derogation from Human Rights' (n. 17 above) at p. 18.

[19] Macdonald concludes that (in relation to the 1950 Convention) 'a state of emergency declared not to further democracy, but to destroy or repress it would be invalid under article 15': Macdonald, 'Derogations under Article 15' (n. 17 above) p. 249. Macdonald was referring to a state of emergency in the territory of the State itself. This principle would apply, *a fortiori*, to territory which that State occupies.

[20] See the 1950 Convention, Art. 15; 1966 Covenant, Art. 4; American Convention on Human Rights, San Jos, 22 November 1969, in force 18 July 1978, (1970) 9 ILM 673, Art. 27; Arab Charter on Human Rights 1994, Art. 4; *Cyprus* v. *Turkey* (1982) 4 EHRR 552–3; *Abella* v. *Argentina*, Report No. 55/97, Case 11.137, 18 November 1997, at para. 170. A purported derogation in breach of international humanitarian law (depending upon the nature of the armed conflict) would show a breach of both families of treaties: *Abella*, Report No. 55/97 above. See also the Siracusa Principles and the Paris Minimum Standards of Human Rights Norms in a State of Emergency (n. 17 above).

Once a derogation notice is issued it enables a State to achieve an effect similar to that produced by a suitable reservation. It has the advantage, however, of providing a means for a State to tailor the rights it wishes to deny to individuals during a specific international armed conflict. It can be amended or withdrawn at any time. This advantage can be compared with a reservation to treaties. Once a reservation is made by a State at the time of its ratification it cannot be altered thereafter, nor can one be added once ratification has taken place.[21] It can also be contrasted with a denunciation of the relevant treaty. There are normally limits on the power of a State to denounce a treaty in both the human rights and international humanitarian law fields.[22]

It is now accepted[23] that during an international armed conflict both families of treaty apply, subject to any reservations or, in the case of human rights treaties, to any derogations and to the limits of their jurisdiction set out in each individual treaty. A consequence of this position may well be that States will issue a derogation notice where permitted by the relevant human rights treaty should they become involved in an international armed conflict. No derogation notice under the European Convention on Human Rights 1950 was issued in respect of the Falklands/Malvinas conflict 1982, the Gulf war 1990–1 or in respect of NATO action in the Balkans in the 1990s or in respect of the attack and occupation of Iraq in 2003. To some extent this might be understandable since in the Gulf war,

---

[21] In the United Kingdom the opposition party has proposed that the United Kingdom should denounce the 1950 Convention and subsequently accede to it with a suitable reservation concerning the applicability of the Convention to military discipline.

[22] The 1966 Covenant has no provisions for denunciation. Compare the First Optional Protocol 1966, Art. 12. Of the other major human rights instruments only the 1950 Convention, Art. 58 provides for denunciation. The Geneva Conventions 1949 and Additional Protocol I 1977, can be denounced (with restrictions): see Arts. 63, 62, 142 and 158 respectively of the 1949 Conventions (Geneva Convention for the amelioration of the condition of the wounded and sick in armed forces in the field, Geneva, 12 August 1949, in force 21 October 1950, 75 UNTS 31 ('First Geneva Convention 1949'); Geneva Convention for the amelioration of the condition of wounded, sick and shipwrecked members of armed forces at sea, Geneva, 12 August 1949, in force 21 October 1950, 75 UNTS 85 ('Second Geneva Convention 1949'); Geneva Convention relative to the treatment of prisoners of war, Geneva, 12 August 1949, in force 21 October 1950, 75 UNTS 135 ('Third Geneva Convention 1949'); Geneva Convention relative to the protection of civilian persons in time of war, Geneva, 12 August 1949, in force 21 October 1950, 75 UNTS 287 ('Fourth Geneva Convention 1949')), and Art. 99 of Additional Protocol I 1977.

[23] See *Bankovic* (n. 13 above) had Art. 1 applied; *Legality of the Threat or Use of Nuclear Weapons* (1996) para. 25 (see n. 13 above); *Coard* v. United States, Report No. 109/99, Case 10.951, 29 September 1999 at para. 39; *Abella* v. *Argentina*, Report No. 55/97, Case 11.137, 18 November 1997 at para. 158.

the Balkans and in Iraq the conflict occurred in the territories of States not party to the 1950 Convention. This was not, however, the case of the conflict which took place on the territory of a dependant territory of the United Kingdom, the Falklands (Malvinas) Islands in 1982.[24] The fact of non-derogation has been argued so as to show that the Convention does not apply during an international armed conflict, or at least to show that it does not apply when the acts of the armed forces of States party to it occur on the territory of a non-State party.[25] No derogation notices have been issued under the International Covenant on Civil and Political Rights 1966 or under any other human rights treaty in respect of an international armed conflict, other than where states of emergency brought about by border incidents have been declared.

The extent of the jurisdiction of each human rights treaty varies. All of them are, however, as a group in sharp contrast with the Geneva Conventions 1949 and Additional Protocol I 1977. The 1949 Conventions impose an obligation on States party to 'undertake to respect and to ensure respect for the [Conventions] in all circumstances'.[26] This phrase has been interpreted widely as involving an obligation on States party to ensure that they and all other States party to the 1949 Conventions respect the Conventions in all circumstances.[27] There are no jurisdictional or territorial limits on this obligation. The effect is that States take this obligation with them wherever their armed forces operate, during an international armed conflict, whether on national territory or outside such territory.[28] This has never been seen as a problem; indeed it is a strength of these Conventions (and the whole of international humanitarian law applying during

---

[24] The 1950 Convention was applicable to the Falkland Islands through express declaration to the Secretariat of the Council of Europe, dated 30 June 1969, as was the 1966 Covenant. There is a further question, namely, whether the acts occurring on the territory of the Falkland Islands/Malvinas came within the jurisdiction of those islands or the United Kingdom, or both. In relation to the sinking of the Argentine warship, the *General Belgrano*, the European Court of Human Rights (on 19 July 2000) declared the application of Luisa de Ibanez (Application No. 58692/00) to be inadmissible due to the lateness of the submission of her application.

[25] See *Bankovic* (n. 13 above), at para. 62.

[26] Common Art. 1 to the 1949 Conventions and Art. 1(1) of Additional Protocol I 1977. These treaties come into operation in the circumstances of common Arts. 2 and 1(3) respectively.

[27] See Y. Sandoz, C. Swinarski and B. Zimmerman (eds.), *Commentary on the Additional Protocols of 8 June 1977 to the Geneva Conventions of 12 August 1949* (Geneva: International Committee of the Red Cross, 1987), para. 43.

[28] See also the Secretary-General's Bulletin: Observance by United Nations Forces of International Humanitarian Law (1999) 38 ILM 1656.

an international armed conflict). The fact that this principle eschews 'jurisdiction' as a basis for it has avoided the difficulties inherent within that terminology under international law. Any comparison between the Geneva Conventions 1949 and human rights treaties drawn solely on the basis that the former imposes personal liabilities on members of the armed forces and the latter give rights to 'victims' is not satisfying. The 1949 Conventions and Additional Protocol I do impose many obligations on members of the armed forces to 'respect', for instance, women and children[29] but they also appear to give rights to particular groups of individuals.[30]

The reach of the relevant human rights treaties, on the other hand, is based upon 'jurisdiction'[31] although Article 2 of the 1966 Covenant imposes a further limitation on the part of the State, that of undertaking to respect and to ensure respect to individuals 'within its territory' (which is discussed below). Given that international armed conflicts normally[32] involve the armed forces of at least one State operating outside its territorial limits this issue is crucial in determining whether such a State owes obligations under a relevant human rights treaty to those with whom it comes into contact. A State is free to consent to the exercise of jurisdiction by another on its territory. In relation to the armed forces this is normally achieved by a status of forces agreement or by a memorandum

---

[29] Arts. 76, 77 respectively of Additional Protocol I 1977.

[30] See, for example, Art. 75 of Additional Protocol I 1977; chapter III of the third Geneva Convention 1949. For further discussion see chapter 1.

[31] 1966 Covenant, Art. 2; 1950 Convention, Art. 1; American Convention on Human Rights 1969, Art. 1; Arab Charter on Human Rights 1994, Art. 2; African Charter on Human and Peoples' Rights, Nairobi, 27 June 1981, in force 21 October 1986; (1982) 21 ILM 59, Art. 1 (States 'undertake to adopt legislative or other measures to give effect to [rights and duties])'.

[32] The position of an occupying State is anomalous in this context, since it will possess *some* of the obligations of the sovereign State by virtue of its occupation of that territory. A State may also keep its own armed forces within its boundaries but wield overall control over an organised armed group within another State. In this case the group may be treated as belonging to the State, see *Prosecutor* v. *Tadic*, Judgment of the Appeals Chamber, International Criminal Tribunal for the Former Yugoslavia, IT-94-1-A, 15 July 1999 at para. 145 (1999) 38 ILM 1518; *Prosecutor* v. *Aleksovski*, Judgment of the Appeals Chamber, International Criminal Tribunal for the Former Yugoslavia, 24 March 2000, para. 143; *Cyprus* v. *Turkey* (2002) 35 EHRR 35, at para. 77. The State may also be liable for a breach of the 1966 Covenant committed by those whom it controls, see CCPR/C/79/Add.15, paras. 7, 9.

of understanding between (or among) the States concerned.[33] Where such an agreement or memorandum is in force it will generally permit the sending State to exercise its military jurisdiction over members of its armed forces in the territory of the receiving State.[34] This may occur during an international armed conflict where allies from the sending State are based[35] in the receiving State or where, for example, prisoners of war are transferred to the receiving State by an ally and soldiers from the sending State remain there as guards.[36]

Where a State has not consented to the presence of foreign armed forces on, or over, its territory such as where an armed conflict is taking place between them, general principles of international law provide guidelines in determining the limits of the jurisdiction of the sending State. The position cannot be that that State brings everyone with whom its armed forces come into contact on the territory of another State within its human rights treaty obligations. To accept this proposition would be to ignore both the term 'within the jurisdiction' contained in human rights treaties and the (factual) distinction which exists between the 'effective control' of an area outside its national territory[37] of a State as evidenced, for example

---

[33] There may be occasions when no status of forces agreement is in existence, see S. Gibson, 'Lack of Extraterritorial Jurisdiction over Civilians: a New Look at Old Problems' (1995) 148 *Military Law Review* 114, 156 (where the author refers to the lack of a status of forces agreement between the United States and the Kingdom of Saudi Arabia, despite the presence for many years of United States forces in that State). For the position in respect of warships see *Cheung Chi Cheung* v. *R* [1939] AC 160.

[34] See, generally, D. Fleck (ed.), *The Handbook of the Law of Visiting Forces* (Oxford: Oxford University Press, 2002); J. Woodliffe, *The Peacetime Use of Foreign Military Installations under Modern International Law* (Dordrecht: Nijhoff, 1992). Depending upon the terms of the relevant status of forces agreement the visiting soldiers may not be within the criminal jurisdiction of the receiving State, although on its territory. For further examples of a separation between jurisdiction and territory see D. McGoldrick, 'The Extra-Territorial Application of the International Covenant on Civil and Political Rights' in Fons Coomans, Menno and Kamminga (eds.), *The Extra-Territorial Application of Human Rights Treaties* (Antwerp: Intersentia, 2004), p. 41.

[35] See, for example, the United States of America (Visiting Forces) Act 1942. For further examples see Fleck, *Handbook of the Law of Visiting Forces*. The related issue of whether this may involve the *receiving* State being in breach of its human rights obligations through the actions of the sending State on the territory of the former is discussed in chapter 3.

[36] An example occurred in the Gulf war 1990–1 where prisoners of war were transferred to Saudi Arabia.

[37] *Loizidou* v. *Turkey (Preliminary Objections)* (1995) 20 EHRR 99 at para. 62. This principle was also accepted by the Inter-American Commission on Human Rights in *Alejandre et al.* v. *Cuba*, Report No. 86/99, Case 11.589, 29 September 1999 at para. 24 and by the Human Rights Committee in General Comment No. 31, 'The Nature of the Legal Obligation

by the occupation of territory[38] and fighting on or over territory.[39] In the case of an occupation the occupying State not only has the physical power to enforce its wishes; it has also the legal responsibility to protect the inhabitants (who will be non-nationals)[40] of that territory. Where territory is being fought over some degree of 'control' of part of that territory will normally be exercised by the invading State. They may have men and equipment in an area supported by logistics through a supply line. This control over an area may be insufficient for the purposes of establishing that the invading forces have occupied the territory of another State (in whole or in part) or to show that their control enables the State to secure in 'such an area' the rights and freedoms set out in the Convention. In such a case it is difficult to accept that the invading armed forces have established the jurisdiction of their State over this area of foreign land.[41]

It will be shown that different human rights bodies may take different views over this preliminary issue of jurisdiction. A State may be found to have jurisdiction within the territory of another when it exercises effective control over the territory and its inhabitants so as to exercise public powers in that territory.[42] One way of exercising such control would be through the occupation of that territory but it is unlikely that a human rights

Imposed on States Parties to the Covenant', CCPR/C/21/Rev/Add.13, 26 May 2004, para. 10.

[38] Hague Regulations 1907, Art. 42; Geneva Conventions 1949, common Art. 2. The latter may come into play before the former.

[39] In *Bankovic* v. *Belgium et al.* (n. 13 above) the European Court of Human Rights decided, in effect, that control of the airspace over Belgrade in 1999 did not bring those who were killed or injured by a NATO airstrike on the RTS TV station within the jurisdiction of the NATO States.

[40] See the fourth Geneva Convention 1949, Art. 4. This obligation does not, however, depend upon occupation of territory. See, however, A. Orakhelashvili, 'Restrictive Interpretation of Human Rights Treaties in the Recent Jurisprudence of the European Court of Human Rights' (2003) 14 *European Journal of International Law* 529, 545.

[41] Compare, however, A. Cassese, *International Law* (Oxford: Oxford University Press, 2001), p. 363 who refers to 'any exercise of power, however limited in time (for instance, the use of belligerent force in an armed conflict)'; K.Watkin, 'Controlling the Use of Force: A Role for Human Rights Norms in Contemporary Armed Conflict' (2004) 98 *America Journal of International Law* 1, 33; the position of Moldova in *Ilascu* v. *Moldova and Russia*, Application No. 48787/99, Judgment, 8 July 2004, para. 335. Given that there will be an armed conflict in existence the Geneva Conventions 1949 and Additional Protocol I 1977 can apply.

[42] See *Bankovic* v. *Belgium et al.* (n. 13 above) at para. 71 and see para. 73. Compare the wider view in *Issa* v. *Turkey*, Application No. 31821/96, Judgment, 16 November 2004, paras. 68–71. This requirement of not only the physical ability to exercise public

body would confine the degree of control required over the territory to establish the jurisdiction of another State to cases of occupation.[43] An obvious case would be the detention of civilians who have taken a direct part in the armed conflict (which might or might not lead to the territory being occupied). The detaining State will have physical control over such individuals and will therefore have brought them within the jurisdiction of that State in the same way as if all the events had occurred in the territory of that State.[44] In the absence of a suitable derogation notice it will owe them the human rights obligations which it has accepted as applying to all individuals within its jurisdiction.[45]

powers but their actual use will be sufficient to establish the necessary degree of control by the non-territorial State over that territory and its inhabitants. Concentration on the control of territory has also been considered by the Human Rights Committee to be crucial. A State will not owe rights under the 1966 Covenant to individuals outside its control, CCPR/C/79/Add.88, para. 3; although compare CCPR/C/79/Add.14, para. 4 and see, generally, McGoldrick, 'The Extra-Territorial Application' in F. Coomans and M. Kamminga (eds.), *Extra-Territorial Application of Human Rights Treaties* (Antwerp: Intersentia, 2004), p. 41.

[43] See, for example, *Ilascu v. Moldova and Russia*, Application No. 48787/99, Judgment 8 July 2004, in respect of Russia, para. 394; CCPR/C/79/Add.99, para. 14; CCPR/C/79/Add.93, para. 10. For a similar view taken by the Inter-American Commission on Human Rights see *Alejandre et al. v. Cuba*, Report No. 86/99, Case 11.589, 29 September 1999 (direct victims shot down by Cuban military aircraft in international airspace). Compare the United Kingdom as a respondent State in *Bankovic v. Belgium et al.* (n. 13 above) which observed that 'military operations by the forces of one State in the territory of another State . . . do not alter the jurisdiction of the latter State over persons within its territory, so long as that State is able to exercise its authority over them. Only when the territory is occupied by the former State . . . is the population considered to be within the jurisdiction of the former State': *Observations of the United Kingdom Regarding the Admissibility of the Application*, 2 May 2001, para. 21; United Kingdom Ministry of Defence, *The Manual of the Law of Armed Conflict*, para. 11.19. See also C. Greenwood, contribution to 'Bombing for Peace: Collateral Damage and Human Rights' (2002) *Proceedings American Society of International Law* 95, 101; M. O'Boyle, 'A Comment on "Life After Bankovic"' in F. Coomans and M. Kamminga (eds.), *Extra-Territorial Application of Human Rights Treaties*, p. 125.

[44] For an example, otherwise than under occupation, of the exercise outside the territory of the State concerned of authority over individuals, thereby bringing them 'within the jurisdiction' of the 1950 Convention, see *X v. United Kingdom* (1977) 12 DR 73 at 74. See also *Coard et al. United States*, Report No. 109/99, Case 10.951, 29 September 1999, at para. 37.

[45] It will also owe them obligations under the fourth Geneva Convention 1949, from which it cannot derogate. The same principle would apply to the capture of prisoners of war, although human rights issues are unlikely to be of such prominence given the obligation in the third Geneva Convention 1949 to detain prisoners of war until the end of active hostilities. Compare, however, where judicial proceedings are taken against prisoners of war during their detention.

The control over civilians during the course of an international armed conflict can be compared with the acts of State organs operating outside their own territory to arrest and detain a national. It has been accepted by the European Court of Human Rights, the Human Rights Committee and the Inter-American Commission on Human Rights that such individuals come within the jurisdiction of their State of nationality acting extra-territorially.[46] The reason for State organs acting in this way will often (although not always) be because the captured person is a national. The crucial factor is, however, the control over the individual.[47] *Lopez Burgos* v. *Uruguay* also shows that it is no defence for a State responding to a communication brought before the Human Rights Committee to argue that its only obligation under the 1966 Covenant relates to acts committed within its territory.[48]

During the course of an international armed conflict a State may occupy territory and pass to the local administration for trial those whom it has detained. In whose jurisdiction will the individual fall if he is denied the right to a fair trial under a human rights instrument to which there has been no derogation? In Iraq in 2003 civilians arrested during the period of occupation by the United Kingdom armed forces were handed over to the Iraqi civilian authorities for trial.[49] It would appear that an accused person would come within the jurisdiction of both the United Kingdom and Iraq. Since the former has direct control over individuals in that part of Iraq occupied by the United Kingdom it can decide how trials will be conducted. It could withdraw the right of the civil courts to administer justice or amend their procedure at any time. Once an individual has been handed over to the Iraqi civil authorities he is within the jurisdiction (also) of an Iraqi State organ. That an individual may, simultaneously, be under the jurisdiction of more than one State is not unknown under international law. It frequently occurs where a status of forces agreement

---

[46] See respectively, *Ocalan* v. *Turkey* (judgment and merits) (2003) 37 EHRR 10 and by the Grand Chamber, 12 May 2005 at para. 91; *López Burgos* v. *Uruguay* (1985) 68 ILR 29, CCPR/C/13/D/52/1979 at paras. 12.1–12.3 and *Coard et al.* v. *United States*, Report No. 109/99, Case No. 10.951, 29 September 1999, at para. 37.

[47] See 68 ILR 29, CCPR/C/13/D/52/1979, para. 12.1. Compare the individual opinion of Mr Tomuschat, who drew attention to 'wilful and deliberate attacks against the freedom and personal integrity of *their citizens* (emphasis supplied) abroad'.

[48] *Ibid.*

[49] *The Times*, 9 May 2003. See also the handing over of individuals to the Grenadian and Caribbean Peacekeeping Force following the United States military operation in Granada in 1983, *Coard et al.* v. *United States*, Report No. 109/99, Case 10.951, 29 September 1999 at paras. 1, 19. A judicial review of the detention may have to be provided by the initial detaining State, see *Coard*, para. 58.

is in place, the effect of which is that both the sending and receiving States share jurisdiction over members of the visiting force subject to some mechanism, such as a system of primary rights, to try an individual. It is, therefore, not satisfying to deny that an individual comes within the jurisdiction of a particular State simply because he would thereby be under the jurisdiction of more than one State.[50]

This issue of the jurisdiction of a State may be contrasted with the responsibility of a State under international law. The liability of a State to make reparations for the acts of a State organ is well established.[51] In this context, the acts on foreign territory of the armed forces of a State will engage the responsibility of that State where they cause damage to any non-national.[52] The difference between the jurisdiction of a State and the responsibility in international law of that State may be illustrated in the following manner. The aircrew of a bomber aircraft discharging a missile onto a building such as the embassy of a neutral State during an international armed conflict will engage the responsibility of the State to which they belong towards the neutral State.[53] This will be so whether the State to which the aircraft belongs has, or has not, effective control over the airspace of the territory on which the target was located. Something more needs to be shown to lead to the conclusion that the actions of the bomber aircraft bring the victims of its actions within the jurisdiction of that foreign State for the purposes of a human rights treaty.

It is axiomatic that the jurisdiction of a State is essentially territorial, which includes its territorial sea and airspace. It may exercise extraterritorial jurisdiction in respect of war crimes and a number of other criminal offences.[54] In these cases, however, the State will exercise its

---

[50] Compare Greenwood, 'Bombing for Peace' at p. 102. Note, however, the position of Russia in *Ilascu* v. *Moldova and Russia*, Judgment, 8 July 2004, para. 384.

[51] See, generally, the Articles on the Responsibility of the State for Internationally Wrongful Acts, UNGA Resolution 56/83, UN Doc. A/Res/56/83 (2001) annex, Art. 4; Crawford, *International Law*.

[52] See Crawford, *International Law*.

[53] I am grateful to Professor Françoise Hampson for drawing my attention to this point. An example would be the bombing of the Chinese Embassy in Belgrade in 1999: compensation was paid to China by the United States. See Murphy, 'Contemporary Practice'. For a view as to the importance of distinguishing 'jurisdiction' from 'responsibility' see the dissenting opinion of Judges Golcuk and Pettiti in *Loizidou* v. *Turkey (Preliminary Objections)* 20 EHRR 99 and Judge Kovler (dissenting) in *Ilascu* v. *Moldova and Russia*, Judgment, 8 July 2004.

[54] It may exercise this jurisdiction over nationals and non-nationals. A treaty may give wide jurisdiction upon States. For wide claims to jurisdiction see N. Boister, 'The ICJ in the *Belgian Arrest Warrant* Case: Arresting the Development of International Criminal Law'

jurisdiction in the form of criminal proceedings on its *own* territory. There might be an issue of a conflict of jurisdiction between that State and the State on whose territory the alleged offence was committed, or, indeed, among other States who seek to exercise their own extra-territorial jurisdiction. These issues will be open for resolution by way of extradition proceedings, unless a status of forces agreement applies to all relevant States to resolve such conflicts of jurisdiction.

It is a considerable leap from this position to argue that the activities of the armed forces of a State acting on foreign territory can bring non-nationals within its jurisdiction there and then so as to extend to them the human rights obligations of that State. If occupation of territory has actually taken place there can be little objection to the occupier bringing within its jurisdiction those over whom it can now exercise State control (through the exercise of public powers) through its armed forces. By so doing the occupier has, effectively, denied the opportunity for the citizens of that territory to rely upon their own State to protect their human rights. A refusal to accept that the invading State exercises its jurisdiction over the occupied territory would mean that the inhabitants of the sovereign State would lose the opportunity they may have possessed before the occupation of making a complaint against their own State.[55] Where there is, on the other hand, no occupation of territory something more than presence of these armed forces is required. This extra requirement, for these purposes, will be the degree and extent of the control exercised by these armed forces over territory or individuals in this foreign territory.

It may well be that the degree of control the invading armed forces have over individuals is of much greater significance than its control over territory. Questions of fact are likely to loom large where the control is purportedly exercised by armed forces in foreign territory. There is, for example, a considerable difference between killing a civilian in detention

---

(2002) 7 *Journal of Conflict and Security Law* 293; D. Turns, 'Arrest Warrant of 11 April 2000 (Democratic Republic of Congo v Belgium) The International Court of Justice's Failure to Take a Stand on Universal Jurisdiction' (2002) 3 *Melbourne Journal of International Law* 383; *Certain Criminal Proceedings in France (Republic of Congo v. France)* 29 April 2003, ICJ.

[55] See, for an example, the decision by the European Court of Human Rights to hold Turkey liable for acts of its armed forces in Northern Cyprus, which it occupied, *Loizidou v. Turkey (Preliminary Objections)* (1995) 20 EHRR 99; *Cyprus v. Turkey* (2002) 35 EHRR 30. The effect of this proposition is that inhabitants of the invaded State may be able to take the benefit of a human rights treaty to which the invading State, but not the invaded State is a party. This is the effect of *R. (Al Skeini and others) v. Secretary of State for Defence* [2005] 2 WLR 1401. Compare the rights of those in occupied territory to communicate with the Protecting Power or the ICRC, fourth Convention 1949, Art. 30.

and his death by gunfire in the street. Concentration on this degree of control over individuals is likely to avoid the difficulties of a human rights body having to apply detailed rules of international humanitarian law such as those relating to targeting. It may well be that individual cases will have to be worked out over a period of time.[56]

Human rights treaties are, by their very nature, concerned with the rights of individuals vis-à-vis a State. These rights would, however, be sound in theory rather than in practical reality if the State under whose control they are was unable to carry out its obligations under the relevant human rights treaty towards such individuals. To be able to do this it must be in a position to control the activities of its armed forces in respect of individuals in this foreign territory and it must be able (whether it does so in practice or not) to grant rights to them enforceable against the State.

A practical difficulty in concluding that the State should make it possible for foreign nationals in the situation under discussion to enforce their human rights against that State relates to the issue of the exhaustion of domestic remedies.[57] This may well be impossible as a practical matter for a victim. The victim, not being a national of the State concerned, may not have available to him legal advice relating to the pursuit of a claim in that State, he may not be permitted to cross the border[58] to pursue any such claim, he may not have the funds to do so[59] or the State itself may deny such claims on the basis of sovereign immunity.[60]

An alternative for the State concerned is to establish its own courts (or a claims process)[61] in the territory of the State in which they are present, for the specific purpose of providing a forum for an alleged victim to pursue a domestic remedy. In order to ensure that any such courts

---

[56] See *Issa* v. *Turkey*, Application No. 31821/96, Judgment, 16 November 2004, paras. 77, 81.

[57] See the 1950 Convention, Art. 35; First Optional Protocol to the 1966 Covenant, Art. 2.

[58] This assumes that the two States are contiguous. Where they are not the problem is much greater.

[59] There may also be language difficulties. The European Court of Human Rights has taken a very pragmatic view of the requirement to exhaust domestic remedies: see *Ilascu et al.* v. *Moldova and the Russian Federation*, Application No. 48787/99, Admissibility decision of 4 July 2001, para. IV; *Issa* v. *Turkey*, Application No. 31821/96, Admissibility decision of 30 May 2000. The burden of proof is upon the respondent State, *ibid*. See also *Alejandre et al.* v. *Cuba*, Report No. 86/99, Case 11.589 at para. 27, 'the Cuban State has tacitly declined to make an objection asserting the non-exhaustion of domestic remedies'; Report No. 31/93, Case No. 10.573, 14 October 1993, para. 9.

[60] See, for example, Report No. 31/93, Case No. 10.573, 14 October 1993, para. 8.

[61] *Ibid*. Following the United States military action in Panama in 1989 claims were granted in respect of injury or damage caused otherwise than by military action.

are independent and impartial they would have to be entirely composed of civilian judges applying the law of their own State.[62] The practical problems of establishing such courts in territory which is not occupied would be too great for most, if not all, States. There would have to be some legal basis in the home State for the exercise of such jurisdiction outside its territory, the security of the members of the court and lawyers would need to be considered. Finally, it is unlikely that the full range of legal procedures would be available to a victim in his own territory, such as an appeal mechanism. Where the territory is brought under a state of occupation, as determined by international humanitarian law,[63] these difficulties may well be overcome, especially if it is foreseen that the occupation may last for some time.

Unlike the family of treaties known as international humanitarian law, some human rights treaties are regionally based. In this category would fall the American Declaration on the Rights and Duties of Man 1948, the European Convention on Human Rights 1950, the American Convention on Human Rights 1969 and the African Charter on Human and Peoples' Rights 1981. When addressing this regional issue there is less difficulty where the international armed conflict is contained within that region. Suppose, however, it spreads beyond the region. Is the effect of this that the treaty no longer applies? The position can be seen more clearly if examples are posed. French armed forces are engaged in an international armed conflict in Africa or the armed forces of the United Kingdom are similarly engaged in the Gulf region. In both these cases the armed conflict is taking place outside the territorial borders of any member of the Council of Europe. Can it be said that the European Convention on Human Rights has no reach into this conflict? The fact that neither of the 'receiving' States in the examples posed above (i.e. in Africa or in the Gulf region respectively) is a party to the 1950 Convention is, it is suggested, irrelevant. This Convention is not based upon reciprocity as between or among States but upon a treaty obligation owed to the victims within the jurisdiction of a State party's action and to all other States party to the Convention. Although the European Court of Human Rights has concluded that the

---

[62] For discussion of the issues involved with military courts see chapter 4. Compare the more limited obligations in the fourth Geneva Convention 1949, Art. 66, dealing with a trial for breach of the law promulgated by the occupying power, as to which see below.

[63] See the Hague Regulations 1907, Art. 42. It is not uncommon for a State to deny that it is occupying territory and thus deny the applicability of the fourth Geneva Convention 1949.

Convention was intended to cover the 'legal space (*espace juridique*) of the Contracting States ... and was not designed to be applied throughout the world, even in respect of the conduct of Contracting States'[64] it is difficult to follow this line of reasoning. No exception to it can be taken if the Court meant to say that the Convention does not apply where the victim is outside the jurisdiction of a relevant contracting State. He is not then 'within their jurisdiction' under Article 1 of the Convention and no question of its applicability to that particular victim can arise. If, however, as the Court itself recognised, such jurisdiction can be established where a contracting State has effective control over foreign territory there would appear to be no reason in logic why this must occur in the territory of a State party to the Convention.[65] The mere fact that the alleged breach of the Convention has occurred outside the territorial boundaries of the member States of the Council of Europe does not prevent any other State party referring any such breach of the Convention to the Court.[66] The obligations of the contracting State can then still be enforced by other contracting States.

If this argument is accepted no issue arises as to the imposition of the Convention obligations on non-contracting States involved in an international armed conflict with a contracting State.[67] There was, for instance, no suggestion that Kenya owed any obligations under the European Convention on Human Rights when it handed a Turkish national over to agents of the Turkish government in Kenya.[68]

It cannot be assumed that the limits of these human rights treaties, based as they are upon individuals being within the jurisdiction of the

---

[64] See *Bankovic* (n. 13 above), para. 80. Compare, however, the Court in *Issa* v. *Turkey*, Judgment, 16 November 2004, which, had the facts been otherwise, would have been likely to hold Turkey liable for the acts of its armed forces in northern Iraq. See also the French version of Art. 1 referred to by Burnton J in *R. (on the application of Carson)* v. *Secretary of State for Work and Pensions* 2002 WL 820019, at para. 21.

[65] *Issa* v. *Turkey*, Judgment, 16 November 2004, para. 71; *Ilascu* v. *Moldva and Russia*, Application No. 48787/99, Judgment, 8 July 2004, dissenting view of Judge Loucaides. Compare the view of the High Court in England and Wales in *R. (Al Skeini and others)* v. *Secretary of State for Defence* [2005] 2 WLR 1401. At para. 265 the Court recognised that 'it may well be that there is more than one school of thought at Strasbourg'. It was referring to *Issa* v. *Turkey*, para. 71.

[66] Art. 33.

[67] See *Soering* v. *United Kingdom* (1989) 11 EHRR 439 at para. 86.

[68] *Ocalan* v. *Turkey*, Judgment (merits and satisfaction) 12 March 2003, Grand Chamber, 12 May 2005, para. 91. There was no international armed conflict occurring in Kenya at the time. Nor was it shown that any breach of the applicant's rights occurred in Kenya.

relevant State, are identical for all such treaties.[69] The 1966 Covenant specifies that a State owes an obligation to those individuals who are 'within its territory and subject to its jurisdiction'.[70] If, however, jurisdiction can be exercised, albeit exceptionally, in the territory of another State as discussed above the term 'within its territory' adds little by way of limitation to the applicability of the Covenant in such circumstances.[71] In giving scope to a disjunctive interpretation of this phrase the Human Rights Committee has come to the view that Uruguay was responsible for the acts of its agents directed against a Uruguayan national abroad.[72] Moreover, in 2004 that Committee interpreted Article 2(1) as meaning that 'State parties are required . . . to respect and ensure the Covenant rights to all persons who may be within their territory and to all persons subject to their jurisdiction' and ensure the rights laid down in the Covenant to anyone within the power or effective control of that State Party, even if not situated within the territory of the State Party.'[73] Indeed, the Optional Protocol to the 1966 Covenant eschews any reference to acts of the State 'within its territory' and permits communications from individuals 'subject to its jurisdiction'.[74] The conclusion may therefore be drawn that the scope of human rights instruments can extend beyond the territory of the

---

[69] See *Bankovic* v. *Belgium et al.* (n. 13 above) para. 78. See also *Coard* v. *USA* (n. 23 above) (reach of United States extended to Granada) although this was not an issue raised by the parties (para. 27). In the *Nuclear Weapons* Advisory Opinion (n. 13 above) the ICJ did not discuss the issue of 'jurisdiction' before coming to the view that international humanitarian law was the *lex specialis* in relation to the 1966 Covenant, Art. 6.

[70] Article 2(1) (emphasis added). See also the Arab Charter on Human Rights 1994, Art. 2. For the traditional view as to the reach of the Covenant see Schindler, 'Human Rights' 939.

[71] Provost, *International Human Rights*, p. 19 concludes that the word 'jurisdiction' has 'been taken to refer to the State's power rather than the geographical or territorial limitation of this power'; McGoldrick, 'The Extra-Territorial Application'. The *travaux preparatoires* of the 1950 Convention show the change of wording in Art. 1 from 'all persons residing within their territories' to 'everyone within their jurisdiction' was recommended because it was considered that 'there were good grounds for extending the benefits of the Convention to all persons in the territories of the signatory States', quoted in *Bankovic* v. *Belgium et al.* (n. 13 above) at para. 19. This suggests that insertion of the term 'within the territory' into Art. 1 would have been tautologous given the presence there of the term, 'jurisdiction'.

[72] See *Lopez Burgos* v. *Uruguay* (n. 46 above). For the debate over the interpretation of Art. 2 of the 1966 Covenant see Provost, *International Human Rights* at pp. 22–3.

[73] 'The Nature of the General Legal Obligation Imposed on States Parties to the Covenant', CCPR/C/21/Rev.1/Add.13 (General Comments), 26 May 2004, para. 10; *Legal Consequences of the Construction of a Wall in the Occupied Territory*, ICJ Advisory Opinion, 9 July 2004, paras. 109–11.

[74] At the time of writing there are 104 States party to this Protocol. Neither the United States nor the United Kingdom is a party to it.

State party itself but not so far as to result in a 'cause and effect notion of jurisdiction'.[75] For many States more than one relevant[76] human rights treaty will be applicable simultaneously. Thus, a State party to the European Convention on Human Rights 1950 or to the American Convention on Human Rights 1969 may also be a party to the International Covenant on Civil and Political Rights 1966.

The role of national law

Members of the armed forces will invariably take some of the national law of the State with them when operating outside their territorial limits. However this is achieved,[77] it may encompass some of the human rights obligations of the individual State, if embedded, in an appropriate form, within national law. A soldier who infringed this (national) law may well find himself charged with an offence against his national criminal law or the disciplinary code of his armed forces. The relevant prohibited conduct might not be specified as a breach of human rights but as a breach of military standing orders or some other military offence. Moreover, the nature of military law in many States is wide, encompassing acts or omissions which would not necessarily be punishable under civilian disciplinary codes or under the criminal law. It is therefore distinctly possible that the military law obligations placed on soldiers during an international armed conflict in which they are operating outside the boundaries of their State is wider, in practical terms, than the obligations of a relevant human rights treaty. An example might suffice. The standing orders of a military unit require soldiers to treat all foreign civilians who they hold for questioning in a way that, in effect, does not subject them to torture, degrading or inhuman treatment. A soldier will be subjected to military discipline if he does not comply with this standing order. It may be that there is some

[75] See *Bankovic* v. *Belgium et al.* (n. 13 above), para. 75. This view is also supported by those authorities which suggest a wide interpretation of 'jurisdiction'. For the Inter-American Commission on Human Rights see *Coard* v. *USA* (n. 23 above); Report No. 31/93 Case No. 10.573, 14 October 1993.

[76] This refers to a human rights treaty whose rights are most relevant during an international armed conflict. This might include the Rights of the Child 1989 and its Optional Protocol 2000 relating to the recruitment and care of children in armed conflict.

[77] Through the direct applicability of treaties within the national law of a State or through the implementation of treaties by national legislation. J. Simpson, *Law Applicable to Canadian Forces in Somalia 1992/93* (Ottawa: Public Works and Government Services Canadian Publishing, 1997), chapter 1, did not seek to argue that the Canadian Charter of Rights and Freedoms (Part I, Constitution Act 1982) applied to Canadian forces in Somalia so as to protect those against whom those forces came into contact.

argument that the civilians do not come within the jurisdiction of the State for the purposes of Article 1 of the 1950 Convention. The 'victim' of the soldier's actions may have no redress under the 1950 Convention[78] but the soldier remains bound by his military law and it is this body of law which can enforce the treatment ordered for him by the soldier's military superiors.

The national law will be relevant also as to whether the victim is able to secure a remedy under it and whether he has exhausted such a remedy. In addition, individual States may assume jurisdiction, whether of a civil or criminal nature, over the acts of non-nationals committed abroad.[79]

Applying human rights treaties during an international armed conflict

The right to life

It will be assumed that the victim is within the jurisdiction of the State (as discussed above) and that the relevant human rights treaty (or treaties) is (or are) applicable.[80] The 1950 Convention and the 1966 Covenant approach the issue in quite different ways. The former permits a person to be deprived of his life if the force used is no more than 'absolutely necessary (a) in defence of any person from unlawful violence; (b) in order to effect a lawful arrest or to prevent the escape of a person lawfully detained; (c) in action lawfully taken for the purpose of quelling a riot or insurrection'.[81] The latter provides that 'no one shall be arbitrarily deprived of his life'.[82] Where, under the 1950 Convention, a State derogates from the right to life it is permitted to deprive a person of his life if this results from 'lawful acts of war'.[83] International humanitarian law becomes the *lex specialis*, as it will be in respect of the 1966 Covenant which forbids the deprivation of life 'arbitrarily'.[84] The only difference,

---

[78] For an example see R. *(Al Skeini and others)* v. *Secretary of State for Defence* [2005] 2 WLR 1401 relating to the death of a civilian allegedly killed by British armed forces in Iraq.

[79] For an excellent account of the acceptance of jurisdiction in these circumstances, see A. Cassese, *International Law* (2nd edn, Oxford: Oxford University Press, 2005) p. 435.

[80] It will also be assumed that a State party only to the 1966 Covenant is also a party to the Optional Protocol 1966.

[81] Art. 2(2).

[82] Art. 4. This is similar to the American Convention on Human Rights 1969, Art. 4 and the African Charter on Human and Peoples' Rights 1981, Art. 4.

[83] Article 15(2).

[84] For the 1966 Covenant see the *Legality of the Threat or Use of Nuclear Weapons*, Advisory Opinion, 1996 ICJ Reports 226, para. 25.

in this connection, between these two approaches to the right to life is that under the 1950 Convention a State must actually issue a derogation notice. If it fails to do so its scope for depriving a person of his life will be that set out in Article 2(2).[85] This will be adequate to cover the situation during an international armed conflict where a State holds individuals in some form of detention (either as protected civilians or as prisoners of war) or where it seeks to detain such individuals[86] but not where it is actually fighting against lawful combatants in territory it occupies.[87] In this latter situation the *lex specialis* (international humanitarian law) *permits* a lawful combatant to kill another lawful combatant[88] providing the means of doing so are not, themselves, prohibited under that law.[89] There is clearly no requirement that under international humanitarian law the force used should be 'absolutely necessary', let alone be for one of the purposes set out in Article 2(2). To apply these terms consistently with the obligations and this 'right' to attack individuals in international humanitarian law is quite unrealistic. To argue, for instance, that an attack by a territorial State's armed forces on an enemy military command and control centre (which, in the circumstances, is without doubt a military objective) is 'no more than absolutely necessary . . . in defence of a person from unlawful violence' would be to impose strains both on language[90] and on the acceptability to members of armed forces of legal norms applying during an international armed conflict. If the conclusion from this

---

[85] It may fail to do for a number of reasons. It may consider that the 1950 Convention is not applicable to the conflict at all (as it is taking place outside the territorial limits of any Council of Europe State) or it may omit to make such a derogation, or decide not to do so for political reasons.

[86] It may use weapons against escaping prisoners of war in accordance with Art. 42 of the third Geneva Convention 1949. It must avoid any 'physical suffering' of protected civilians under the fourth Geneva Convention 1949, Art. 32. The death of a prisoner of war or a protected civilian internee must be investigated, Third Convention, Art. 121, Fourth Convention, Art. 131.

[87] Or in territory over which it has sufficient control to justify a finding that the State is exercising its jurisdiction within foreign territory. For discussion of the 'jurisdiction' issue see above.

[88] In addition a lawful combatant may attack a civilian who is taking a direct part in hostilities, Additional Protocol I 1977, Art. 51(3).

[89] Examples would include the killing of a combatant through the use of poison gas or a dumdum bullet, the 1925 Geneva Gas Protocol; the 1899 Hague Declaration 3 Concerning Expanding Bullets, the Rome Statute 1998, Art. 8(2)(b)(xviii), (xix).

[90] Violence by combatants against other combatants is not 'unlawful'. If the attacked force has been in the practice of using 'unlawful' violence against civilians a strong causative link would have to be shown between the attack on the command and control centre and the defence of such civilians from this unlawful violence.

example is that, in the absence of a suitable notice of derogation, such an attack would infringe the right to life of those killed during it and thus lead to a right on the part of relatives to seek a remedy the obligations of the State concerned are at variance with those it has accepted under international humanitarian law. In terms, therefore, of its human rights obligations a State will be considerably more restricted in its actions where it has not issued a notice of derogation than where it has done so.

It will be assumed for the remainder of this discussion that an appropriate notice of derogation has been made and the position under the 1950 Convention and the 1966 Covenant is the same, namely, that it will be governed by international humanitarian law and, in particular, by determining whether the death results from 'lawful acts of war'.[91]

Depriving a person, during an international armed conflict, of his life may occur otherwise than through the direct attack by one or more[92] members of the armed forces on a combatant or on a military objective. Civilians may be killed as a result of lawful acts of war (or non-arbitrary killing) where their deaths are not 'expected' to be 'excessive in relation to the concrete and direct military advantage anticipated'.[93] Such deaths may occur as a direct result of the attack itself or as an indirect consequence of it. Thus the attack on a conventional power station, assuming it to be a military objective, might lead to the breakdown of sewage pumping facilities with consequent loss of life of weak and vulnerable civilians through waterborne diseases.[94] The loss of life as a direct or an indirect consequence of an attack on a military objective will need to be assessed in line with the limitations imposed by Article 51(5)(b) of Additional Protocol I 1977[95] to determine whether the attack itself

---

[91] It will be assumed also that this term is co-terminous with non-arbitrary deprivation of life.

[92] Unlike in a prosecution for genocide, crime against humanity or a war crime it is the State which will be responsible for human rights breaches. It will, therefore, be of less significance that the individual who bore the greatest responsibility for the loss of life was the commander (who may be many miles distant from the acts carried out) rather than his subordinates.

[93] Additional Protocol I 1977, Art. 51(5)(b). See, generally, A. P. V. Rogers, *Law on the Battlefield* (2nd edn, Manchester: Manchester University Press, 2004).

[94] See, generally, R. Normand and C. Jochnick, 'The Legitimation of Violence: A Critical Analysis of the Gulf War' (1994) 35 *Harvard International Law Journal* 387, 403.

[95] This is generally understood to reflect customary international law, see C. Greenwood, 'Customary Law Status of the 1977 Additional Protocols' in A. Delissen and G. Tanya (eds.), *Humanitarian Law of Armed Conflict: Challenges Ahead* (Dordrecht: Nijhoff, 1991), pp. 93, 108–9; J.-M. Henckaerts and L. Doswald-Beck (eds.), *Customary International Humanitarian Law* (3 vols., Cambridge: Cambridge University Press, 2005).

was a 'lawful act of war'. If the loss of civilian life was expected to be excessive in relation to the concrete and direct military advantage anticipated this will also indicate an infringement of the right to life of such[96] individuals.

Could the soldier, himself, be a victim of a breach of his right to life by his own State?[97] It has been shown in chapter 1 that a soldier retains his human rights when he becomes a member of the armed forces, although such rights must be considered in a military context. The right to life is one of these rights. During peacetime it can hardly be doubted that the State to which he belongs owes him this right. In the course of an international armed conflict he may lawfully be deprived of this right to life as a result of lawful acts of war carried out by enemy nationals. He may also be ordered to carry out military operations by his superior officers which may involve a risk to his own life to a greater or lesser extent. Suppose he is ordered to attack an enemy fortification which is adjudged by himself and his superiors to involve a very high degree of probability of his being killed during the course of it. He is, of course, obliged to obey lawful orders of his superiors and will be subject to disciplinary punishment if he does not do so.[98] He is thus subject to punishment if he does not act at great risk to his life.[99] The concept of 'lawful acts of war' is concerned with the obligations a State owes to those (normally non-nationals) against whom it is engaged in an international armed conflict and not its own soldiers.[100]

---

[96] A practical issue arises here. If there has been a breach of Art. 51(5)(b) the loss of *some* lives will be lawful, the loss of others unlawful due to it being expected that such losses would occur. Which lives come within the lawful and which within the unlawful categories will pose a difficult decision for any human rights body to make.

[97] I am grateful to Col Charles Garraway, CBE (formerly, United Kingdom Army Legal Services) for drawing this point to my attention. The views expressed are those of the author.

[98] For the purposes of this discussion, it is assumed that the soldier has been ordered and has not 'volunteered' to take part in the military operation. The suggestion by M. Osiel, *Obeying Orders* (New Brunswick: Transaction Publishers, 1999), at p. 216 that 'inferiors had to be reasoned with and persuaded concerning the merits of a risky course of action' might be applicable in some, but not all, circumstances.

[99] The manner in which this military obligation to obey military orders is manifested will vary among the armed forces of different States, but the underlying obligation is common in most, if not all, armed forces. The death penalty for an offence (however described) involving military disobedience may also be available to the military authorities. For further discussion of the death penalty see below.

[100] See, however, the rule against making use of flags, military emblems, insignia or uniforms of 'adverse Parties while engaging in attacks . . .': Additional Protocol I 1977, Art. 39(2). The purpose of this rule, which appears designed to protect a State's own soldiers, is discussed by P. Rowe in 'The Use of Special Forces and the Laws of War: Wearing the

The right to life which the State owes its own soldiers continues from its peacetime position and although construed in the new military context of wartime must therefore be taken into account unaffected by any derogation.

Depending upon the degree of risk of loss of life and the nature of the compulsion (through the medium of military punishment for refusing to obey orders) it is possible to foresee a situation where a soldier may arbitrarily be deprived of his life.[101] An extreme example may illustrate the point. A commander has taken very little care over a plan to attack an enemy military installation with large numbers of his own soldiers. He expects that very many of them will be killed in the attack. If, however, any reasonable commander had thought through the planned operation he would have concluded that the loss of life of his own soldiers would clearly be excessive compared with the concrete and direct military advantage to be gained from the attack.[102] It might not be difficult to conclude here that some[103] of his men have been deprived of their lives arbitrarily. If this is the case it may well be that a soldier concerned would be able to challenge the order to attack on the ground that it infringed his right to life.[104] In modern conditions of warfare during an international armed conflict this may be an unlikely example but the real issue is one of degree. At what stage does an order by a commander risk breach of the right to

Uniform of the Enemy or Civilian Clothing and of Spying and Assassination' (1994) 33 *Revue de Droit Militaire et de Droit de la Guerre* 209, 213–15.

[101] Considered under Art. 6 of the 1966 Covenant. Article 2 of the 1950 Convention may be thought to produce a different result since, apart from Art. 2(2) and the execution of a duly passed death sentence (neither of which apply in the circumstances under discussion), the Article is concerned with *intentional* killing. This is not, however, the case since the Article has been considered wide enough to cover those who ought to have guarded against the real risk of an intentional killing by others, or those who kill unintentionally: see, respectively, *Osman* v. *United Kingdom* (2000) 29 EHRR 245; *Stewart* v. *United Kingdom* (1984) 39 DR 162, Commission.

[102] The analogy is drawn with Additional Protocol I 1977, Art. 51(5)(b). An example might be the use of ground forces without close air support in the case of a defended assault on land positions. For an excellent account of a commander's responsibilities during an international armed conflict see Rogers, *Law on the Battlefield*, chapter 7.

[103] See the practical point made in n. 96 above.

[104] Whether there was a legal challenge that could be made would depend upon the military law system of the State concerned. It is also possible to foresee that the positing of a challenge to the legality of the order to attack on the ground suggested in the text is not a practical proposition in the circumstances of a particular case.

life of a subordinate soldier?[105] If such an order has this effect what can the soldier lawfully do to protect his right to life?[106]

There are dangers involved in concentrating upon the right to life of the soldier of one's own armed forces. In protecting his life the lives of enemy civilians may disproportionately be put at risk. Greater use may be made of air attacks with the attendant risk of life to civilians rather than that of ground troops.[107]

Closely linked to the protection of the life of a State's own soldiers is the issue of the protection of their lives from the military acts of an ally. Allied armed forces may mistake friendly forces as being those of the enemy and attack them. These, so-called 'friendly fire' incidents have occurred to a greater or lesser extent in all modern armed conflicts. The issue here is whether the State, to which the soldiers belong, is under an obligation to protect their right to life from the activities of an allied State. The State concerned clearly has no jurisdiction over the armed forces of an allied State but it would be expected to 'take measures within the scope of [its] powers which, judged reasonably, might have been expected to avoid that risk'.[108] The provision of electronic identifiers on tanks and other mobile military equipment might solve such a problem where such equipment is prone to attack from high altitude allied aircraft.[109]

A variation on these 'friendly fire' incidents is where soldiers kill civilians, who are nationals of an allied State, on the territory of that State. The most likely instance of this is where one State calls upon another to

[105] *Quaere* whether it would apply to an order to the aircrew of military aircraft to attack targets from low altitude where the risk of being shot down was very high, or an order to 'fight to the last man' or an order to stay with a stricken warship while enemy forces are attempting to sink it. For an allegation that reserve soldiers were not properly trained in firearms handling before deployment to the Iraq war in 2003 with the consequence that one soldier was shot by another, see *The Times*, 22 October 2004.

[106] It is, perhaps, unusual to think of the soldier having to take a legal avenue to protect his right to life in the absence of a lawfully imposed death sentence being imposed upon him.

[107] See, generally, A. P. V. Rogers, 'Zero Casualty Warfare' (2000) 82 *International Review of the Red Cross* 165.

[108] *Osman* v. *United Kingdom* (n. 101 above), para. 116 (a decision under the 1950 Convention) which requires the risk to be known at the time to have been 'real and immediate' to the lives of individuals.

[109] Placing aircrew on trial by court-martial by their own State for manslaughter and dereliction of duty is a measure of how seriously a State takes its obligations to avoid 'friendly fire'. For the court-martial of two United States pilots for a 'friendly fire' incident in Afghanistan in 2002, see *The Times*, 17 January 2003.

assist it by way of self-defence against attack from another State.[110] The position is unlikely to be different from that posited above. The fact that in neither case would the individuals be protected persons under the Geneva Conventions 1949 is not relevant.[111]

A State may impose the death penalty for offences committed during an international armed conflict. Its national law may provide for this as a penalty for a wide range of offences.[112] Those States which have abolished the death penalty may revive it in these circumstances, providing this is included within their legislation and judicial framework.[113] A State may therefore be in a position to impose this penalty lawfully upon its own soldiers or its own civilians; prisoners of war (or other members of the armed forces of an enemy State) and civilians protected under the fourth Geneva Convention 1949 for the commission of offences before or after capture.

In so far as its own soldiers are concerned the State may perceive the need to protect military discipline and thus feel it necessary to make the death penalty available to its military courts for a wider or a lesser range of military offences. The history, in Europe at least, has been to reduce and even to eliminate this penalty for military offences, even for those committed during an international armed conflict.[114] It is likely that, in most States, the range of offences committed during an international armed conflict and for which civilians may be sentenced to death will be smaller than for members of the armed forces. In both cases such a penalty may be revived (if it has previously been abolished) during wartime.[115]

---

[110] Modern examples would include the presence of United States forces in South Vietnam during the Vietnam war and coalition forces in Kuwait following the invasion of that country by Iraq in 1990. For an excellent account of the trial of United States servicemen for crimes committed against South Vietnamese civilians see G. Solis, *Son Thang: An American War Crime* (Annapolis: Naval Institute Press, 1997).

[111] In relation to civilians see Art. 4(2) of the Fourth Convention. No question of protected person status arises in respect of allied armed forces in the circumstances discussed, although see the discussion of 'nationality' by the International Criminal Tribunal for the Former Yugoslavia in n. 177 below.

[112] See Art. 6 of the 1966 Covenant; Art. 2 of the 1950 Convention; Art. 4 of the American Convention on Human Rights 1969.

[113] See Sixth Protocol (1983) to the 1950 Convention, Art. 2; Protocol to the American Convention on Human Rights to Abolish the Death Penalty (1990), Art. 2. These Articles are not identical.

[114] See discussion in chapter 3.

[115] There may, however, be specific restrictions on the use of the death penalty: see Arts. 76(3), 77(5) of Additional Protocol I 1977; Human Rights Committee General Comment No. 6 CCPR/C/21/Rev.1/Add.11, 31 August 2001, para. 15. See, generally, W. Schabas, *The Abolition of the Death Penalty in International Law* (3rd edn, Cambridge: Cambridge University Press, 2002) chapter 5.

Prisoners of war (and members of enemy armed forces not entitled to this status), along with protected civilians, may also be sentenced to death. By the nature of their status they will be in the hands of a State of which they are not nationals. International humanitarian law will provide the main guidelines as to when this punishment may be imposed, although national law may also be necessary to implement this international law if the nature of the State's legal system requires it. International humanitarian law does not prohibit the imposition of the death penalty by the detaining State. A prisoner of war may lawfully be sentenced to death by the courts of the detaining power for acts committed prior to, or after, capture, subject to a number of safeguards.[116] Since a prisoner of war may be subjected to the same penalties as a member of the armed forces of the detaining power[117] he is at risk of receiving the death penalty only if he is detained by a State with such a legal structure. The third Geneva Convention 1949 leaves it to the State concerned to determine which offences are punishable by the death penalty. There is no requirement in the Convention to confine such offences to those which are the most serious. In theory, therefore, a State could impose the death penalty on a prisoner of war (and comply with the Convention) for insulting a superior officer, or the symbols, of the armed forces, providing a soldier of the detaining power is also subject to the death penalty for such an offence.[118] It is not difficult to speculate on a range of other offences, from those which might be considered to be minor to those considered serious by any State, in order to see the limited protection which the Convention gives a prisoner of war in this respect.

Whether a prisoner of war is offered more protection from the death penalty from human rights instruments to which the detaining State is a party will depend on which instrument is applicable, assuming that this penalty has been retained or revived by the State concerned. Under the 1966 Covenant the death penalty may be imposed only for the 'most

---

[116] The act concerned must not merely be a breach of discipline committed after capture, third Geneva Convention 1949, Art. 89. Further safeguards are contained in Chapter III of that Convention. The right of fair trial is discussed below.

[117] Third Geneva Convention 1949, Arts. 87, 100 (and see, in particular, para. 3).

[118] The detaining State would have to show that it was appropriate to classify such an offence as a judicial, rather than a disciplinary, offence: see third Geneva Convention 1949, Art. 83. This should be read in the light of Art. 100(3): see J. Pictet (ed.), *Commentary on Geneva Convention* III *Relative to the Treatment of Prisoners of War* (Geneva: International Committee of the Red Cross, 1960), p. 411 (referring to the 'honourable motives' of those who have become prisoners of war).

serious crimes'[119] and, under the Optional Protocol Aiming at the Abolition of the Death Penalty 1989, a State may enter a reservation providing for the application of the death penalty 'in time of war . . . for a most serious crime of a military nature committed during wartime'.[120] The 1950 Convention makes no reference to the seriousness of the crime for which the death penalty may be imposed for acts committed 'in time of war' nor to the minimum age or whether the person is pregnant.[121] The American Convention of 1969 provides that the penalty should not be imposed for 'political offenses or related common crimes'.[122] In its Protocol to Abolish the Death Penalty 1990 it permits States party to 'reserve the right to apply the death penalty in wartime . . . for extremely serious crimes of a military nature'.[123] There is no reference to the death penalty in the African Charter on Human and Peoples' Rights 1981.

Where a State is a party to one (or both) the Protocols of 1990 it must actually make a reservation at the time of ratification or accession permitting it to impose the death sentence as limited by the respective Protocol. If it does not do so it cannot insert such a power into its national law at a later date, such as when it is engaged in an international armed conflict. A State may see this as a serious limitation on its legislative powers during a particular armed conflict, especially where prisoners of war have killed guards or innocent civilians with whom they have come into contact. Unlike in the domestic arena where a person may be sentenced to life imprisonment for murder (and may spend the rest of his life in imprisonment), such a punishment might be seen as unrealistic if imposed upon a prisoner of war. Although it will not be a breach of the third Geneva Convention 1949 to retain a prisoner of war in imprisonment after the end of the conflict[124] there may be political pressures[125] to release all

---

[119] Article 6(2). It may not be carried out on prisoners of war under the age of eighteen or on pregnant women. It is possible that a prisoner of war could fit into either or both categories.

[120] Article 2. At the time of writing there are fifty-one States party to this Protocol. Only Azerbaijan and Greece currently maintain such a reservation (although France and other States have entered an objection to the purported reservation entered by Azerbaijan).

[121] In respect of those States party to the Sixth Protocol 1983, see Art. 2. See, however, Protocol 13 to the 1950 Convention Concerning the Abolition of the Death Penalty in All Circumstances 2002.

[122] Article 4(4).

[123] Article 2(1). There are currently eight States party to this Protocol.

[124] Article 119.

[125] By way of a peace treaty or settlement of the conflict by a neutral body, such as the United Nations. The practical realities of such a treaty or settlement may outweigh the legal right of a State to retain a prisoner of war.

prisoners of war or at least to repatriate them on condition that they serve the remainder of their sentences in their home State.[126] Since there is no express power to denounce or withdraw from either of these Protocols a State may not do so.[127]

The effect of this is that a State party to one of the Protocols discussed above could not impose the death penalty on a prisoner of war (even though the third[128] Geneva Convention 1949 did not prohibit it) unless it had entered a reservation at the time of ratification or accession and the offence was a 'most serious crime of a military nature' or an 'extremely serious crime of a military nature'.[129] Where a State is not a party to either of these Protocols it will be the relevant Geneva Convention 1949 which will provide the limitations on the imposition of the death penalty. Depending upon the position of any derogation notices a relevant human rights instrument will apply to the trial processes leading to its imposition and to the death penalty itself.

The activities of a particular type of individual have traditionally attracted the death penalty on capture.[130] This has been the expected fate of the spy, whether he has been a member of the armed forces or a civilian. Where a member of the armed forces engaged in espionage falls into the power of the enemy he will not be entitled to the protection of the third Geneva Conventions 1949, as discussed above.[131] The reason for this is that he is entitled to no more than a trial before punishment

---

[126] See, for example, the Council of Europe Convention for the Transfer of Sentences Prisoners 1983 and its Additional Protocol of 1997.

[127] See Vienna Convention on the Law of Treaties 1969, Art. 56. It is unlikely that such a right was intended by the parties to each Protocol or that all States party to it would consent to a State withdrawing (Art. 54).

[128] See also the fourth Convention 1949 relating to civilians, Art. 68 (referring to serious offences).

[129] The State concerned must also have notified the appropriate office of the relevant legislation: see Second Optional Protocol to the 1966 Covenant, Art. 2(2); Protocol to the American Convention on Human Rights to Abolish the Death Penalty 1990, Art. 2(2). Although these Articles impose the obligation to notify 'national legislation applicable during wartime' at the time of ratification or accession it must be accepted that such legislation is subject to change from time to time and that a State must notify the most up-to-date national law applicable. It may therefore increase the range of offences for which it has imposed the death penalty as a punishment provided it makes the appropriate notification (and does not increase the number or range of such offences after it has detained prisoners of war, third Geneva Convention 1949, Art. 100(2)). Other States are then given an opportunity to express a view as to whether a particular offence is 'extremely serious' or a 'most serious crime' of a 'military nature'.

[130] See the Lieber Code 1863, Art. 88.

[131] Additional Protocol I 1977, Art. 46(1). The mercenary attracts the same legal consequence, see *ibid.*, Art. 47(1), as does a member of the armed forces who wears civilian clothes during

is imposed on him,[132] where he may have the opportunity to deny that he was engaged in espionage. The detaining State will only be entitled to impose the death penalty upon a convicted spy if it meets the requirements set out above, both in relation to the trial and to the imposition of the death penalty, in the human rights instruments to which it is a party.[133]

The availability of the death penalty in one State which may be imposed upon a prisoner of war may lead to difficulties in the transfer of a prisoner of war from one State to another. This is permitted by the third Geneva Convention 1949[134] and was a feature of the Gulf war in 1991, where the armed forces of particular States took responsibility for the detention of prisoners of war, who had surrendered to the armed forces of other States. A State which has abolished the death penalty might be unwilling to transfer prisoners of war, which it holds, to another State where they may be subjected to the death penalty for 'inappropriate' offences. The obligation of the transferring State under the third Geneva Convention 1949 continues after the transfer in so far as it becomes aware of a failure on the part of the transferee State 'to carry out any of the provisions of the Convention in any important respect'.[135] It has been commented above that the third Geneva Convention does not impose restrictions on the imposition of the death penalty against prisoners of war, providing that such a penalty is available for the members of the armed forces of the detaining State. Were it to be the case that the potential transferee State contains in its law a large number of offences which may be committed by members of its armed forces and which attract the death penalty there

---

an attack without properly distinguishing himself, *ibid.*, Art. 44(4), although he is entitled to some protection under that Protocol. As to the position prior to Additional Protocol I 1977, see *Ex parte Richard Quirin*, 317 US 1 (1942); *Mohamed Ali* v. *Public Prosecutor* [1968] 1 All ER 488. For the position of civilians see the fourth Geneva Convention 1949, Arts. 5 and 68(2); Pictet, *Commentary*, p. 57. The civilian spy is in a better position than his counterpart in the armed forces since there are some limitations imposed upon the detaining State under the fourth Geneva Convention 1949.

[132] Regulations Annexed to the Hague Convention IV Respecting the Laws and Customs of War on Land 1907, Art. 30. See *Mohamed Ali* v. *Public Prosecutor* [1968] 3 All ER 488, at 493–4, Viscount Dilhorne. His trial would be required to comply with the State's human rights obligations (subject to a derogation notice) should it wish to comply with its international obligations.

[133] *Quaere* whether the carrying out of the death penalty against a convicted spy is a 'lawful act of war' within the meaning of the derogation provisions of the 1950 Convention, Art. 15. Compare the 1966 Covenant, Art. 4 (as interpreted by the *Legality of the Threat or Use of Nuclear Weapons* case (n. 13 above).

[134] Article 12.   [135] *Ibid.*

would be no breach of the third Geneva Convention merely through the courts of the transferee State sentencing prisoners of war to death. If the potential transferor State considered that the transferred prisoners of war would suffer torture, inhuman or degrading treatment[136] through being kept on 'death row' after sentence of death[137] it would be likely to refuse to transfer them since the transferee State is required to treat all prisoners of war humanely.[138]

In similar vein a State repatriating prisoners of war at the close of active hostilities may need to consider the reception to be accorded to them by their home State. It is accepted that, despite the mandatory language of Article 118 of the third Geneva Convention 1949, a State is under no legal obligation forcibly to repatriate prisoners of war.[139] The State may have an independent obligation to consider whether there is a real risk of a prisoner of war being killed upon his repatriation. This can pose serious difficulties for a State following the conclusion of hostilities.

The nature of the risk may run through a number of possibilities. Thus, the repatriated prisoner may be killed merely because he is of a particular ethnic group; he may be placed in confinement where death is likely to result; or he may be put on trial for a capital offence of 'desertion' from his own armed forces. The most that can be said is that the detaining State must actively consider this issue prior to repatriation and take account of its human rights obligations.[140]

States are expected to establish independent investigations where it is alleged that one or more individuals have been deprived of their right to life as a result of the actions of the armed forces (or other State agents).[141]

---

[136] See *Soering* v. *United Kingdom* (1989) 11 EHRR 439, at para. 111.

[137] The third Geneva Convention 1949, Art. 101 requires a six-month postponement of the execution of a death sentence passed on a prisoner of war to enable the protecting power to make any representations it may wish to the detaining State.

[138] *Ibid.*, Art. 13. See also the 1966 Covenant, Art. 7; the 1950 Convention, Art. 3; the American Convention on Human Rights, Art. 5; the African Charter on Human and Peoples' Rights 1981, Art. 5.

[139] See the declaration to Additional Protocol I 1977, made by the Republic of South Korea (declaration 2) which may not have been strictly necessary and see T. Meron, 'The Humanization of Humanitarian Law' (2000) 94 *American Journal of International Law* 239, 253.

[140] It will also need to consider these issues if a third State requests the extradition of a prisoner of war in order to place him on trial for acts committed prior to capture, see the third Geneva Convention 1949, Art. 119. A third State may claim jurisdiction if the prisoner of war was alleged to have committed an offence under the Rome Statute 1998, Arts. 6–8 on its territory.

[141] See *Aksoy* v. *Turkey* (1997) 23 EHRR 553, para. 98; *Cyprus* v. *Turkey* (2002) 35, EHRR 35, at para. 131; *Ozkan* v. *Turkey* Application No. 21689/93, Judgment, 6 April 2004, para. 319; *Abella* v. *Argentina* Report No. 55/97, Case 11.137, 18 November 1997, at para. 412.

Whilst this has become well established under various human rights instruments following internal disturbances it would be more difficult to apply it in practice where the deaths occurred during an international armed conflict. It has been shown above that this issue may arise where a State has not made a derogation in respect of Article 2 of the 1950 Convention or it is alleged to have killed individuals whom it has detained. It is assumed that the individuals concerned were within the jurisdiction of the Convention State immediately prior to their deaths.

A key feature of an independent investigation is that it is not carried out by those alleged to have taken part in the killings. It is not necessary that the police or some body distinct from the armed forces carry out the investigation and it would therefore appear that a branch of the armed forces separate from the chain of command[142] of those alleged to have taken part in the events under investigation would suffice.[143] This may be a practical solution where the events have taken place outside the territory of the State. Whoever carries out the investigation may well be faced with difficulties of obtaining evidence from those involved in the incidents, not only because such procedures are unlikely to have been established for deaths of non-nationals occurring during an international armed conflict but also because of the possible difficulty of securing the presence of individuals involved.[144] In addition, an investigation may be carried out by the armed forces themselves or by the civilian police for the purposes of deciding whether to prosecute any individuals for a crime of war.[145]

---

[142] The acceptance by human rights bodies of military courts to try members of the armed forces is based upon the principle that the minimum requirement for an independent body in such circumstances is independence from the chain of command, see chapter 3; *McKerr* v. *United Kingdom* (2002) 34 EHRR 20, para. 112 (drawing attention to 'a lack of hierarchical or institutional connection').

[143] This may be a more effective body to carry out such an investigation since the armed forces of a State may be more willing to co-operate with another branch of those forces than with a civilian organisation. There is a further advantage, namely, that the investigators, depending upon their status within the armed forces, may be able to issue military orders to those whom they wish to co-operate with them. For a disadvantage see *Abella* v. *Argentina* Report No. 55/97, Case 11.137, 18 November 1997, para. 420.

[144] They may be involved in actual military operations, have been killed or otherwise be unavailable to the investigators. In addition, an individual may wish to raise the issue of privilege against self-incrimination (or its equivalent in the law of the State concerned).

[145] This may be in relation to one of the offences set out in Arts. 6–8 of the Rome Statute 1998, depending upon the form of implementation of that Statute within the law of the State, or for any offence over which the State concerned has national jurisdiction.

The requirement to conduct such an investigation where there is a possibility that an individual has been deprived of life during an international armed conflict in breach of a human rights instrument is likely to be seen by the armed forces, except in the most obvious cases where a criminal investigation is mounted, to be an unwelcome bureaucratic procedure. The limitations of the jurisdictional reaches of the various instruments will, however, narrow the field for investigations to situations similar to those existing during a non-international armed conflict or during tensions and disturbances falling short of this. Thus, the killing of a prisoner of war or a suspected combatant in occupied territory is not dissimilar in kind from the killing of civilians detained by the armed forces or the killing of suspected terrorists during a period of civil disorder. In practice, a State which takes its international obligations seriously and which is a party to the Rome Statute 1998 will be likely to mount a criminal investigation where the circumstances of a killing suggest that a war crime has been committed.[146] Such an investigation may, in practice, also suffice for human rights[147] purposes, given that the issue is likely to be similar, namely was the killing carried out in accordance with international humanitarian law?

Torture, degrading or inhuman treatment

In the various human rights instruments a State may not derogate from its obligations to protect those within its jurisdiction from torture, degrading or inhuman treatment.[148] The grave breach provisions of the Geneva Conventions 1949 and of Additional Protocol I 1977 provide similar

---

[146] The effect of the Rome Statute 1998, Art. 17 may be to encourage States party to conduct investigations into potential war crimes more frequently than in the past, so as to retain jurisdiction over members of their armed forces in national hands, rather than in the hands of the Court's prosecutor. A State may take the view that were it to hand such investigations over to the latter the morale of its armed forces would suffer, particularly during the currency of an international armed conflict. For similar thinking see the issue of retention of jurisdiction by a sending state where it is a visiting force on the territory of a receiving State. It is for the State concerned, however, to choose the charge to be framed against an accused. It may elect to charge a soldier with murder (before a civilian or a military court) rather than with a war crime.

[147] In addition to the obligation of a State to carry out an investigation into the death of a prisoner of war and of a civilian internee: the third Geneva Convention 1949, Art. 121, fourth Geneva Convention 1949, Art. 131, respectively. An occupying State may consider that financial compensation for civilians killed by its armed forces is sufficient: see note 11.

[148] The 1966 Covenant, Art. 7; the 1950 Convention, Art. 3; the American Convention on Human Rights 1969, Art. 5; the African Charter on Human and Peoples' Rights 1981,

injunctions.[149] In addition, the 1949 Conventions require protected persons to be treated 'humanely'[150] and the Rome Statute incorporates the grave breach provisions of the Geneva Conventions 1949 into its list of war crimes.[151] There is, therefore, considerable overlap between the human rights instruments and international humanitarian law in this area. In neither family of treaties can there be any derogation from the obligations owed by States.

The International Criminal Tribunal for the Former Yugoslavia has considered these terms within the framework of its own jurisdiction[152] and has shown some of the circumstances in which these acts can occur during a recent international armed conflict.[153] In terms of the human rights instruments there is little difference in kind between the position of those detained by the armed forces during some form of internal disturbance and those held by them during an international armed conflict. The protection of human rights in this situation is discussed in chapter 6.

Human rights when persons are detained

It is almost inevitable that States engaged in an international armed conflict will detain prisoners of war.[154] Their protection is provided for by the third Geneva Convention 1949 from 'the time they fall into the power

Art. 5. See also the torture conventions: Convention Against Torture and other Cruel, Inhuman or Degrading Treatment or Punishment 1984 particularly Arts. 2(2) and 12 (where an investigation is required); the European Convention for the Prevention of Torture and Inhuman or Degrading Treatment or Punishment 1987 and their two Protocols (1993); the Inter-American Convention to Prevent and Abolish Torture 1985, particularly Art. 5. Both the 1984 and the 1985 Conventions require States party to provide jurisdiction within their national legal systems. For the United Kingdom see the Criminal Justice Act 1988, s. 134. For a discussion of the conditions in Abu Ghraib prison in Iraq controlled by United States armed forces see S. Hersh, *Chain of Command. The Road from 9/11 to Abu Ghraib* (London: Penguin, 2004), chapter 1 and for the conviction of a soldier for acts committed there, *The Times*, 22 October 2004.

[149] Articles 50, 51, 130 and 147 respectively of each of the four Conventions 1949; Arts. 11(4) and 85 of Additional Protocol I 1977. There is, however, no reference to 'degrading' treatment. An example of degrading treatment might be the forced shaving of a prisoner of war's facial hair which has been grown for religious purposes or the forcing of a person to eat particular food prohibited by his religion.

[150] Articles 12, 12, 13 and 27 respectively of each Convention. See also the third Convention 1949, Art. 17, fourth Convention 1949, Art. 31.

[151] Article 8(2)(a). See, in particular, Art. 8(2)(a)(ii).

[152] See the Statute of the International Tribunal 1993, Arts. 2(b), 5(i).

[153] See, for example, *Prosecutor* v. *Furundzija*, Appeals Chamber, 21 July 2000, at para. 114.

[154] The nature of the conflict will often determine the numbers of prisoners of war. If the conflict is mainly fought by one side from the air the number will be small, if a land war is fought the numbers might be large.

of the enemy . . . until their final release and repatriation'.[155] They will, however, also be able to take the benefits of the human rights instruments to which the detaining State is a party, on the assumption that the State has not issued a valid derogation notice in respect of the right to liberty and that the prisoners of war come 'within the jurisdiction' of the detaining State, as discussed above.[156] Each treaty takes a different approach to this particular right. The 1966 Covenant requires the detention to be in 'accordance with such procedures as are established by law'[157] whereas under the 1950 Convention the detention will only be justified if it comes within the cases specified in the relevant Article, none of which cover expressly the situation of prisoners of war.[158] The only means by which the detention of a prisoner of war might be brought within any of the cases mentioned is that such detention is 'in order to secure the fulfilment of any obligation prescribed by law'.[159] This 'obligation' is that contained in the third Geneva Convention 1949, namely, to detain prisoners of war under the conditions set out in that Convention.[160]

The detention of prisoners of war during an international armed conflict is, nevertheless, difficult to fit within the regime of the human rights instruments. First, it will be of uncertain duration; it may last months or years and is unrelated to any acts on the part of the prisoner of war. He is not entitled to release and repatriation until the cessation of active hostilities.[161] At the beginning of captivity it will almost always be impossible to determine when this will occur. Deprivation of liberty without time limit

---

[155] Article 5(1).

[156] A consistent phrase is that the derogation must be 'strictly required by the exigencies of the situation': see 1966 Covenant, Art. 4; 1950 Convention, Art. 15.

[157] Article 9(1). For a similar approach see also the American Convention on Human Rights 1969, Art. 7(1); the African Charter on Human and Peoples' Rights 1981, Art. 6.

[158] Article 5(1). In the Arab Charter on Human Rights 1994 there is merely a requirement that a person deprived of his liberty be treated humanely.

[159] Article 5(1)(b). This conclusion is supported by the comment that 'an international instrument must be interpreted and applied within the overall framework of the juridical system in force at the time of the interpretation': *Coard* v. *United States*, Report No. 109/99, Case 10.951, 29 September 1999 (Inter-American Commission on Human Rights), at para. 40 quoting *Legal Consequences for States of the Continued Presence of South Africa in Namibia (South West Africa)*, Advisory Opinion, 1971 ICJ Reports 16, 31. Compare the basis of the detention of prisoners of war accepted in *Cyprus* v. *Turkey* (1976) 4 EHRR 482, at para. 313.

[160] *Quaere* whether a State has an 'obligation' to *detain* prisoners of war. There is no legal impediment in the Convention to a State releasing healthy prisoners of war prior to the conclusion of hostilities. This became the practice in the Falklands/Malvinas conflict in 1982. The early release of sick and wounded prisoners of war is provided for by Arts. 109–17.

[161] Third Geneva Convention 1949, Art. 118.

would be found unacceptable if imposed in peacetime against soldier or civilian. Secondly, the vast majority of prisoners of war will have no wish to take proceedings to determine the lawfulness of their detention.[162] This is because prisoner of war status is, apart from being repatriated, much preferred[163] than any of the alternatives.

A member of the armed forces captured by an enemy State may be denied prisoner of war status by his captors on the grounds that he is alleged to be a mercenary or he has failed to distinguish himself, by his clothing or actions, from the civilian population.[164] If such an individual does 'take proceedings by which the lawfulness of his detention might be decided by a court' he will, ironically, be arguing that he *should be* detained (as a prisoner of war). The State will need to provide a 'court' for this purpose. A military board will not amount to a court unless it possesses the guarantees of independence and impartiality from the military chain of command expected of a trial court.[165]

The third Geneva Convention 1949[166] and, by implication,[167] the human rights instruments require a State to account for individual prisoners of war whom it detains. Relatives of those who cannot be traced may themselves become victims and may be able to take some form of action under the most appropriate human rights instrument.[168]

Civilians (or persons who are not members of the armed forces of a party to the armed conflict[169]) may also be detained during an international armed conflict. They will be owed obligations under the fourth Geneva Convention 1949[170] if they come within the category of 'protected

---

[162] See the 1966 Covenant, Art. 9(4); the 1950 Convention, Art. 5(4); the American Convention on Human Rights, 1969, Art. 7(6); the African Charter on Human and Peoples' Rights 1981, Art. 6 (by implication).

[163] This is on the assumption that the conditions mandated by the third Geneva Convention 1949 are implemented in respect of prisoners of war.

[164] As to the mercenary see Additional Protocol I 1977, Art. 47, and as to failing properly to distinguish himself from a civilian (and therefore a non-combatant) see *ibid.*, Art. 44(3).

[165] For discussion of these requirements see chapter 3.

[166] Article 122 and note the work of the Central Tracing Agency, Geneva.

[167] The requirement to provide a court to determine the lawfulness of detention leads to an implication that court (and prison) records will be kept.

[168] For an example under the 1950 Convention see *Cyprus* v. *Turkey* (2002) 35 EHRR 35, at para. 156. Compare where a State has issued a derogation notice in respect of the relevant Article dealing with the deprivation of liberty. It is unlikely to be able to derogate from a duty to account for detained individuals.

[169] See Additional Protocol I 1977, Art. 50.

[170] See Arts. 5 and 66–76. For the internment of alien civilians in the territory of a party to the conflict see *ibid.*, Arts. 41, 42 and, in occupied territory, Art. 78. They may also be arrested on suspicion of certain offences by the State of whom they are not nationals, see

persons',[171] which in most cases will mean that they are non-nationals of the State in whose hands they are. If they are interned their treatment will be similar to that of prisoners of war, although they may be expected to challenge more vigorously their detention. Their rights under the appropriate human rights instrument will be the same, *mutatis mutandis*, as those of prisoners of war.

Modern forms of conflict have shown the existence of a 'hybrid' form of fighter, the civilian who, on an organised basis, takes part in a substantial way in the conflict. Organised resistance groups operating in or out of occupied territory have gradually been brought within the category of lawful combatant.[172] The civilian who has undergone extensive military-type training and who is fighting not on behalf of his State but for some other purpose appeared on the scene in a dramatic fashion on 11 September 2001 when civilian aircraft were deliberately flown into buildings in New York and Washington. This is accepted as being the work of individuals belonging to the al Qaeda organisation, based in Afghanistan.

Although the relationship between al Qaeda and the Afghan government at the time is not entirely clear it is unlikely that the former were members of the armed forces of Afghanistan or 'belonged to a Party to the conflict'[173] entitling them to prisoner of war status if captured. A number of al Qaeda members were taken into custody by United States forces when they launched an attack against Afghanistan in 2001–2 and taken to the United States military base in Guantanamo Bay, Cuba, where they were held in detention.[174] If they were not to be classified as prisoners of war were they to be presumed to be so until their status was determined by a competent tribunal?[175] The answer would appear strictly to be in the negative since no 'doubt' had arisen as to whether they fell within any of the categories of prisoner of war set out in the third Geneva Convention

Arts. 5, 66–76. *Quaere* the effect of UNSCR 1546 (2004) para. 10; HC 436 (UK) 2005, para. 12.

[171] Article 4. See, however, the view of the International Criminal Tribunal for the Former Yugoslavia at n. 177 below.

[172] Hague Convention IV 1907, Art. 1; third Geneva Convention 1949, Art. 4(2), Additional Protocol I 1977, Art. 44.

[173] Third Geneva Convention 1949, Art. 4(1), (2). See, generally, H.-P. Gasser, 'Acts of Terror, "Terrorism" and International Humanitarian Law' (2002) 84 *International Review of the Red Cross* 547, 567; R. Cryer, 'The Fine Art of Friendship: *Jus in Bello* in Afghanistan' (2002) 7 *Journal of Conflict and Security Law* 37, 68; P. Rowe, 'Responses to Terror: the "New War"' (2002) 3 *Melbourne Journal of International Law* 301, 314.

[174] At this stage it was clear that the Geneva Conventions 1949 were applicable. See G. Aldrich, 'The Taliban, Al Qaeda, and the Determination of Illegal Combatants' (2002) 96 *American Journal of International Law* 891, 893.

[175] The third Geneva Convention 1949, Art. 5.

1949. Although Additional Protocol I 1977 had widened the scope of the presumption of prisoner of war status, neither the United States nor Afghanistan was, at the time, a party to it.[176]

The effect of the non-applicability of prisoner of war status[177] to these individuals leads to the conclusion that unless they are entitled to the benefit of any applicable human rights treaty they will be in a legal vacuum with no rights or means of protection at all.[178] For the reasons it has been argued above these detainees are within the jurisdiction of United States armed forces for the purposes of human rights instruments to which that State is a party even though they are not detained in the territory of the United States itself.[179]

The situation of the detainees at Guantanamo Bay may well be repeated in some form or other. Unlike a person who is clearly a prisoner of war the detainee in these circumstances will wish to have his detention considered by a judicial officer and to put his case before a court to determine the lawfulness[180] of his detention with the hope that his release will be ordered.

---

[176] See Art. 45(1). The issue is whether this Article reflects customary international law and thus is binding upon the United States as such.

[177] It is unlikely that all detainees will be protected persons under the fourth Geneva Convention 1949 since many will be nationals of States with whom the United States has normal diplomatic relations: Art. 4(2). Compare, however, the view of the Appeals Chamber of the ICTY in *Prosecutor* v. *Delalic* IT-96-21-T Judgment, 16 November 1998, para. 263 that nationality was not the test of whether the fourth Geneva Convention 1949, Art. 4 applied; *Prosecutor* v. *Tadic* IT-94-1-A, 15 July 1999 at para. 166 (1999) 38 ILM 1518. For those under the age of eighteen when captured the Convention on the Rights of the Child, 20 November 1989, in force 2 September 1990, (1989) 28 ILM 1448 and its Optional Protocol of 2000 offer little in the way of relevant specific rights to the child, assuming that the issue is not one of under-age recruitment.

[178] See chapter 4.

[179] The Inter-American Commission on Human Rights, 12 March 2002 has requested that the United States take the 'measures necessary to have the legal status of the detainees at Guantanamo Bay determined by a competent tribunal'. This is not, however, a complete answer to the issue since the denial of prisoner of war status by a competent tribunal will not necessarily determine whether the United States owes them obligations under a human rights instrument. The detainees are within the jurisdiction of the United States for these purposes, see *R (Abassi)* v. *Secretary of State for Foreign and Commonwealth Affairs and Secretary of State for the Home Department* [2002] EWCA Civ 1598, at para. 66.

[180] The detaining State may have to provide some form of judicial oversight of detention, see *Coard* v. *United States* (n. 23) at para. 58. Should it be argued that the 'lawfulness' of the detention is based upon international law (such as the third or fourth Geneva Conventions 1949) this ground will expire at the close of hostilities, unless a criminal (judicial) charge is pending or a sentence is being served: third Convention, Arts. 118, 119; fourth Convention, Art. 133 (internees). For an application of the fourth Convention (Art. 78) in this regard see *Coard* v. *United States* Report (n. 23 above). The fourth

In the absence of an appropriate derogation notice a failure to provide a court for this purpose will be a breach of the detainee's human rights. It will, of course, be otherwise where the detainee has been convicted by a court[181] of the detaining State for acts committed before capture.

Finally, the treatment of those who have been detained may breach other human rights obligations,[182] such as the right to life or the prohibition on torture or inhuman treatment. Neither of these rights can be subject to a derogation in the circumstances of a detention by the armed forces of a foreign State.

Right to a fair trial

The right to a fair trial and to fair trial procedures is a central feature of all human rights instruments.[183] In the absence of an appropriate derogation notice (where this is permissible) and assuming that foreign individuals are within the jurisdiction of the State this right will apply during an international armed conflict or in occupied territory.

There are a number of situations where international humanitarian law imposes an *obligation* on a State to place a detained person before a tribunal or other judicial process. It may hold a person whom it alleges is a spy,[184] who claims to be treated as a prisoner of war,[185] who, as a prisoner of war, is to be tried for a crime committed before or after capture,[186] or who as a civilian is to be tried for an offence against the security of the detaining State as the occupying power.[187]

Convention 1949 will continue to operate in certain respects if the territory remains occupied. The case that the fourth Geneva Convention should apply also to a detainee who is not a protected person by either of these Conventions, is a strong one. Where the 'lawfulness' is based upon national law it will normally have to involve an offence with extraterritorial jurisdiction, unless the offence is committed on the territory of the detaining State itself.

[181] This is on the assumption that such a court and the procedure it adopts is otherwise consistent with human rights provisions. This cannot be assumed if, for instance, the court is a military one. See, generally, chapter 4.

[182] In addition to a State's obligations under the Geneva Conventions 1949. See, for example, Arts. 13, 17, 130 of the third Convention and Arts. 31–4 and 147 of the fourth Convention.

[183] See the 1966 Covenant, Arts. 14, 15; the 1950 Convention, Arts. 6, 7; the American Convention on Human Rights 1969, Arts. 8, 9, the African Charter on Human and Peoples' Rights 1981, Art. 7; compare the Arab Charter on Human Rights 1994 which makes no mention of 'an independent and impartial' court or tribunal.

[184] See Regulations Annexed to the Hague Convention IV 1907, Art. 30.

[185] Third Geneva Convention 1949, Art. 5; Additional Protocol I 1977, Art. 45.

[186] Third Geneva Convention 1949, Arts. 82–108.

[187] Fourth Geneva Convention 1949, Arts. 66–75.

International humanitarian law goes on to provide some basic trial safeguards[188] whilst imposing an additional obligation on the part of the detaining State to respect 'the generally recognised principles of regular judicial procedure'.[189] These principles will also have been developed by the various human rights instruments. In the event that the detaining State has issued a derogation notice in respect of fair trial rights under a relevant human rights instrument it would be expected to have regard to international humanitarian law in formulating its court procedure in order to comply with the requirements of Article 75 of Additional Protocol I.[190] A failure, in these circumstances, to apply international humanitarian law principles of fair trial would show both a breach of the relevant human rights treaty since the derogation notice would be invalid and of international humanitarian law.[191]

The practice, however, in modern armed conflicts has been not to issue a derogation notice in respect of the fair trial provisions. The effect is that the fair trials provisions in the various human rights instruments will continue to apply alongside those of international humanitarian law. Given this to be so, a person placed on trial and faced with a 'choice' of fair trial rights may well argue for the precedence of the former.[192] Where the 1950 Convention is the relevant human rights instrument a person on trial will not only be able to argue that fair trial rights given in that Convention apply to his trial but also seek 'just satisfaction' if his rights are denied to him.[193]

The major difference between these two families of treaties lies in the type of court in which a person is entitled to have his case judged. Under international humanitarian law this court must be the same as would judge members of the armed forces of the detaining State,[194] or be 'a

---

[188] See third Geneva Convention 1949, Art. 105; Additional Protocol I 1977, Art. 75. Note also the obligation to notify the protecting power, third Geneva Convention 1949, Art. 104.

[189] Additional Protocol I 1977, Art. 75(4).

[190] This is considered to reflect customary international law and therefore binding on States not party to the Protocol, see Greenwood, 'Customary Law Status', p. 93.

[191] See *Abella* v. *Argentina*, Report No. 55/97, Case 11.137, 18 November 1997, at para. 170. The derogation notice would be invalid since the State would fail to comply with 'its other obligations under international law', (common terminology in respect of derogation), i.e., international humanitarian law.

[192] This choice is based upon the person on trial being a 'protected person' under the third or fourth Geneva Conventions 1949 and Additional Protocol I 1977.

[193] Article 41. Under other instruments the human rights committee (or other body) may investigate his case following a communication from him.

[194] Third Geneva Convention 1949, Art. 102. For the position of internees see fourth Convention 1949, Art. 117. For a right of appeal see Arts. 106, 73 respectively.

properly constituted non-political military court'[195] or be an 'impartial and regularly constituted court'.[196] The requirement in the human rights instruments for an 'independent and impartial' court or tribunal imposes a more strict standard, on the basis that the word 'independent' adds something to a requirement to be 'impartial'. When it is considered that, in practice, these courts are likely to be[197] courts-martial the potential for an abuse of human rights of the defendant,[198] given that the individual will be detained by military personnel and be tried by military courts, is considerable.[199]

The requirement in Article 75 of Additional Protocol I that the court be 'regularly constituted' suggests not only that it must be established by law but also that it is given jurisdiction to sit in territory outside the national borders of the State. The armed forces of that State may, for instance, detain prisoners of war in the area in which they are engaged in an international armed conflict. This was the case during the Gulf war in 1991 when a number of coalition forces States held prisoners of war in the Gulf region.[200] It may also capture outside the borders of its own State those whom it considers to be spies. Should no court of the detaining State possess extra-territorial jurisdiction to try the alleged spy any purported court convened for this purpose would not be 'regularly constituted'.[201]

It has been argued above that a State may carry its human rights obligations with it outside its territorial jurisdiction, at least where it has control

---

[195] Fourth Geneva Convention 1949, Art. 66.

[196] Additional Protocol I 1977, Art. 75(4). This Article does not draw any distinctions between the different categories of protected persons.

[197] This will not, of course, always be the case but during an international armed conflict the possibility of being put before a court-martial is greater than it would be in peacetime. For the right of a protected person to have his case considered by a 'court or administrative board' see the fourth Geneva Convention 1949, Arts. 35(2), 43(1). In this type of case Additional Protocol I 1977, Art. 75 will not apply. The human rights instruments would, however, apply to the nature of the court, see the 1966 Covenant, Art. 14; the 1950 Convention, Art. 6; the American Convention on Human Rights 1969, Art. 8; the African Charter on Human and Peoples' Rights 1981, Art. 7.

[198] A State may argue that the normal trial procedures should not apply in time of international armed conflict even to its own soldiers because of considerations of 'national security' or 'military necessity'. The prisoner of war would be entitled to a trial process no 'better' than a soldier of the detaining State.

[199] For discussion of how military courts may be considered to be 'independent' see chapter 3 and for the trial of civilians by military courts, see chapter 4.

[200] Prisoners of war were also held in England during this conflict, see G. Risius, in P. Rowe (ed.), The Gulf War 1990–91 in International and English Law (London: Routledge, Sweet & Maxwell, 1993), chapter 14.

[201] To send a protected person from occupied territory to the territory of the occupying State for trial or other purpose is a grave breach of the fourth Geneva Convention 1949, Art. 147 (and Art. 49).

over territory or over non-nationals. It will clearly owe these rights also to anyone within its territory, subject to any appropriate notice of derogation. Where no such derogation has taken place the relevant human rights treaty will have considerable impact during an international armed conflict on the right to a fair trial for an offence connected with that conflict.

It was envisaged that any trial of a prisoner of war would be carried out by the detaining power itself unless he is transferred to another party to the third Geneva Convention 1949. The fourth Convention 1949 provides for the trial by the occupying power of civilians for breach of the penal provisions promulgated by it.[202] It assumes the occupying power will hand over to the courts in the occupied territory 'ordinary' criminals who have come into its hands. If, however, it has brought all the inhabitants of the territory it occupies within its jurisdiction under a human rights instrument it will owe them, *inter alia*, the right to a fair trial. If it knows that the courts of the occupied territory cannot provide such a trial process it is likely to be in breach of its human rights obligations if it hands such individuals over for trial.[203]

Finally, a wilful deprivation of the 'rights of fair and regular trial' of a prisoner of war or a protected person under the Fourth Geneva Convention 1949 is a grave breach of the relevant Convention[204] and also a war crime under the Rome Statute.[205] The rights of fair and regular trial are those set out in the respective 1949 Conventions and do not, therefore, extend to those greater rights which may be applicable to the individual through a relevant human rights instrument.

Rights to the protection of property

It is in the nature of war itself that property will be destroyed or be requisitioned by armed forces. To destroy or seize the enemy's property in the necessary course of military operations is not prohibited under international

---

[202] Article 66.
[203] See, by analogy, *Soering* v. *United Kingdom* (1989) 11 EHRR 439. It is assumed that an interpretation of the other human rights instruments would lead to a similar conclusion. For the attitude of the British armed forces to the courts being held in occupied Iraq see *The Times*, 21 May 2003. In *Coard* v. *United States*, Report No. 109/99, Case No. 10.951, 29 September 1999, the Inter-American Commission on Human Rights was asked to decide on the detention of individuals by United States armed forces in Grenada in 1983 and not on their subsequent trial by the courts in Grenada.
[204] Arts. 130 and 147, respectively, of the third and fourth Geneva Conventions 1949.
[205] Article 8(2)(a)(vi).

humanitarian law.[206] The protection of property, as a human right, would appear to be of lesser importance than some other human rights and, where it exists, is tied in with the general principles of international law or the 'provisions of appropriate laws'.[207]

In the absence of a derogation notice the right of a person to the protection of his property from the acts of military forces during an international armed conflict will tie in with the obligation of those soldiers not to destroy or seize property which cannot be justified by military necessity.[208]

Right of free movement

The right to leave a State is a recognised human right, although it can be restricted.[209] In such terms it is similar to the right given to an alien to leave the territory of a party to the conflict under the fourth Geneva Convention 1949.[210] The expulsion of an alien from territory is subject to procedural guarantees in the human rights instruments,[211] or is prohibited if it is

[206] Regulations Annexed to the Hague Convention IV 1907, Art. 23(g); the Rome Statute 1998, Art. 8(2)(b)(xiii). See, however, the provisions relating to pillage and the non-confiscation of private property in occupied territory, Regulations, Arts. 47 and 46 respectively, or of the destruction of any property unless rendered absolutely necessary, fourth Geneva Convention 1949, Art. 53. Other prohibitions relating to, for instance, the natural environment (Additional Protocol I 1977, Arts. 35(3), 55) or attack on civilian objects may involve individual property rights.

[207] There is no reference to a right to protection of property, as such, in the 1966 Covenant. It is a right given in the 1950 Convention (First Protocol 1952, Art. 1). For an example see *Cyprus* v. *Turkey* (2002) 35 EHRR 30; the American Convention on Human Rights 1969, Art. 21 and the African Charter on Human and Peoples' Rights 1981, Art. 14. It is common to provide that the destruction of property during warlike actions of a State will not give rise to compensation in the courts of the State. For examples see *El-Shifa Pharmaceutical Industries Co.* v. *United States* (2004) 378 F. 3d 1346; War Damage Act 1965 (United Kingdom).

[208] Failure to comply with this obligation could lead to a charge of committing a war crime, see the Rome Statute 1998, Art. 8(2)(b)(xiii) or Art. 8(2)(a)(iv) if the destruction of property is 'extensive'. The link with international law (in this case international humanitarian law) would also apply in respect of personal property. A derogation notice could not have the effect of overriding international humanitarian law. If it purported to do so it would be invalid, see *Abella* v. *Argentina*, Report No. 55/97, Case 11.137, 18 November 1997, at para. 170.

[209] See the 1966 Covenant, Art. 12(2); the 1950 Convention, Fourth Protocol 1963, Art. 2.2; the American Convention on Human Rights 1969, Art. 22(2); the African Charter on Human and Peoples' Rights 1981, Art. 12(2). A curfew could be justified in the circumstances, see *Cyprus* v. *Turkey* (1976) 4 EHRR 482.

[210] Fourth Geneva Convention 1949, Art. 35.

[211] See the 1966 Covenant, Art. 13; the American Convention on Human Rights 1969, Art. 22(6); the African Charter on Human and Peoples' Rights 1981, Art. 12(4).

a collective expulsion.[212] It is, however, only prohibited by international humanitarian law where the protected person is in occupied territory.[213] In the absence of an appropriate derogation notice, therefore, the collective expulsion of aliens from the territory of a party to the conflict (and where that State has not been occupied) would be a breach of some of the human rights instruments but not a breach of international humanitarian law. An individual who wished to remain in such territory would therefore have to rely on any available human rights instrument to protect him (in so far as it could) from expulsion.

Human rights under occupation

The obligations of an occupying State towards the civilian population (in which is included individual civilians) are fairly well developed in international humanitarian law.[214] Such occupation might last for some time[215] and be relatively peaceful. The issue of the liability of the occupying State to the human rights obligations assumed by the sovereign State[216] will arise in three types of case. First, where both the sovereign State and the occupying State are parties to the same human rights instrument(s); secondly, where the sovereign State is a party to a human rights instrument but the occupying State is not; thirdly, where the occupying State is a party to a human rights treaty to which the sovereign State is not a party.

---

[212] The 1950 Convention (Fourth Protocol 1963), Art. 3; the African Charter on Human and Peoples' Rights 1981, Art. 12(5).

[213] Fourth Convention 1949, Art. 49. To do so is a grave breach of Additional Protocol I 1977, Art. 85(4)(a) and a war crime under the Rome Statute 1998, Art. 8(2)(a)(vii).

[214] See Regulations Annexed to Hague Convention IV 1907, Section III; the fourth Geneva Convention 1949, Section III. For analysis of the occupation of Iraq in 2003 see J. Paust, 'The U.S. as Occupying Power Over Portions of Iraq and Relevant Responsibilities Under the Laws of War' (May 2003) at http://www.nimj.com/documents/occupation.doc and, generally, A. Roberts 'What is a Military Occupation?' (1984) 55 *British Yearbook of International Law* 249 (who analyses 'seventeen types of occupation'). For the purposes of this chapter no distinction is drawn between occupying the territory of another State and annexing that territory.

[215] The obligations (either in part or in full) of the occupying State will continue after the armed conflict is concluded if the occupation continues: fourth Geneva Convention 1949, Art. 6; Additional Protocol I 1977, Art. 3(b). A practical difficulty is the refusal of a State to accept that the fourth Geneva Convention 1949 is applicable. This is the current position of Israel over some of the territories occupied by it from 1967.

[216] This term is taken to refer to the State in the form it was prior to occupation.

The prime issue is whether the inhabitants of the occupied State are within the jurisdiction (certainly where this is the only condition precedent to the application of a human rights instrument) of the occupying State. For the reasons given earlier in this chapter the answer may (depending on the facts) be in the affirmative.[217] First, where both States are parties to the same human rights treaty(ies) the inhabitants of the occupied State can look to the occupier to secure to them their rights under the relevant treaty. This was the situation when Turkey occupied Northern Cyprus from 1974.[218] A (Greek) Cypriot civilian who had been excluded from her premises by the Turkish armed forces could look to Turkey for redress of her rights to possession of her property, even though she was, at the time of application, an inhabitant of that part of Cyprus not occupied by Turkey since it was 'obvious from the large number of troops engaged in active duties in Northern Cyprus . . . that her army exercises effective control over that part of the Island'.[219] Had the European Court of Human Rights decided that the applicant was not within the jurisdiction of Turkey she would have been denied the rights she would have had against the sovereign State (Cyprus) if the occupation had not taken place.

The status of any reservations or derogation notice may also fall to be considered. In doing so the nature of the occupying State's obligation to secure to those within the occupied territory the rights under an appropriate human rights instrument will need to be explored. Does this State's obligation arise merely because it is a party to the relevant human rights treaty or because, through the act of occupation, it now stands in the shoes of the sovereign State? The answer must be the former of these two positions since, as it will be argued below, a State cannot become a party to a treaty merely through the occupation of territory and thus be required to assume the treaty obligations of the sovereign State. The effect of this conclusion is that a reservation or derogation notice issued by the

---

[217] Compare Provost, *International Human Rights*, p. 56 who concludes that 'the granting of individual rights against an occupying State . . . would clearly signal a convergence between human rights and humanitarian law'. Such rights arise, however, through the human rights obligations of the occupying State and not through international humanitarian law.

[218] Turkey became a party to the European Convention on Human Rights 1950 in 1954 and Cyprus in 1962.

[219] *Loizidou* v. *Turkey* (1997) 23 EHRR 513, para. 56. Compare *Ilascu* v. *Moldova and Russia*, Judgment, 8 July 2004 where both Moldova and Russia were able to exercise jurisdiction over the 'Moldovian Republic of Transdniestria' for the purposes of Art. 1 of the Convention.

sovereign State goes with the disappearance from the scene of that State. The reservation or derogation notice effective in the occupied territory will therefore be that adopted (if any) by the occupying State.

The second case is where the sovereign State is a party to a particular human rights instrument but the occupying State is not. Does the latter take over the treaty obligations of the former while it is occupying the territory? If it does not the inhabitants of the occupied territory will lose the rights which, prior to the occupation they had. Where, however, those rights have been incorporated in some form in the national law of the occupied State the inhabitants will not lose them unless the occupying State repeals this law. Under international humanitarian law there is no restriction on the power of the occupying force to do this, or to amend such laws.[220] In doing so it may argue that such a course of action is necessary in the interests of the security of the occupying forces or, if it purports to annex the territory, to bring the national law of that territory into line with its home State.[221] The occupying State cannot, however, become a party to a human rights treaty in the place of the sovereign State merely by the fact of occupation of its territory.[222] The effect of this is that the inhabitants may lose their human rights protection and those which they gain through the medium of international humanitarian law are much less extensive. The right to receive visits from delegates of the protecting power or the International Committee of the Red Cross[223] may go some way to ensure that the inhabitants of occupied territory are able to secure the more limited conditions required to be established by the occupying State.[224] This right to receive visits cannot be equated with the right to make an application either to a court of human rights or to a human rights committee under the relevant human rights treaty.

The third case involves the occupying State but not the sovereign State being a party to a human rights treaty. In the light of the discussion

---

[220] It can impose new penal laws, repeal or suspend existing penal laws but there is no reference to a similar ability to do this in respect of civil rights and obligations: fourth Geneva Convention 1949, Art. 64.

[221] Annexation was the intended object of the Indonesia control of East Timor in 1976 (although recognised by Australia) (1978–80) 8 *Australian Yearbook of International Law* 281, the Argentine invasion of the Falkland/Malvinas Islands in 1982 and the Iraqi invasion of Kuwait in 1990. Compare the occupation by the United States and the United Kingdom of Iraq in 2003.

[222] It is unlikely that the United Kingdom Ministry of Defence, *The Manual of the Law of Armed Conflict*, intended this in para. 11.19.

[223] The delegates of the protecting power or the ICRC are given rights of visit, fourth Geneva Convention 1949, Arts. 76, 143.

[224] Under the fourth Geneva Convention 1949.

above the inhabitants of the occupied territory may (depending on the individual human rights treaty) gain the full protection of this treaty, unless the former State has issued an appropriate notice of derogation. It will clearly gain those rights from which derogation is not possible. Moreover, it will be for the occupying State to show why a derogation notice is necessary. It may be able to do this where there is resistance to the occupier by armed groups operating in the territory itself. In this situation the occupier's position is not dissimilar to that of a State fighting 'rebels' or 'terrorists' within its own borders.[225] Any denunciation of the human rights treaty can take effect if it is permitted by the treaty[226] itself or, if so, only after a fixed period.[227]

Amnesty

At the conclusion of an international armed conflict, which has not resulted in the occupation of territory, the possibility of granting an amnesty to the political or military leaders of one or more of the States concerned might arise. Although each of the Geneva Conventions 1949[228] provides that protected persons may not renounce the rights secured to them by the Convention there is an obligation upon States to 'search for persons alleged to have committed . . . grave breaches'.[229] There is no relief granted to a State to set aside this obligation in the interests, for instance, of securing a peace treaty or agreed terms by which hostilities will be brought to an end. The practice of States has, however, been quite different. It has not been uncommon for offers of immunity in respect of alleged war crimes to be made to political leaders. It is likely that, in a suitable case, the Prosecutor of the International Criminal Court will override any purported immunity and issue an indictment against such a person.[230]

Given that a breach of human rights during an international armed conflict gives rights to the individual and, in many cases, rights also to invoke the machinery of a human rights body, any purported immunity of

---

[225] See, generally, chapter 6.
[226] There is no provision in the 1966 Covenant for denunciation. For the non-withdrawal from a treaty which does not provide for such an event see the Vienna Convention on the Law of Treaties 1969, Art. 56.
[227] See the 1950 Convention, Art. 58 (six months); the American Convention on Human Rights 1969, Art. 78 (one year).
[228] For an example, see the third Convention 1949, Art. 7.
[229] *Ibid.*, Art. 129.
[230] Compare, however, the Rome Statute 1998, Art. 15. For the position of a purported amnesty following a non-international armed conflict see chapter 6.

a State for human rights breaches during the international armed conflict will have no legal basis. Nor should States grant immunity under their national law, provide for a defence of compliance with superior orders to individuals for such breaches or impose 'unreasonably short periods of statutory limitation'.[231]

---

[231] 'The Nature of the Legal Obligation Imposed on States Parties to the Covenant, CCPR/C/21/Rev.1/Add.13 (general comments), 26 May 2004, para. 18. See, generally, M. Zeidy, 'The Principle of Complementarity: A New Machinery to Implement International Criminal Law' (2002) 23 *Michigan Journal of International Law* 869, 940; J. Gavron, 'Amnesties in the Light of Developments in International Law and the Establishment of the International Criminal Court' (2002) 51 *International and Comparative Law Quarterly* 91.

6

Human rights, non-international armed conflict and civil disorder

The use by a State of its armed forces within the boundaries of that State on what might be termed 'combat' activities places on the shoulders of the soldiers involved an often conflicting set of 'laws' as to how they should behave. Thus, military law, national law and human rights law will, and international humanitarian law may, have some bearing on their activities, although the relationship among these various sources of legal obligation will vary and their boundaries may be unclear in any particular case.

Discussion, for instance, of the legal consequences flowing from a non-international armed conflict suggests that this type of conflict can be easily distinguished from an international one or, indeed, from disorder within a State which does not amount to an armed conflict at all. In some cases this may be possible[1] but in others there will be room for disagreement.[2] The State concerned may deny that an armed conflict is taking place at all.[3] Moreover, an armed conflict may be deemed[4] to be of an international character or be international at one level and non-international at another

---

[1] See the Falklands/Malvinas conflict in 1982, the use of armed force to expel Iraq from Kuwait in 1991 and the attack on Iraq in 2003 which were clearly international armed conflicts.

[2] See the disagreement in the Appeals Chamber of the International Criminal Tribunal for the Former Yugoslavia, *Prosecutor* v. *Tadic* IT-94-1-AR 72, 2 October 1995, para. 97, (1996) 35 ILM 35 and note the approach of the Appeals Chamber decision in the same of 15 July 1999; *Prosecutor* v. *Aleksovski*, Appeals Chamber, 24 March 2000.

[3] See, generally, T. Meron, 'Towards a Humanitarian Declaration on Internal Strife' (1998) 78 *American Journal of International Law* 859; J.-M. Henckaerts, 'Binding Armed Opposition Groups Through Humanitarian Treaty Law and Customary Law' in *Relevance of International Humanitarian Law to Non-State Actors* (Proceedings of the Bruges Colloquium, 25–6 October 2002, Collegium, Special Edition, No. 27 (2003), Bruges: College of Europe and International Committee of the Red Cross), p. 123. Compare *Third Report on the Human Rights Situation in Columbia*, OEA/Ser.L/V/II.102, Doc. 9 rev. 1, 26 February 1999, para. 20 (Columbia accepted that a non-international armed conflict was in existence).

[4] Protocol Additional to the Geneva Conventions of 12 August 1949, and relating to the protection of victims of international armed conflicts (Protocol I) Geneva, 8 June 1977, in force 7 December 1978, (1977) 16 *International Legal Materials* (ILM) 1391, Art. 1(4).

or it may transform itself from the one to the other[5] or into internal disorder. It may even involve non-State actors operating across national boundaries.[6]

Where it is accepted that armed conflict is occurring within a State international humanitarian law and human rights law will, in addition to national and military law, apply to govern (in so far as law can) the actions of the armed forces[7] of the State. The liability of rebels[8] to international humanitarian law and the State's liability under human rights law for their actions are discussed below under the heading 'The position of the rebels'.

Whilst international humanitarian law may impose a uniform approach to controlling those who use force during an armed conflict the same cannot always be said for human rights law with its different regional treaty and enforcement arrangements. International humanitarian law and human rights law do, however, borrow principles from each other. They share a common purpose, to protect the 'human dignity' of every person.[9] Both systems expect the perpetrator of breaches to be punished and, under human rights law, the victim to be compensated and

---

[5] See, for example, the change in the nature of the armed conflict in Afghanistan in 2001–2 from an attack against that State by armed forces led by the United States to one of co-operation with the new government of Afghanistan in the armed conflict against the former Taliban and the al Qaeda fighters within that State. A further example followed the end of the occupation in Iraq in 2004 when the armed forces of the United States and the United Kingdom remained in Iraq to assist the provisional government to restore order. A non-international armed conflict continued in part of that State.

[6] There is a growing literature analysing the actions of al Qaeda principally for its attacks on the United States on 11 September 2001. See, generally, D. McGoldrick, *From '9–11' to the Iraq War 2003* (Oxford: Hart, 2004); K. Watkin, 'Controlling the Use of Force: A Role for Human Rights Norms in Contemporary Armed Conflict' (2004) 98 *American Journal of International Law* 1, pp. 3–9.

[7] This chapter will concentrate on the role of the armed forces. The term 'armed forces' is considered in its widest form as to include organisations which may, under the law of the State, be treated as a branch of the armed forces, such as border guards. The actions of the armed forces on the ground may be indistinguishable from those of the police, or other security forces. In many States they are subject to a disciplinary and command system different from those of other security forces. See CAT/C/47/Add.3, 16 July 2001, para. 59 where in 'response to the public criticism against the police being a part of the armed forces, the Indonesian Government in 2001 made the police completely independent from the armed forces'.

[8] This term is used in a generic sense to include all forms of organised resistance against the government of a State and carried out by means of a non-international armed conflict or through civil disorder. Alternative expressions would be 'armed groups' or 'dissident armed groups' or 'insurgents'. Armed groups may also be engaged in armed conflict against each other. It is not uncommon to see more pejorative terms used, such as 'bandits' or 'terrorists'.

[9] See *Prosecutor* v. *Furundzija*, Case No. IT-95-17/I-T at para. 183. Broadly, however, the international humanitarian approach involves the use of the judicial process either under

the State to prevent recurrences. The importance of punishment of those responsible for human rights breaches and the compensation of victims has been stressed in a number of cases.[10]

This chapter is concerned principally with the application of human rights law during a non-international armed conflict or in civil disorder. The idea that this law (assisted, where possible, by international humanitarian law) could prevent all breaches of it by soldiers is as fanciful as the idea that national law could prevent criminal activity in all its forms. Breaches of human rights in these situations often tend to be on a much greater scale than that with which even a remedies-based system can cope. Publicity of soldiers' actions and pressure from other States may be needed to supplement individual petitions (where these are permissible under the relevant human rights treaty) as a means of greater adherence to the human rights obligations which the State has accepted.[11]

There is, however, a danger that the norms of human rights may be invested by some with more weight than they can reasonably bear.[12] It is true that some are non-derogable but others may be derogated from by the

national or international law to bring those to account directly while the human rights approach may (or may not) involve direct judicial proceedings although it requires States to provide an effective remedy. For an example of the alleged politicisation of the Human Rights Committee see *The Times*, 16 March 1989 (alleged use of chemical weapons by Iraq against its own Kurdish population).

[10] See, for example, Report No. 62/01, Case 11.654, *Riofrio Massacre (Columbia)* Report No. 62/01, Case 11.654, 6 April 2001, para. 384; arguments by petitioners in admissibility proceedings in *Khashiyev and Akayeva v. Russia* (Application No. 57942/00, 19 December 2002 (admissibility)) (2002) 23 *Human Rights Law Journal* 474; *Mentese v. Turkey* (Application No. 36217/97, 23 March 2004 (admissibility)). In addition, the Inter-American Commission on Human Rights has stressed that the victim has the 'right to know the truth about incidents . . . as well as the identity of those who participated in them': *Cea v. El Salvador*, Report No. 1/99, Case 10.480, 27 January 1999 at para. 148. The possibility, however, of amicable settlements cannot be ignored. For an example, see *Association pour la Defence des Droits de l'Homme et des Libertés v. Djibouti* (African Commission on Human and Peoples' Rights), Communication No. 133/94, 11 May 2000, in which it was alleged that government troops had carried out extra-judicial executions, torture and rape. Article 75 of the Rome Statute of the International Criminal Court, Rome, 17 July 1998, (1998) 37 ILM 999 does permit the International Criminal Court to award compensation (as defined) following a conviction. See also the views of the Inter-American Court on Human Rights in *Juan Sanchez Case* (2003) Ser. C, No. 99, para. 149.

[11] See Council of Europe Resolution 1323 (2003), para. 7. Moreover, non-compliance by States at all or in a speedy fashion with reports from human rights bodies is often evident. Reports from these bodies do not generally attract the same degree of publicity as criminal trials for breach of international humanitarian law.

[12] See, generally, C. Doebbler, 'Overlegalizing Human Rights' (2002) *Proceedings. American Society of International Law* 381 (who argues to the contrary); R. McCorquodale, 'Overlegalizing Silences: Human Rights and Non-State Actors' in *Proceedings, American Society of International Law* at p. 384.

State and they have their own (fairly extensive) limitations, upon which the national law of the State will be relevant. It may be necessary, therefore, to consider this law before coming to a firm conclusion as to whether the State concerned is in breach of its human rights obligations. This is important in relation to the armed forces since this body is frequently deployed to 'protect national security', a common ground justifying a limitation on a particular human right. Moreover, where a soldier is involved in armed conflict (or civil disorder) the real physical risks to him must be taken into account as well, of course, as the harm caused to the victim of his actions.[13]

The legal effects of a non-international armed conflict

Where the classification of an armed conflict, or even its existence, is difficult to establish the armed forces may be unclear as to the legal basis upon which their actions should be based. They will have been trained to know that if the conflict is an international one they can kill or wound any enemy combatant, without having to rely upon specific grounds to do so, merely because of this classification. There are no limits to the number of enemy combatants who may be killed, although there are restrictions against killing or wounding such individuals in breach of international humanitarian law. The armed forces may also destroy property if such destruction can be justified by military necessity. In most States those who perform 'their duty' well, for instance, by killing large numbers of enemy combatants,[14] may receive gallantry awards and enhanced status. Those who are not so effective or efficient at doing so may well be killed themselves.[15]

In this type of armed conflict the enemy is usually clearly distinguishable from the armed forces it is fighting and from the civilian population. Those who are captured are entitled to be treated as prisoners of war

---

[13] Compare the position, as discussed in chapters 1–3, where the human rights concern is one of the soldier and his own armed forces. If there is a breach of human rights the soldier is the 'victim'.

[14] The system of describing a fighter pilot as an 'ace' was dependent on the number of 'kills' he had achieved over enemy aircraft. It was not, however, necessary to show that the enemy aircrew had been killed.

[15] The old adage of 'kill or be killed' is well established in the psyche of those who take part in armed conflicts. See, generally, S. Noy, 'Combat Stress Reactions' in R. Gal and A. Mangelsdorff (eds.), *A Handbook of Military Psychology* (Chichester: John Wiley and Sons, 1991), pp. 491, 511.

and will normally be detained until the end of active hostilities when the detaining State is under an obligation to repatriate them.

For the individual members of the armed forces fighting what is clearly a non-international armed conflict the position is quite different. First, the national law of the State will continue to apply, although it is likely to be modified by some form of emergency legislation.[16] In many States the national law will incorporate human rights norms,[17] but these may be abridged, to some extent, by this emergency legislation. Soldiers, well trained in the basic principles of international humanitarian law, may know very little about the human rights obligations of the State for whom they will be State agents.[18] Especially will this be the case where these human rights obligations are in conflict with the national law whether affected by a permissible derogation notice or declaration upon ratification of a human rights instrument or not.[19] Even where there is a

---

[16] Such legislation may be short- or long-lived. As an example of the latter, see CCPR/C/ISR/2001/2, 4 December 2001, para. 71 which comments that 'the State of Israel has remained in an officially proclaimed state of public emergency since May 19, 1948 . . . until the present day'. It may involve the formal suspension of constitutional rights.

[17] In some States these norms may have been directly incorporated, in others a State may take the view that its national law is consistent with such norms. In some States human rights norms formally take precedence over internal law, see CCPR/C/81/Add.7, 3 April 1995, para. 26 (Guatemala).

[18] See, however, the statement of the Government of Sri Lanka that the Army 'has established special units . . . with a mandate in ensuring the adherence of military personnel particularly those serving in operational areas to international human rights norms in the discharge of their duty', CCPR/C/LKA/2002/4, 18 September 2002, para. 182; CAT/C/47/Add.3, 16 July 2001, para. 62 for an account of the 'stern measures against security personnel who violate human rights' relating to Aceh.

[19] For an example of a failure to issue a derogation notice and reliance on emergency law see CCPR/C/79/Add.81, 4 August 1997 (India). A derogation notice must not infringe some aspect of international humanitarian law or peremptory norms of international law, General Comment No. 29, CCPR/C/21/Rev.1/Add.11, 31 August 2001, paras. 9, 11; *Abella* v. *Argentina*, Case 11.137, Report No. 55/97, 18 November 1997 at para. 170. See also the Siracusa Principles (dealing with the 1966 Covenant) (1985) 7 *Human Rights Quarterly* 3; the Paris Minimum Standards of Human Rights Norms in a State of Emergency (dealing with the 1966 Covenant and the 1950 Convention) (1985) 79 *American Journal of International Law* 1072; E/CN.4/2001/91. See, however, T. Meron, *Human Rights Law-Making in the United Nations: a Critique of Instruments and Process* (Oxford: Clarendon Press, 1986) p. 86.

The Human Rights Committee welcomed 'the establishment in 1996 of the Ugandan Human Rights Commission, which is endowed with powers to address human rights violations and seeks to adhere to the Paris Principles', CCPR/CO/80/UGA, 4 May 2004, para. 4. See, for example, Israel's declaration on ratification of the 1966 Covenant in respect of Art. 9 and CCPR/C/SR.1676, 28 September 1998, para. 50, stated in the form of a derogation. Compare General Comment No. 29 on Art. 4: 'measures derogating from the

derogation the 'State party must comply with the fundamental obligation . . . to provide a remedy that is effective'.[20]

Secondly, since the national law (as enhanced by emergency legislation)
will continue to apply, those who take up arms against the armed forces of
the State will remain subject to it. The very act of taking part in the armed
conflict will lead to the commission of a variety of criminal offences from
treason and murder downwards.[21] If captured, such fighters will be dealt
with under the criminal procedures of the State, subject to any existing
human rights protections offered by the national law or under a relevant
human rights instrument. Unlike the prisoner of war a civilian arrested
by the armed forces (or other security forces) is not entitled merely to be
detained in a place other than a civilian prison until the armed conflict is
at an end and then be released.

Thirdly, those whom the individual soldier is fighting will, by the nature
of the conflict, be civilians. Such individuals are unlikely to have been
trained as the soldier has or be subject to a military discipline system.
The whole of international humanitarian law may be quite unknown to
them.[22]

Even if they are aware of these two branches of law and breach them
there may be no effective means of enforcing it among the rebels. They
will, in most cases, be indistinguishable from the civilian population and
may carry out their normal civilian occupation by day and be a 'terrorist'
at night. The very fact of being indistinguishable from the civilian population, who do not take part in the conflict, places at risk the lives and
property of these individuals to a much greater extent than would be the
case if the armed conflict had been of an international character.

Fourthly, whereas during an international armed conflict the combatants on each side may have a respect for each other (although this is not, of
course, always the case) this is unlikely to occur during a non-international

provisions of the Covenant must be of an exceptional and temporary nature'. There can
be no derogation from the African Charter on Human and Peoples' Rights 1981 (African
Charter on Human and Peoples' Rights, Nairobi, 27 June 1981, in force 21 October 1986,
(1982) 21 ILM 59).

[20] HRC General Comment No. 29 (see n. 19 above) at para. 14.

[21] Given the seriousness of such offences rebels may consider that there is no incentive to
comply with international humanitarian law or human rights law, see A. Cassese, 'The
Status of Rebels under the 1977 Geneva Protocol on Non-International Armed Conflicts'
(1981) 30 *International and Comparative Law Quarterly* 416, 434.

[22] The leaders may, however, publicly confirm they will abide by such rules, see the statement
by the FMLN leaders (that is the National Liberation Party) in El Salvador in 1998, referred
to by Judge Cassese in *Prosecutor* v. *Tadic*, Appeals Chamber, IT-94-1-AR 72, 2 October
1995 at para. 107, (1996) 35 ILM 35.

armed conflict. In this type of conflict an attack on soldiers is more likely to come from an unexpected source and, which if it had taken place in an international armed conflict, would be considered to be 'treacherous' or 'perfidious', both of which are prohibited forms of conduct.[23] Rebels may be ascribed as 'terrorists', a term which conjures up notions of an unacceptable form of conducting an armed conflict since it implies these prohibited forms of conduct.[24]

Fifthly, individual civilians or parts of the civilian population need only to be suspected of involvement in some form[25] with the rebels or their cause to run the risk of attack or arrest by soldiers. By way of contrast during an international armed conflict civilians are at risk[26] of attack or arrest by soldiers only if they take a direct part in hostilities, are killed or injured as a consequence of an attack upon a military objective or an individual protected person is 'definitely suspected' of being engaged in 'activities hostile to the security of the State'.[27]

Finally, soldiers will normally train with the weapons most suitable for taking part in an international armed conflict. It is likely that in a non-international armed conflict they will be equipped with high-powered rifles and may have access to armoured vehicles and attack helicopters.[28] The rebels will often be able to match the personal weapons of soldiers, along with grenades, mortars and anti-personnel mines[29] but they are unlikely to possess attack helicopters or other aircraft. This concentration during the training of the soldier on fighting international armed conflicts along with an imbalance of equipment has a tendency to lead to excesses on both sides. Once this begins it attains a momentum of its own and

---

[23] See the Regulations Annexed to the Hague Convention IV 1907, Art. 23(b); Additional Protocol I 1977, Art. 37 respectively.

[24] The State may also describe them as 'criminals' which conjures up a similar notion of unacceptable conduct.

[25] This could involve a suspicion of even minor activities such as omitting to tell the authorities of sightings of rebels.

[26] Assuming the armed forces act within international humanitarian law.

[27] Geneva Convention relative to the protection of civilian persons in time of war, Geneva, 12 August 1949, in force 21 October 1950, 75 *United Nations Treaty Series* (UNTS) 287 (fourth Geneva Convention 1949), Art. 5. Civilians may also be interned in accordance with the Convention, see Arts. 79–141.

[28] They may also have access to anti-personnel mines dependent upon whether the State to which they belong is a party to the Ottawa Convention on the Prohibition of the Use, Stockpiling, Production and Transfer of Anti-Personnel Mines and on their Destruction 1997. See also Basic Principles on the Use of Force and Firearms by Law Enforcement Officials 1990, para. 2.

[29] There may, despite the Ottawa Convention 1997, be sufficient numbers of anti-personnel mines in existence for the rebels to acquire them.

it becomes progressively more difficult for individual soldiers or rebels to restrain themselves. Once the armed conflict has been in existence for some time the limit of what military commanders see as acceptable conduct on the part of their soldiers becomes wider with a de jure or a de facto change in the rules of engagement. In turn, the rebels may see that, against such military hardware possessed by the armed forces, the instillation of fear on the part of the individual soldiers through the unpredictable nature of guerrilla warfare is their only real hope of success. To them a high number of casualties on the part of the armed forces may be seen as the only means by which their objective might be achieved.

This contrast with an international armed conflict illustrates the much greater degree of risk of harm faced by individual civilians (who are not involved with the rebels) during a non-international armed conflict. It also shows how casualties on the part of the armed forces may also be higher than during an international armed conflict since, unlike the latter type of conflict a campaign fought by the armed forces through the medium of air attacks alone (and thus the chances of fighting a war with few casualties) is unlikely to be a realistic option.[30]

Non-international armed conflicts can take a number of different forms. Thus, it can involve rebels attempting to topple the existing government in order to take its place.[31] Alternatively, the rebels may wish to secede from the State and to establish their own State[32] or to create a semi-autonomous region or merely to control territory for the purpose of extracting the wealth from it for the personal benefit of its leaders.[33]

---

[30] Compare the Kosovo campaign in 1999 where the NATO action was almost exclusively carried out by air attacks on what were asserted to be military objectives in the Federal Republic of Yugoslavia. See generally, A. Rogers, 'Zero Casualty Warfare' (2000) 82 *International Review of the Red Cross* 165.

[31] An example might be in Sierra Leone between 1991 and 2001. For background to the conflict see the separate opinion of Justice Robertson in *Prosecutor* v. *Kondewa*, Case No. SCSL-2004-14-AR72(E), 25 May 2004 at paras. 5–6.

[32] See, for example, the armed conflicts in Bosnia/Herzegovina, in Croatia and in Slovenia against the Federal Republic of Yugoslavia before each became a separate State in 1992.

[33] See K. Nossal, 'Bulls to Bears: The Privatisation of War in the 1990s' *Forum, War, Money and Survival* (Geneva: International Committee of the Red Cross, 2000), p. 36. For the allegation that Charles Taylor (at one time President of the Republic of Liberia) committed 'crimes against humanity and grave [*sic*] breaches of the Geneva Conventions, with intent "to obtain access to the mineral wealth of the Republic of Sierra Leone . . . and to destabilize the State"' see *Prosecutor* v. *Taylor*, Case No. SCSL-2003-01-I, 31 May 2004 at para. 5. For the link between the aims of rebels and organised crime see *Third Report on the Human Rights Situation in Columbia* (n. 3, above), para. 25.

A further possibility is that sections of the armed forces attempt a *coup d'état* and engage in fighting those parts of the armed forces loyal to the government or they use military force for their own private ends.[34] Again, rebels may engage in armed conflict against other rebels with the State armed forces being used to restore order or in siding with one of the rebel groups. The State may even be accused of aiding rebels to carry out the political aims of the State itself.[35]

The importance of analysing the different types of non-international armed conflict lies in the nature of the aims of the rebels and, through this, in the way in which they are likely to conduct their side of the conflict. It may be reasoned from this that rebel groups who aim to replace the government of the State may (although this is not always the case) wish to be seen by other governments as behaving responsibly in the manner of the conduct of the armed conflict, despite the fact that they have used armed conflict as a method to replace the existing government. In doing so their chances of being accepted as the legitimate government of the State if they succeed will be greater than if they achieved this through large-scale abuses of human rights. The same may be said of the secessionists who will wish to gain recognition as a separate State from other States as quickly as possible should they succeed in controlling the territory in question. Armed conflicts carried out where rebels (or members of the armed forces) are attempting to achieve any of the other aims discussed above are, perhaps, more likely to involve widespread abuses of human rights. A real danger is that both sides convince themselves that it is a 'war' that they are fighting in which human rights have, in consequence, no place.[36]

In some States the government may not have secure control over the armed forces. It may fear that an exhortation to the armed forces to apply human rights during the conflict or civil disorder will result in, or the threat of, a military coup. A possible consequence of such a belief is that the State may tolerate what are clear breaches of human rights carried out

---

[34] See *Abella* v. *Argentina*, Report No. 55/97, Case 11.137, Inter-American Commission on Human Rights, 18 November 1997.

[35] An example would be the alleged relationship between the Government of Sudan and the Janjaweed rebels active in 2004 in the Darfur region. See United Nations Security Council (UNSC) Resolution 1556 (2004) which demanded that the Government of Sudan fulfil its commitments to disarm the Janjaweed militias, para. 6; Decision on Darfur, Assembly of the African Union, 6–8 July 2004, para. 3.

[36] See, for example, *Juan Sanchez Case* (Inter-American Court of Human Rights), (2003) Ser. C. No. 99, para. 44.

by the armed forces and thereby create a feeling of impunity on the part of the soldiers concerned.[37]

States have generally been wary of accepting that international law has any part to play in armed conflicts occurring within the boundaries of their States where no other States[38] are involved. The position has moved from a 'minimalist' approach in common Article 3 of the Geneva Conventions 1949 to greater scope in Additional Protocol II 1977, to the establishment of the International Criminal Tribunal for Rwanda (1994), the development of war crimes liability by the International Criminal Tribunal for the Former Yugoslavia in 1995 and, ultimately, by the Rome Statute 1998 of the International Criminal Court.

These treaties (and the International Criminal Tribunal for the Former Yugoslavia) require there to be in existence a non-international conflict.[39] Establishing whether such a conflict is in existence can prove to be problematic. Additional Protocol II 1977 tackles the issue by a mix of positive and negative features. This Protocol requires the rebels, 'under responsible command, [to] exercise such control over a part of [the] territory as to

---

[37] *Ibid.*, para. 110. This impunity may involve 'lack of investigation, prosecution, capture, trial and conviction of those responsible for violations of the rights protected by the American Convention' (para. 143). Failure by the armed forces to produce documents (such as logs recording military activities) or to provide oral evidence on the grounds of national security (or official secrets) also has the same effect, *Myrna Chang Case* (Inter-American Court of Human Rights) (2003) Ser. C. No. 101, para. 159(f); *Genie Lacayo Case* (1997) Ser. C. No. 30, para. 76. Where journalists are able to carry out their work the risks of impunity may become less, *Saavedra* v. *Peru*, Report No. 38/97 Case 10.548, 16 October 1997 at para. 92. It is difficult for a State to argue that a junior-ranking soldier has acted outside what his superiors expected of him if there are no investigations or prosecutions for his actions, see *Myrna Chang Case*, para. 146.

[38] See the discussion by Judge Cassese of the position of El Salvador in 1987, *Prosecutor* v. *Tadic*, Appeals Chamber, 2 October 1995, IT-94-1-AR 72 at para. 117, (1996) 35 ILM 35. An international court may conclude that the control exercised over the rebels by another State suggests that, in reality, that State is a participant in the armed conflict thus making the armed conflict an international one. See, for example, *Prosecutor* v. *Tadic*, Appeals Chamber, IT-94-1-A, 15 July 1999 (1999) ILM 1518 and chapter 5.

[39] Or an 'armed conflict not of an international character', Geneva Conventions 1949 (Geneva Convention for the amelioration of the condition of the wounded and sick in armed forces in the field, Geneva, 12 August 1949, in force 21 October 1950, 75 UNTS 31; Geneva Convention for the amelioration of the condition of wounded, sick and shipwrecked members of armed forces at sea, Geneva, 12 August 1949, in force 21 October 1950, 75 UNTS 85; Geneva Convention relative to the treatment of prisoners of war, Geneva, 12 August 1949, in force 21 October 1950, 75 UNTS 135; Geneva Convention relative to the protection of civilian persons in time of war, Geneva, 12 August 1949, in force 21 October 1950, 75 UNTS 287), common Art. 3. Under the Rome Statute 1998 the crimes of genocide and crimes against humanity do not require an armed conflict to be in existence.

enable them to carry out sustained and concerted military operations.[40] The negative features involve an attempt to distinguish an armed conflict from internal disturbances, tensions and riots.[41] The Rome Statute 1998 adopts these negative but not the positive features in setting out the conditions for war crimes liability during a non-international armed conflict.[42] Whilst these two treaties appear to set different standards by which to judge whether a non-international armed conflict is taking place or not the practical reality is that, often, there will be uncertainty over whether an armed conflict is taking place and whether, if so, this is of an international or non-international character.[43] The Appeals Chamber of the Special Court in Sierra Leone in 2004 concluded that 'the *phase of armed conflict* was of such a degree as to be recognised as an insurgency, passing beyond the threshold of a rebellion that could be dealt with internally as a matter of domestic security and to be regulated by domestic law, to a level of conflict that had to be regulated by Common Article 3 of the Geneva Conventions'.[44] This is to confuse recognition of insurgency by other States with the factual presence of an armed conflict. Whilst the events in Sierra Leone may have fallen within this description of an insurgency it is difficult to argue that all cases in which common Article 3 has been considered to apply would have gone beyond a 'rebellion' and have amounted to an 'insurgency'.[45]

The nature and extent of the involvement of another State may be crucial in determining whether it has sufficient control over the rebels to lead to the conclusion that the conflict is an international one.[46] This may not be clear for some time after the start of the armed conflict.

---

[40] Article 1(1). This Article also requires them to be capable of implementing the Protocol. This is a high threshold. There may be doubt in a particular case whether, as a result, the Protocol applies or continues to apply.

[41] Article 1(2).   [42] Article 8(2)(c) and (d).

[43] The effect of the Geneva Conventions 1949, common Art. 3, which is binding on virtually every State in the world, is that this is the only requirement. See, generally, C. Byron, 'Armed Conflicts: International or Non-International?' (2001) 6 *Journal of Conflict and Security Law* 63.

[44] *Prosecutor v. Kallon and Kamara*, Case No. SCSL-2004-15-AR72(E) at para. 17.

[45] A further problem involved in the formulation by the Appeals Chamber is a definition of 'insurgency' and 'rebellion'. See, generally, B. Roth, *Governmental Illegitimacy in International Law* (Oxford: Clarendon Press, 1999), p. 173. Compare the events in Rwanda which led to the establishment of the International Criminal Tribunal for Rwanda in 1994, whose jurisdiction assumed that an *armed conflict* 'not of an international character' had occurred there in 1994: see Art. 4 of its Statute; J. Pictet (ed.), *Commentary on Geneva Convention I* (Geneva: International Committee of the Red Cross, 1952), p. 50.

[46] It may take a court to decide on the facts presented to it whether such a degree of control exists. See n. 2 above.

It should not be assumed that every non-international armed conflict is similar in intensity and scale to an international one save that it takes place within a State. It may be taking place within a region of the State and other parts of the State may be totally unaffected by it. For the reasons mentioned above, it is likely to involve action on the ground by relatively small numbers of participants rather than in the air or in territorial waters. The actual fighting may be sporadic and be of short duration on each occasion. As a result it may not be easy to determine whether there is in existence an armed conflict at all in the absence of the State declaring that such a conflict is taking place.

This problem was considered by the Inter-American Commission on Human Rights in 1997 when it concluded that 'the most difficult problem regarding the application of Common Article 3 is not at the upper end of the spectrum of domestic violence, but rather at the lower end'.[47] In this case the Commission decided that an armed conflict had taken place when in 1989, forty-three armed individuals attacked an army base in La Tablada, near Buenos Aires. Their stated aim was to prevent a *coup d'état* which they believed was being planned within the barracks. The Commission went on to explain that what 'differentiates the events at the La Tablada base from [a situation of internal disturbances] are the concerted nature of the hostile acts undertaken by the attackers, the direct involvement of governmental armed forces, and the nature and level of the violence attending the events in question'.[48] The Commission was impressed by the fact that the attackers had 'executed an armed attack, i.e., a military operation, against a quintessential military objective – a military base'.[49] The result was that 'despite its brief duration, the violent clash between the attackers and members of the Argentine armed forces triggered application of the provisions of Common Article 3, as well as other rules relevant to the conduct of internal hostilities'.[50]

Armed action taken by a group of individuals for some political purpose may not so easily fall within the category of an armed conflict. There were

---

[47] Case 11.137, *Abella* v. *Argentina*, Report No. 55/97, 18 November 1997, para. 153. For discussion of whether the Commission had jurisdiction to apply international humanitarian law see L. Zegweld, 'The Inter-American Commission on Human Rights and International Humanitarian Law: A Comment on the *Tablada* Case' (1998) 324 *International Review of the Red Cross* 505 and for subsequent interpretations on this point see L. Moir, 'Law and the Inter-American Human Rights System' (2003) 25 *Human Rights Quarterly* 182.

[48] *Abella* v. *Argentina* (n. 47 above) at para. 155.

[49] *Ibid.*

[50] *Ibid.*, para. 156. Compare the long-running 'internal armed conflict' in Guatemala, *Myrna Chang Case* (Inter-American Court of Human Rights) (2003) Ser. C, No. 101, para. 134.8.

a number of distinct features in the La Tablada case. There was the attack on a military base, which was repulsed by the use of military equipment; to an observer it clearly looked like an armed attack, even though it did not last long. There was also the fact that the purpose of the attack was to prevent a *coup d'état*. The finding of the Commission might have been different if, instead of the type of attack which took place on La Tablada, a number of separate attacks had taken place by smaller groups of individuals, with longer-term political objectives, on a range of targets at different times.[51]

For the purpose of this chapter it will be assumed that an armed conflict is occurring within a State and that that part of international humanitarian law applying to non-international armed conflicts and the relevant human rights instrument apply together. It is likely that some form of national emergency law will also be in place (at least where the armed conflict is other than of short duration) giving soldiers legal powers which they might not otherwise possess under the law.[52]

The role of human rights may be more important in a non-international armed conflict than in its international counterpart.[53] For the reasons expressed above the likelihood of civilians being, or being suspected of being, caught up in the conflict is much greater than in an international armed conflict. They may, for instance, be at risk from the actions of soldiers even though there is no actual fighting taking place between the rebel group and the armed forces of the State.[54] They may be arrested, subjected to deprivation of liberty, summarily executed or tortured on the basis of a suspicion of involvement in some form with the rebels.

---

[51] *Quaere* whether a court applying international humanitarian law would have found an 'armed conflict' to have been in existence in these circumstances, see *Prosecutor* v. *Delalic et al.*, Case No. IT-96-21, Trial Chamber, 16 November 1998 at para. 184.

[52] Emergency legislation is also likely to be brought into existence where the internal disturbances do not reach the level of an armed conflict.

[53] In *Abella* v. *Argentina*, see n. 47 above, para. 160, the Inter-American Commission concluded that that it was 'during situations of internal armed conflict that these two branches of international law most converge and reinforce each other': Report No. 26/97, Case 11.142, 30 September 1997 (Columbia), para. 174. The preamble to the Protocol Additional to the Geneva Conventions of 12 August 1949, and relating to the protection of victims of non-international armed conflicts (Protocol II), Geneva, 8 June 1977, in force 7 December 1978, (1977) 16 ILM 1442, unlike Additional Protocol I 1977, refers to human rights. See also United Nations General Assembly (UNGA) Resolution 2444 (XXIII), 19 December 1968.

[54] See for example the situation in Chechnya after 1996, *Khashiyev and Akayeva* v. *Russia*, Application No. 5792/00, Judgment European Court of Human Rights, 24 February 2005.

The role of national law

In practice, where law is able to control the actions of a soldier in a non-international armed conflict, this role will fall to the national law (including the military law) of the State concerned. It will be this body of law that will be able to impose the most immediate sanctions on his actions if they are considered by his superiors or by officials of the State to have infringed the law. Any investigations of his conduct are more likely to be held at this level (if held at all).[55] Depending on the law of the State concerned any trial will be by military court or by the national criminal courts. The rank of the soldier may be a relevant factor in the risk to him of an investigation or trial based on his military performance as the actual perpetrator of alleged breaches of the criminal law or of military orders[56] or through his command responsibility (however this is formulated) for such acts.

This, perhaps idealised, role of national law as a restraining influence during a non-international armed conflict may not be matched by reality, for a number of reasons. First, should the armed conflict continue for any length of time a blurring of what is acceptable conduct on the part of the armed forces of the State may occur. Revenge for the loss of colleagues, considered to have been killed 'unfairly', may lead to actions which might have been thought to have been unacceptable at the start of the conflict. Secondly, national law may be amended during the course of the conflict (unlike international humanitarian law). As the conflict increases in intensity the State may take greater powers of action though this law. It is likely to limit the rights of individuals under the relevant human rights instrument or to issue a derogation notice where this is permissible, from its international human rights obligations.[57] National leaders may see the 'risk' of human rights claims as being of a less immediate concern

---

[55] There are many examples of failures to investigate alleged breaches of the right to life or torture. For two examples see *Khashiyev and Akayeva* v. *Russia* (n. 54 above); *Urrutia* v. *Guatemala* (Inter-American Court of Human Rights), Judgment, 27 November 2003, para. 126.

[56] It is, of course, possible that the soldier's military orders may impose greater restraints upon his action than the criminal law actually requires.

[57] Although the Russian Federation did not do so in respect of the armed conflict in Chechnya, see *Isayeva* v. *Russia* (Application No. 57950/00, Judgment, 24 February 2005, para. 119). Any derogation notice must be consistent with the national law of that State, see HRC General Comment No. 29, para. 2. See generally, E/CN.4/2002/103, 20 December 2001, paras. 6–15. The national law must also be consistent with the power to derogate, CCPR/CO/79/LKA, 1 December 2003, para. 8.

than the defeat of the rebels.[58] They may take the view that, in order to achieve their object, national law should even go beyond that permitted by a relevant derogation notice.[59] This is more likely to be the case where international human rights treaty obligations have not been incorporated into the national law.[60]

Thirdly, the nature of national law will affect the soldier's obligation to obey military orders. The military law of the State concerned may provide that he is only required to obey orders which do not infringe national or (perhaps) international law, all other orders being illegal or it may provide that he must follow orders which, although illegal, are not manifestly so. Alternatively, it may give the soldier a complete defence to show he was acting on the order of a superior.[61] In the former case the extent of the national law will normally determine the legality of his actions. Where this permits wide forms of activities on the part of the armed forces, which would otherwise involve breaches of human rights, the scope for an illegal order (or one that is manifestly illegal) under national law is greatly restricted. Even if the chance of a soldier disobeying an order from his superior on the grounds that he considers it to be an unlawful order is, in reality, rare, the scope to do so on the part of the 'thinking soldier' is limited where the national law gives him such extensive powers.

---

[58] The government is likely to take the view that the 'rebels', whatever their purpose, are clothed with illegality to whom fewer 'rights' are owed than to its own legitimate armed forces. The nature of this emergency legislation may, in fact, give the armed forces a feeling of impunity for their actions. For an example, see *Mejía* v. *Peru*, Report No. 5/96, Case 10.970, 1 March 1996.

[59] See, for example, Russian Federation law applying in Chechnya, *Khashiyev and Akayeva* v. *Russia* (see n. 54 above) and, in particular, the national law right to detain individuals in order to determine their identity. Compare the European Convention for the Protection of Human Rights and Fundamental Freedoms, Rome, 4 November 1950, in force 3 September 1953, 213 UNTS 222, ('1950 Convention'), Art. 5, where no such right is given. No derogation was made by the Russian Federation to permit such action.

[60] In the United Kingdom, for instance, the treaty obligations under the 1950 Convention have been incorporated by the Human Rights Act 1998 but not the obligations accepted under the 1966 Covenant. For an example of where a State's 'legal system does not contain provisions which cover all substantive rights set forth in the Covenant', see CCPR/CO/79/LKA, 1 December 2003, para. 7. One practical example would be where the constitutional protections (which map onto the rights given by a human rights instrument) apply only to nationals. A further example might be whether a State party to the Inter-American Convention on Enforced Disappearances of Persons 1994 has implemented the proscription in Art. IX of the trial of soldiers by military jurisdiction for an alleged breach of acts prohibited by the Convention, although note the reservation made by Mexico.

[61] This will show the national law to be incompatible with Art. 2(3) of the Convention Against Torture 1984: see CAT/C/SR.377, 7 May 1999, para. 16.

Fourthly, national law operating through civilian courts, through courts-martial, military summary procedures or through investigations, will require some form of proof of an individual soldier's actions. To a civilian one soldier may look very similar to another. Unlike the police officer who may be identified through a number badge attached to his uniform a soldier will often carry no indicators of his name or even his unit. His identity may be deliberately concealed for some actual or purported[62] military security purpose. Not only will this make it difficult for a victim of the soldier's actions to identify his assailant but it can encourage in soldiers a feeling of anonymity and thus of impunity for their actions. Added to this problem is the psychology of military units and groupings, which cannot be ignored. It will often prove difficult to get one soldier to give evidence against another or to break the bond of loyalty within the group. This will especially be the case where casualties have been taken on their part.[63] Investigations may also be hampered through the absence of a *corpus delicti*, the death of witnesses, potential witnesses feeling intimidated from bringing a complaint,[64] or where soldiers claim to have made a mistake of fact.[65]

Further problems arise in those States where any allegation against a member of the armed forces can only be investigated by the military themselves and any trial of a soldier can take place only before a military court. This is more likely to arise where emergency legislation is in force. The consequence of this arrangement was explained in *Mejía* v. *Peru*[66] where

---

[62] See, for example, *Mejía* v. *Peru*, Report No. 5/96, Case 10.970, 1 March 1996, which involved the use of 'military personnel with their faces covered by ski masks' to abduct an individual.

[63] Despite a 'high incidence of fatalities' the obligation to ensure an effective investigation is not displaced, *Ergi* v. *Turkey* [2001] 32 EHRR 18, para. 85; *Ozkan* v. *Turkey*, Application. No. 21689/93, Judgment, 6 April 2004, para. 319. See, generally, S. Noy, 'Combat Stress', p. 513. It also helps to explain the pattern of acquittals by military courts of soldiers alleged to have killed civilians.

[64] See, for example, CCPR/CO/79/LKA, 1 December 2003, para. 9. Any investigation must deal with the possibility of ethnic prejudice by soldiers against the victim, *Nachova* v. *Bulgaria* (2004) 39 EHRR 37, para. 157.

[65] It is in the nature of this type of conflict that the probability of an individual soldier facing death in military operations is high. A mistake of fact, such as a sudden movement from an unexpected source, might result in him being killed. It is, perhaps, understandable that the individual soldier is unwilling to take this risk. In these situations the chance of an innocent person being killed by the soldier is at its highest. Alternatively, soldiers may assert that the victims were 'guerrillas killed in combat' when the evidence suggests otherwise, see Report No. 23/93, Case 10.456 (Columbia), 12 October 1993, para. 3.

[66] See n. 62 above. The case has been determined by the Inter-American Court of Human Rights as *Lori Berenson Mejía* v. *Peru*, 25 November 2004, in Spanish only. See also Report No. 23/93, Case 10.456 (n. 65 above); Report No. 15/95, Case 11.010 (Columbia),

the Inter-American Commission on Human Rights concluded that 'in virtually no case are individuals accused of sexual abuse and other serious human rights violations convicted'. As a result of the de facto control of the armed forces in an area subject to emergency powers the civil authorities and courts may be powerless to act. It is not unnatural, therefore, that individual soldiers may feel that they can act with impunity and that victims of human rights breaches have no effective remedy through these military procedures. It is, however, dangerous to draw the conclusion from this that the trial of soldiers by military courts for serious human rights abuses will always infringe human rights standards. The Inter-American Commission was concerned with the use of military courts in the circumstances it was considering. Depending on the circumstances there is no logical reason why a military court could not provide an effective trial of a soldier alleged to have committed serious human rights breaches and provide an effective remedy to the victim of his actions.[67]

The scope of national law, modified as necessary by emergency legislation, may be extremely important in determining whether an applicant who has a right to make an individual application to a human rights body has exhausted all domestic remedies. In a number of cases before the European Court of Human Rights the respondent State has been able to argue that national law provides for adequate remedies but the applicant has not exhausted them and, in consequence, the application is inadmissible. The applicant, in turn, will argue that the national law cannot in practice provide a remedy since, for instance, no investigation has been held into deaths allegedly carried out by soldiers.[68] It is well established,

---

13 September 1995, para. D3; *Mapiripan Massacre (Columbia)* Report No. 33/01, Case 12.250, 22 February 2001, paras. 33, 34; *Riofrio Massacre (Columbia)* Report No. 62/01, Case 11.654, 6 April 2001, para. 71; *Durand and Ugarte*, Judgment of 16 August 2000, paras. 117–18 (Inter-American Court of Human Rights); *Amnesty International et al.* v. *Sudan*, Communication No. 48/90, para. 51. For further discussion of this issue see chapter 5.

[67] See the discussion in chapter 4 of the trial of civilians by military courts. Nor should it be thought that concern over human rights in military courts during an armed conflict is centred only around civilians, see *Amnesty International et al.* v. *Sudan*, Communication No. 48/90, para. 66 (execution of soldiers who were denied legal representation). Military courts are, however, an inappropriate forum for holding those to account for enforced disappearances, Declaration on the Protection of All Persons from Enforced Disappearances, UNGA Resolution 47/133, 18 December 1992, Art. 16(2).

[68] See *Durand and Ugarte*, Judgment of 16 August 2000, paras. 125, 126; *Khashiyev and Akayeva* v. *Russia* (see note 57 above); *Abella* v. *Argentina*, Report No. 55/97, Case 11.137, 18 November 1997, para. 410; *Dermit Barbato* v. *Uruquay*, Communication No. 84/1981 at para. 9.6.

however, that an application will not be ruled inadmissible on this ground if the so-called remedy is likely to be ineffective or proceedings would be likely to have no prospect of success.[69] The State may establish a human rights body, to enable it to monitor alleged human rights abuses and to provide 'educational activities'.[70]

The right to life

There is, at the time of writing, no precedent for the issue of a deroga-tion notice from the right to life under the 1950 Convention, although derogations have been made in respect of other rights.[71] In the absence of such a derogation a killing by soldiers (or anyone) can therefore only be justified if the force used was 'absolutely necessary' for one of the pur-poses set out in Article 2(2)(a), (b) or (c). Although the grounds upon which a derogation notice can be issued would apply equally to the right to life as they do to the right of liberty and security any derogation from the former requires the acts to be justified in accordance with 'lawful acts of war'.[72] There is no reason why such a derogation notice could not be issued, especially in the light of the Rome Statute 1998 which makes it a war crime to act in one of the prohibited ways during a non-international armed conflict. There is, therefore, a sufficient argument to show that where a killing was caused during a non-international armed conflict in a way not prohibited by the 1998 Statute it should be classified as a 'lawful act of war'.[73]

It has been shown above[74] that the test for a breach of the right to life under the 1966 Covenant is whether the taking of life during an armed conflict is 'arbitrary'. International humanitarian law is the *lex specialis* to

---

[69] An alternative formulation is that the remedy must be 'adequate and efficacious', *Mejía* v. *Peru* (n. 58 above); *Abubakar* v. *Ghana*, No. 103/93, para. 6, or that it must be 'available, effective and sufficient', *Sir Dawda Jawara* v. *The Gambia* (African Commission on Human and Peoples' Rights), Communication No. 147/95 and 149/95, 11 May 2000, para. 31. For the 'ineffectiveness of the habeas corpus remedy in Honduras' see *Juan Sanchez Case* (n. 10 above), para. 123.

[70] See CCPR/CO/79/LKA, 1 December 2003 (Sri Lanka), para. 4; CCPR/C/81/Add.12, 23 September 1998, (Cambodia) para. 27.

[71] Both the United Kingdom and Turkey have issued derogation notices at various times.

[72] The 1950 Convention, Art. 15.

[73] This is, it is suggested, a practical suggestion since to argue that, nevertheless, the act of killing was unlawful according to the Marten's Clause or through the application of Additional Protocol II 1977, Preamble would create too much uncertainty.

[74] Chapter 5. Decisions of the European Court of Human Rights, such as *McCann* v. *United Kingdom* (1995) 21 EHRR 97, may be helpful in deciding whether a killing was 'arbitrary'.

determine whether a killing is arbitrary. Although this view was set out in the *Legality of the Threat or Use of Nuclear Weapons* Advisory Opinion of the International Court of Justice in 1996[75] and that Court was considering the situation during an international armed conflict, logic and practicality would suggest that no such distinction should be made between these different types of armed conflict.

The opposite argument is that a breach of international humanitarian law applying to a non-international armed conflict could not amount to the 'lawful conduct' of war and would therefore be 'arbitrary'.[76] It would therefore amount to a breach of the right to life. The difficulty in this type of conflict is to determine what method or means of fighting is prohibited if the only individuals involved are soldiers and rebels. It seems clear now that for one of the fighters to kill or wound by resort to treachery or to order that no quarter will be given will be a war crime.[77] In this respect the prohibited methods of conflict applying in this type of conflict are considerably inferior to those applying in an international armed conflict. Whilst it may be interesting to speculate whether the use during a non-international armed conflict of a chemical weapon against other 'combatants'[78] would infringe international humanitarian law[79] in the absence of a specific prohibition to this effect in the Rome Statute 1998[80] the more practical issue is the use of anti-personnel mines.

---

[75] [1996] ICJ Reports 265 at para. 25. For the practical advantages to this approach see Columbia Report 1999 (n. 3 above), para. 12; Report No. 26/97, Case 11.142, 30 September 1997 (Columbia), para. 168.

[76] Arbitrary in the sense of being 'capricious' or 'irregular'.

[77] The Rome Statute 1998, Art. 8(2)(e)(ix), (x). For States not party to the Statute this provision may reflect customary international law. See generally, J.-M. Henckaerts and L. Doswald-Beck (eds.), *Customary International Humanitarian Law* (3 vols., Cambridge: Cambridge University Press, 2005). For an example of the use of a grenade placed on the corpse of a soldier who had been killed, see *Third Report on the Human Rights Situation in Columbia* (n. 3 above), para. 34.

[78] This term is used in the Rome Statute 1998, Art. 8(2)(e)(ix) and should be distinguished from a combatant in Additional Protocol I 1977, Art. 43(2). In the light of the fact that a combatant under the latter instrument has 'the *right* to participate directly in hostilities' whereas an individual has no such right to do so if the armed conflict is a non-international one it is strange that the same noun should be used to describe two quite distinct classes of individual under international law.

[79] See the discussion by Judge Cassese in *Prosecutor* v. *Tadic* (1995) Appeals Chamber, IT-94-1-AR 72, 2 October 1995, paras. 120–4 (1996) 35 ILM 35, who considered the use by the Iraqi armed forces of chemical weapons against its own nationals in 1988. This was clearly an attack on civilians taking no direct part in hostilities.

[80] Compare Art. 8(2)(b)(xviii) applying during an international armed conflict.

Use of these mines is widespread in this type of conflict. They provide a cheap and effective means for one side to try to prevent encroachment by the other into territory they control. For this reason it is not difficult to see why they are attractive to the rebels,[81] in particular, but they may also be to the armed forces. Where the State is a party to one of the relevant treaties[82] there will be restrictions on their use during a non-international armed conflict or a complete prohibition on their use (depending on which treaty applies). In this type of armed conflict it would appear that their use (certainly by soldiers) in some types of location would be unlawful if the effect of their detonation would be indiscriminate.[83] Where the State is not a party to either of these treaties reliance would need to be placed upon customary international law to determine whether their use would be unlawful and would, in consequence, make any killing by this method a breach of the right to life even of 'combatants'.

In the absence of an appropriate derogation notice killing by soldiers of individuals during a non-international armed conflict may occur in a variety of situations, some of which will be similar to the type of combat which takes place during an international conflict.[84] An attack by soldiers on rebels, or vice versa, may not look to the outsider as any different from an attack by members of the armed forces of one State against their counterparts of another State, except for the clothing worn by the rebels. Soldiers may kill the rebels (those who have taken an active or direct part in hostilities[85]) both under international humanitarian law;[86] by doing so they will not be in breach of the right to life of those rebels. This latter proposition is not, however, free of doubt under the 1950 Convention.[87]

---

[81] See below for a discussion of the applicability to the rebels of international humanitarian law and of human rights treaties to which the State is a party.

[82] See the Amended Protocol II (to the Conventional Weapons Convention 1980) on Prohibitions or Restrictions on the Use of Mines, Booby-Traps and Other Devices, 1996; the Ottawa Convention on the Prohibition of the Use, Stockpiling, Production and Transfer of Anti-Personnel Mines and on their Destruction 1997.

[83] Amended Protocol II 1996, Art. 3(8). This Protocol includes booby-traps and other devices.

[84] There can, of course, be a number of breaches of a human rights treaty from, for example, the extra-judicial execution of those not taking part in the conflict, see *Riofrio Massacre (Columbia)* Report No. 62/01, Case 11.654, 6 April 2001; *Myrna Chang Case* (Inter-American Court of Human Rights) (2003) Ser. C, No. 101, para. 158.

[85] '[w]hich practically speaking, means assuming the role of a combatant, either individually or as a member of a group', *Saavedra v. Peru*, Report No. 38/97, Case 10.548, 16 October 1997 at para. 61.

[86] As long as the killing does not occur in the ways prohibited by the Rome Statute 1998, Art. 8(2)(d)(ix) or (x) or under customary international law.

[87] Article 2(2)(a), (b) and (c), in the absence of a suitable derogation notice.

THE RIGHT TO LIFE

It has been argued above that international humanitarian law does not draw any distinction, in this area, between government forces and rebels. Any use of force by either group would be judged on the same legal basis. Unlike, therefore, national law which does draw such a distinction, the use of armed force by the rebels is not unlawful *per se* at the international humanitarian law level. It will, however, be unlawful at the national law level. Through its use of the terms 'lawfully' and 'unlawfully' Article 2(2) of the 1950 Convention must be referring to a test of lawfulness judged at the national law level. This is, of course, consistent with the principle that national law will continue to apply during a non-international armed conflict and that the rebels are not on an equal legal basis with soldiers. The effect of this is that soldiers may lawfully kill rebels where they are engaged in a fight with lethal weapons and where the method of killing is not prohibited but that rebels may not lawfully kill soldiers in this situation.

In terms of human rights this may be of theoretical significance only since a State will, generally, not be responsible for the actions of rebels in killing its soldiers.[88]

It is likely that the majority of individuals killed by soldiers will not involve a soldiers versus rebels firefight. Soldiers may attack what they understand or suspect to be rebel bases[89] by long range munitions, by aircraft,[90] by mortar fire or by other means not involving close contact fighting. It is unlikely,[91] for instance, that laser-guided or other 'smart' weapons will be used in these circumstances. The risk of killing civilians

---

[88] Though compare *Osman* v. *United Kingdom* (2002) 35 EHRR 19 at para. 116; *Cyprus* v. *Turkey* (2002) 35 EHRR 35 at para. 81; *Z et al.* v. *United Kingdom* (2002) 34 EHRR 3 (State liable for ill-treatment of children by their parents). In the *Third Report on the Human Rights Situation in Columbia*, OEA/Ser.L/V/II.102 Doc. 9 rev. 1, 26 February 1999, the Inter-American Commission on Human Rights considered that the Columbian Government would be responsible for the actions of certain paramilitary groups if their illicit acts were 'acquiesced in, condoned or tolerated by the State' (para. 234) or 'when it fails to take reasonable measures to prevent the violation, or subsequently, to investigate and sanction those responsible for the harm caused' (para. 272). See also the Declaration on the Protection of all Persons from Enforced Disappearances, UNGA Resolution 47/133 of 18 December 1992, Art. 5. This was the case in Columbia, certainly in the 1970s and 1980s, where 'State officials supported the growth of the paramilitaries as a means of fighting the armed dissident groups': para. 237. The State may still be required to investigate deaths caused by rebels, *Ergi* v. *Turkey* [2001] 32 EHRR 18, para. 82.

[89] This is taken to refer to what would amount to a military objective (Additional Protocol I 1977, Art. 52), if the armed conflict was of an international type.

[90] See, for example, the *Third Report on the Human Rights Situation in Columbia*, OEA/Ser.L/V/II.102, 26 February 1999, para. 204.

[91] Largely for reasons of lack of availability and cost.

who are not taking any part in the hostilities is much greater in this situation. Although the principle of proportion in attack, as seen through the particular requirements of Article 51(5)(b) in Additional Protocol I 1977 has not been formally[92] translated into a non-international armed conflict it is likely that it would, nevertheless, apply. This would ensure that, at least under the 1966 Covenant, an attack on what is clearly a rebel stronghold which caused the death of a 'proportionate'[93] number of civilians who were not taking part in the hostilities would not be considered as an 'arbitrary' deprivation of life.

The position under the 1950 Convention is more problematic. Since Article 2(2) was envisaged as dealing with individual attempts to enforce the national law it can hardly have imagined an attack by a State's soldiers using, for instance, an attack helicopter on a rebel base. It takes some strain of language to be satisfied that any of the purposes for which lethal force may be used under Article 2(2) would be met in this situation or that the force was 'absolutely necessary' to achieve one of these purposes. Any deprivation of life could fall foul of this Article even if it was caused unintentionally.[94] Where the armed forces attacked the stronghold by way of a surprise operation with the assistance of an attack helicopter or long-range munitions the burden would be on them to show that one of the relevant purposes of Article 2(2) applied both as regards the death of rebels and those not taking any part in the hostilities, even though the attack might be justified under international humanitarian law.

The reach of the 1950 Convention extends to those who planned the operation as well as to those who carried it out. It may therefore be a breach of the Convention if the planning of the raid on the rebel base did not include some alternative means of securing the captivity of the rebels[95] or if it did not consider the type of weapons to be issued to the soldiers to prevent loss of life to innocent bystanders.[96] Should the circumstances

---

[92] Although see Additional Protocol II 1977, Arts. 14–16.

[93] The killing of civilians during an attack on a military objective during the course of an international armed conflict will not infringe international humanitarian law if it was not expected that such losses would occur and which losses were not 'excessive in relation to the concrete and direct military advantage anticipated': Additional Protocol I 1977, Art. 51(5)(b).

[94] *Stewart* v. *United Kingdom* (1984) 39 DR 162 at para. 15 (European Commission on Human Rights). This case involved Art. 2(2)(c) by the killing of a person through the use of a baton round by a soldier to quell 'a riot'.

[95] See *McCann* v. *United Kingdom* (1996) 21 EHRR 97; *Nachova* v. *Bulgaria* (2004) 39 EHRR 37.

[96] *Ergi* v. *Turkey* (2001) 32 EHRR 18; *Gul* v. *Turkey* (2002) 34 EHRR 28.

suggest that the attack was carried out in circumstances that no quarter was to be given the conclusion could be drawn that such an attack would also breach international humanitarian law.[97] The liability of the State for breach of the human rights of those killed may attach not because of the actions of the soldiers on the ground but through those who were involved in its planning or through those who gave the orders or instructions or even the training to the soldiers.[98]

Civilians may often be killed through a failure by soldiers to distinguish them from rebels. Attacks on villages in rural areas and shootings at roadblocks form the background of many particular instances.[99] It will be much easier to show a breach of international humanitarian law and of human rights where a suspected rebel is killed whilst in the hands of soldiers after having been captured.[100] Summary execution can, in some States, become very common.

The European Court of Human Rights (along with other human rights bodies) has shown how important it considers investigations to be into the deaths of individuals at the hands of State authorities as a means of ensuring accountability for their actions.[101] It also expects these to be carried out independently of those alleged to have been involved and at the instigation of State authorities and not merely as a result of action on behalf of a victim.[102]

---

[97] The Rome Statute 1998, Art. 8(2)(e)(x).

[98] In which case the training records might prove to be of significance. I am grateful to Professor Françoise Hampson for drawing my attention to this point.

[99] See, for example, *Third Report on the Human Rights Situation in Columbia*, OEA/Ser.l/V/II.102 Doc. 9 rev. 1, 26 February 1999, para. 190.

[100] A breach of the Geneva Conventions 1949, common Art. 3, may be committed where a rebel has laid down his arms or is *hors de combat*; Additional Protocol II 1977, Art. 4. See, for example, the *Third Report on the Human Rights Situation in Columbia*, 1999 (n. 3 above), para. 196. See also *Abella* v. *Argentina* (see n. 68 above) and *Khashiyev and Akayeva* v. *Russia* (n. 57 above); *Guerrero* v. *Columbia*, Report No. 61/99, Case 11.519, 13 April 1999 at para. 34 and note the attempt to make the victims look as if they had been 'combatants' at paras. 35 and 36.

[101] See, for example, *McKerr* v. *United Kingdom* (2002) 34 EHRR 20 at para. 109. At a practical level the State authorities will need to show (should an application be made in the appropriate forum in connection with a breach of the human rights of the victim) that a full autopsy was carried out and that the records of this are available. I am grateful to Professor Françoise Hampson for drawing my attention to this point.

[102] *McKerr* v. *United Kingdom, ibid.*, para. 112. See, generally, C. Warbrick, 'The Principles of the European Convention on Human Rights and the Response of States to Terrorism' (2002) *European Human Rights Law Review* 287, 293–4. Where death has been caused the family of the deceased are treated as the victim, *Mejía* v. *Peru* (n. 58 above); *Juan Sanchez Case* (n. 36 above) para. 101.

These principles may be practical in the circumstances of the decisions made by the Court, namely, the deaths of one, or a relatively small number of individuals as a result of the action of soldiers. Where the number of deaths increase substantially as a result of the action of the armed forces during a non-international armed conflict practical problems arise, as they would if the armed conflict was of an international character. Thus, establishing the identities of those killed during an attack on a rebel base or determining whether a particular dead person had been taking part in the conflict or was an innocent victim may prove difficult. Added to this may be a reluctance on the part of the victim's family to report the death or disappearance of a family member for fear of being considered to be involved themselves in the conflict. This is not, however, to suggest that this procedure is always impractical or that it cannot provide some form of accountability on the part of the armed forces in respect of their actions. There will, no doubt, be circumstances where it will work effectively but in others investigators may not be able to establish, with a sufficient degree of proof, the facts of a particular event.

In any event, the holding of an effective investigation presupposes that the investigators, or those to whom they report, will be sufficiently independent of mind to pursue prosecutions or other disciplinary measures against the soldiers involved. In an extreme case this may be so but, in practice, few proceedings will be brought against individual soldiers. This may be due to incompetence on the part of the investigators or prosecutors but may also be due to political and psychological factors. The armed conflict may be seen from the standpoint of the armed forces[103] as a 'dirty war' namely, one in which soldiers are killed or wounded through treachery or perfidy and rarely through what might be considered as a 'fair fight'. In these circumstances, maintaining the morale of soldiers will be considered essential to ensure defeat of the rebels. Pejorative terms are likely to be applied to the rebels (of which 'terrorist' might be the mildest) especially if they are drawn from a different ethnic group. A system of 'body counts' may also be introduced with the efficiency (and resultant status) of particular units being measured against them. In these circumstances the reluctance to prosecute individual soldiers may be understandable, although undesirable. The relative control over the armed conflict between politicians on the one hand and senior military commanders on the other hand may explain in some conflicts why the balance of accountability swings

---

[103] It is, perhaps, inevitable that the civilians will also see it in this way as a result of the actions of the armed forces.

one way or the other. At one extreme is a military dictatorship where accountability for deaths may be weakest and at the other an established democracy where the politicians are keen to maintain control over the armed forces and the way in which the conflict is being fought. Effective investigations into the deaths of individuals are more likely in the latter than in the former, although the factors mentioned above cannot be completely ignored whatever the form of government.[104]

A State which has abolished the death penalty, as a result of becoming a party to a particular human rights treaty, may restore it in the circumstances provided by that treaty. This topic is discussed more fully in chapter 5 but a particular issue arises in connection with a non-international armed conflict. This is whether such a conflict can be considered as coming within the term 'war' or 'wartime' justifying a restoration of capital punishment for a 'most serious crime of a military nature'.[105] To invoke this provision a State must have provided for it in its law and, depending upon the human rights instrument involved, have so provided at ratification of, or accession to, it.[106] A State which has not abolished the death penalty cannot derogate, for instance, from the fair trial provisions in the 1966 Covenant in order to secure a conviction leading to the death penalty being imposed.[107]

The right to life may also be breached where the armed forces place restrictions on food supplies reaching an area in which rebels are considered to be located.[108]

---

[104] See *Khashiyev and Akasheva v. Russia* (n. 57 above); *Isayeva v. Russia* (Application No. 57950/00), 24 February 2005, para. 224. A Russian colonel was placed on trial for the murder of a Chechen woman but was found to be insane at the time of the killing, see *The Times*, 17 December 2002.

[105] See the discussion above of applying the term 'war' to a non-international armed conflict under the 1950 Convention, Art. 15. For human rights treaties involving the death penalty see Second Optional Protocol (1990) to the 1966 Covenant, Art. 2; Sixth Protocol 1983 to the 1950 Convention, Art. 2; Protocol to the American Convention on Human Rights to Abolish the Death Penalty 1990, Art. 2. Compare Protocol 13 to the Convention for the Protection of Human Rights and Fundamental Freedoms, Concerning the Abolition of the Death Penalty in all Circumstances 2002 to which no reservations or derogations are permitted.

[106] Compare the Optional Protocol 1990 and the Protocol of 1990 on the one hand with the Sixth Protocol 1983 on the other.

[107] General Comment No. 29 (n. 20 above), para. 15; General Comment No. 6, para. 7; see also Economic and Social Council Resolution 1984/50, 25 May 1984, para. 5.

[108] See the *Third Report on the Human Rights Situation in Columbia* 1999 (n. 3 above), at para. 232 (although the Commission was unable to draw any firm conclusions on this alleged practice).

Torture, inhuman or degrading treatment

At least one form of this breach of human rights is, perhaps, more likely to occur in the course of a non-international armed conflict than in its international variant. Those who have been captured by soldiers and who are suspected of some involvement in the armed conflict are not entitled to prisoner of war status, with which is attached a right not to be coerced into giving any form of information.[109] Those captured in a non-international armed conflict may find themselves held for questioning and they may be prosecuted, depending on the national law, not merely for acts alleged against them but also for failing to supply information.[110] It does not follow that individuals held in these circumstances will be tortured or be subjected to inhuman or degrading treatment. Practice, however, suggests otherwise in a number of cases.[111] In this type of conflict defeat of the rebels is unlikely to take place on a battlefield. It will depend, to a greater or lesser extent, upon obtaining information as to who is involved (particularly the leaders) and their subsequent arrest.[112]

Both international humanitarian law[113] and human rights law prohibit conduct of this kind, from which no derogation is permitted. Those held

---

[109] The third Geneva Convention 1949, Art. 17.

[110] The European Court of Human Rights has been concerned with the claim that a defendant has been compelled to answer questions, see *Saunders* v. *United Kingdom* (1996) 23 EHRR 313, para. 76.

[111] For an analysis of the meaning of 'inhuman' and 'degrading' treatment within the 1950 Convention, see *Ilascu* v. *Moldova and Russia*, Judgment, 8 July 2004, paras. 425–33; *Ocalan* v. *Turkey* (2003) 37 EHRR 10, para. 220 and for its application to handcuffing and blindfolding, see paras. 221–4; for failure to get medical treatment after the applicant was struck by a rifle butt see *Ilhan* v. *Turkey* (2002) 34 EHRR 36, para. 87. For the reclassification of 'torture' as compared with 'degrading' or 'inhuman' treatment see *Selmouni* v. *France* (2000) 29 EHRR 403 at para. 101. For an analysis of 'psychological torture' and 'mental violence' see *Urrutia* v. *Guatemala* (Inter-American Court of Human Rights), 27 November 2003 at para. 92.

[112] See, for example, *Bamaca Velasquez* v. *Guatemala* (2001) 22 *Human Rights Law Journal* 367 at para. 121. The Israeli High Court of Justice decided in 1999 that the Israeli Security Agency was 'no longer authorized . . . to employ certain investigation methods that involve the use of physical pressure against such a suspect': CCPR/C/ISR/2001/2, 4 December 2001, para. 83. It is, however, possible for an interrogator to set up a defence of necessity, CCPR/C/ISR/2001/2, para. 86.

[113] The Geneva Conventions 1949, common Art. 3; Additional Protocol II 1977, Art. 4. Such conduct would also amount to a war crime: see the Rome Statute 1998, Art. 8(2)(c) for States party to this treaty. The definition of torture appears to differ between international humanitarian law and human rights law, see *Prosecutor* v. *Kunarac*, International Criminal Tribunal for the Former Yugoslavia, Trial Chamber, 22 February 2001 at para. 496 (a point not altered on appeal in this case). Its definition in national law may not be identical with that under an international instrument. For an example see CAT/C/47/Add.3, 16 July 2001, para. 69.

in detention can look for some surveillance of their treatment to the International Committee of the Red Cross, which may offer its services to the parties to the conflict[114] or to one of the anti-torture committees established by treaty.[115] Where an individual has been released or where his family know[116] of his treatment an application (where possible) under a relevant human rights treaty may be appropriate. This latter course of action may cause the government, who will be notified of the application, to make inquiries about a particular individual being held by its police or armed forces. Depending on the view taken by government officials of the importance of human rights complaints in individual cases there is the possibility of action being taken by them at a time when some difference in the form of treatment can be made. This may, however, be a counsel of perfection since torture, degrading or inhuman treatment may be occurring on a scale too great for individual petitions to be brought before a human rights body.[117] It may be that the individual does not possess a right of individual petition or complaint against his or her State so that, in such cases, inter-State action before that body or the invocation of universal jurisdiction may be necessary.[118]

It is not uncommon for the armed forces to require one of their medical officers to examine a detained person to determine whether he is fit to be

---

[114] Geneva Conventions 1949, common Art. 3(2).

[115] In addition to the 1950 Convention, the 1966 Covenant, the Human Rights Committee and Commission, see: the Convention Against Torture and Other Cruel, Inhuman or Degrading Treatment or Punishment 1984; its Optional Protocol, 2002; the European Convention for the Prevention of Torture and Inhuman or Degrading Treatment or Punishment, 1987. These processes depend upon the State co-operating with the relevant Committee. For the problem faced by the European Committee for the Prevention of Torture in Chechnya, see Council of Europe Parliamentary Assembly Resolution 1323 (2003) para. 7. See, generally, N. Rodley, *The Treatment of Prisoners under International Law* (2nd edn, Oxford: Oxford University Press, 1999).

[116] A frequent problem is that relatives are denied information as to the location of their family member and are unable to visit him to see or to hear how he has been treated. In a number of cases he may have 'disappeared' in which governmental authorities deny any knowledge of his whereabouts. See, generally, Declaration on the Protection of All Persons from Enforced Disappearances, UNGA Resolution 47/133, 18 December 1992; Inter-American Convention on the Forced Disappearance of Persons 1994; Columbia Report 1999 (n. 3 above) para. 30; *Cea* v. *El Salvador*, Report No. 1/95, Case 10.480, 27 January 1999, para. 114; *Velasquez Rodriguez* Case, Judgment, Inter-American Court of Human Rights, Ser. C., No. 4, 29 July 1988, para. 149.

[117] See the Council of Europe Parliamentary Assembly, Resolution 1323 (2003) para. 7 (relating to Chechnya).

[118] *Ibid.*, para. 10. Compare CCPR/C/78/D/950/2000, 31 July 2003, para. 9.5, where the Human Rights Committee upheld a communication made under the Optional Protocol to the 1966 Covenant to the effect that the forced disappearance of the complainant's son in Sri Lanka amounted to a breach of Art. 7.

'interrogated'. The medical officer, in these circumstances may be faced with a conflict between his military obligations to obey his military superiors and his ethical duties as a medical practitioner. Depending on the nature of the conflict or civil disorder and the practice of the armed forces concerned a doctor may well foresee that his 'patient' will be subjected to torture, degrading or inhuman treatment in the hands of the soldiers 'interrogating' him or at least that his physical or mental health will be adversely affected. It seems likely that, in these circumstances, the medical officer will be in breach of his medical ethics.[119] The (armed forces) group psychology should not be overlooked as a motive for any failure to act as a medical practitioner. Should he be concerned he may take the view that this dilemma can only be resolved by obeying his military orders (if given by someone senior in rank to himself) since punishment for not doing so may be much more immediate than the possibility of being the subject of disciplinary proceedings brought by his medical governing body.

The right to liberty

The right to liberty can be made the subject of derogation in all human rights instruments. It has been shown that a derogation notice must be issued to the appropriate body or person under the human rights treaty arrangements and will not be implied from the circumstances. It may be challenged on the basis that it does not match the requirements in the relevant human rights instrument for a derogation or that its terms are not 'strictly required by the exigencies of the situation'.[120] It is unlikely that a responsible State will derogate from the whole of the relevant human rights provision relating to detention or deprivation of liberty but it may do so to deal with particular difficulties that it is facing during the armed conflict.[121] For the purposes of this section it will be assumed that the State concerned in the armed conflict has made no derogation.

---

[119] Principles of Medical Ethics relevant to the Role of Health Personnel, Particularly Physicians, in the Protection of Prisoners and Detainees against Torture and Other Cruel, Inhuman or Degrading Treatment or Punishment, UNGA Resolution 37/194, 18 December 1982.

[120] The 1966 Covenant, Art. 4; 1950 Convention, Art. 15; American Convention on Human Rights, San José, 22 November 1969, in force 18 July 1978 (1970) 9 ILM 673, Art. 27. For an example, see *Aksoy* v. *Turkey* [1997] 23 EHRR 553, para. 86.

[121] Compare *A and others* v. *Secretary of State for the Home Department* [2005] 2 AC 68 where no armed conflict was in existence.

It will be recalled that national law will continue to apply during a non-international armed conflict and that those who are detained by State authorities are not entitled[122] to be treated as prisoners of war. There are likely, therefore, to be a large number of individuals detained in prisons or other places designed for the detention of alleged or convicted criminals for alleged breaches of national law during the conflict.

A particular problem faced by soldiers who have detained a person suspected of being involved in the conflict is whether they can hold him for as long as necessary to establish his identity for the purposes of determining whether he has been involved in hostilities at some stage. The 1950 Convention does not permit detention for this reason alone.[123] Other human rights instruments are equivocal and would seem to allow it if it is lawful in the national law. The 1950 Convention also requires a person detained for the purpose of placing him on trial to be brought promptly before a judge or other officer exercising judicial power to determine the lawfulness of his detention.[124] Assuming that a judge or other appropriate officer[125] is available to determine the lawfulness of the detention, the Court has determined that the period of detention before appearance before the judicial officer should be measured in hours. A State requiring a longer time to comply with such requirements will need to issue a derogation notice.[126]

In so far as individuals are detained following conviction by a competent court there will be no breach of their human rights. The difficulty

---

[122] A State may detain rebels as prisoners of war and accord to them the benefits of the third Geneva Convention 1949 if it wishes. Political reasons will, however, often compel their treatment in detention according to the national law of the State and not as prisoners of war. See, however, the special agreement (1992) made under Common Art. 3 to the Geneva Conventions 1949, discussed by Judge Cassese in *Prosecutor* v. *Tadic*, Appeals Chamber, IT-94-AR 72, 2 October 1995, para. 136, (1996) ILM 35.

[123] Article 5.

[124] Article 5(3). For an example under the America Convention 1969 see the assessment of the 'arbitrary detention' by the El Salvador Army of individuals, in *Cea* v. *El Salvador*, Report No. 1/99, Case 10.480, 27 January 1999 at para. 101.

[125] Such an individual must at least offer the guarantees of independence and impartiality expected of judicial officers. A soldier's commanding officer could not perform this function in relation to a disciplinary offence since he was also responsible for discipline, see Chapter 3 and *Jordan* v. *United Kingdom* (2001) 31 EHRR 6.

[126] See the derogation notice of the United Kingdom, dated 23 March 1998, in which detention for a period of up to five days was contained within the law of the United Kingdom's Prevention of Terrorism (Temporary Provisions) Act 1984, s. 12, all of which are set out in the Human Rights Act 1998, Schedule 3. For the derogation issued by Turkey in 1990 see *Aksoy* v. *Turkey* [1997] 23 EHRR 553, para. 31 and for its non-application to detention for fourteen days without judicial supervision, para. 84.

here is that this court may be a military one, established in consequence of the armed conflict[127] or be an existing military court whose jurisdiction is drawn in such a way as to encompass civilian defendants. The issue of whether a military court established to try civilians will fall foul of human rights instruments is discussed in chapter 4. Under international humanitarian law a State is obliged to ensure a form of trial procedures not dissimilar to those applying by way of human rights instruments.[128]

It is not unknown during non-international armed conflicts for individuals to be detained by the military authorities without any form of proper judicial assessment of the lawfulness of the detention. A particular problem is that of disappearances where individuals are detained by military authorities (or the police) and are never heard of again. Since there may be no records of individual cases there is no accountability on the part of the military authorities for their actions against these individuals, whose fate invariably involves summary execution. The International Committee of the Red Cross is likely to wish to play a role in observing conditions of detention, monitoring the records of individuals (including passing on of messages to their families) and, where necessary, putting pressure on the State to comply with (at least) the minimum conditions of detention.[129] Whilst the International Committee of the Red Cross will normally act on a confidential basis towards the State[130] concerned human rights organisations often take the view that world publicity of the situation of detainees is equally effective in putting pressure on the State to comply with its human rights obligations.

Right to a fair trial

Under international humanitarian law the right to a fair trial during a non-international armed conflict is similar to the human rights standards. Whilst common Article 3 to the Geneva Conventions 1949 directs

---

[127] It may, for instance, be styled a 'security' court or some similar phrase but include in its membership members of the armed forces.

[128] See Additional Protocol II 1977, Art. 6. This Article also requires a court to 'offer the essential guarantees of independence and impartiality'.

[129] These minimum conditions may be drawn from international humanitarian law or from human rights law although, strictly, the mandate of the International Committee of the Red Cross (ICRC) to act internationally is given by the Geneva Conventions 1949 and their Additional Protocols of 1977.

[130] See, however, the statements of the ICRC concerning the detainees at Guantanamo Bay on their website, www.icrc.org

that the court should be 'regularly constituted' Additional Protocol II 1977 requires it to offer the 'essential guarantees of independence and impartiality'.[131] Where a court is shown to be both independent from the executive (in its various forms) and impartial the basic ingredients of a fair trial are likely to be present even if the court is a military one or is a mixed military and civilian court. As a means of offering protection to those placed on trial for activities connected with the conflict these norms will be of little value unless they have been included, in some form, within the national law of the State. Since a State may not have foreseen the possibility of a non-international armed conflict occurring on its territory the implementation of Additional Protocol II 1977 may have been ignored. The obligations owed by the State under the relevant human rights instrument will apply in all circumstances, unless an appropriate derogation has been made. It is likely, however, that the right to a fair trial given by a human rights instrument will continue to apply to detainees during a non-international armed conflict. There would be little point in a State issuing a derogation notice to the effect that it could not comply with the obligation to provide an independent and impartial tribunal since this requirement is also present in Additional Protocol II 1977 (assuming the State is a party) and a derogation notice must not be inconsistent with the State's other obligations under international law.[132]

Where, however, the State may have a difficulty is in the structure of the fact-finding process. Should this normally be by a jury of lay people an issue might arise of the possibility of the jury members being threatened by rebel members and their consequent unwillingness to serve or their fear of bringing in a guilty verdict. The most practical solution will be to restructure this process to provide for a judge or a panel of judges to make the finding and to pass sentence. There is nothing in international humanitarian law or in the human rights instruments requiring any particular form of fact-finding or sentencing process, apart from the obligation to ensure that the court or tribunal is independent and impartial.

---

[131] Article 6(2).This assumes that the State concerned is a party to the Protocol.

[132] See also the other obligations of the State in respect of the trial, Art. 6(2)(a)–(f) of Additional Protocol II 1977, none of which may be the subject of derogation. These requirements do not map completely onto the equivalent human right to a fair trial. See also the Siracusa Principles on the Limitation and Derogation of Provisions in the International Covenant on Civil and Political Rights, Annex, UN Doc. E/CN.4/1984/4 (1984); Report on Terrorism and Human Rights OEA/Ser. L/V/11.116, 22 October 2002, para. 246.

The trial and detention of a person suspected of taking part in the conflict and, in consequence, of breaking the national law of the State is markedly different from the position where an 'ordinary' suspected criminal is tried and detained upon conviction. First, the nature and scale of the former's breaches of the law is likely to be much greater than the 'ordinary' criminal. He may be tried for treason or for killing more than one soldier or for causing much greater property damage than would be expected of a single individual carrying out a criminal purpose for private gain. Secondly, unless the rebels can be defeated within a reasonable time scale, the State and the rebel organisation may have a mutual interest to negotiate some form of settlement. This could include an amnesty for those detained prior to or after conviction, or for those held outside this process.[133] Additional Protocol II 1977 encourages this result, although at the end of hostilities.[134] Were this to occur (and not subsequently be challenged) the rebels[135] would be in a better position than any human rights instrument could provide. When the conflict is over it will be to the human rights obligations of the State that attention will be drawn, particularly where the State seeks to join international organisations or to secure foreign aid.

Destruction of property

The destruction of property during a non-international armed conflict may appear less dramatic than during an international armed conflict, where sustained aerial or long-range bombardment is more likely[136] to occur. In the former type of conflict it will typically involve the destruction of houses, means of transport and livestock. Where such destruction is carried out by soldiers the reasons for doing so may range from the necessity to do so to attack rebels actually located in their vicinity, to prevent their use in the future by rebels and as a punishment for assisting or

---

[133] There is no restriction in Additional Protocol II 1977, on the power of a State to intern those whom it considers to be a security risk although, in the absence of an appropriate derogation notice, such action would conflict with a State's human rights obligations. See below for more detailed discussion of an amnesty.

[134] Article 6(5).

[135] *Quaere* whether any amnesty would apply equally to soldiers imprisoned by the State authorities for acts committed during the hostilities.

[136] Compare, however, the bombardment from the air and from long-range weapons during the Chechnya fighting between the Russian armed forces and Chechen rebels. For the allegations of such bombardment see *Khashiyeva* v. *Russia* (n. 54 above).

supporting the rebels.[137] The armed forces may argue that this destruction of property was 'imperatively demanded by the necessities of the conflict' and thus not a war crime.[138] It is more difficult to challenge this opinion where the conflict is non-international since its very nature is often antithetical to an ordered armed conflict with both combatants and military objectives being distinctive. It will, however, be less difficult to do so where the destruction is justified on the basis that it was a punishment for assisting or supporting the rebels, especially where the destruction is not linked to a proven cause and effect.[139]

In the absence of a suitable derogation notice some human rights instruments give a person a right to the enjoyment of his property, subject to certain limitations.[140] He will have little of which to complain if his property has been seized as a result of lawful action by his State[141] but if his house has been destroyed or damaged by soldiers without any military necessity for doing so (as discussed above) he could pursue any remedy available to him under the relevant human rights instrument.[142] Given that this is likely to be a person's principal asset and as its value (along with loss of contents and non-pecuniary loss) can be ascertained relatively easily this may be of real practical value to him if he has the right of individual petition.[143]

---

[137] For the procedure to be followed under Israeli law for the destruction of houses used by 'terrorists' see CCPR/C/SR.1677, 27 July 1998, para. 48.

[138] The Rome Statute 1998, Art. 8(2)(e)(xii).

[139] Note the emphasis, although in the context of penal prosecutions, of individual penal responsibility, Additional Protocol II 1977, Art. 6(2)(b) and the protection offered to civilians until 'such time as *they* take a *direct part in hostilities*': Art. 13(3). See also the provisions in the Rome Statute 1998, Art. 8(2)(e)(ii), (iii), (iv) relating to public property or to property belonging to organisations.

[140] See Art. 1 of the First Protocol (1952) to the 1950 Convention; the American Convention on Human Rights 1969, Art. 21.

[141] Such as a requisitioning order in respect of a vehicle. For an example, see the Army Act 1955, s. 165, which could be justified as being in the public interest (see s. 175 of the 1955 Act).

[142] Including his right to respect for his family and home; see, for example, the 1966 Covenant, Art. 17.

[143] Compared with the (unlikely) satisfaction of seeing the soldiers being prosecuted either within their State or by the International Criminal Court (where the State is a party to the Rome Statute 1998). See *Ayder et al.* v. *Turkey* (Application No.23656/94) Judgment, 8 January 2004; *Akdivar et al.* v. *Turkey* (1997) 23 EHRR 143, para. 88. See also (2003) CCPR/CO/78/ISR, para. 16 (Israel). The practical difficulties of identifying the actual soldiers who destroyed his house will be a further issue where a criminal prosecution is brought following a possible investigation. The State may, however, claim that the destruction was caused by the rebels and thus thwart any possible investigation, which, in turn, will strengthen any feeling of impunity felt by the armed forces.

Movement of individuals

Should State authorities[144] attempt to expel some of its own nationals from its territory it will clearly be in breach of international humanitarian law.[145] This is more likely to take the form of systematic attacks on a part of the population of a different ethnic origin by the armed forces with the purpose of encouraging them to leave the territory rather than any form of direct transportation by the State itself.[146] Similarly, displacement of the civilian population is also prohibited unless their security or imperative military reasons so demand.[147] In the absence of any appropriate derogation notice the individual (whether national or not[148]) subjected to this treatment by the State would find his protection under the relevant human rights instrument to be of more importance than any obligation on the State not to expel civilians.[149] There would, in any eventuality, be little he could do prior to his expulsion to prevent it[150] and so an *ex post facto* application to the relevant human rights body, should this be available to him, may be the only avenue open, difficult although this may be in practice.

---

[144] For the position if the rebels act in such a fashion see below.

[145] See Additional Protocol II 1977, Art. 17(2); Rome Statute 1998, Art. 8(2)(e)(viii).

[146] An example would be the activities of the Belgrade authorities in their attacks on ethnic Albanians with (at least) one purpose being to drive them out of the Kosovo region of the Federal Republic of Yugoslavia into Albania in 1999. There can be little doubt but that this would amount to a form of compelling those individuals to leave their territory.

[147] Additional Protocol II 1977, Art. 17(1); Rome Statute 1998, Art. 8(2)(e)(viii).

[148] The right of a State, however, to expel individual aliens by virtue of its national law is unaffected by international humanitarian law (Y. Sandoz, C. Swinarski and B. Zimmerman, *Commentary on the Additional Protocols of 8 June 1977 to the Geneva Conventions of 12 August 1949* (Geneva: International Committee of the Red Cross, 1987), para. 4868 or by human rights instruments (1966 Covenant, Art. 13; Fourth Protocol to the 1950 Convention, Art. 4; American Convention on Human Rights 1969, Art. 22(6); African Charter on Human and Peoples' Rights 1981, Art. 12(4)). See, however, *Fédération Internationale des Ligues des Droits de l'Homme* v. *Angola*, Communication No. 159/96 (expulsion of West Africans from Angola), para. 16.

[149] Assuming there is an effective enforcement mechanism under that human rights instrument, although there are limited rights to interfere with this right contained within the relevant article. The displacement of an individual could involve a breach of Art. 12(1) of the 1966 Covenant; Art. 2(1) of the Fourth Protocol (1963) to the 1950 Convention; Art. 22(1) of the American Convention on Human Rights 1969; Art. 12(2) of the African Charter on Human and Peoples' Rights 1981 and an interference with his right to family and private life and/or the protection of his property. In addition, any displacement may be discriminatory. For an example see *Dogan et al.* v. *Turkey*, Application No. 8803/02, Judgment, 29 June 2004, at para. 143.

[150] Unless his human right is implemented in the national law and he is able to bring court proceedings to challenge the legality under that law of his expulsion.

The State may, however, consider that the movement of parts of the civilian population to camps is necessary for their protection from rebels. In this case it should take 'immediate and effective measures to protect the right to life and liberty of the civilians' confined in such camps where they are 'constantly exposed to attacks by [rebels]'.[151]

The position of the rebels

It would be misleading to consider the legal controls operating upon the State authorities, in particular the armed forces only. Since the conflict under discussion is a non-international one it will on the ground, in many aspects, resemble its international counterpart. Both the armed forces of the State and the rebels may perform similar activities. The rebels will deprive soldiers[152] of the right to life, detain those whom they capture and so on. Although they may exercise some form of disciplinary control over their members the rebels are unlikely, however, to have in place a disciplinary system similar to that applying to soldiers. This has two consequences. First, the rebel organisation will usually not have a comparable means of enforcing a standard of conduct as to the means of carrying out the conflict. The organisational structure is unlikely to be in place for this and the standard of knowledge of the limits imposed by international humanitarian law on those who take part in a non-international armed conflict may not be well known. Secondly, an individual member of the rebel group may be denied his human rights by his rebel organisation during the course of the conflict. If he is to be disciplined for an infraction of the rules of the organisation and be subjected to some form of serious penalty he will, for instance, find it difficult to secure an independent and impartial tribunal to determine his guilt or innocence.[153] He can hardly look to his State for such protection.

---

[151] CCPR/CO/80/UGA, 4 May 2004. The HRC was concerned about attacks made on camps by the Lord's Resistance Army in Uganda.

[152] It will not only be soldiers who are attacked by rebels. Since international humanitarian law in this area concentrates on those who take no 'active part in the hostilities' or those who do not take a 'direct part in the hostilities' there is considerable scope for uncertainty as to which officials of the State may be lawfully attacked in just the same way as the uncertainty over who may be attacked by soldiers. See *Ends and Means: Human Rights Approaches to Armed Groups* (Versoix: International Council on Human Rights Policy, 2000), pp. 63–4.

[153] For discussion of court-martial of a State's soldier and whether it can comply with human rights obligations see chapter 3.

The rebel organisation may take the view that neither international humanitarian law nor the human rights obligations of the State (assuming that State is a party to a human rights instrument) apply to them since these are, by their very nature, matters solely within the competence of States. In relation to the former, it is accepted that such a view would be mistaken since in common Article 3 to the Geneva Conventions 1949 (although not in Additional Protocol II 1977), obligations are placed on the *Parties* to the conflict.[154] This term must refer to rebels as well as to the State organs or it would otherwise have no meaning.[155] This conclusion may be challenged by some rebel organisations on the (political) ground that their organisation refuses to accept that the authority of the government runs to the territory which they physically control and thus its national and international laws do not apply there.[156] This is hardly a wise approach to take since international humanitarian law has at least the ability[157] to control the actions of the State armed forces and thus to provide some protection for those who do not take a part in the hostilities[158] or those who have become *hors de combat*. Moreover, the actions of an individual member of the rebel organisation may be subjected to the gaze of the prosecutor of the International Criminal Court, where the State concerned is a party to the Rome Statute 1998, if a crime against

[154] The threshold of this Protocol, however, requires the organised armed groups involved to be able to 'implement this Protocol', Art. 1(1).

[155] See the Appeals Chamber, Special Court for Sierra Leone, *Prosecutor v. Norman*, Case No. SCSL-2004-14-AR72(E), 31 May 2004 at para. 22; *Prosecutor v. Kallon and Kamara*, Case No. SCSL-2004-15-AR72(E), 13 March 2004, para. 45; the Convention on the Rights of the Child, Optional Protocol, 2000, Art. 4 (referring to 'armed groups that are distinct from the armed forces of a State'); *Third Report on the Human Rights Situation in Columbia*, OEA/Ser. L/V/II.102 Doc. 9 rev. 1, 26 February 1999, paras. 13, 234 and generally, Sandoz, *Commentary on the Additional Protocols*, para. 4442; Cassese, 'The Status of Rebels' (n. 21 above); T. Meron, 'International Criminalization of Internal Atrocities' (1995) 89 *American Journal of International Law* 554; L. Moir, *The Law of Internal Armed Conflict* (Cambridge: Cambridge University Press, 2002), p. 65. *Quaere* the statement of the Government of Sri Lanka that *in 'terms of the Ceasefire Agreement* [2002] the parties to the conflict are bound by international law that prohibits hostile acts on civilian population [sic]' [emphasis supplied] CCPR/C/LKA/2002/4, 18 October 2002, para. 543.

[156] See *Ends and Means*, p. 59. They may also argue that there is a lack of reciprocity since a rebel organisation, unlike a State, cannot enter any reservations or understandings on ratification or accession to a treaty.

[157] In so far as it is complied with and enforced by the State. Whether the State can engage in reprisals against the rebels is discussed in Cassese (n. 21 above) at pp. 437–9.

[158] Field agreements may be made between humanitarian agencies and rebels (as well as with the State concerned), see 'Promotion and Protection of Human Rights', Commission on Human Rights, E/CN.4/2001/91, 12 January 2001, paras. 41–5.

humanity or a war crime is alleged against him.[159] The risk of prosecution before his State courts or the International Criminal Court may, however, be considered remote until such time as a rebel is captured by his State's armed forces or he comes otherwise within the jurisdiction of the Court. Depending on how senior this individual is in the rebel organisation there is the further possibility that any peace negotiating process between his organisation and the State may result in an amnesty being offered to him.[160]

The aims of the rebels may, on the other hand, cause them to assert that international humanitarian law does apply to them. This may be because they seek to make political capital (and gain some international 'status') out of the assertion that, as an organisation, they owe international obligations not merely to their own State but to all other States party to the relevant international treaties.[161] By taking such an approach the rebels may convince themselves and those whom they seek to support them[162] that the organisation is not merely a criminal gang but a responsible organisation seeking to achieve an objective which international law itself does not prohibit, namely, the change of a government of a State by rebellion.[163]

---

[159] Articles 7 and 8(2)(c) and (e) of the Rome Statute 1998. The crime of genocide is also a theoretical possibility.

[160] Such an amnesty will not be binding upon the Court but if the State is unwilling to place him on trial (because of the amnesty) or to extradite him and if the individual does not leave the security of his State there may be little the Court can do to bring him to trial. For further discussion of the legal consequences of an amnesty see under the heading 'Amnesty' below.

[161] They may even be moved to describe government soldiers as 'prisoners of war' and seek the assistance of the International Committee of the Red Cross for their return, see T. Jenatsch, 'The ICRC as a Humanitarian Mediator in the Columbian Conflict' (1998) 323 *International Review of the Red Cross* 303 at 304. They may, on the other hand, see no advantage to them of complying with the Protocol, see Cassese (n. 21 above) at p. 434. For the liability of States to 'the international community as a whole' for breach of an international obligations, see commentary to Art. 48(1) of the International Law Commission's Draft Articles of Responsibility of the State for Internationally Wrongful Acts, 2001: J. Crawford, *The International Law Commission's Articles on State Responsibility* (Cambridge: Cambridge University Press, 2002).

[162] The formal legal status as rebels cannot be altered even if the State concerned enters into special agreements with them, common Art. 3 to the Geneva Conventions 1949; Additional Protocol II 1977, Art. 3(1).

[163] See M. Shaw, *International Law* (5th edn, Cambridge: Cambridge University Press, 2003), p. 1040 cited with approval in *Prosecutor v. Kallon and Kamara*, Case No. SCSL-2004-15-AR72(E), 13 March 2004 (Appeals Chamber) at para. 20. In some conflicts, however, the political objectives and criminality (through drug dealing, protection rackets etc.) may not be clearly distinguished.

It is not so clear whether rebel organisations are bound by the human rights instruments entered into by the State concerned. Unlike international humanitarian treaties[164] the former make express reference only to the State (acting through a variety of its organs) who, alone, will be bound by the treaty obligations.[165] In very limited circumstances the State may be liable for the actions of private individuals if it acquiesces or connives in their actions, through, for instance, relying on the actions of paramilitaries or of militias.[166] The very nature of a non-international armed conflict shows that rebels, opposed to the State, are unlikely to make the State liable for their actions, although the State retains the obligation to investigate acts of the rebels and to attempt to try those considered responsible.[167]

The imbalance in the protection of the human rights instruments becomes immediately apparent. The actions of the State organs (including its armed forces) will attract the liability of the State but not (generally) the actions of the rebels. Rebels can expect to be treated in accordance with human rights principles if captured by soldiers but not vice versa. Thus, soldiers who fall into the hands of the rebels can expect relatively little by way of legal protection. Under international humanitarian law they become *hors de combat* and should not be treated in ways prohibited by common Article 3 to the Geneva Conventions 1949 or by Additional Protocol II 1977.[168] This conclusion is based upon the premise that the

---

[164] Including relevant parts of customary international law.

[165] The Inter-American Commission has 'consistently refused to formally examine or condemn human rights violations by non-governmental actors such as terrorists': V. Iyer, 'States of Emergency-Moderating Their Effect on Human Rights' (1999) 32 *Dalhousie Law Journal* 125, 140. In its declaration to the Optional Protocol to the Rights of the Child 2000, Mexico has confirmed that the responsibility of armed groups who recruit children under the age of eighteen to take part in hostilities 'lies solely with such groups and shall not be applicable to the Mexican State as such'.

[166] See *Cyprus v. Turkey* (2002) 35 EHRR 35, at para. 81. For examples see *Riofrio Massacre* (Columbia), Report No. 62/01, Case 11.654, 6 April 2001 at para. 49; UNSC Resolution 1556 (2004) concerning the responsibility of Sudan for the actions of the Janjaweed; OEA/Ser. L/V/II.77 rev. 1, Doc. 18, 8 May 1990, para. 174 (Haiti); Columbia Report 1999 (n. 3 above) para. 250 'in these cases of joint activity between the paramilitaries, particularly when carried out with the knowledge of superiors, the members of the paramilitary groups clearly act as State agents': *Mapiripan Massacre*, Report No. 23/01, Case 12.250, 22 February 2001 (admissibility); Crawford, *International Law* at p. 110.

[167] See the Columbia Report 1999 (n. 3 above) para. 314; *Amnesty International et al. v. Sudan* (n. 66 above) para. 50; McCorquodale, *'Overlegalizing Silences'* (n. 12 above). See, however, R. McCorquodale and R. La Forgia, 'Taking Off the Blindfolds: Torture by Non-State Actors' (2001) 1 *Human Rights Law Review* 189.

[168] Article 5.

rebels accept the applicability of this law to themselves. They may be placed on trial by the rebels but it will, as a matter of practice, be difficult for them to show that any 'court' they establish for this purpose is able to offer 'the essential guarantees of independence and impartiality'.[169] It is very unlikely that they could, for the same reason, be offered any real human rights protection by the rebel organisation in whose hands they are.[170]

It will be recalled that rebel organisations differ in their objectives and should not be thought of as being monolithic. Should it suit the political ambitions of a particular rebel organisation to treat captured soldiers well it may, of course do so. In other cases hatred may build up between soldiers and the rebels to such an extent that captured soldiers are treated badly and captured rebels are routinely denied their human rights (along with breaches by the State of its obligations under international humanitarian law) with the result that neither soldiers nor rebels are willing to run the risk of being captured. In these circumstances it is not surprising to see international law having little or no effect on the conduct of the armed conflict.

It may also suit the rebel organisation to be seen by the outside world as responsible in its conduct of the armed conflict through its avoidance of human rights 'abuses'. For it to be able to achieve this status it will have to behave in a way similar to a State in respect of its armed forces. An enforceable disciplinary code will be required to ensure that its fighters (the rebels) comply with international humanitarian law and human rights standards and that these fighters are not denied their human rights by their own organisation. The organisation will, for this purpose, have to determine for itself which human rights standards it wishes to apply. It could accept those rights adopted by the State itself with or without any reservations to the relevant treaty or derogation notices issued. It could, for instance, refuse to sanction the death penalty after a 'trial' for any captured soldier or one of its own members despite the State using this penalty.[171]

---

[169] Article 6(2). By common Art. 3 to the Geneva Conventions 1949 such a court must be 'regularly constituted', a much more difficult prerequisite to show.

[170] For the execution of Russian soldiers by Chechen rebels see *Amnesty International News Service* 126/96, 10 July 1996.

[171] The State may not have abolished the death penalty or, in keeping with the relevant human rights treaty, restored it during the conflict. For discussion as to whether human rights treaties permit restoration of this penalty during a non-international armed conflict see above.

The actual practice of rebel organisations suggests that many do not act like this. With no means of enforcing their will save violence or the threat of it they invariably deny, de facto, a range of human rights to individuals with whom they come into contact, whether soldiers, civilians taking no part in the hostilities or their own fighters.[172] The effect of this is to place such individuals in a worse position than the inhabitants of a State under occupation by the armed forces of another State. In this situation the occupying State will be responsible for the human rights of the inhabitants, certainly when it detains them.[173] They will not lose out in the protection of their human rights by a State (although that State will not be one of which they are nationals).[174] They may do so in practice, however, if the territory in which they are living comes under the actual control of a rebel organisation, whose members act in such a way as to deny the human rights of the inhabitants.[175]

One particular group of individuals who may suffer at the hands of the rebels are children, recruited into their organisation to perform duties from actual fighting, suicide bombing to acts of servitude (sexual and otherwise). In areas controlled by the rebels parents may even be offered inducements to persuade them to encourage their children to join the rebel organisation. Alternatively, they are kidnapped. The Sri Lanka Government summed up the attractiveness to the rebels (Liberation Tigers of Tamil Eelam) of recruiting child soldiers who were 'receptive to indoctrination fine tuned to their level of maturity, willing to engage in high risk operations, obedient and can easily use weapons such as M16, AK-47 and T-56 which are light in weight, easy to fire and maintain and require minimum training'.[176]

It may, at first glance, appear illogical to argue that, at the international level, rebels are bound by international humanitarian law but not

---

[172] Such breaches of human rights towards civilians can include, of course, all of the rights as discussed above from the standpoint of soldiers, including destruction of their property and forced movement or expulsion.

[173] Within the limits discussed in chapter 5.

[174] This was a concern of the European Court of Human Rights following the occupation by Turkey of Northern Cyprus, see *Loizidou* v. *Turkey* (1997) 23 EHRR 513 at para. 57.

[175] Despite the sovereign State retaining its jurisdiction over an area controlled by rebels, see *Ilascu* v. *Moldova and Russia*, Judgment, 8 July 2004 (the position of Moldova); *Assanidze* v. *Georgia* (2004) 39 EHRR 32, paras. 142, 143.

[176] CCPR/C/LKA/2002/4, 18 October 2003, para. 461. The Government estimates that of the rebels killed in 'combat . . . at least 40 per cent of the fighting force consist of girls and boys between the ages of 9 and 18 years' (*ibid.*). See also 'Children and Armed Conflict: Report of the Secretary-General' A/58/546-S/2003/1053, 10 November 2003, para. 42. See, generally, chapter 1.

by human rights treaties to which the State is a party. The difference can, however, be explained by the fact that the former imposes direct obligations on individuals whilst the latter does so, at the international level, only on the State (although the State has an obligation to investigate and prosecute individuals for what are, effectively, breaches of human rights). This analysis breaks down, however, where the State 'structures no longer exist or where States are unable or unwilling to mete out punishment for crimes committed by' rebels.[177] In this case (and at the international level) only through international humanitarian law procedures, including international tribunals, can individual actors be brought to account.

Disorder not amounting to an armed conflict within a State

It has been seen that international humanitarian law accepts that there is a threshold of public disorder[178] within a State before it can have any influence over events. Common Article 3 to the Geneva Conventions 1949 draws this threshold at the level of a non-international armed conflict whilst Additional Protocol II 1977, picks up this reluctance on the part of a number of States to accept, except in clear cases, international standards applying to the way in which they manage what they see as their own law and order problem.[179] The Protocol requires organised armed forces to control territory for the purposes set out there. It also excludes 'internal disturbances and tensions, such as riots, isolated and sporadic acts of violence and other acts of a similar nature'.[180]

The key to determining whether international humanitarian law applies to a particular factual situation is whether what is taking place there amounts to an 'armed conflict'. A State could deny that the events taking place within its territory amounted to an armed conflict and argue that they were criminal activities, all be it on a larger scale than normal and

---

[177] See 'Promotion and Protection of Human Rights', Human Rights Commission, E/CN.4/1999/92, 18 December 1998, para. 13.

[178] This term is chosen deliberately so as to avoid any confusion with an armed conflict. It may also be styled as a state of siege or of emergency. See, generally, J. Fitzpatrick, 'States of Emergency in the Inter-American Human Rights System' in D. Harris and S. Livingstone (eds.), *The Inter-American System of Human Rights* (Oxford: Clarendon, 1998), p. 371.

[179] A State is always free to withhold signature or ratification of Additional Protocol II 1977, or to enter reservations to it. In this event, it may have to consider carefully whether it can become a party to the Rome Statute 1998 with its liability for war crimes having been extended to non-international armed conflicts.

[180] Additional Protocol II 1977, Art. 1(2). See also the Rome Statute 1998, Art. 8(2)(d) and (f), which adds 'sporadic acts of violence'.

carried out with a political motive.[181] Were that State to be a party to the Rome Statute 1998 the prosecutor of the International Criminal Court might take a different view. He or she might wish to begin an investigation into the activities of soldiers or the rebels with a view to prosecution for a war crime. To provide the ground for doing so it will be necessary for a decision (subject always to that of the Court) to be made that the events occurring within a State do, in fact, amount to an armed conflict. The State may wish to challenge the admissibility of the case before the Court but it will make the final decision.[182]

If it is now assumed that there has been no such determination of an armed conflict by the Court or by the State itself international human-itarian law will have no scope for application unless the acts of one or more of the parties involved amounts to genocide or to a crime against humanity.[183] National law and any human rights instruments will deter-mine the legality, or otherwise, of the actions of soldiers and the 'rioters' during such disturbances.[184]

In many[185] States members of the armed forces will only be deployed by the government for law enforcement where the disorder reaches a level at which the normal police forces[186] are unable to manage to control it or where the weapons used by the rioters can only be matched by those possessed by the armed forces. In some cases the action by soldiers will look very much like a non-international armed conflict. Soldiers will use

---

[181] It may take the view that it would prefer to treat the rioters as common criminals rather than to appear to give them some political credibility by elevating the events to a dispute about political objectives. On the other hand, to accept the status of the dispute as an armed conflict would impose the limitations of international humanitarian law on the actions of the rebels.

[182] See Arts. 13(c), 15, 19. Note that victims may also submit observations to the Court, Art. 19(3).

[183] See the Rome Statute 1998, Arts. 6 and 7. It is likely in this event that the Court would also hold that an armed conflict is taking place, see the Statute of the International Tribunal for Rwanda 1994, Arts. 2–4 for an example.

[184] This term is used to denote those who, for political reasons, engage in acts contrary to the national criminal law of the State and which involve a degree of violence to persons or property. The motives of the rebels may, however, be mixed since a breakdown of order often enables rebel organisations to acquire funds through activities, normally considered illegal, such as drug selling or protection rackets.

[185] In some States it may be contrary to the constitution for the armed forces to be used in such circumstances within the State itself. For the position, for example, of Germany see G. Nolte and H. Krieger, 'Military Law in Germany' in G. Nolte (ed.), *European Military Law Systems* (Berlin: De Gruyter Recht, 2003), pp. 350–2.

[186] A State may, for instance, have available to it some form of paramilitary police force in addition to its 'ordinary' police force.

their standard issue of high velocity rifles, which are designed to kill; they may also use armoured vehicles and even attack helicopters. There is nothing surprising in this since had the political will been there the activities on the ground would have been accepted as an armed conflict. At the other end of the spectrum will be those cases where the actions of the rioters may be more sporadic without the use of violence and the role of the soldiers will be limited to assisting the police to arrest individuals.

It is a high risk policy for a State to involve its soldiers in situations of disorder. They are not trained as police officers and will generally be supplied with equipment suitable only for their principal role of taking part in armed conflict or in 'warlike' situations such as a peacekeeping mission where armed groups may attack them. It is therefore particularly important to develop for the soldiers appropriate rules of engagement. These will enable military commanders to think through the situations in which a soldier would be permitted by the national law (including any human rights obligations) to use lethal force and when they may detain someone.[187] These rules will not usually have force as a legal instrument but will be subordinate to the soldier's obligation to obey national law. They will, in effect, be equivalent in legal standing to the order of a superior officer.

The role of national law is particularly important. In practice States have not shown themselves to be anxious to classify the internal disorder they are experiencing as a non-international armed conflict or as 'mere' internal disturbances. There will, however, often be little difficulty in passing emergency legislation to enable the security forces to act within the law in a way which would be unlawful had no such legislation been passed. This legislation may give legal powers to the security forces to kill those committing crimes linked with the disturbances where to do so is 'necessary' or even 'absolutely necessary' to prevent the crime concerned. Concentration should be placed not solely on whether the use of force is necessary or absolutely necessary but on the nature of the crime against which the force is permitted. There is, for instance, considerable difference between killing a potential bomber who is in the process of planting a bomb in a building in which there are many innocent people and permitting lethal force as 'necessary' or 'absolutely necessary' to prevent the

---

[187] See, generally, S. Rose, 'Crafting the Rules of Engagement for Haiti' in M. Schmitt (ed.) *The Law of Military Operations*, International Law Studies, vol. 72 (Newport: Naval War College Press, 1998), p. 225.

activities of a proscribed organisation[188] by killing a person merely on the ground that he is a member of that organisation. The national law of a State may draw a link between the degree of force that is legally permissible and the seriousness of the crime being prevented, but it may do so only in some cases or not at all. In this latter type of situation the risk to those mistakenly thought to be involved in any form of activity prohibited by the 'ordinary' criminal law or by emergency law is much greater. The law cannot, of course, do much to prevent illegal activity on the part of the security forces if they deliberately flout it and it will be assumed that this is not the case.

This emergency legislation is also likely to give security forces powers (or increased powers) of arrest, detention, search, seizure and destruction of property and of restriction of movement. It may also provide for different types of court to deal with alleged offenders. In many States armed forces have no such powers over their own citizens other than against other members of the armed forces and should it be constitutionally permissible such powers will have to be given by some legal means.

This chapter considers the position solely from the standpoint of the armed forces, although it is recognised that they may be acting jointly[189] with the police or other forms of security services. This position is considered justified since the armed forces generally possess a disciplinary and command system stronger than other forces, have access to (military) equipment not available to other security forces and often have political power or influence greater than any other group. Indeed, where serious internal disturbances have occurred on a large scale the possibilities of a military *coup d'état* may increase in some States.[190]

Moreover, the armed forces may also possess three unique features compared with other forms of security forces. First, the national law of the State concerned might require that the actions of soldiers in quelling disturbances be brought only before military and not civil courts. Where this is the case a reluctance to prosecute individual soldiers can be foreseen

---

[188] This term is used to refer to the organisations to which those engaged in disorder against the State for political purposes belong. It is common practice for such organisations to be proscribed by law.

[189] Although they may carry out distinctly separate functions. The Basic Principles on the Use of Force and Firearms by Law Enforcement Officers 1990 encompasses soldiers also acting in this role. The armed forces may actually control the police, which, in turn, may intimidate judges, see *Juan Sanchez Case* (Inter-American Court of Human Rights) (2003) Ser. C, No. 99, para. 97.

[190] See, generally, S. E. Finer, *The Man on Horseback: the Role of the Military in Politics* (2nd enlarged edn, Harmondsworth, Baltimore: Penguin, 1976).

if to do so would lead to senior officers also being prosecuted or being criticised for their decisions.[191] There is, in addition, a potential for lack of any transparency in showing that soldiers are also subject to the law, given that it will not be difficult to declare that 'security' considerations require secrecy. This will also be the position, *a fortiori*, if the emergency legislation were to declare that the armed forces are not subject to the civilian law at all but only to military law. Secondly, this legislation may make civilians subject to the jurisdiction of military courts for some or all of the offences encompassed by it. Should it do so it may also provide that a civilian convicted by a military court should be handed over to the civilian authorities to serve any period of imprisonment or for any fine or confiscation of property to be implemented or it may provide that the individual will remain in military custody.[192]

Finally, the law of some States[193] may provide that the armed forces themselves can proclaim the existence of martial law. Should the conditions be met for such a proclamation the most senior military officer with responsibility to maintain law and order in the area can, in effect, proclaim it to be illegal to do anything he so decides. He can also provide for any form of trial and punishment he considers necessary to restore order and to return the area to the law applicable prior to his proclamation.

A proclamation of martial law gives scope for soldiers to set aside the civilian law (although not their own military law) in pursuit of what is perceived by their commanders to be the priority goal of restoring order within the area concerned. There is no counterpart to this under international humanitarian law, i.e., where soldiers may set aside that law in order to achieve their goal of victory during an armed conflict.[194] This statement does not, however, give a fully accurate picture since during an international armed conflict a soldier may kill as many lawful combatants as he is physically able to and during a non-international armed conflict there is no restriction on killing those who are taking an active part in the hostilities. Given that during the conduct of their operations following

---

[191] Compare the situation where a soldier has acted in breach of his orders. In drawing the line between lawful and unlawful action the contents of rules of engagement become particularly important.

[192] It may then carry out any order of the military court for the seizure or destruction of property. See, generally, chapter 4 for the trial of civilians by military court.

[193] This exists under the common law of the United Kingdom. For further discussion see chapter 4.

[194] The purported justification of military necessity will not be permitted to relieve a soldier of his obligations under international humanitarian law unless this is specifically provided in a particular norm itself.

a proclamation of martial law soldiers will be likely to have breached the national law obtaining prior to the proclamation (in the absence or otherwise of emergency legislation) it is not uncommon for a State to pass an Act of Parliament to grant immunity from prosecution or to indemnify soldiers for their actions carried out in good faith.[195]

In the absence of an armed conflict there will be no scope for the application of international humanitarian law unless the State concerned decides to apply part of it. It will need to weigh the political consequence, for instance, of treating arrested members of a proscribed organisation as if they were prisoners of war.[196] Experience suggests, however, that whilst lawyers might feel unhappy if they cannot draw a clear distinction in a particular case between an armed conflict and disorder within a State not amounting to an armed conflict politicians and others, such as the International Committee of the Red Cross, do not. It is not therefore uncommon for delegates of the International Committee of the Red Cross to inspect detention facilities and communicate with individual prisoners despite the non-acceptance of the State that an armed conflict is taking place. Reports following visits are made confidentially to the State.

Experience has also shown that where a State engaged in civil disorder is party to a human rights instrument, under which it faces penalties for breach, the impact of that treaty has been considerable. A good example of such a treaty is the European Convention on Human Rights 1950, particularly in its approach to the disorder occurring in Northern Ireland from 1969–95 and in Turkey from 1974. In both cases the loss of life has been considerable and on a scale not comparable with 'ordinary' criminal activities. The State may be ordered by the European Court of Human Rights to pay 'just satisfaction' to the victims of its breach. In the absence of any legislation providing otherwise, individuals acting on behalf of the State and those acting on behalf of a proscribed organisation will be subject to, and be judged by, the same national law.[197]

A State permitted to issue a derogation notice under a relevant human rights instrument may find it more difficult to show the conditions for its application are met when the disorder in the State does not reach the level

---

[195] See discussion below on the effect of an amnesty agreement.
[196] Were the State to accept that there was in existence a non-international armed conflict common Art. 3(2) to the Geneva Conventions 1949 enables it to enter into special agreements to bring into existence some or all of the other provisions of the Conventions.
[197] This may be so in theory. In reality, however, the soldier will (normally) be acting to uphold that national law and a member of a proscribed organisation will be in breach of it. The scope for legal justification for acts committed by a soldier in these circumstances will be greater than for acts committed by a member of a proscribed organisation.

properly to be classified as a non-international armed conflict. To make a derogation the State will have to show that there is in existence a 'public emergency which threatens the life of the nation'.[198] This phrase might be construed to mean that the public emergency must threaten the whole of the territory of a State (as a war would do) and the very existence of the State (as a war would do). Were this to be the correct analysis of this phrase it could apply only very rarely in the absence of an international armed conflict.

The issue of a derogation notice may be challenged by a State party to the human rights instrument under which it is made but this occurs rarely,[199] although it may be challenged by the individual applicant. The human rights bodies (in which is included the European Court of Human Rights) have given a wide latitude to States to issue a derogation notice where serious disorder is occurring on the territory of their States or where it threatens to do so.

An example of this wide margin of appreciation given to States under the 1950 Convention is the case of the United Kingdom which issued a derogation notice in 1988 in respect of the activities occurring in Northern Ireland. It described these as 'campaigns of organised terrorism' which have 'manifested themselves in activities which have included repeated murder, attempted murder, maiming, intimidation and violent civil disturbance and in repeated bombing and fire raising which have resulted in death, injury and widespread destruction of property. As a result a public emergency within the meaning of Article 15(1) of the Convention exists in the United Kingdom.' Having shown the conditions for the power to issue a derogation notice existed,[200] the United Kingdom went on to derogate from Article 5(3) of the Convention giving to itself the right to detain a person for up to five days before bringing him before a judge or other judicial officer. With the decrease in activities of these 'terrorist organisations' following the Belfast Agreement (1998) the United Kingdom withdrew its derogation notice in February 2001.[201]

---

[198] The 1966 Covenant, Art. 4(1); the 1950 Convention, Art. 15(1); the American Convention on Human Rights 1969, Art. 27 (although all have slightly different wording).

[199] *Ireland* v. *United Kingdom* (1978) 2 EHRR 25 at para. 224.

[200] Since activities by proscribed organisations (mainly, although not exclusively, the Irish Republican Army (IRA)) took place in England as well as in Northern Ireland the civil disorder was not confined to a relatively small part of the United Kingdom, although the vast majority of the deaths and other activities occurred in that province. See also, *Aksoy* v. *Turkey* (1997) 23 EHRR 553, para. 70.

[201] Council of Europe Press Release, 22 February 2001.

In contrast with this is the derogation issued by the same State in December 2001,[202] following the attacks in the United States:

> 'The terrorist attacks in New York, Washington, D.C. and Pennsylvania on 11th September 2001 resulted in several thousand deaths, including many British victims . . . there exists a threat to the United Kingdom from persons suspected of involvement in international terrorism. In particular, there are foreign nationals present in the United Kingdom who are suspected of being concerned . . . in acts of international terrorism, of being members of organisations or groups . . . and who are a threat to the security of the United Kingdom. As a result a public emergency, within the meaning of Article 15(1) of the Convention, exists in the United Kingdom.'

The power to arrest and detain a foreign national where it is not possible to deport him is then given by legislation.[203]

At the date of this derogation made in 2001 there had not been, unlike in Northern Ireland, any terrorist activity resulting in the loss of life or destruction of property although the possibility of such action was clearly foreseeable. There was no actual civil disorder, let alone an armed conflict with the United Kingdom on one side and these international terrorists on the other.[204]

It is currently foreseeable that international terrorism could result in the deaths of very large numbers of people if a weapon of mass destruction (of a chemical, biological or nuclear nature) was used. If such an event were to occur it is also foreseeable that a State which had abolished the death penalty might wish to restore it.[205] Should it be a party to a human rights instrument providing for its restoration it will be necessary to show that the acts of the terrorists were 'committed in time of war pursuant to a conviction for a most serious crime of a military nature committed during wartime'.[206] It would be difficult to show this if the ordinary meaning is

---

[202] The Human Rights Act 1998 (Designated Derogation) Order 2001 (SI 2001 No. 3644).

[203] The Anti-Terrorism, Crime and Security Act 2001, s. 23. No other State party to the 1950 Convention has, at the date of writing, taken a similar course. A declaration of incompatibility between s. 23 of the 2001 Act and Arts. 5 and 14 of the Convention was made in *A and others* v. *Secretary of State for the Home Department* [2005] 2 AC 68.

[204] This is not to suggest that the attacks on 11 September 2001 in the United States did not amount to an armed conflict between that State and the Taliban government of Afghanistan. Although there were British victims of those events it would be difficult to argue that there was an international armed conflict in existence then between the United Kingdom and the Taliban government of Afghanistan.

[205] It is also likely to issue further derogation notices under the relevant Convention.

[206] Second Optional Protocol (1990) to the 1966 Protocol, Art. 2 providing the State has made a reservation to this effect. See also the Sixth Protocol (1983) to the 1950 Convention,

given to the terms 'war' and crime of a 'military nature'. In addition, there is a requirement, other than under the 1950 Convention, for a State wishing to restore the death penalty to have made a reservation at the appropriate time.

During a period of civil disorder, however intense it is, a State will not be able to derogate from the right to life (where this is permitted in the relevant human rights instrument) since to do so it would have to show that the person was killed as a result of a 'lawful act of war', a phrase totally inapplicable in this context.[207] A similar result follows from consideration of the 1966 Covenant which requires that 'no one shall be arbitrarily deprived of his life' from which no derogation is permitted. Here[208] an 'arbitrary' deprivation of life must mean a killing that is not justified by the national law concerned and by the principles of human rights set out in the Covenant.[209]

The jurisprudence developed under the European Convention on Human Rights 1950 provides a useful paradigm for a study of the human rights under that Convention of individuals with whom soldiers, as State actors, have come into contact. Both the United Kingdom and Turkey have been respondent States on many occasions before the European Commission on Human Rights[210] and before the Court of Human Rights. Both States have faced violent actions by organisations whose aims have been political and both have had to use soldiers to try and contain this violence. Although the principles upon which the Commission and the Court act have been discussed in relation to both an international and, more particularly, a non-international armed conflict they apply *mutatis mutandis* where the disorder within a State has not reached the level of intensity to be properly described as an armed conflict. It is, perhaps, pertinent to make some additional comments relevant to disorder alone.

Art. 2 (no reservation required); Protocol to the American Convention on Human Rights to Abolish the Death Penalty 1990, Art. 2 (reservation required). Compare Protocol 13 (2002) to the 1950 Convention, concerning the abolition of the death penalty in all circumstances.

[207] The 1950 Convention, Art. 15(2).

[208] Compare where international humanitarian law is applicable. See above.

[209] It would be clearly inconsistent with the Covenant, for instance, to conclude that a killing was justified by the national law which permitted a soldier to kill a person of a particular ethnic origin in circumstances where he would not be permitted to kill someone of a different ethnic origin.

[210] This body ceased to exist in 1998 and is now amalgamated into the European Court of Human Rights. See, generally, A. Reidy, 'The Approach of the European Commission and Court of Human Rights to International Humanitarian Law' (1998) 324 *International Review of the Red Cross* 513.

It has been shown above that the practice (and law) of States will vary as to the circumstances in which soldiers may be called in to assist the police or other security forces in controlling such violence. Indeed, there may be no clear line recognisable by other States between members of the armed forces and other security forces. Where civil disorder takes place within a State it is unlikely to reach a level immediately where soldiers (who are not normally involved in law enforcement) are called in to assist the police or other security forces. Should it be foreseeable that they will be deployed training for such a role will need to be undertaken to ensure, as far as possible, the human rights (however this is expressed) of those with whom they will come into contact. Equally important (at least from the standpoint of the armed forces) will be the protection of the right to life of those soldiers themselves. The history of Northern Ireland in particular has shown how vulnerable soldiers are to being killed by members of a proscribed organisation. Those members can work individually or in small groups, are not distinguishable in appearance from innocent civilians and are unlikely to be disciplined by their organisation if they are able to kill a soldier by whatever means (even if this would be prohibited during an international armed conflict). They can disappear easily into the surrounding countryside or urban area from where they draw political or other support (whether voluntarily or not).

The events of Northern Ireland have also shown that since 1969 more British soldiers have been killed while on duty there than in all the international armed conflicts in which they have been engaged since then.[211] The soldier can look to his commanders to provide protective equipment such as a flak-jacket and to develop tactics to preserve as far as possible his right to life whilst recognising that he has a duty to perform. He can also expect that they will develop rules of engagement (by whatever name they are called)[212] to ensure that the soldier also stays within national law and any human rights obligations owed to those with whom he comes into contact.[213] This is probably the most difficult type of operation faced by soldiers, given that the line between a killing which can be justified under the law and one which cannot is much more difficult to draw than

---

[211] These are principally the Falklands/Malvinas conflict 1982, the Gulf war 1990–1, Kosovo 1999, Afghanistan 2002, Iraq 2003.

[212] In the Northern Ireland situation they were known as the 'Yellow Card'. They were issued to soldiers in the form of a card which could easily be carried and referred to by the soldier.

[213] Where these human rights obligations are not fully incorporated within the national law it may be necessary to incorporate them instead within the rules of engagement.

in an armed conflict. Soldiers will be expected to protect innocent civilians from violence (such as through the use by members of a proscribed organisation of bombs in buildings or in vehicles) as well as to defend themselves.

Not only does the soldier run the risk of being killed in this type of operation but if his commanders do not give him orders that are compliant with national law and international human rights he runs the risk of being deprived of his liberty should he be prosecuted for what is later adjudged to have been an unlawful killing.[214] It will, generally, be no defence for him to say that he was following orders.[215] A number of soldiers have been prosecuted for murder or manslaughter in relation to acts committed whilst on duty. A small number have been convicted of murder and sentenced to life imprisonment.[216] A larger number were disciplined for committing military offences while on duty which did not amount to criminal offences. Thus, a soldier who fired an unaimed shot or who negligently discharged his weapon could be charged with a military offence and dealt with by his commanding officer or be tried by court-martial. The power, in particular, of a commanding officer to

[214] For serious criminal offences committed in Northern Ireland soldiers were primarily subject to the jurisdiction of the ordinary criminal courts and not courts-martial. Civilians could only be tried by the civilian courts.

[215] Whether this defence exists at all or in some form will depend upon the national law of the State concerned. For its application to the shooting by border guards of a person attempting to escape from East Berlin see *K-H.W.* v. *Germany* (2003) 36 EHRR 59, para. 75 where the European Court of Human Rights took 'the view that even a private soldier should not show total, blind obedience to orders which flagrantly infringe not only the GDR's [German Democratic Republic] own legal principles but also internationally recognised human rights, in particular, the right to life, which is the supreme value in the hierarchy of human rights'. A communication under the Optional Protocol by a former border guard alleging breaches of Arts. 15 and 26 of the 1966 Covenant was dismissed, CCPR/C/78/D/960/2000, 19 September 2003. For a case involving the leaders of the GDR at the time see *Streletz, Kessler and Kreuz* (2001) 33 EHRR 31. Where the rules of engagement reflect accurately the limits of the criminal law it is less likely, in practical terms, that a soldier will be given an illegal order by a military superior.

[216] Offences of this nature were tried by judge alone and not by the normal process of trial by jury. For an example see *R.* v. *Clegg* [1995] 1 AC 482, who was released on licence after a period of imprisonment. It is probable that he *thought* he was doing what was *expected* of him by his superiors (although he had no direct orders) when he opened fire. This might be compared with one or more cases were soldiers killed civilians using their military equipment for their own private motives, see the Memorandum for Mr Seamus Mallon, MP to the Select Committee on the Armed Forces Bill 1985–86, *Report* (1986 HC 170), p. 255. Compare the Memorandum from the Ministry of Defence at p. 263. For the position of Israeli soldiers prosecuted before military tribunals for 'using their weapons in a manner contrary to military instructions': CCPR/C/SR.1676, 28 September 1998, para. 31.

impose restrictions on his soldiers by way of standing orders (or some similar means) on the use of weapons, the degree of force to be used or the treatment of those whom they arrest should not be underestimated as a means of protecting innocent civilians. Such orders can supplement the rules of engagement and can be drawn in such a way that a soldier who follows these orders will be acting clearly inside the law.

An alternative approach was for victims or their relatives to sue the Ministry of Defence as being vicariously liable for the actions of soldiers whilst on duty and seek an award of damages. This tort route proved itself to be a popular one although the soldier concerned was not 'punished' purely through this process. Damages were awarded and the burden of proof (in effect) shifted to the soldier to prove that the force he had used was reasonable in the circumstances.[217] Where the court could not be sure of whether he had used reasonable force or that he genuinely believed the facts which, if true, would have shown the force used to have been justified within the law, he would lose and the plaintiff would win.[218]

In addition, as shown above, a number of cases were brought before the European Court of Human Rights.[219] The Court has shown that, in relation to the justifications for shooting an individual Article 2 is not different in substance from the law of Northern Ireland.[220] The Court did, however, face a particular difficulty given that some applicants before the Court admitted that they were members of a proscribed organisation and that they had been engaged in unlawful activity. If the Court was to determine that they had been treated in breach of their human rights should compensation be awarded to them or to their next of kin who, in the case of a person killed, had brought the application before the Court? It might be argued that if the soldiers caused a breach of the human rights of an applicant before the Court it should be irrelevant to take into account the fact that he, himself, was acting unlawfully. To some extent, the courts in Northern Ireland had been faced with a similar issue. In the law of tort the defence of *ex turpi causa* can deny a claim where the plaintiff has been involved in illegality. The courts there have been reluctant to apply it to the case of those seeking compensation under the law of tort for fear

---

[217] This was based upon the Criminal Law (Northern Ireland) Act 1967.

[218] For an example see *Doherty* v. *Ministry of Defence* (1981) 44 *Modern Law Review* 466. A number of cases were settled by the parties before reaching court. Such cases, unlike relevant criminal prosecutions, were tried by judge and jury.

[219] Along with cases before the European Commission on Human Rights when it was in existence. It ceased to exist on 1 November 1998 when Protocol 11 of the 1950 Convention came into force.

[220] *McCann et al.* v. *United Kingdom* (1995) 21 EHRR 97.

of drawing the conclusion that a member of a proscribed organisation cannot succeed in a claim simply because he is a member of an illegal organisation.[221]

The European Court has been willing to draw a clear distinction between, on the one hand, declaring that the State has been in breach of its human rights obligations and, on the other, awarding compensation by way of just satisfaction. Where it considers appropriate it will decide that a breach has occurred but that no compensation should be awarded.[222] It has taken a similar course where a person has been convicted by a military court, which the Court later decides acted so as to breach the applicant's right to a fair trial.[223]

From the above discussion it can be seen that some form of judicial process is likely, although not universal, where soldiers are engaged in situations of civil disorder, more rare where a non-international armed conflict is taking place and very rare where that armed conflict is of an international nature. Apart from the element of restorative justice involved a court (whether in criminal, tort or court-martial proceedings) will be required to form its own judgment of the legality in the circumstances of a particular action by one or more soldiers, which has been challenged. The insertion within the Geneva Conventions 1949 of judicial proceedings in the course of the handling of civilians by armed forces illustrates also the desirability of imposing some check upon the physical power of armed forces.[224]

It may appear obvious that a court can often see through a false line of reasoning offered by military commanders and it can, in consequence, restore the position under law. So, when senior commanders of the German border guards of the former German Democratic Republic (GDR) ordered guards to shoot and, if necessary, kill escaping GDR citizens they were acting contrary to the law of the GDR itself. Had the matter been brought to a court earlier than it was, the human rights of those attempting to escape might have been better protected as might those of the border guards themselves.[225] The guards who followed their orders and who succeeded in preventing an escape of one of their own citizens

---

[221] *Farrell* v. *Secretary of State for Defence* [1980] 1 All ER 166. See also *McCann* v. *United Kingdom* (2004) 39 EHRR 37 where it was held that alleged terrorists had been deprived of their right to life by British soldiers; McCorquodale, *'Overlegalizing Silences'* at p. 387.

[222] For an example see *McCann et al.* v. *United Kingdom* (1995) 21 EHRR 97.

[223] For full discussion of this issue see chapter 3.

[224] See, for example, the third Convention, Art. 5; Additional Protocol I 1977, Art. 45 and the Regulations Annexed to the Hague Convention (IV) 1907, Art. 30.

[225] See *K-H. W.* v. *Germany* (2003) 36 EHRR 59.

were rewarded with a medal and additional pay. Had they not been successful in preventing an escape they could have expected a detailed investigation with the possibility of disciplinary proceedings being brought against them. The court proceedings in the (later re-united) Germany showed a particular guard to have broken the law of his State, although he was following the orders of his commanders, the consequence of which he was sentenced to a form of imprisonment. Although the person whom he killed was the principal victim it is not an exaggeration to say that the border guard was, to some extent, a victim also of his military system.

It should not be thought that the actions of the armed forces during civil disorder will attract only the attention of the courts. In a democracy parliament and the media also have a role in checking the actions of the armed forces. Pressure may be brought, for instance, to hold an inquiry into the actions of the armed forces on a particular occasion. This occurred in the United Kingdom following the events of 'Bloody Sunday' on 30 January 1972 when British soldiers shot and killed thirteen unarmed individuals who were taking part in a protest march in Northern Ireland. An inquiry was established in the same year by the British Government under the chairmanship of Lord Widgery, the chief justice of England and Wales. It concluded that the soldiers were not at fault in opening fire when they did. Following the peace negotiations which led to the Belfast Agreement of 1998 the British Government agreed to set up a further inquiry into the events of Bloody Sunday. This inquiry is, at the time of writing, continuing. It has called the former Prime Minister Sir Edward Heath to give evidence as to the orders, which had been passed to the army commander in Northern Ireland from his office at the time.[226]

Other situations

The armed forces may be deployed in another State and at its request to assist it with a non-international armed conflict or civil disorder occurring there, although this is not a common occurrence.[227] Foreign armed forces may be involved in training on the territory of another State, also with the consent of that State. In both cases the human rights of those they come into contact with may be affected by their actions. For the reasons discussed in chapter 5 the sending State may bring in the inhabitants of the

---

[226] See *The Times*, 15 January 2003.
[227] An example would be the direct action of the armed forces of the United Kingdom, at the request of the government of Sierra Leone in 2000 to defeat rebels in that State.

receiving State within their jurisdiction for the purposes of human rights instruments. There is a stronger argument for doing so in these cases. This is that the receiving State would, otherwise, leave its inhabitants without any recourse to the relevant human rights body since the actions of which they make complaint are not those of the territorial State.

The sending of units of its armed forces to the territory of another State for training is common. In the vast majority of cases there is unlikely to be any interference with the local population so as to give rise to any human rights issues. Accidental injury or damage to the property of the inhabitants of the receiving State will normally be regulated by a status of forces agreement or memorandum of understanding between the States involved. The firing of live ammunition during training sessions in another State is likely to be carried out within areas from which the local population have been excluded, at least for the period of the live firing. The danger arises when individuals come into contact with spent munitions and are killed or injured as a result.

The immediate concern may be one of compensation for loss of life or injury.[228] Whilst the human rights of the victims may be a broad ground for arguing that compensation should be paid to them it might also arise as a separate issue. From the discussion above it will be necessary to argue that the victims are within the jurisdiction of the visiting armed forces for the purposes of a relevant human rights instrument. The position is not, however, so clear as it would be if the visiting force had been in occupation of the territory or if the victims had actually come into the hands of this military force. The visiting force will take measures to exclude the local population from the area where the munitions are being fired and from where they land. In this sense it may be argued that they have assumed jurisdiction (with the consent of the receiving State) over the territory controlled in this way. It is likely, however, that the visiting force will have left the territory when its inhabitants come into contact with the discarded munitions and any assumed jurisdiction over the area will have been returned to the receiving State.

This situation is little different in principle from that where an international armed conflict has resulted in an occupying force (or at least a force with some control over the territory of another State in which it has been fighting) leaving discarded munitions in the area which puts the

---

[228] In July 2002 the United Kingdom Ministry of Defence 'agreed to pay 233 victims a total of about £4.5 million' following allegations that they were injured as a result of munitions discarded by British armed forces during live weapons training in Kenya: *The Times*, 7 November 2003.

lives of the inhabitants at risk when they return to use the land. Modern armed conflicts are replete with examples. The munitions may have been abandoned without being used; they may have been used but are part of the predicted failure rate; or they may remain dangerous to the local population despite having achieved their intended military purpose.[229]

There is a growing trend within the field of international humanitarian law to impose a duty upon States to remove or to render safe any munitions they use during an armed conflict as a result of the indiscriminate damage they may cause after the armed conflict has ended.[230] There are, however, considerable practical difficulties in doing so especially where the munitions have failed to detonate or have done so but remain dangerous. Even if an international body, acting as an intermediary between the territorial State and other States involved in the armed conflict, can be appointed to oversee the process these practical difficulties will remain.

Should the problem be looked at from a human rights point of view it will be necessary to argue that the time at which the victim must be within the jurisdiction of the State if, indeed, he could be is not when he is killed by the discarded weapon but when the armed forces of the State caused that weapon to be placed there, even though it may take some time before it actually deprives someone of his or her right to life. At the time it explodes the State responsible for its emplacement is likely to be long gone from the territory. This situation can be distinguished from one where the act of the State causes injury to an individual when he is clearly within the jurisdiction of that State but he dies later when outside the jurisdiction. It is suggested that in this case a human rights body would hold the State responsible for depriving the individual of his right to life. It is, however, much more difficult to accept that if both the injury and the death occur whilst the victim is not within the jurisdiction of that State the victim's representatives can hold the State responsible for its breach of human rights to the deceased.

The alternative view, that the victim's representatives have no human rights claim against the State responsible for the emplacement of the weapon simply because the victim was not within the jurisdiction of that

---

[229] Such as a weapon containing depleted uranium. See, generally, J. Beckett, 'Interim Legality: A Mistaken Assumption? – An Analysis of Depleted Uranium Munitions under Contemporary International Humanitarian Law' (2004) 3 *Chinese Journal of International Law* 43.

[230] This is one of the reasons behind the attempt to prohibit the possession and use of anti-personnel mines: Ottawa Convention 1997. See also the Protocol on Explosive Remnants of War (Protocol V to the 1980 Convention) 2003.

State when he was killed by it, would lead to the conclusion that no State bears any responsibility in these circumstances. The territorial State will, of course, argue that it is not responsible since it did not discharge the weapon which caused the death of the individual. This is clearly the case where the munitions are discharged during the course of an international armed conflict and the responsible State was not an ally. The territorial State may, however, be argued to bear some responsibility where it has consented to a visiting force being on its territory and it is aware of the risk of the threat to life of the inhabitants from discarded munitions and fails to reduce or to eliminate this risk.

It is suggested, therefore, that the territorial State will be responsible for the deprivation of the right to life of an inhabitant of that State (who will clearly have been at the time of his injury, which has resulted in death within the jurisdiction of that State) where there is a sufficiently high degree of fault on its part[231] or where the State has been shown to have failed in its 'positive obligations'.[232] This may occur in the following circumstances. First, where as a result of an international armed conflict, the territorial State is aware of dangerous munitions, whichever State caused their emplacement, and it could with reasonable effort have rendered such munitions harmless but fails to do so. There will be some munitions which are easily discovered and those which are not. There is, therefore, a difference between a State being obliged to clear discarded weapons lying on the surface in open terrain and such weapons having been deliberately concealed (such as land mines) or having landed in terrain in which it is difficult to locate them. Secondly, where the territorial State has invited a visiting force onto its territory, *inter alia*, for training purposes and it becomes aware that discarded munitions may cause death

---

[231] The European Court of Human Rights has developed the principle that a State may be liable for the acts of private individuals where 'the authorities knew or ought to have known at the time of the existence of a real and immediate risk to the life of an identified individual or individuals from the criminal acts of a third party and they failed to take measures within the scope of their powers which, judged reasonably, might have been expected to avoid the risk': *Osman* v. *United Kingdom* (2002) 35 EHRR 19 at para. 116. See also *Cyprus* v. *Turkey* (2002) 35 EHRR 35 at para. 81; *Kaya* v. *Turkey* (1998) 28 ERRR 1; *Yavuz* v. *Turkey* (Application No. 29870/96), Admissibility, 25 May 2000. It is suggested that other cases cited show the reference in *Osman* v. *United Kingdom* to 'an identified individual' is not a prerequisite of the liability of the State for the actions of non-State actors. Given the facts, the Inter-American Commission in *Abella* (n. 68 above) at para. 175, was not stating a contrary position. Compare K. Watkin, 'Controlling the Use of Force: A Role for Human Rights Norms in Contemporary Armed Conflict' (2004) 98 *American Journal of International Law* 1, 30.

[232] *Ilascu* v. *Moldova and Russia*, Judgment, 8 July 2004, para. 352 (in relation to Moldova).

to the inhabitants of that State and it fails to insist that the visiting force remove them or it fails to do this itself. In both cases the territorial State is in a better position to render them harmless than the State responsible for their emplacement since it, alone, is likely to have access to the site where they are to be found and it can, if necessary, prohibit entry to that area until such time as it is rendered safe. In the absence of evidence that the victim was within the jurisdiction of the State responsible for the emplacement of the weapon at the time it caused at least the injury from which he or she subsequently died, it is likely that the victim must look to the territorial State alone as being responsible for a breach of this right to life.

The argument above will, if it is accepted, cover only those who have been deprived of their right to life. It will not deal with those injured by such munitions since, in these circumstances, it will be difficult to show a breach of a specific human right granted by a human rights instrument.[233] It will, for instance, be difficult to argue that an injury caused by an unexploded bomb which results in the loss of a leg amounts to 'torture, degrading or inhuman treatment'. More so will this be the case if contact with the discarded weapon (such as one containing depleted uranium) could be shown to cause, at worst, the risk at some time in the future of illness or a premature death.

A State may deploy its armed forces to prevent what it perceives to be illegal immigration where the circumstances suggest that a military option is required, even though no disorder has occurred. An example is the activities of the Australian Defence Force in 2001 in preventing the landing by boat in Australia of those who claimed to be refugees.[234]

Amnesty

Following the end of a non-international armed conflict or a state of emergency it is not uncommon for the State to grant an amnesty to military personnel,[235] either generally or by declaring that the acts of the

---

[233] Although compare the right to privacy, *Guerra* v. *Italy* (1998) 26 EHRR 357, para. 60; Convention on the Rights of the Child 1989, Art. 19.

[234] The Written Submission of the Human Rights and Equal Opportunity Commission to the Coroner's Court of Western Australia, 22 November 2002, recommended that the standard operating instructions to the Royal Australian Navy make a 'specific reference to the right to life contained in article 6 of the [1966 Covenant]': para. 4.1, http://www.humanrights.gov.au/legal/ashmore.

[235] A change of government may result in the amnesty laws being repealed or the courts may interpret them strictly. As to the former, see *The Times*, 22 August 2003, reporting

armed forces are deemed to have been committed on duty making them liable to military processes only.[236] Indeed, following an armed conflict to which Protocol II 1977 to the Geneva Conventions 1949 applies States are encouraged to 'grant the broadest possible amnesty to persons who have participated in the armed conflict'.[237] Given the context of Article 6 of that Protocol it would appear to apply to those fighting against the government. If the government is encouraged by international humanitarian law to grant such amnesties it is not surprising to find that an amnesty may also exonerate its own armed forces or other officials.[238] Whether this would, however, have any effect before a human rights body so as to exclude the liability of that State for (at least) serious violations of human rights by State actors is doubtful.[239] It could not prevent the Prosecutor

the vote of the Senate in Argentina 'to annul laws granting immunity from prosecution to former military officers'. The Supreme Court of Chile held on 26 August 2004 that General Pinochet was not immune from prosecution for crimes against humanity: [2004] *International Law in Brief* (31 August). See also the declared intention of the President of Uganda to the Prosecutor of the International Criminal Court (press release, 29 January 2004) to amend the Amnesty Act 2000 (Uganda) 'so as to exclude the leadership of the LRA [Lord's Resistance Army]' from the amnesty granted to 'any Ugandan' by s. 3(1) of the Act.

[236] An example is Report No. 28/92, Case 10.147 (Uruguay) 2 October 1992, para. 2.

[237] Article 6(5). See *Cea v. El Salvador*, Report No. 1/99, Case 10.480, 27 January 1999 at para. 116, which proclaimed that this article 'seeks to be an amnesty for those who have violated international humanitarian law'. This must be too broad a view.

[238] For the view that the amnesty provisions in the Lomé Accord (1999) between the Government of Sierra Leone and the Revolutionary Front of Sierra Leone were intended to apply to 'combatants on either side of the conflict' see the separate opinion of Justice Robertson in *Prosecutor v. Kondewa*, Case No. SCSL-2004-14-AR72(E), 25 May 2004 at para. 7. Even if an amnesty agreement did not grant immunity to members of its own armed forces there is the possibility that individual soldiers charged before their own military courts may find themselves before a 'show trial', but one in which the accused will suffer no or little penalty. Alternatively, a soldier may be 'pardoned' by the Head of State (often the commander-in-chief of the armed forces, whose security may depend on those armed forces) or short time limits may be imposed for any prosecutions. These possibilities contribute 'to the impunity which such personnel enjoy against punishment for serious human rights violations': Concluding Observations of the Human Rights Committee: Chile, CCPR/C/79/Add.104, 30 March 1999, para. 9.

[239] See Human Rights Committee General Comment No. 20, para. 15. For examples see Report No. 28/92, Case 10.147, (Argentina), 2 October 1992; Report No. 29/92, Case 10.029 (Uruguay) 2 October 1992, (1992) 13 *Human Rights Law Journal* 340. For the arguments against an amnesty see *Saavedra v. Peru*, Report No. 38/97, Case 10.548, 16 October 1997, para. 48. See also the Declaration on the Protection of all Persons from Enforced Disappearance, UNGA Resolution 47/133, 18 December 1992, Art. 18; E/CN.4/Sub.2/1998/53 (1998); Report of the Secretary-General to the Security Council on the Protection of Civilians in Armed Conflict, 26 November 2002, S/2002/1300, para. 47.

of the International Criminal Court from investigating a particular case, although he or she may decide not to continue an investigation in the light of an amnesty.[240] Since, however, an amnesty agreement may, in practical terms, be an important bargaining tool between the government and the rebels to bring about an end to the fighting its compatibility with the human rights obligations of the State should be considered on an individual basis. There may, for instance, be a stronger case for granting an amnesty from prosecution to rebels than members of the armed forces (or other security forces). On the other hand, giving effect to a large-scale amnesty on the part of the armed forces and of those who took violent action against the State might be justified where, as part of the peace process, a truth and reconciliation commission is established.[241]

The peace agreement, on the other hand, may make no reference to an amnesty. The rebels may wish to be incorporated into the armed forces of the State and this may be seen as the only realistic way of bringing an end to the conflict. Where this is agreed the effect is the same. Except possibly for egregious breaches of human rights by identified individuals no investigation is likely to be held into the acts of individual former rebels who have become soldiers of the State.[242]

---

[240] The argument for non-prosecution would be based upon an assertion that to do so would be an abuse of the process of a court. For discussion of this argument see *Prosecutor v. Kallon and Kamara*, Case No. SCSL-2004-15-AR72(E), 13 March 2004, paras. 75–85. See, generally, R. Slye, 'The Legitimacy of Amnesties under International Law and General Principles of Anglo-American Law: Is a Legitimate Amnesty Possible? (2002) 43 *Virginia Journal of International Law* 240; D. Majzub, 'Peace or Justice? Amnesties and the International Criminal Court' (2002) 3 *Melbourne Journal of International Law* 247, who refers specifically to Arts. 16 and 53 of the Rome Statute 1998 to uphold the effect of a particular amnesty. See also the Appeals Chamber of the Special Court for Sierra Leone, *Prosecutor v. Kallon and Kamara*, above, which decided that the amnesty provisions in the Lomé Accord (1999) did not bind an *international* court. See also the powerful separate opinion of Justice Robertson in *Prosecutor v. Kondewa* (n. 238 above) in which the learned judge stated 'immunity [through an amnesty] for perpetrators of serious crime is a betrayal both of the rule of law and of innocent victims of the crime' (at para. 20). He also drew attention to the effect of a breach (by a resumption of the conflict) of an amnesty agreement.

[241] Majzub (n. 240 above) at pp. 272–7 (dealing specifically with the truth commissions established in Sierra Leone and in East Timor). See the commission established by Argentina which 'investigated and documented the disappearances that occurred during the so-called "dirty war"': Report No. 28/92 (n. 239 above) at para. 42. None had been established in Uruguay, Report No. 29/92 (n. 239 above) at para. 36.

[242] For the re-integration of ex-combatants into society in Sierra Leone see Eighteenth Report of the Secretary-General on the United Nations Mission in Sierra Leone, 23 June 2003, S/2003/663, para. 18.

Closely linked with the issue of an amnesty is the purported immunity of a head of State or of senior government ministers for their actions (or inactions) during a non-international armed conflict or a period of disorder. An international court will not accept such immunity.[243] Not only can such individuals be prosecuted[244] before an international court but the State would be in breach of its international human rights obligations were it to permit such impunity for breaches of human rights by the individuals concerned.[245]

---

[243] *Prosecutor* v. *Taylor*, Case No. SCSL-2003-01-I, 31 May 2004.

[244] The significance, in this context, of the Rome Statute 1998, Art. 28 (responsibility of commanders and other superiors) should not be overlooked where leaders, through their inaction, have permitted others to commit crimes set out in the Statute. They may also be sued in the courts of a foreign State, if that State's national law permits it, see *Xuncax* v. *Gramajo* (1995) 886 F Supp 162.

[245] Thus, in *McKerr* v. *United Kingdom* (n. 101 above), the European Court of Human Rights based the requirement for an investigation into a breach of the right to life on the need 'to ensure the accountability of [State agents]', para. 111.

7

Human rights during multinational operations

This chapter will consider the human rights of those with whom the armed forces of States forming part of a multinational force operation come into contact during the course of the operation. It will be concerned with the presence of armed forces, usually in multinational contingents, present on the territory of another State, whether their presence results from a United Nations Security Council resolution, by agreement with another international organisation or through an inter-State arrangement between or among the States involved.

The ostensible purpose of deploying armed forces to a multinational force is not to engage in military operations but to protect the lives of civilians. Indeed, it is not unusual to find human rights organisations requesting the United Nations Secretary-General to send a United Nations force to a particular region in order to protect the civilian population from opposing militia groups and to enable humanitarian assistance to be delivered where it is needed.[1] The main function of the armed forces will differ, therefore, from those situations where armed forces are deployed to take part in an armed conflict or during a period of disorder within a State. The protection by armed forces of the basic human rights of the civilian population (and possibly the use of military logistical support to those providing humanitarian assistance) is not a by-product of the operation but of its very nature.[2]

---

[1] See, for example, the joint letter from Amnesty International and Human Rights Watch requesting the deployment of a 'rapid reaction force' to the Ituri region of the Democratic Republic of the Congo, 21 May 2003 (http://www.africaaction.org/docs03/conk0305.htm). The link between a stable security environment in which there is a national army 'well-trained, well-equipped and regularly paid' and the protection of the human rights of the civilian population is drawn in the Report of the Secretary-General to the Security Council on the Protection of Civilians in Armed Conflict, 26 November 2002, S/2002/1300, paras. 42–3.

[2] Other functions may include assistance with HIV/AIDS awareness by the civilian population, see Eighteenth Report of the Secretary-General on the United Nations Mission in

It is usually the practice for the States involved to negotiate a status of forces agreement or a memorandum of understanding detailing the arrangements for the entry and exit of members of the visiting force, exemptions from taxation, conflicts of jurisdiction over members of the visiting force, the payment of compensation in the event of damage, and so on.[3] The normal practice will be for each visiting force[4] to be granted the right to exercise its military jurisdiction over its own members in the territory of the receiving (or host) State. Its soldiers will therefore be subject to their own military law according to the procedures which would be followed within their home State.[5] The degree to which soldiers act as a disciplined body whilst forming part of a multinational force will largely determine the success of the operation in relation to the respect due to the civilian population.

The idea of establishing a unified disciplinary system applying to all military contingents in a multinational force operation sounds attractive. Soldiers from different national contingents will, at least in some operations, be working alongside each other. It would, it is often argued, be much more effective if the soldiers were made liable to a unified system of military law to which everyone would be subject, irrespective of their nationality. Such a system is unlikely to come about in the near future since the variations among the different contingents can be quite considerable, ranging from permitted hours of work, holiday entitlement to the right in some cases not to obey orders and to differences in the disciplinary systems themselves. Any possibility of the United Nations taking disciplinary action against its peacekeepers is non-existent, despite the issue of misconduct being raised on a number of occasions.[6]

Sierra Leone, 23 June 2003, S/2003/663, para. 54; United Nations Security Council (UNSC) Resolution 1327, 2000, para. I.

[3] This may not be possible if no governmental authority exists in the territorial State or where action is taken by the United Nations under Chapter VII of the United Nations Charter. It is not unknown for a status of forces agreement not to be in existence or to be entered into after the foreign armed forces have been deployed.

[4] This term refers to the armed forces contingent of a sending State on the territory of the receiving State with its permission.

[5] See, generally, P. Rowe, 'Maintaining Discipline in United Nations Peace Support Operations: The Legal Quagmire for Military Contingents (2000) 5 *Journal of Conflict and Security Law* 45 for more detailed treatment of the issues.

[6] See the 'Ten Rules: Code of Personal Conduct for Blue Helmets', United Nations Department of Peacekeeping Operations Training Unit, which are directed to member States to enforce: 'Report of the Secretary-General to the Security Council on the Protection of Civilians in Armed Conflict', 26 November 2002, S/2002/1300, para. 57 (which includes a suggestion for the appointment of an ombudsman to deal with complaints); 'Special Measures for

Similarly, the possibility of a unit or contingent of one nationality being placed under the command of a foreign officer has proved to be limited.[7] Whilst it is common for a senior officer to be placed in command of the multinational forces as a whole the reality of the situation is that he will pass his orders to the national commanders who then, in turn, will command their own national contingents. In this way the normal military structures operating within each national contingent can continue to operate in terms of the superior/subordinate relationship as they would were the contingent operating by itself.[8] The only relationship to change in this simple model is that between the overall commander and his immediate subordinates. The latter individuals can then be instructed by their national superior officers to obey the orders of the overall commander.[9]

There can be further variations between or among the different national contingents. The equipment, food and facilities available to one may not be matched by another. Alcohol, in particular, may be denied to one contingent and be available to another within certain limits. It should not be thought therefore that the separate national contingents in a multinational force somehow meld seamlessly into a single armed force comparable to the army of a single nation.

In some multinational forces it may be expected that fighting with rebels will take place from time to time or that, on occasion, force may need to be used in self-defence for the protection of members of the force or those whom it has a duty to protect. In others, as in peace monitoring missions, the use of military force is not reasonably anticipated. It will be common for individual States contributing forces to draft rules of engagement for their national contingents to indicate in what circumstances force can be used and how any threat to the force or those whom it has a duty to protect should be met. One of the advantages of drafting rules of engagement is that commanders can work through various possibilities which may occur

Protection from Sexual Exploitation and Sexual Abuse', Report of the Secretary-General, A/58/777, 23 April 2004, para. 14; CCPR/C/SR.1707 (Summary Record) 27 October 1998 relating to Belgian soldiers in Somalia.

[7] See the Comprehensive Report on Lessons Learned from United Nations Operation in Somalia (UNOSOM), paras. 44–6; M. Kleine, 'Integrated Bi- and Multinational Military Units in Europe' in G. Nolte (ed.), *European Military Law Systems* (Berlin: De Gruyter, 2003), chapter 13. For the position of command over United States armed forces see 'US: Administration Policy on Reforming Multinational Peace Operations' (1994) 33 *International Legal Materials* (ILM) 795 at 807.

[8] This is based upon a simple structure. There may, of course, be variations in structures.

[9] For discussion of the varying constitutional positions in Europe see G. Nolte and H. Krieger, 'Comparisons of European Military Systems' in Nolte, *European Military Law*, p. 120.

in the situation facing them and how they should respond. Their preferred mode of response will also determine the equipment needed to do so. In some cases it may be considered appropriate to respond to demonstrations with riot shields and batons rather than issuing the soldiers with firearms. In other cases firearms and armoured vehicles may be necessary to protect the soldiers should they come under attack. Helmets rather than berets may be considered appropriate.

The rules of engagement issued to a national contingent will be designed to ensure that its soldiers comply with their own national law[10] (including military law) in addition to any applicable principles of international law, the nature of the mandate for the operation, or terms agreed within a status of forces agreement. Just as the national law of a State may vary as to the circumstances when lethal force may be used by a soldier, so may the rules of engagement among the different contingents, with the possibility of making joint operations difficult and hazardous to the individual soldiers.[11] The national law of one or more States may, for instance, not permit lethal force to be used to protect property whatever the nature of it. In its eyes there may be no distinction between, say, the use of force to prevent a vehicle being stolen and the theft of vital medical supplies or food in a situation where people are starving to death.

It is usually not anticipated that an armed conflict will take place during a multinational operation and so international humanitarian law will have no application. States are naturally reluctant to commit their troops to such operations where an armed conflict (whether of an international or a non-international character) is taking place for fear of incurring unacceptable numbers of casualties. They may, however, be willing to contribute troops where an armed conflict is taking place but on the basis that the multinational force operation will not take part in that conflict. Should the national contingent be operating under a United Nations mandate the opportunity may be taken to incorporate by reference some of the applicable international law and the terms of the mandate into the

---

[10] The national law may provide, for instance, that weapons may only be used in self-defence of its soldiers or those whom they have a duty to protect. See, in relation to Japanese troops serving in Iraq, *The Times*, 12 January 2004. See the rules of engagement issues to British soldiers in Iraq in the period following the completion of major combat operations and prior to the assumption of authority by the Iraqi interim government in *R. (Al Skeini and others)* v. *Secretary of State for Defence* [2005] 2 WLR 1401 para. 45.

[11] See Fifth Report of the Secretary-General on the United Nations Mission in Sierra Leone S/2000/751, 31 July 2000, para. 54 and compare para. 56; J. Cerone, 'Minding the Gap: Outlining KFOR Accountability in Post-Conflict Kosovo' (2001) 12 *European Journal of International Law* 469, 486.

rules of engagement.[12] The Secretary-General's Bulletin of 1999 appears to confuse the circumstances when international humanitarian law will apply by including the situation where United Nations forces use force by way of self-defence without becoming combatants in an existing armed conflict.[13] The status of forces agreement might also impose some limitations on soldiers of the visiting force in their treatment, for example, of women.

Although the rules of engagement may differ as between the different national contingents to the multinational force there is likely to be a common core. Where there are any differences a commander will be able to judge which contingent will be able to carry out a particular operation and which would be prevented by its rules of engagement from doing so.[14]

International law applicable to a national contingent

If it is assumed that a contingent of the armed forces of a visiting State is present on the territory of the receiving State with its consent for the purposes of a multinational force operation, a primary issue for consideration is the legal basis upon which it treats civilians with whom it comes into contact. Individual members of the contingent will be bound by their rules of engagement, in which should be incorporated at least by reference, any liability of such a member to the law of the receiving State. It is, however, common for the States concerned to agree that in these circumstances the members of the sending State will be subject to the exclusive jurisdiction of their own State.[15] In practice, therefore, it is

---

[12] Convention on the Safety of United Nations and Associated Personnel, 1994. This requires the States concerned to enter into a separate status of forces agreement: Art. 4. See also the United Nations Secretary-General's Bulletin on Observance by United Nations Forces of International Humanitarian Law 1999 (1999) 38 *International Legal Materials* 1656.

[13] Section 1.1.

[14] This optimistic view may not always be matched on the ground. See, for instance the 'Comprehensive Report on Lessons Learned from United Nations Operation in Somalia (UNOSOM) (n. 7 above) at para. 46, which deals with conflicting orders given to a contingent commander from his national capital; C. Gray, 'Peacekeeping after the *Brahimi Report*: is there a Crisis of Credibility for the UN?' (2001) 6 *Journal of Conflict and Security Law* 267 at 285–7.

[15] Whether jurisdiction for the commission of a crime by a member of a visiting force is shared or given exclusively to that force depends, to a large extent, on the relative bargaining positions of the State concerned. Two broad situations can be compared. The first is where the sending State seeks permission to station its forces on the territory of another State essentially for its own military purposes with no comparable interest in the receiving State. The second is where the primary interest is in the receiving State for its own military purposes or for the protection of that State. In each case the bargaining position

much more likely that the individual soldier will be bound solely by his own national law (in so far as it travels with him) in his treatment of civilians. It will be recalled that in the likely absence of an armed conflict international humanitarian law will have no application unless force is used in self-defence, as discussed above. In this case, and on the assumption that the contingent involved is acting under United Nations command and control, the principles of international humanitarian law set out in the United Nations Secretary-General's Bulletin 1999 will be expected to apply.[16]

It has, however, been argued that the mere presence of a national contingent on the territory of another State will bring into operation the fourth Geneva Convention 1949 relating to civilians.[17] There is an understandable reason for arguing in this fashion. If the 1949 Convention is applicable those who come into the hands of the contingent concerned will be protected persons under the Convention. Should they be treated in the manner prohibited by Article 147 of that Convention the person concerned will have committed a grave breach of the Convention and can be prosecuted for this by his own State or, indeed, any State and, should the receiving State or the sending State be a party to the Rome Statute 1998, through the mechanism of the International Criminal Court.

Should the fourth Geneva Convention 1949 apply so will the third Convention dealing with prisoners of war. Their application brings the further advantage to the armed forces of a degree of certainty in the legal regime. They are normally trained to apply the Geneva Conventions if they are serving outside their own State where some degree of military force may be required.

of the receiving State may be different. The real bargaining position may, of course, be affected by the offer of military assistance by a sending State. The pressure on a State to prevent the loss of military assistance is often very strong. See, for example, concerns by some States over Art. 98 (of the Rome Statute of the International Criminal Court, Rome, 17 July 1998 (1998) 37 ILM 999) agreements with the United States.

[16] See n. 12 above. See also Sections 2 and 3 of the Bulletin. *Quaere* whether it will have been incorporated into rules of engagement of a particular national contingent.

[17] See J. Simpson, *Law Applicable to Canadian Forces in Somalia 1992/93* (a study prepared for the Commission of Inquiry into the Deployment of Canadian Forces to Somalia) (Canada, Minister of Public Works and Government Services, 1997), chapter 2; M. Kelly, *Restoring and Maintaining Order in Complex Peace Operations, the Search for a Legal Framework* (The Hague: Kluwer Law International, 1999); J. Cerone, 'Minding the Gap: Outlining KFOR Accountability in Post-Conflict Kosovo' (2001) 12 *European Journal of International Law* 469 at 485. See also the 'Report on the Expert Meeting on Multinational Peace Operations' (2004) 86 *International Review of the Red Cross* 207 at 209; The Comprehensive Report on Lessons to be Learned from United Nations Operation In Somalia (UNOSOM) (n. 14 above), para. 57.

The Geneva Conventions 1949 will, however, only apply if there is in existence an armed conflict between two or more States or a partial or total occupation of the territory of a State even if the occupation meets no resistance. Since the multinational force operation will be present with that State's consent it is unlikely to be a party to any armed conflict which might be occurring with another State. It is also unrealistic, from a legal point of view, to argue that the armed forces comprising the multinational force are in 'occupation' of the territory on which they are based. There must be a difference of legal regime between, on the one hand, the stationing of a visiting force on a long- or short-term basis or its presence there for a multinational force operation and, on the other hand, the actual occupation of territory by the armed forces of another State. In the first category the territorial sovereign will have consented to the presence of the foreign armed forces while in the second this will be without such consent. For occupation to occur the 'territory must be placed under the actual authority of the hostile army . . . with the authority of the legitimate authority having passed into the hands of the occupant'.[18] It would be surprising if the territorial State had intended this to occur. Even where the territorial State had no physical control over that part of the territory prior to the entry of the foreign armed forces it remains difficult to accept that the latter is in 'occupation' of the territory despite the fact that the only means of securing public order and safety lies with it.[19]

Were one to take a teleological or purposive approach to the 1949 Conventions, as the International Criminal Tribunal for the Former Yugoslavia has done,[20] and to argue that the Conventions should apply since their main purpose is to aid the victims of armed conflicts (in this case, principally, civilians) the result would remain unsatisfactory. This is because these Conventions require, as a prerequisite to their application, an international armed conflict if the basis of their applicability is not an occupation of territory. It is in the nature of multinational forces that what might be described as an 'armed conflict' will begin and end on an uncertain basis. If the applicability of the Conventions requires there to be an armed conflict in existence they will only apply when there is an armed conflict and cease to apply when there is not. Admittedly, the fourth Convention is different in this respect from the third one since it will continue to apply

---

[18] Regulations Annexed to the Hague Convention IV 1907, Arts. 42 and 43.
[19] See, for example, the position of coalition forces who were present in Iraq at the request of the sovereign Interim Government of Iraq on 30 June 2004 when 'the occupation will end': UNSC Resolution 1546, 8 June 2004.
[20] *Prosecutor* v. *Tadic* IT-94-1-A, 15 July 1999, (1999) 38 ILM 1518 at para. 160.

in certain respects after an armed conflict is concluded. This will occur, however only in occupied territory and it will be necessary to show this.[21] There is an additional difficulty with the third Geneva Convention 1949 relating to prisoners of war. Even if this Convention is assumed to apply those persons detained by members of the armed forces of the multinational force operation will not normally be entitled to prisoner of war status since they will not belong to the armed forces of a State (or national liberation movement) party to the conflict.[22]

Another approach is to accept that, strictly, the Geneva Conventions 1949[23] do not apply in the absence of international or a non-international armed conflict, but that they should be applied 'in principle'. In this way those detained by the national contingent would be treated *as if* they were prisoners of war and others would be accorded the treatment owing to civilians who come under the control of the armed forces of a State of which they are not nationals.

This approach is not a satisfactory one. The Geneva Conventions 1949 and their Additional Protocols were drawn up, as discussed above, on the basis of the existence of an armed conflict or an occupation of territory. They permit combatants and those taking part in an armed conflict to be attacked without any further justification. They also accept that prisoners of war can be detained for the duration of the conflict with no right to earlier release.[24] There is limited judicial oversight of the treatment of prisoners of war and civilians.[25] This is quite different in substance and not merely in degree from the circumstances in which a multinational force operation is usually carried out.

An alternative approach is to require soldiers of the multinational force to treat those with whom they come into contact in accordance with any

---

[21] See Art. 6; Protocol Additional to the Geneva Conventions of 12 August 1949, and relating to the protection of victims of international armed conflicts (Protocol I) Geneva, 8 June 1977, in force 7 December 1978 (1977) 16 ILM 1391, ('Additional Protocol I'), Art. 3(b). See also *R v. Brocklebank* (1996) 134 DLR (4th) 377, Decary JA at para. 54; C. Greenwood, 'International Humanitarian Law and United Nations Military Operations' (1998) 1 *Yearbook of International Humanitarian Law* 3 at 30.

[22] Article 4 (or any of the other grounds listed in this Article). Nor will Additional Protocol I 1977, Art. 45 necessarily assist them.

[23] Along with Additional Protocol I 1977 if the sending State is a party to it.

[24] Civilians may be interned, see Geneva Convention relative to the protection of civilian persons in time of war: Geneva, 12 August 1949, in force 21 October 1950, 75 *United Nations Treaty Series* (UNTS) 287, ('fourth Geneva Convention'), Section IV.

[25] See, for example, Geneva Convention relative to the treatment of prisoners of war, Geneva, 12 August 1949, in force 21 October 1950, 75 UNTS 135, ('third Geneva Convention 1949'), Art. 5; fourth Geneva Convention 1949, Arts. 66–78.

human rights obligations owed by their State.[26] This also has the merit of consistency with the application of the national law and the military law of the State to determine how soldiers should deal with civilians in their area of operations. There may well, however, be inconsistency among the different national contingents but this is both inevitable and unlikely to lead to substantial differences in treatment providing all peacekeeping contingents belong to States party to a human rights instrument. Recent practice, however, shows that a number of major troop-contributing States to United Nations peacekeeping forces are not parties to any relevant human rights instrument.[27] Even if they are they may take the view that the 1966 Covenant does not apply to the actions of their armed forces outside their own territory.[28] Since these armed forces are not organs of the territorial State a lacuna in human rights provision might occur, whether or not the territorial State is a party to a human rights instrument. Thus, the multinational force in Iraq after 30 June 2004 has power to intern insurgents 'where this is necessary for imperative reasons of security'.[29]

[26] Compare the view, expressed in United Nations mandates (along with the Charter itself), that civilians in the territorial State be accorded treatment consistent with 'international human rights standards'. This presumably means standards set out in the Universal Declaration of Human Rights 1948, in the absence of the visiting State being a party to a human rights instrument. The 'rights' of the civilians become, in reality the obligations (perhaps unenforceable) of the soldiers of the visiting State.

[27] At 31 August 2004, Pakistan was supplying 8,300 troops to peacekeeping forces. It is not a party to the 1966 Covenant (International Covenant on Civil and Political Rights, 16 December 1966, in force 23 March 1976, 999 UNTS 171), nor are the following contributing States: China; Fiji; Indonesia; Malaysia; Moldova. See, however, *Improving the Operation of Human Rights Bodies* HRI/MC/MC/1998/4 (Chairpersons Meeting) para. 13 which called for the provision of 'human rights training to UN personnel in the field'.

[28] See, however, General Comment No. 31 CCPR/C/21/Rev.1/Add.13, 26 May 2004, para. 10 which concluded that the Covenant applied to those 'within the power or effective control of the forces of a State Party acting outside its territory . . . such as forces constituting a national contingent of a State Party assigned to an international peacekeeping or peace enforcement action'. Note also the commitment of some States, such as that made by Poland, 'to respect the rights recognized in the Covenant to all individuals subject to its jurisdiction in situations where its troops operate abroad, particularly in the context of peacekeeping and peace-restoration missions': CCPR/CO/82/POL/Rev.1 (Concluding Observations/Comments) 5 November 2004, para. 3. Compare the view of Belgium and that of the Human Rights Committee, CCPR/CO/81/BEL (Concluding Observations/Comments) 12 August 2004, para. 6. The position would appear to be stronger where a State is a party to the First Optional Protocol 1966. For discussion of the extra-territorial application of the [European] Convention for the Protection of Human Rights and Fundamental Freedoms, Rome, 4 November 1950, in force 3 September 1953, 213 UNTS 222 ('1950 Convention'), see chapter 5 and *Bankovic v. Belgium et al.* (2002) 41 ILM 517 at para. 71 and, in particular, the consent of the territorial State to the exercise of some public powers.

[29] UNSC Resolution 1546, 8 June 2004, Annex.

Should an alleged insurgent be interned by United States armed forces that State may assert that the 1966 Covenant has no application outside the territory of the United States. Iraq, in turn, may claim that the individual has not been interned by its armed forces, even though the Government of Iraq has 'authority to commit Iraqi security forces to the multinational force to engage in operations with it'.[30]

In applying the human rights obligations of the visiting force to inhabitants of the territory of another State the issue of whether the latter are within the jurisdiction of the former will arise. It has been argued in chapter 5 that, depending upon the human rights instrument involved, an individual may come within the jurisdiction of another State if that State has control over the territory or over that individual. This would clearly be the case where a civilian comes into the hands of soldiers, certainly with the intent to detain him for more than a very short period.[31] If this view is correct it would be irrelevant that the territorial State is not a party to the particular human rights instrument and that the instrument has been 'transported' out of the territory of the State party to it.

The primary form of legal restraint on the actions of soldiers in a multinational force will be the limitations of action set out in their rules of engagement. It has been shown above that these will be expected to be compiled from the national, military law and any human rights obligations of the State.[32] It has also been shown that, in practice, only a soldier's own State can discipline him.

Although the soldier may be liable, in theory, for his actions to a criminal jurisdiction other than his own the exercise of this jurisdiction is

---

[30] Ibid., para. 11. Iraq is a party to the 1966 Covenant.

[31] General Comment No. 31 (see n. 28 above) requires that the 1966 Covenant rights apply to 'anyone within the power or effective control of that State Party'. Compare where a civilian is held merely for the purpose of handing him over to the armed forces of another State or to the civilian authorities. See Ocalan v. Turkey (2003) 37 EHRR 10 and the position of the Kenyan officials: para. 96, Grand Chamber, 12 May 2005, para. 91. The position is not, however, entirely clear since little consideration would have been given by the Court to the responsibility of the Kenyan authorities since that State was not a party to the 1950 Convention.

[32] It is possible that for any one contingent the State's human rights obligations have not been incorporated into national law and may not appear also in the rules of engagement. Similarly instruments such as the Basic Principles on the Use of Force by Law Enforcement Officials, 1990 (adopted by the Eighth United Nations Congress on the Prevention of Crime and the Treatment of Offenders) which includes military forces within the term 'law enforcement officials' may not be incorporated. A State may, however, have incorporated the crime of torture into its criminal law and it may take the view that its ordinary criminal law will cover the main breaches of a human rights instrument to which it is a party committed by its armed forces.

unlikely to occur. The territorial State, as shown above, will normally cede exclusive jurisdiction to the visiting force in any status of forces agreement. The extra-territorial reach of the criminal law of a State might encompass the activities of a soldier within another State, especially where this involves torture.[33] The soldier may be at risk from the exercise of some form of criminal process if he later visits a State claiming such jurisdiction and he is arrested. Depending upon the extent of the extra-territorial effect of the jurisdiction he might find himself being prosecuted in that State or be the subject of extradition proceedings to another State with such extensive jurisdiction. The soldier might also find himself the subject of an investigation by the prosecutor of the International Criminal Court if either the State in which he was serving in his multinational force role or his home State are parties to the Rome Statute.[34] This risk is, however, considered to be small since in the multinational forces under consideration the soldier is unlikely to be involved in an international or a non-international armed conflict.[35]

This relationship between the national law, military law and human rights obligations of the visiting force on the one hand and the national law and human rights obligations of the receiving State on the other is a complex one. In addition, the terms of any mandate will also need to be considered. Whilst the status of forces agreement will deal, *inter alia*, with the issue of jurisdiction from the point of view of the criminal liability of the visiting soldiers and the liability of the visiting force in respect of any damage caused it is unlikely to deal with details such as powers of arrest and detention by the soldiers of the visiting force. The law of the receiving State may be quite different from that of the visiting State and quite different from any system of law imposed by a United Nations mandate.[36] The receiving State may not be a party to any human rights instrument or it might have made a relevant reservation to its position.

[33] The Convention Against Torture and other Cruel, Inhuman or Degrading Treatment or Punishment 1984, Art. 5 of which requires a State party to enact extra-territorial jurisdiction in respect of torture committed by its nationals. Some States have gone beyond this.

[34] See, however, in relation to the United States, the American Service-Members' Act 2002 and UNSC Resolution 1422 (2002), Resolution 1487 (2003). No similar resolution was passed in 2004.

[35] See the Rome Statute 1998, Art. 8(2), where it is alleged the armed conflict is of a non-international character see Art. 8(2)(f).

[36] I am grateful to Lt Col Justin McClelland, United Kingdom Army Legal Services for drawing my attention to this point. Views expressed are those of the author. For a recent example, see UNSC Resolution 1545 (2004), para. 5. For discussion of problems of the mandate to 'enable it to be translated into a detailed operational plan', see Gray, 'Peacekeeping', p. 271 (n. 14 above); UNSC Resolution 1327 (2000).

From all of this, procedures will need to be developed to guide the soldier as to the powers to arrest and detain that he will possess. Whatever law upon which such powers are based it is clear that they must be based on law, rather than merely upon the soldier's physical ability to arrest and detain individuals. If these powers are given by the mandate itself it must be assumed that the receiving State has in practice consented to them.

Can this United Nations mandate operate as a basis of law? It can certainly determine the international obligations and duties of States in upholding the decisions of the Security Council. The point at issue here is whether a mandate, which gives United Nations forces the right to arrest and detain individuals, replaces the national law of the visiting force (whose members will do the arresting and detaining) and that of the receiving State so as to become the governing law. Lawyers from common law States may find it difficult to accept that even a decision of the Security Council can become part of the national law of a common law State in the absence of some specific instrument incorporating it within the national law. They would look to something like a United Nations Act to see whether the mandate has been incorporated in the national law.[37] In practice this may not prove to be the case.

Liability of the State when its armed forces are part of a multinational contingent

The liability of a State, party to an international human rights instrument, for a breach of human rights by members of its armed forces if applicable will not be extinguished merely because the armed forces are assigned to a multinational force. Those armed forces may come under the command of a senior officer from another State who may direct that individuals in the hands of the armed forces under his command are to be treated in a particular way. The rules of engagement of the armed forces alleged to have committed a breach of human rights may be silent on such detail or be drawn in such a way that they pose no impediment to obedience of the orders of the foreign commander. It is also a strong possibility that the commander may be a national of a State not party to any international human rights instrument. He may not have human rights issues foremost in his mind.

---

[37] An example is the United Nations Act 1946 (United Kingdom) but this is limited to measures not involving armed force. Less so is it likely to be the case if the multinational action is on behalf of NATO or some other regional arrangement.

Despite armed forces taking part in operations outside the boundaries of their State and under the command of a foreign senior officer ultimately they will remain subject to the control of their own State. The treaty regime of a particular human rights instrument is unlikely to accept that a participating State can be permitted to pass its responsibility under that treaty to another State or to an international organisation, such as the United Nations or NATO.

The killing of an attacker

A person who attacks a member of a United Nations force or its property will commit a war crime providing his act takes place during an armed conflict.[38] A State party to the Convention on the Safety of United Nations and Associated Personnel 1994 is required to make an attack on United Nations personnel a crime against its national law.[39] Whether it is an offence for a person to attack a member of a United Nations force or not will not determine the legality or otherwise of the actions of the soldier who shoots and kills the attacker in order to defend himself or those for whom he is responsible. The national law of the soldier concerned will determine this and it is desirable that this law is set out, in effect, in the soldier's rules of engagement.

In many States the national law in this connection will be no different in its application to any other criminal activity such as where the soldier is involved in dealing with serious disorder within his own State, discussed in chapter 6. Although it may turn out that the soldier has a justification[40] for killing the attacker under his national law he may still be disciplined under his military law if he has, for instance, failed to comply with standing orders in the circumstances surrounding the shooting. It

---

[38] Rome Statute of the International Criminal Court (n. 15 above), Art. 8(2)(e)(iii). *Quaere* where the State of which he is a national is not a party to the Rome Statute 1998.

[39] Article 9. See also UNGA Resolution 57/28, 19 November 2002, para. 3; 'Report of the Ad Hoc Committee on the Scope of the Legal Protection under the Convention on the Safety of United Nations and Associated Personnel', Supplement No. 52 (A/58/52), 2003.

[40] This justification may be based on self-defence of the soldier himself, of those whom it is his duty to protect, to prevent a serious crime of violence being committed or a mistake of fact. See also *V.J.F.G (Konrad Khalid v. Paracommando Soldier)* 1995 and *D. A. Maria Pierre (Osman Somow v. Paracommando Soldier)* both decisions of a Belgian Military Court, referred to by A. Cassese, *International Criminal Law* (Oxford: Oxford University Press, 2003), p. 236, n. 12; CCPR/C/SR.1707, 27 October 1998. A claim for damages was brought successfully against the United Kingdom Ministry of Defence in respect of British peacekeepers who shot and killed a civilian in Kosovo: *Bici* v. *Ministry of Defence* [2004] EWHC 786 (QB). On the facts the concept of combat immunity did not apply.

is also possible that soldiers superior in rank to the soldier who shot and killed the attacker may be disciplined for their own breaches of military law in the circumstances surrounding the shooting.[41] The practical difficulties involved in the concept of liability (perhaps only) to the national law, including the military law, of the visiting State include the obvious fact that that State may, in practice, exercise little effective control over the discipline of its soldiers. In addition, its military justice system might work imperfectly since an inadequate number of trained investigators may not have been deployed with the force.[42]

Whether this killing amounts to a breach of the right to life of the attacker will turn on the relevant human rights instrument. The first issue to consider, however, is whether the attacker was within the jurisdiction of the soldier's State at the time he was shot and killed. For the reasons discussed in chapter 5 (and above in this chapter) this is a preliminary issue before the merits can be considered. The fact that the contingent is there with the consent of the territorial State is an important, but not decisive factor.[43] The practical reality of the situation suggests that those who are merely within the area controlled by a particular national contingent do not necessarily come within its jurisdiction for the purposes of the 1950 Convention.[44] Even if they do a soldier is unlikely to cause a breach of the right to life of the attacker if he has complied with his rules of engagement.[45]

---

[41] An example would be where military orders or procedures binding on the superior had been ignored by him. See, for example, *R. v. Mathieu* (unreported) discussed by Decary JA in *R. v. Brocklebank* (n. 21) at para. 16, where the accused, the commander of the battalion, had been charged with (but acquitted of) negligent performance of a military duty under the Canadian National Defence Act 1985.

[42] Many of these practical issues are discussed in *Dishonoured Legacy, Report of the Commission of Inquiry into the Deployment of Canadian Forces to Somalia* (Canadian Government Publishing, 1977) vol. 5, para. 40. See, generally, R. Young and M. Molina, 'IHL and Peace Operations: Sharing Lessons Learned from Somalia' (1998) 1 *Yearbook of International Humanitarian Law* 362.

[43] It may be relevant, for example, under the 1950 Convention but not under the 1966 Covenant in determining whether the victim was within the jurisdiction of the soldiers of the contingent concerned, Compare *Bankovic v. Belgium et al.* (2002) 41 ILM 517 at para. 71 with General Comment No. 31.

[44] It is suggested that the same result would apply if the relevant treaties were, respectively, the 1966 Covenant or the American Convention on Human Rights, San José, 22 November 1969, in force 18 July 1978, (1970) 9 ILM 673.

[45] Since the killing is then unlikely to be 'arbitrary' within the 1966 Covenant, and it is likely to fall within the exceptions to the 1950 Convention, Art. 2, as to which see *McCann v. United Kingdom* (1995) 21 EHRR 97. The rules of engagement are likely to set out the basis upon which the soldier can act by way of self-defence.

Individuals might, however, look to their own State's human rights obligations to protect their right to life. The effect of granting permission to another State to base its armed forces on the territory of that other State will not necessarily break the chain of responsibility which the receiving State owes to those within its territory. The difficulty to be faced by the representatives of the attacker of the visiting force who has been killed is that the organs of the State which killed him were those of the visiting force and not those of the receiving State. It is highly unlikely that the responsibility for a breach of the right to life committed by the armed forces of one State could be imputed to another State.[46]

A civilian in the hands of the foreign armed forces

A civilian in the hands (or under the control) of a member of the visiting armed forces is in a different legal position from someone who is not, but who is affected by the actions of its soldiers. It has been argued in chapter 5 that where a person comes within the control of a soldier belonging to a foreign armed force he is, by that fact, brought within the jurisdiction of the State concerned for the purposes of a relevant human rights instrument. Where, however, this occurs outside the territory of the State (as in this case) there may be difficulty in showing that the detaining State considers the 1966 Covenant to apply.[47] It has also been shown that this legal status of the civilian in these circumstances is distinct from that of State responsibility under international law. Whilst the State will be responsible for any actions of its armed forces having effects outside its own territory it will bear responsibility for its human right breaches only to those within its jurisdiction or within its territory, depending on the particular instrument and its subsequent interpretation.

Should anyone be killed whilst in the hands of a member of the visiting force it is clear that the victim would have suffered a deprivation of his right to life. The killing would be described as 'arbitrary'[48] or as not 'absolutely necessary' to achieve one of the stated objects in the 1950 Convention.[49]

---

[46] By way of comparison, see the liability of the State for the actions of private individuals and for rebel groups, discussed in chapter 5, and for visiting forces, chapter 6.

[47] See discussion in chapter 5.

[48] See the 1966 Covenant, Art. 6; the American Convention on Human Rights 1969, Art. 4(1). For an example of deprivation of liberty following arrest by United States soldiers in Grenada see *Coard* v. *United States*, Report No. 109/99, Case 10.951, 29 September 1999 and by Russian soldiers in Moldova: *Ilascu* v. *Moldova and Russia*, Judgment, 8 July 2004.

[49] Article 2(2). The potential conflicts of jurisdiction between the sending and the receiving States may have been settled in a status of forces agreement. It has been argued above that

The soldiers concerned are likely also to have broken their own national law and may be tried by a military court at the *locus in quo* or be repatriated for trial depending on the terms of the status of forces agreement.[50]

In like manner a soldier who subjects anyone to torture, degrading or inhuman treatment will cause his State to be in breach of its human rights obligations to him, should the relevant human rights instrument not require that the act take place on its territory. He will almost certainly also be in breach of his national and military laws.

Soldiers of the visiting force may be given the power by the status of forces agreement to arrest and detain those who are suspected of interfering with their duties. The nature of the mission and the circumstances existing on the ground will determine the extent of such a power. It may merely be to detain an individual for a short period in order to identify him so as to hand him over to the security forces of the receiving State if he is suspected of an offence against the law of that State. It may be for a longer period in order formally to question him about a specific offence or to gain intelligence. The law under which the soldiers are operating would be expected to be clearly formulated, incorporated at least in its main points in the rules of engagement and be consistent with the legal structure of both the sending and the receiving States.

The grounds for a lawful arrest and the degree of force which is permitted to prevent a person escaping from lawful arrest may vary as between the law of the visiting and receiving States and a United Nations mandate. The key point here is whether a soldier would be legally justified in firing at (and killing) a person who had been arrested by him or by any other member of the United Nations force or, indeed, by the security forces of the territorial State and who escapes from arrest. Different answers may be given depending on how similar are the different systems of law. The problem for the soldier is, however, that if he fires at an individual with a high-powered rifle he is very likely to kill him. In order to provide some grounds of justification for killing him it will be necessary for the soldier to give some explanation of the risks he perceived if the person escaped compared with the risk of killing him then and there. Different national legal systems may express this concept in different ways. Some may require

in a multinational operation it is more than likely that these States will have agreed to the sending State having exclusive jurisdiction over the members of its own armed forces. This will cover situations where one member commits a crime against another as well as where a soldier commits a crime against an inhabitant of the receiving State.

[50] See, for example, the court-martial of a United States soldier, Staff Sergeant Horne, for murder in killing a wounded Iraqi, *The Times*, 11 December 2004.

a prosecution to prove that the soldier's actions amounted to an unreasonable degree of force, others that the harm done was disproportionate to the risks perceived or that that degree of force was not necessary. It is likely also that the relevant national law will permit the deciders of guilt or innocence of the soldier to take into account the nature of any risks faced by the soldier if an alternative to firing at the escaping detainee could have been adopted. A soldier, for instance, who chases after an escaping detainee may place himself, depending upon the circumstances, at considerable risk if he becomes detached from his unit. If his own national law has not been amended by the terms of the mandate a soldier would be well advised to act in accordance with his own national law where his powers to act appear to be different in the United Nations mandate.

A further complication for the application of the relevant human rights instrument in these circumstances is whether the fact that a detainee has escaped from detention shows that he is no longer under the control and, therefore, the jurisdiction for human rights purposes of the State which had, until his escape, detained him. This would appear to be the position and it would place the escaping detainee, legally, in the same position as the civilian who attacks United Nations force members (discussed above).

The mere act of detaining a civilian will not necessarily amount to a deprivation of his liberty. For a soldier to stop a civilian for as much time as is needed to inspect his identity papers will not do so. Nor, for the same reasons, will the imposition of a curfew. To place him under lock and key whilst checks are made as to his identity or to obtain information from him will, however, amount to a deprivation of liberty. Such a ground for depriving him of his liberty as such is not provided for in the relevant human rights treaties.[51] A State which considers this power essential for the efficient discharge of its duties will have to issue a derogation notice stipulating the law which permits such detention.[52] If the detention is for the purposes of questioning him about a specific offence he will need to be brought before a judicial officer promptly. The detaining State may provide a judicial officer, with legal advice to the individual being given by its own military lawyers. The judicial officer should preferably be a civilian in order to show objectively that the judicial process is independent of the military authorities and that the judge is impartial. The possibility of

---

[51] The 1950 Convention and the American Convention on Human Rights 1969.
[52] See the discussion above concerning the issue of which law will apply to the acts of the soldiers.

video links with a civilian judicial officer sitting in the home State of the visiting force may enable this function to be carried out by a civilian but if not it will be necessary to show that any military officer (usually a lawyer) acting as a judicial officer is seen to be independent of other soldiers acting in an executive capacity.

The broad circumstances under which a soldier may cause a civilian to be detained for any length of time have been sketched out above. If we consider the position of this detainee for a moment we can see that uncertainty as to the legal basis of his treatment becomes apparent. Even if it is assumed that only one State is involved in his arrest and detention[53] issues such as his right to legal advice, the legality of his arrest, whether he is to be charged with an offence (by whom and for what offence?), how soon he is to be placed before a judicial officer, his right to communicate with his family or friends, whether he can refuse to be transferred to his own State's security forces and the circumstances in which he may make a valid confession, will arise. To determine the answer to these questions it will be necessary to be clear, just as it must if armed force is to be used by soldiers, as to which law applies. Will it be his national law, the terms of the mandate and any human rights obligations (including any permitted declarations or reservations made at the time of becoming a party to the instrument) of the detaining State or a combination of two or more of these? In addition, what law will determine the length, and conditions, of detention?

It is likely, however, that the United Nations (or other) force will not wish to detain individuals for any length of time and will seek to hand over someone arrested as quickly as possible to the security forces of the territorial State. This may not, however, always be possible. The latter State may be in a condition of actual or near collapse; it may not be able to provide the basic infrastructure to enable it to detain individuals in the area where they have been arrested; it may have a poor track record of treating them in accordance with basic standards or it may have very slow trial processes. Detainees may not wish to be transferred to the territorial State for fear of the treatment that may be accorded to them there and a detaining State may be concerned about transferring individuals to the territorial State because of the risk that they may be subjected to torture,

---

[53] He may have been arrested by soldiers of one national contingent and transferred to another national contingent. The guidelines for the detention of Somalia were 'confused': see The Comprehensive Report on Lessons Learned from United Nations Operation in Somalia (UNOSOM) (n. 7 above), para. 73.

degrading or other treatment. This treatment may result from proper or improper actions by the territorial State. The actions may be 'proper' if the national law of that State provides, for instance, for some form of physical mutilation as punishment for certain activities and improper if the treatment of detainees breaches the law of the State.

The visiting force may, in consequence, have to face detaining individuals who are suspected of having committed an offence against the law of the territorial State (such as assault or serious destruction of property) or who have interfered with the military operations of the visiting force. In these circumstances the visiting force will wish to ensure that it complies with any human rights obligations it may owe to those within its jurisdiction,[54] such as these detainees, in addition, to its own national law. In addition, it will have to apply the law of the territorial State, where it can, to avoid the imposition of retroactive law.[55] The consent of the territorial State to changes in its law or in its procedures applying during detention will not, by itself, cure the problem of retroactivity of laws imposed by the visiting force but compliance by it with any human rights obligations it owes is likely to be seen as the paramount consideration.[56]

To achieve this standard of treatment it will have to create an infrastructure of legal advisers, courts and detention facilities for those convicted. This is likely to be an unwelcome addition to the responsibilities of the visiting force and it may deter some States from contributing a national contingent to a multinational force. A potential contributing State may also be unclear as to how any detainees are to be dealt with after the State ends any contribution made to the force. Will it be able to transfer detainees to another national contingent (assuming there is another which is willing to accept them) or to the territorial State whatever the human rights record of that State or will it consider that it has no option

---

[54] Assuming the State accepts that its human rights obligations apply outside its national territory.

[55] See, for example, the 1950 Convention, Art. 7; the American Convention on Human Rights 1969, Art. 9. Even if territory is occupied an occupier is not permitted to create retroactive laws: Geneva Convention 1949, Art. 65. For discussion of the desirability, or otherwise, of importing model codes, see B. Oswald, 'Model Codes for Criminal Justice and Peace Operations: Some Legal Issues' (2004) 9 *Journal of Conflict and Security Law* 253; compare the Brahimi Report, UN Doc. A/55/305, S/2000/809, Annex III, para. 6, (2000) 39 ILM 1432. For particular problems in reconciling human rights standards and the national law in East Timor see B. Kondoch, 'The United Nations Administration of East Timor' (2001) *Journal of Conflict and Security Law* 245 at pp. 249–50.

[56] This will apply more strongly where the UNSC establishes a transitional administration in the territory, as it did with East Timor, by Resolution 1272 (1999) and in Iraq by Resolution 1511 (2003).

but to grant them asylum in its home State? A State owing human rights obligations to those outside its own territory will have to choose the first and third options posed here if it comes to the conclusion that the territorial State would cause detainees to be subjected to torture, degrading or inhuman treatment.[57]

An alternative approach for a State faced with this situation is to treat detainees as if they were prisoners of war and to apply the third Geneva Convention 1949 to them.[58] The advantage to the detaining State of doing so is that it need only provide appropriate facilities of detention commensurate with that Convention. It need not, therefore, have to provide a court structure or a system of legal advisers to detainees on the same basis as discussed above. It may, however, wish to establish a procedure where a person could challenge the legal basis of his detention, on terms similar to Article 5 of the third Geneva Convention 1949.[59] Should a detainee make a challenge the only ground upon which he could be released would be that his detention resulted from a mistake of fact. He will continue to be detained if the military[60] or other authorities of that State determine that he was involved in the acts alleged against him so as to warrant arrest and detention. If he is to be treated as a prisoner of war no attempt will be made to determine his guilt or innocence of a particular charge and he will be detained until this quasi-legal position comes to an end.

For a State, party to a relevant human rights treaty which applies to detainees outside its territory, to treat individuals as prisoners of war may involve an infringement of its human rights obligations owed to such individuals. The rights given to freedom from a deprivation of liberty and to a fair trial are the most obvious rights involved.

A further alternative is to keep the detainees securely within some form of detention facility (as compared with a local prison) but to deny

---

[57] See *Soering* v. *United Kingdom* (1989) 11 EHRR 439. In CCPR/C/78/D/829/1998, 13 August 2003 the Committee decided that a State which had abolished the death penalty could not transfer a prisoner to a State which had not done so 'without ensuring that the death penalty would not be carried out' (para. 10.4).

[58] For its applicability in such circumstances by United States forces in Haiti in 1994 see T. Meron 'Extraterritoriality of Human Rights Treaties' (1995) 89 *American Journal of International Law* 78. Should United Nations soldiers be detained by rebels they are entitled to be treated in accordance with the 'principles and spirit of the Geneva Conventions 1949': Convention on the Safety of United Nations and Associated Personnel 1994, Art. 8 (assuming the territorial State is a party).

[59] Or Art. 45 of Additional Protocol I 1977.

[60] *Quaere* whether a particular military board, court or tribunal is, in fact, sufficiently independent and impartial to determine this issue against a civilian. See chapter 5.

the applicability of the third Geneva Convention 1949 and to deny also that the human rights obligations of the detaining State apply to them.[61] Were a State to take this course it is, however, likely in practice to use the third Geneva Convention 1949 as the framework document in providing the standard of treatment of the detainees.[62] It can also, on an *ex gratia*, basis invite the International Committee of the Red Cross to inspect the detention facilities and to communicate with the detainees.

This discussion would suggest that a State contributing units of its armed forces to a multinational force operation enters a legal minefield where it and its individual soldiers face risks perhaps greater than at first sight might appear. To some extent the potential legal problems have not surfaced until now. There are various reasons for this. In some cases it has been unclear as to which legal regime applies. In this uncertainty practices and procedures dictated by legal regulation may not have been firmly established, unlike the position where individuals have been arrested and detained in the State's home territory. It will be common for practices and procedures to be put in place since armed forces are used to operating in such a way. These practices and procedures are, however, likely to be of an administrative rather than a legal nature.[63] The visiting force may think its military role as being of an 'active service' nature rather than as a substitute police force. In consequence it may be encouraged to think that the acts of its soldiers are not subject to legal proceedings against them unless the soldiers fail to comply in an obvious way with their rules of engagement. The news media may not be as attentive to the actions of soldiers acting in a multinational force mission as they would be to the activities of soldiers in their home State.[64]

In some situations United Nations 'peacekeeping operations are multidimensional, and besides the military, they could have humanitarian, civilian police, civil affairs, electoral, rehabilitation and repatriation

---

[61] On the ground that the relevant human rights instrument applied only to those within its territory, as to which see the 1966 Covenant, Art. 2, discussed in chapter 5. Compare, however, the American Convention on Human Rights 1969, Art. 1, to which the United States is not a party.

[62] See discussion of detainees by the United States in Guantanamo Bay, Cuba from 2002, in chapter 4.

[63] To the individual detained this distinction may be thought to have little practical significance. The significance can lie in the fact that administrative procedures may be changed or even ignored more easily than procedures dictated by national law.

[64] If soldiers are acting to quell civil disorder within their own State the role of a free press can be a significant factor in trying to ensure an acceptable standard of conduct on their behalf.

components, each intimately linked to the other'.[65] Where the infrastructure exists a military contingent may be able to hand detainees over to the civilian police and ultimately see them placed on trial by a court established by the United Nations.[66] Troop-contributing States may well be advised to discuss with the organisation (such as the United Nations or NATO) prior to deployment how detainees are to be placed on trial where, for one reason or another, they cannot be handed over to the territorial State. The structure of most armed forces is not designed for the placing on trial by the use of military procedures civilians whom they detain in the course of a multinational operation.[67]

Those who are detained will, of course, not be nationals of the detaining State. Even if they are able to secure legal advice the lawyers (if they are practitioners in the territorial State[68]) are unlikely to be able to offer advice as to the national law of the detaining State. There may be little or no legal aid or assistance to invoke remedies in the latter State.

Once the detainee is released he may be unsure which State is responsible for the deprivation of his right to liberty, the State which detained him or his own State. Although, in theory, he may be tempted to bring proceedings in the courts of his own State, or even in the courts of the detaining State, this is unlikely unless he has the funding to do so himself or obtains legal assistance to do so or a human rights organisation takes up his case on his behalf. In any event, the number of cases in which some form of legal proceedings are brought is likely to be very small indeed. That is not to say that one particular case may not become of profound significance but the position is quite different from the deprivation of the liberty of a number of individuals within the national territory. All those subject to an alleged unlawful deprivation of liberty are likely to take proceedings in some form against the State concerned.

It is not beyond the realms of foreseeability that a State acting as a contingent member of a multinational force operation will face more legal action in the future from those with whom its soldiers come into contact where that State's human rights obligations reach into the territory of another State. To avoid applications being brought a State might wish

---

[65] The Comprehensive Report on Lessons Learned from United Nations Operation in Somalia (UNOSOM) (n. 7 above), para. 94.

[66] See, for example, the Special Panel of the District Court of Dili, East Timor: S. Linton, 'Prosecuting Atrocities at the District Court of Dili' (2001) 2 *Melbourne Journal of International Law* 414.

[67] See chapter 4 for discussion of the difficulties of placing civilians before military courts.

[68] The detaining State may provide its own military lawyers to advise detainees.

to consider specifically how its procedures, principally for the detention of civilians are consistent with its human rights obligations to them. It would, in many cases, be difficult for the force contingent to perform its mission if it could not, where appropriate, use or threaten force or arrest those threatening those whom it is their duty to protect. It is in the realm of detaining civilians where its human rights obligations will be most significant.

Have soldiers a duty to intervene?

Multinational force soldiers may be faced with a clear breach of human rights[69] of the civilian population by the armed forces of the territorial State or by rebels. Do they have a duty to intervene to prevent such a breach? To argue in the affirmative is to accept that failure to do so would entail some personal liability under their national law on the part of the soldiers concerned. Many, but not all, legal systems will not make a mere omission to act in these circumstances a criminal or a military offence.[70] Alternatively, if the armed forces forming part of the multinational forces owe human rights obligations under their own treaty arrangement to the individuals concerned their failure to act in circumstances where they could have prevented,[71] for example, arbitrary killing, would be a breach of their own human rights obligations to those individuals. For the reasons discussed above it may, however, be difficult to show that any such human rights obligations are owed by the multinational contingent to the victims. Whether there is a breach of some legal obligations or not, a failure to act may have significant political consequences.[72]

---

[69] This phrase is taken to mean acts having consequences which would be a breach of human rights under any human rights instrument had they been committed by State organs even though the territorial State is not a party to any such instrument.

[70] Those States which have implemented Art. 28 of the Rome Statute 1998 will not be able to prosecute their contingent military commander since the crimes will be committed by persons not under his effective command or control. Military law may, however, be more willing to punish acts of omission as separate military offences. See, for example, *R* v. *Mathieu* discussed in n. 41.

[71] Compare circumstances where the lives of the soldiers of the multinational force would be put to an unacceptable risk by any intervention. See chapter 5 for discussion of the right to life of the soldiers themselves.

[72] See R. Siekmann, 'The Fall of Srebrenica and the Attitude of Dutchbat From an International Legal Perspective' (1998) 1 *Yearbook of International Humanitarian Law* 301 at 310. Report of the Secretary-General pursuant to G. A. Resolution 53/35: the Fall of Srebrenica, 15 November 1999, A/54/549; CCPR/CO/72/NET (Concluding

Humanitarian missions

The armed forces of a State may be required by their government to play a role in providing humanitarian assistance to the population in the area allocated to them in a multinational force mission. They may be in charge of 'life and death properties', such as food and medicines, as well as taking part in multinational force operations.[73] The armed forces may also be sent abroad, with the consent of the territorial State, solely to provide humanitarian assistance in the wake of some natural disaster. In these circumstances the soldiers are likely to carry out their functions unarmed and will not generally envisage any use of force or any deprivation of liberty of the local population. Arrangements will usually be made with the security forces of the territorial State to work closely with the visiting armed forces contingent in the event of a need to enforce the national law of the territorial State. Nevertheless, it is possible that civilians will try to steal food or medical supplies guarded by the visiting armed forces. Whilst the theft of food or medical supplies may not lead to the risks of those thereby deprived of such supplies dying as a direct consequence of such action in the States supplying the armed forces the risks are very real in a humanitarian mission.

The most likely area of difficulty will be whether the soldiers will be justified in firing at (and killing) civilians who are in the process of stealing these supplies if no alternative method of preventing the theft is possible. This will be determined solely by the national law of the State supplying the armed forces on the assumption that both the sending and receiving States have entered into a status of forces agreement whereby the former is to have exclusive jurisdiction over the members of its own armed forces on the territory of the latter.[74]

It is also, of course, foreseeable that a civilian caught by a visiting force soldier cannot be handed over to the security forces of the territorial

Observations/Comments), 27 August 2001, para. 8 which called upon the Netherlands to 'complete its investigations as to the involvement of its armed forces in Srebrenica as soon as possible, publicize these findings widely and examine the conclusions to determine any appropriate criminal or disciplinary action'. For the Gallo Commission established by the Italian Government to investigate the activities of its armed forces in Somalia, see CAT/C/SR.374 (Summary Record), 18 October 1999, para. 23.

[73] An example would be the deployment of contingents of foreign armed forces to States affected by the tsunami on 26 December 2004, see *The Times*, 3 January 2005.

[74] For the reasons expressed above it is unlikely that a relevant human rights instrument will apply where the individual is not within the hands of the armed forces of the visiting State. For an example see *R. v. Brocklebank* (1996) 134 DLR (4th) 377.

State because of the possibility of him being dealt with in such a way as to breach any human rights obligations of the visiting force State.[75] The latter State will have to consider how it will deal with such an individual. One possibility is to agree procedures with the territorial State's police or armed forces that any arrest is to be made by those forces rather than by the armed forces of the visiting force.

Since the consent of the territorial State will be required for the presence of foreign armed forces on its soil both States will have to agree beforehand as to the nature of the humanitarian operation. Thus, a territorial State which sought humanitarian assistance in order to supply a particular group in its State with these necessary supplies but to deny it to others is unlikely to gain the co-operation of other States. Other States may take the view that the territorial State is unwilling or unable to ensure adequate food and medical supplies to a section of its population. That State is also unlikely to consent to the presence of members of a foreign armed force on its territory. In these circumstances one or more States have felt compelled to drop food supplies by their air forces for the benefit of a particular section of the population denied them. Whilst this may not have been expressed in human rights terms an underlying principle of human rights, that all persons be treated equally, is clearly one of the reasons for a foreign State to act in this way.

It may seem ironic that soldiers performing humanitarian functions, such as delivering food or medicines to the local civilian population, may cause difficulties for foreign civilian humanitarian missions. There is a risk that the latter might be seen by the local population as being linked with the armed forces and thereby attract to themselves any opprobrium attaching to those foreign armed forces.

Derogations

It is very unlikely that a State, permitted by a treaty regime to derogate from its human rights obligations would, or could, do so in the circumstances discussed in this chapter. It would, for instance, have considerable difficulty in showing a 'war' or other 'public emergency threatening the

---

[75] It may, for instance, be known by the visiting force that the territorial State deals very harshly (which term is intended to include torture, degrading or inhuman treatment or punishment) with those stealing such life and death properties. *Quaere* whether the visiting force will have control over the arrested person for the purposes of the jurisdiction of a human rights instrument if there is no intention to detain him: see above.

life of the nation' in most of the circumstances in which the deployment of armed forces to multinational forces would occur. It is possible, of course, that armed forces forming part of a multinational force might be engaged in 'war' where they become parties to an armed conflict but the practice of States has been not to issue a derogation notice in such circumstances.

INDEX